THE GATEWAY TO HISTORY

Allan Nevins is De Witt Clinton Professor Emeritus of American History at Columbia University, a position he held actively from 1931 to 1958, and a senior associate of the Huntington Library, San Marino, California. He was born in 1890 and educated at the University of Illinois and at Columbia. Professor Nevins' first work in American history appeared in 1914 and he has written widely in the field to the present time. His biographies, *Grover Cleveland: A Study in Courage* and *Hamilton Fish: The Inner History of the Grant Administration,* were awarded Pulitzer Prizes in 1932 and 1937, and *Ordeal of the Union,* published in 1947, earned him the Scribner Centennial Prize and the Bancroft Prize. Other major studies include *John D. Rockefeller: The Heroic Age of American Enterprise; The Emergence of Lincoln; Ford: The Times, The Man, The Company;* and *Ford: Expansion and Challenge.* His most recent history, *War for the Union,* appeared in 1959, and in 1960 he was editor of President Kennedy's collected papers on *The Strategy of Peace. The Gateway to History,* which was first published in 1938, has been revised and brought up to date by Professor Nevins for this Anchor Edition.

THE GATEWAY
TO HISTORY

Joseph Allan Nevins

New, revised edition

ANCHOR BOOKS
DOUBLEDAY & COMPANY, INC.
GARDEN CITY, NEW YORK

ACKNOWLEDGMENTS

Excerpt from a review of *Hitler Confronts England*
by Rear Admiral Walter Ansel is reprinted by permission from *The Times Literary Supplement* of
April 14, 1961.

Material quoted from *Eisenhower's Six Great Decisions* by Walter Bedell Smith. Copyright 1956, and
reprinted with permission of David McKay Company,
Inc., publishers.

Preface

THIS IS a revision of a volume first issued just before the last great war; a revision in which the original structure has been retained, but several important parts of the text have been completely recomposed, and many minor changes have been made. I can still assert, as I did in 1938, that the book is written by an amateur of history in the hope that it may assist other amateurs. It is written with the wish that more people would read history widely, and that more of them would do so with intelligence and passion, not as a mere pastime, or as a means to some limited end. For this reason I have tried to make history seem attractive. I have tried also to express my conviction that the writing of history, while a difficult and responsible undertaking, ought to be kept a reasonably free and joyous pursuit, unsaddled by dogma, and varied, mutable, catholic, and progressive in character. This volume will, I hope, help some general readers to realize how much history has been written for them, what a wealth of talent and genius has been poured into it, what a tremendous conquest of perplexities and obstacles it represents, and how pregnant with ideas the best of it is. I hope it may afford a little counsel and encouragement to writers of history, and particularly the beginners.

In my Preface to the first edition I made a statement which it seems now important to recall. I wrote:

> Once historical study in America was tremendously alive. If it were as alive and energetic today as it should

8

PREFACE

be, we would have in this country two enterprises which do not now exist. We would have a popular historical magazine, published monthly, written for the multitude and not the learned few, and full of articles relating the past (particularly the American past) to the present. We would also have some organization which made a systematic attempt to obtain, from the lips and papers of living Americans who have led significant lives, a fuller record of their participation in the political, economic, and cultural life of the last sixty years; a period in which America has been built into the richest and most powerful nation the world has ever seen, and socially and economically has not only been transformed, but re-transformed.

When these lines were written they were a dream, a hope, a vision. It is pleasant now to reflect that the country has the magazine of history, more successful than its founders at first believed possible, in *American Heritage;* and that we have also the other agency here described in the efficient Oral History Office of Columbia University, which has been or is being copied from the Atlantic to the Pacific, and indeed overseas.

ALLAN NEVINS

The Huntington Library

Contents

	Preface	7
I	A Proud Word for History	13
II	The Varieties of History	35
III	Primitive Materials for History	65
IV	Modern Materials for History	97
V	The Cheating Document	137
VI	The Dubious Document	159
VII	Pilate on Evidence	189
VIII	Problems in History	227
IX	Ideas in History	261
X	Man's Home and His History	301
XI	Sociologist, Economist, and Historian	323
XII	Biography and History	347
XIII	Literary Aspects of History	371
XIV	The Reading of History	393
	Notes	413
	Bibliographical Aids to Research	419
	Index	431

Contents

I. ... and Myth for History
II. The Meaning of History 33
III. Standards Materials for History 63
IV. Modern Materials for History 97
The following Programme 127
VI. The Dubious Departure 159
VII. ... state to Reasoning 189
VIII. Problems to Causes 229
IX. Ideas in History 261
X. Main Items and ... History 291
XI. Sociology, Economic and History 325
XII. Biography and History 357
XIII. Literary Art of History 375
XIV. The Recurrent History 397
Notes 410
Bibliographical ... Research 418
Index 424

THE GATEWAY TO HISTORY

I

A Proud Word for History

A CARTRIDGE BAG is unstrapped from the sweaty horse, and a brown hand pulls out a thick volume; it is Theodore Roosevelt in East Africa about to give half an hour at the end of a day's hunting to Carlyle's *Frederick the Great*. His object—relaxation, entertainment, instruction. A clean-cut naval officer in blue uniform sits in the English Club in Lima, Peru, a history of Rome on his knee, pondering, and then opens the book again at a chapter telling how Hannibal crossed the Alps. He is Alfred T. Mahan, he has reflected how much more easily the Carthaginian army might have reached Central Italy by water, and he looks for more facts on a theory that has just struck him—the idea of the decisive potency of sea power in wars. An earnest woman of sensitive face looks up from a page of manuscript which she is intently writing, and quickly consults a book labeled Parkman; it is Willa Cather halfway through *Shadows on the Rock*, and trying to recall a bit of color in *The Old Regime in Canada*. A schoolboy emits a merry laugh; he has just found J. J. Jusserand's account of medieval vagabonds, minstrels, outlaws, and peddlers in *English Wayfaring Life* richly comic.

The uses of history are almost endless. It may be read for a hundred reasons, and when read merely for amusement, or for its rich pageantry and drama alone, it insensibly serves other ends. But to understand its more important values we must approach it on an elevated level, and measure it not in relation to individuals, but to societies and nations.

Although when we use the word history we instinctively think of the past, this is an error, for history is actually a bridge connecting the past with the present, and pointing the road to the future. This fact Daniel Webster wrapped into the majestic exordium of his reply to Hayne. "Mr. President," he began, "when the mariner has tossed for many days in thick weather, and on an unknown sea, he naturally avails himself of the first pause in the storm, the earliest glance of the sun, to take his latitude and ascertain how far the elements have driven him from his true course." Webster here indicated one of the cardinal utilities of history. Since mankind is always more or less storm-driven, history is the sextant of states which, tossed by wind and current, would be lost in confusion if they could not fix their position.

History enables bewildered bodies of human beings to grasp their relationship with their past, and helps them chart on general lines their immediate forward course. And it does more than this. By giving peoples a sense of continuity in all their efforts, red-flagging error, and chronicling immortal worth, it confers on them a consciousness of unity, a realization of the value of individual achievement, and a comprehension of the importance of planned effort as contrasted with aimless drifting.

This conception of history as a lantern carried by the side of man, moving forward with every step taken, is of course far ampler than the concept of a mere interesting tale to be told, a vivid scene to be described, or a group of picturesque characters to be delineated. It is essentially western and modern. To the Oriental, and even to the ancient Greek, history was an incomprehensible chaos of happenings, or a repetitive wallpaper pattern. Present-day citizens of America, Britain, and France, however, especially when harried and perplexed by the sweep of events, peer earnestly into history for some illumination of their predicament and prospects. They may only read magazine articles or listen to TV discussions upon what Lincoln or

Theodore Roosevelt did in some analogous crisis, or they may verse themselves as deeply in history as Woodrow Wilson and Winston Churchill did; but at any rate, they feel the meaning of history for the present.

It is when great events rouse men to their most responsible temper, and fierce ordeals awaken them to a new sense of their capacities, that they turn readily to the writing of history, for they wish to instruct, and to its reading, for they want to learn. Nineteen hundred years ago the Greek essayist Lucian was writing: "From the beginning of the present excitements—the barbarian war, the Armenian disaster, the succession of victories—you cannot find a man but who is writing history; nay, everyone you meet is a Thucydides, a Herodotus, a Xenophon." It was no accident that the First World War fostered such an interest in history that for a time the number of books devoted to it in English exceeded the titles in fiction; that much the same phenomenon appeared after the Second World War; and that the period between the two conflicts produced a number of the most ambitious efforts ever made to find a meaning in the whole course of world history, ranging from H. G. Wells's *Outline of History* to Arnold Toynbee's *The Study of History,* both in very different ways enormously popular.

Democratic peoples of wide popular education, where the feeling of progress toward some goal is strong, inevitably display a specially keen interest in history as an illuminant of present and future. Democracy gives every thoughtful citizen a sense of being a participator in history, education sharpens his curiosity, and belief in progress teaches him to look for continuing patterns. The United States was born at a time when a tradition of interest in history was easily established. Modern historical writing in spirit and method is largely a product of the nineteenth century Enlightenment, and it was just as the Enlightenment began to merge in the Industrial Revolution that the republic emerged. Various writers, such as Lord Morley in his *Voltaire* and *Burke,* have pointed out how great a part historical composition played in the mature phases of the Enlightenment.

The literate generation contemporaneous with the American and French Revolutions in Western Europe and the United States steeped itself in history. When the eighteenth century ended no gentleman's library was complete without Thucydides, Livy, and Tacitus, and few cultivated men on either side of the Atlantic could not discuss the historical works of Hume, Voltaire, Mabillon, and Gibbon. Henry Adams in his life of John Randolph of Roanoke speaks of the immutable "literary standards" of the day to which Randolph's education conformed: "He read his Gibbon, Hume, and Burke; knew English history. . . ." Even at an earlier period three works, Raleigh's eloquent *History of the World,* Bishop Burnet's *History of the Reformation,* and Clarendon's history of the Puritan rebellion, had been widely diffused throughout the American colonies. But as the Enlightenment widened its appeal to the intellectual aristocracy of the time, and the currents of political revolt stimulated a search for precedents, books written on a higher plane came into use. Young John Adams slaked a burning thirst in More's *Wolsey,* Clarendon, Hume, Walton's biographies, and Goldsmith's historical compilations. John Dickinson in Pennsylvania and George Mason in Virginia were not behind him.

In short, the men who took the leadership of our nation, believing in history as an exponent of current events, were well acquainted with the works then standard. Law and political thought were their primary study, but history maintained an almost equal place.

Thus it was that we find Washington after the Revolution ordering from England a small library of historical works: Robertson's *Charles V* and *History of America;* Voltaire's *Charles XII;* Sully's *Memoirs;* lives of Peter the Great, Louis XV, and Gustavus Adolphus, and histories of Rome and Portugal.[1] Hence it is that we find John Adams, in describing the qualifications of a good Secretary of State, writing a little later: "He ought to be a Man of universal reading in Laws, Governments, History."[2] Thus it is, again, that we find Chancellor Kent stating in his autobiography that in 1782, at Poughkeepsie, he brightened his study of law by reading Smollett's and Rapin's histories of England.

"The same year I procured Hume's *History*, and his profound reflections and admirable eloquence struck most
deeply on my youthful mind." Alexander Hamilton's library included not only Greek and Roman historians, but
well-thumbed sets of Gibbon, Hume, and Robertson. Few
well-educated Americans, indeed—ministers, editors, attorneys, physicians as well as political leaders—then failed to
regard history as a necessary discipline. Most of them
would have agreed with Jefferson, himself a lover of the
best British historians, in what he wrote of the proper requirements of Virginia's educational law:

> But of the views of this law none is more important,
> none more legitimate, than that of rendering the peo-
> ple the safe, as they are the ultimate, guardians of their
> own liberty. For this purpose the reading in the first
> stage, where *they* will receive their whole education, is
> proposed, as has been said, to be chiefly historical. His-
> tory, by apprising them of the past, will enable them
> to judge of the future; it will avail them of the experi-
> ence of other times and other nations; it will qualify
> them as judges of the actions and designs of men; it will
> enable them to know ambition under every guise it
> may assume; and knowing it, to defeat its views.[3]

The spell which history, not as entertainment but as an
interpretive guide, exercised over the better instructed
groups of Americans, remained undiminished for generations. Charles Sumner, for example, with a career as statesman in view, wrote a friend just after his Harvard gradua-
tion in 1830: "I have marked out for myself a course of
study which will fully occupy my time—namely, a course
of mathematics, Juvenal, Tacitus, a course of modern history, Hallam's *Middle Ages* and *Constitutional History*,
Roscoe's *Leo* and *Lorenzo*, and Robertson's *Charles V.*"[4]
Even pioneer America felt that a familiarity with history
befitted the leader; after the log cabin campaign Webster
spent a weary day deleting Greek heroes and Roman consuls from William Henry Harrison's inaugural address. We
might extend the roster to the first Roosevelt and Woodrow Wilson, who wrote history as well as read it omnivo-

rously, and acted steadily by its light; to Harry Truman, who referred part of his confidence in discharging his Presidential labors to a wide early reading of history, and who when he faced the intractable MacArthur thought of what Lincoln had done with the intractable McClellan; and to John F. Kennedy, whose *Profiles in Courage* covered a wide historical range, and whose general knowledge of the American and European past is not easily matched.

I

But history is more than a guide for men in their daily round; it is a creator of their future. The conception which men have of their record in generations past shapes their dreams and ambitions for the generations to come. The Israel that Herzl helped to found owed most of its force to the Zionist image of the older Israel, as the new Italy of which Mussolini dreamed was partly a reincarnation of Rome of the Caesars.

Consider how great a purpose history has served as a womb or matrix of nations. The strongest element in the creation of any human organization of complex character and enduring strength is the establishment of a common tradition by the narration of its history. The common literature may be important, especially a common poetry; a common religion will knit its members together by its gospel. But even literature and religion contain historical elements; and members of a nation of uneven literary tastes and of mixed religions can be tightly bound together by reverence for the tale of their past. The Greek who thrilled over Thermopylae, the Roman exulting over the devotion of Curtius or the conquests of Caesar, the Briton reading of Nelson at Trafalgar, the American following the epic story of pioneering from Captain John Smith to Kit Carson, have all responded to the same emotion. When Treitschke resolved to revive the national spirit of the Germans he began by writing their history; when Vienna wished to hinder the growth of patriotism among the Czechs it threw obstacles before the publication of Palacky's history of Bohemia.

To give a people a full sense of their future we need first the historians who give them a full sense of their past. The school texts that told of Plymouth Rock, Valley Forge, and the Alamo, the rhetorical pages of George Bancroft, the historical poems of Longfellow on Miles Standish and Paul Revere, and Cooper's historical romance *The Spy*, helped immeasurably in making America a nation. Turner's essay on the historical influence of the frontier, by deepening our understanding of the uniqueness of our past, strengthened our nationalist feeling. "Laws die, books never"—and the nation-builder may well say that he cares not who writes the laws of a country so long as he can write its history.

If history has been a maker of nations, her role as their continuing inspirer is almost equally important. The nature of the inspiration is highly varied, but its central importance is this, that it tends to make each individual a sharer in the great deeds, ideas, and movements of his ancestors or forerunners, and to awaken an emulative passion in his breast. It tends also, since history tells a very mixed tale, to awaken healthy doubts, repulsions, and condemnations, which may be nearly as valuable; but the positive side is more important than the negative. "My only regret is that I have but one life to give for my country"—the country schoolmaster who said that had done his country service in braving almost certain death to gain information for the patriot armies. But in flinging that golden sentence to the historians, to be repeated till every child knows it, he performed a service far greater. We could add many illustrations of the kind. The best inspiration of history, however, outruns mere national feeling and applies to all humanity, fortifying its higher resolves.

"All learners, all inquiring minds of every order," wrote Carlyle of history, "are gathered round her footstool, and reverently pondering her lessons as the true basis of wisdom." But more than wisdom resides in her teachings. The grandeur of the historical record confers a certain grandeur upon ourselves. All thoughtful men tend in some degree to identify themselves with the figures and forces of history. We realize that each individual mind is one more incarnation of a universal mind. The past was wrought by men and women basically like ourselves. What Shakespeare and Lincoln accomplished, what Caesar Borgia and Stalin perpetrated, what Hannibal and Gustavus Adolphus dared and endured, are illustrations of the powers, debasements, and fortitudes of our common human nature. In the larger accomplishments of the race we feel we have a share. "We sympathize in the great moments of history," writes Emerson, "in the great discoveries, the great resistances, the great prosperities of men; because there law was enacted, the sea was searched, the land was found, or the blow was struck, *for us,* as we ourselves would have done in that place or have applauded."[5]

This conception of history as a creative and inspiring force has always been essentially a literary conception. Such history can effect little unless it is widely read, which means that it must possess color, suspense, warm human interest, and an infusion of romance or poetry. James Anthony Froude deliberately essayed to nurture patriotic feeling by his history of England from the accession of Queen Elizabeth, and by such essays as his stirring account of "England's Forgotten Worthies," a resuscitation of the exploits of Tudor captains like Drake, Hawkins, and Raleigh. Possessing vigorous literary talent, and able to simplify and dramatize complex transactions effectively, he won and still holds a wide following. Guizot in his history of France, written primarily for precocious youth, had a similar goal in view. George Bancroft envisaged his history of the English colonies in America, their developing freedom, and their final struggle for complete liberty as a sort of prose epic, he too telling an oversimplified and sometimes melodramatic story for its inspiring effect. His success in his own long generation was enormous, and hard as it may seem to believe now, it was primarily a literary success.

All the eminent literary historians of the nineteenth century, in fact, believed earnestly in history as a guide to the present and a shaper of the future. Such a writer as Macaulay wished to instill a feeling for Whig and liberal values in English civilization. Because he passionately desired to see these values prevail in the future, he believed he could illustrate their validity by an examination of the past. Anxious for all literate persons to read his work, he thought that the art of Walter Scott's historical romances could be combined with the severe truthfulness of the annalist, and plumed himself on the fact that his history displaced the latest novel on the dressing table of fashionable women. Such glowing literary artists as Motley and Parkman were less consciously and obviously, but just as firmly, animated by a like ambition. Each celebrated in his own way a triumph of the ideals of free, democratic, and Protestant New England, which they hoped would continue to prevail; Motley the victory of Dutch and English libertarians over Spain, Parkman the victory of the free individualistic Anglo-Saxons over the regimentation and intolerance of New France.

Indeed, literary history used for inspiration as well as instruction and entertainment once became a great popular possession in the United States, as in other lands. It is a salient and creditable fact of the American cultural record that from 1830 to 1880 history was one of the most continuously popular forms. Prescott's *Conquest of Mexico* sold 5000 copies in four months in the United States, and went through edition after edition; his *Conquest of Peru* sold 7500 copies in the same brief period; his Spanish histories, indicting obscurantism and tyranny, nearly as well. The works of Bancroft and Motley never ceased to sell. Irving's life of Washington, the ablest study of the Revolution made up to that time, was one of the notable successes of American publishing prior to the Civil War. When we recall that meanwhile the histories of Macaulay, Carlyle, and Grote were not merely brought out by authorized publishers but extensively pirated, while translated works like Charles Rollin's ancient history sold widely, we can comprehend why the American mind received a distinct historical bias during most of the century.

Whenever history is invoked to shape the present and future, however, it obviously runs very real perils. Any participant in current affairs must face some rough hauling and buffeting. The Behistun Rock on the road from Babylon to Ecbatana carries an inscription by Darius the Great asserting that he had destroyed "the Reign of the Lie"; the currency, that is, of a view of history propagated by a usurper who had claimed that he was the son of Cyrus and hence the rightful ruler of the Persian Empire. Every fresh political campaign in democratic lands finds candidates assailing "the reign of the lie"—that is, the misrepresentations of rivals with respect to the history of recent events. We live amid a constant clash of ideas, and they all grow out of historic experience. It is almost impossible to name a political, economic, or social preconception which is not molded and colored by history. It is equally impossible to name a piece of real history which is not molded and colored by political, economic, or social beliefs. The two interact.

II

Written history shapes the world in which we live. It is because the people of India hold a special view of written history that they denounce imperialism. This is not the view that Lord Cromer took when he wrote his thoughtful book on *Ancient and Modern Imperialism,* or that most Britons and Frenchmen take. But the policies of Indian leaders from Nehru down and the speeches of Indian representatives in the United Nations are governed by this view. In the American South, it is because many people have a certain historical view of "the Southern way of life," State Rights, and Reconstruction, that they resist racial integration. They appeal not to sociologists or educators, but to John C. Calhoun, Robert Toombs, and Jefferson Davis—that is, to history. Their opponents also appeal to history; and the Supreme Court decision of 1953 in the school-integration case was based largely on historical grounds, after the judges had heard attorneys exhaustively debate the intent of the authors of the Fourteenth Amendment. It is often supposed that Nasser of Egypt and various Arab leaders took their intransigent attitude toward Israel because they wished to destroy it, or at least to cater to Arab mob passions bent on its destruction, but this is an oversimplified view. They were intransigent partly because they read the history of the preceding ten years as a record of Israeli threats and aggression—the Israelis, of course, reading it as a record of Arab menaces and attacks.

It is obvious that the fusion of past and present in historical study results in an unending controversy over many aspects of written history, and in a constant coloration or perversion of historical truth. History is never above the melee. It is not allowed to be neutral, but forced to enlist in every army. Lincoln sadly pointed out during the Civil War that both sides prayed to the same God for victory. Each side also appealed to the same national history for support of their belief that a just God would give the victory to its special tenets: the belief of Southerners that the American past justified a people in battling for self-determination and independence, the belief of Northerners that the past required a struggle to vindicate national integrity. The conviction of Darius that he had to combat a lie is paralleled by the conviction of Western nations in the twentieth century that they too must overthrow foul and potent lies. A great deal of national policy in Britain and America during the last generation is, from one point of view, an implementation of historical criticism.

The Nazi lie, propagated by Hitler with the aid of a tremendous apparatus, was an imperialist claim that history proved Germans to be a *Volk* of superior gifts and discipline, entitled to rule as a master race over inferior peoples. It was an assertion that after suffering a long series of terrible historical wrongs, this master race should assert its power, and reduce to vassalage the Gauls, the Slavs, the Jews, and the colored hordes. Teutonic domination, in an empire to last a thousand years, would crown civilization with new glories. The racial interpretations of history presented by Count Gobineau, Houston Stewart Chamberlain, and others were mingled with the anti-Christian, anti-humanitarian interpretations of Nietzsche, and the classic exaltations of German virtues by Hans Zwiedineck von Südenhorst and Wilhelm Oncken. Standards of accepted morality were cast aside as historically unjustified. Anything that promoted Nazi ambition was inherently

good, while anything which obstructed it was wicked. Had
Hitler conquered Europe, a vast amount of history would
have been rewritten in an effort to make the Nazi lie
stand as truth.   *Russia*

The reinterpretation of history meanwhile introduced by
Soviet Russia proved equally sweeping and much more
complex. It made no boast of a master race; instead, it
appealed to an ideal of universal equality and fraternity,
and aimed specially at enlisting the neglected, impover-
ished, and handicapped. But it interpreted all history in
the light of a materialist motivation, and of a class war
which set the proletariat against the bourgeoisie, the wage-
earner against the capitalist employer, and the black or
yellow man against his white exploiter. It essayed to destroy the old bourgeois morality based on religion. Whatever promoted the Soviet regime in power was good, to
be praised and propagated by novel, play, poem, and
chronicle, and whatever impeded it was evil. The ease with
which history could be rewritten in the interests of a new
"truth" was demonstrated long before Khrushchev swept
his eraser across the long-accepted tale of Stalin's genius,
virtues, and achievements. It had to be thus rewritten, for
history was the principal key to domination of the Russian
mind.

The Nazi falsification of history was transient. The Soviet
falsification proved much tougher and more persistent.
Both went far beyond the mere coloration of written history for party, sectarian, or class purposes with which
other nations had always been familiar—beyond the line
which no democratic historian who valued his reputation
would pass. In its chameleon changes and protean slip-
periness, the Soviet lie offers a particularly interesting study
of the interplay between political pressures and historical
interpretation. It demonstrates the vital part that written
history plays on the stage of current affairs, and still more
strikingly illustrates the perils which may beset it in such
a role.

III

When the Communists gained ascendency in Russia just after the First World War, they found the historical scene dominated by such able old-school historians as Miliukov, V. O. Kliuchevsky, and Platonov. These men were promptly turned out of the Soviet house, and their works banned. However eminent, they were contemptuously termed old-school bourgeois writers, and their books dismissed as "capitalistic." Lenin and his associates made a veteran Marxist historian, M. Pokrovsky, the most influential figure in what was to be an entirely new school of historians. A firm believer in economic determinism, he had written a series of volumes giving a materialist interpretation of European development, with emphasis on the class struggle. The government made him head of the Academic Council, with authority to regiment all historical teaching and writing, and forthwith, the historical profession was unabashedly mobilized in the service of party politics. Most of the historians genuinely interested in truth fled the country or dropped their pens, but a few, like the Napoleonic scholar Eugene Tarle, prostituted their talents to the new order.

For about fifteen years the new school was given free rein, Lenin himself writing an enthusiastic preface to Pokrovsky's *History of Russia*. The official Soviet view was that the nation's historians had nothing to learn from the Western writers, whose democratic and capitalistic preconceptions prevented them from seeing the past clearly even when given every opportunity. Thus M. A. Alpatov, a leading Soviet historian who specialized in French historiography, asserted that the work of Alexis de Tocqueville on the *ancien régime*, and that of Fustel de Coulanges on ancient cities, were consciously distorted in the interests of wealth and property-holders. He also declared that after the publication of Marx's and Engels's *Communist Manifesto* in 1848, the historians of Western Europe had all become reactionary, and had given themselves up to deliberate falsification of events. Others followed the same

party line, so that under Pokrovsky in the era of Lenin and
of Stalin's first years in power, Russian historical writing
became hopelessly constricted and barren. Various scholars, to be sure, made some advances in the use of sociology
and economics, neglected by their predecessors. But they
were so subservient to the Communist ideologists that they
falsified everything they touched, and devitalized even the
most colorful and dramatic periods of Russian development.

Of course the tendentious absurdities of the Pokrovsky
regime could not endure. After his death, the mid-thirties
witnessed a sharp reaction against him. He was sweep-
ingly condemned for what the review *Voprosy Istorii*
called his vulgar simplifications and errors.

For a time efforts were made to bring forward new,
livelier, and more penetrating writers, but always within
the cast-iron Communist Party lines. After 1935, it was
thought wise to rescue from eclipse the folk heroes of Russia, such as Ivan IV, Suvorov, Kutuzov, and Admiral
Nakhimov, and they were brought under the blazing light
of glorification. Histories which emphasized the "progressive" social character of their achievements were cultivated.
But the Stalin regime soon cast aside this fashion in turn.
And as one new set of demands on Soviet historians followed another writers and students became fearful of
touching history at all. An excessive amount of candor or
an indiscretion in emphasis might cost an author dear.
Even a satisfactory piece of writing, if it became offensive
when Communist Party policy altered, might consign a
scholar to prison, exile, or death. Since it was wise to avoid
history, especially that of modern times, men turned to
other areas.

Thus in Russia history became the handmaid of politics,
and a handmaid whose virtue was always suspect. In the
spring of 1952, for example, the principal Soviet dailies,
Pravda and *Izvestia*, opened a fusillade against the historians of the Crimea, which was reinforced by the duller
thunder of guns in the monthly *Voprosy Istorii*. The journals charged these writers with suppressing the "fact" that
the Slavs had always been the principal element in Crimean history. Among careful historians, the racial identity

of the aboriginal Scythian inhabitants had been a controversial subject. Now the controversy was closed: the party pronounced them full-blooded Slavs. Official spokesmen declared that the Tatars who had taken their places were of comparatively recent date, with no valid claim to an important position in the history of the peninsula. The Kremlin summoned a conference of historians at Sinferopol, where various bureaucrats instructed the scholars in their duty. Thereafter, it was decreed, the Slavs must be given the central credit for shaping Crimean development, while the idea that the Tatar khans had performed any work of value must be discarded as a fable of bourgeois nationalism. Crimean history must be completely rewritten.

Why this sudden reinterpretation of a well-known chapter of the Russian past? First, because the Tatars had to be discredited. During the Second World War they had behaved disloyally, collaborating with the Germans, so that their autonomous republic had been abolished, and many of them had been exiled. Now they were to be exposed as the mongrel, inferior folk they really were! And in the second place, the rewriting of Crimean history fulfilled a larger purpose. The Stalinist leadership in Moscow had decided that the sixteen republics of the Soviet Union must be cemented into one solid block, a process which required weakening their peculiar national traditions and their separatist ideas. Centripetal tendencies should be fostered at the expense of centrifugal impulses. At the same time, the Stalin-Molotov regime decided that to justify Soviet foreign policy, all the annexations of territory by the old Czarist governments, which it had recently denounced as outrageous acts of imperialist aggression, ought to be represented as just and beneficent steps in national expansion.

This last motive for rewriting history seemed to the outside world peculiarly significant, for it touched the central philosophy of the Soviet Government. During the long decades of Communist agitation against the Czars, the imperial seizures of lands and peoples from Peter the Great to Nicholas II had been indicted as a manifestation of capitalist greed for revenue and power. Just as Russian domestic history was presented as a grim conflict between bloodsucking patricians and exploited plebeians, between the nobility, gentry, and military on one side and the toiling masses on the other, so the record in foreign affairs had been treated as a manifestation of robbery and oppression. Communist historians had asserted that the Czars, not satisfied with enslaving their own people, had to dominate and exhaust other peoples as well. By intrigues, blackmail, and war, they clutched neighboring lands and ground their populations underfoot to create a conglomerate Russian Empire. For fifteen years after Lenin gained his primacy, Pokrovsky and his school had pursued this line of exposition. But now, suddenly, historians were expected to sanctify the Czarist empire. They were set to justifying the methods by which it had been gained, and expounding the historical absurdity of nationalist sentiment in Lithuania, Georgia, and the Ukraine.

This crude policy of deforming history to suit an ideological purpose, and using the weapons of totalitarian compulsion to enforce an arbitrary view of the past, of course soon defeats itself. Free minds, even among unlearned peasants and workers, see its contradictions and artificialities, and reject it. It merits all the savage satire that George Orwell gave it in his volume 1984. It should be noted that it is not merely an outgrowth of the desire of the Communist state to mold the present and future. It is the more vicious because it is the product of a Materialist theory of human history, the Marx-Engels principle that the causes of all social and political change are to be sought not in men's minds, nor men's growing insight into eternal truth, "but in changes in the modes of production and exchange." This principle creates a universe governed not by fact but by theory, and impervious to every bit of data, every idea, which is not in harmony with itself.

IV

The only history that can truly nourish, inspire, and guide a people over a long period of time is written in a different spirit. It is produced with a high, not a low, intention; in an earnest effort to ascertain the truth objectively. The servant of truth cannot be slave of party or nation. If men allowed history to sink for long to the fascist or communist level, we would have not an integral European history, but a West German type of history written for West Germans, a French type of history written for Frenchmen, and a Scottish type of history written for Scots. To an unfortunate extent, such distorted history does exist, but not with the sanction of true scholars or tolerance of critical readers. No greater place exists for a Spanish type of European history, or an Italian or Dutch type, than for an Italian physics and a Dutch physics. Of course perfect objectivity is never achieved, but English historians of integrity, like Lecky and George Otto Trevelyan, have gone a long way toward it in granting the justice of the patriot cause in the Revolution, while American historians have gone equally far in granting the purity and strength of the Tory cause.

Not only is the intention of true history high, but the method is scientific. The historian, that is, collects his data fairly, observes it systematically, organizes it logically, and tests its parts thoroughly. Then by inductive logic and the use of hypothesis he reaches provisional generalizations, and only when he has carried out a final search for new data, and made fresh tests, does he commit final conclusions to paper. In all this he casts off, so far as possible, the prejudices of race, nationality, class, and faction. If his method falls short of the test-tube precision of the chemist, it is at any rate as scientific as he can make it. He will go to the primary sources for as many facts as possible, and restrict his reliance on secondary accounts. He will give each category of evidence its proper valuation: the official document, the letter, the memoir, the newspaper story, the pamphlet, the artifact. He will put every witness, every scrap of paper, under cross-examination. And when he finishes his reconstruction of the past, he will give it as veracious a glow of life as his art can encompass.

This standard history is the only type that a cultivated people will in the long run cherish. Fortunately it exists for Western nations in abundance. Our shelves are loaded with its treasures. Some of its values change with the climate of opinion, but the value of its basic integrity remains immutable. It stands ready to give the casual reader sound amusement, the student instruction, the philosopher ideas, and the statesman parallels and prophecies; ready, more importantly, to give any nation a sense of the union of past, present, and future.

Its vitality is constantly quickened by the interaction of past and present, and the changing hues which each gives the other. It is obviously clear that we can learn something about the frenzy of McCarthyism and its faked exposure of plots from a careful reading of Macaulay upon the frenzy that surrounded Titus Oates and his particular faked conspiracy. We can learn a good deal about the criminal folly of Hitler's maltreatment of the Jews from a study of the criminal folly of the Spanish expulsion of the Moors as related by Henry Charles Lea in his vivid book on the Moriscoes. The interaction, however, often gives us a converse profit. Thus one English historian has remarked that it is no longer easy to call the mild repressions and exactions of Charles I "tyranny," as older writers did, since Hitler and Stalin have shown how monstrous a tyranny can really be under a modern dictator. We have to take a more moderate view of Stuart oppressions—or those of George III. It is certainly easier now to understand the history of ideological conflict in sixteenth-century Europe over religious beliefs, for we have the history of twentieth-century ideological conflict over politico-economic beliefs to cast light upon it. In each instance the struggle aroused profound and bitter emotion, making men ready to kill and be killed.

Nearly all historians of the first rank have reflected this complex relationship of yesterday, today, and tomorrow, making their work a bridge. Why did Gibbon choose his particular subject of the *Decline and Fall*? A man of independent means, philosophical outlook, and contemplative pleasure in learning for learning's sake, he might have regarded his theme as divorced from all current interests. Actually he did not. He chose it in part because he believed that a harmonious relationship and even general resemblance existed between Rome of the Antonines, and

Britain of the Hanoverians, and he felt confident that great numbers of literate people in Western Europe would be interested in a delineation of Roman politics and society which brought out the resemblance. He was also fascinated by the question whether any of the causes which had brought about the fall of Rome could operate to bring about the fall of British civilization, and thought that an exploration of this question would also interest many readers. He was right. It was not alone his mastery of facts, his critical angle of vision, or his style which gave his history an immense vogue; it was its close relationship to the situation of Britain at the time. Men may read it even today thinking of a resemblance between the positions of the Roman and American nations.

History, over the long period since Hume and Voltaire, has become steadily more useful to peoples as it has broadened its scope, and gained an eclectic use of new tools. It has learned to take all possible profit from the other social studies—statistics, sociology, economics, psychology, geography—in presenting a complete and exact picture of the past. It has employed new ideas and tools in writing of the state, which is usually the greatest common denominator of society, and in delineating political movements. It has turned to the long-neglected field of industrial and business history, with due attention to science and technology. In doing so it has not forgotten that because even business cannot be interpreted solely by figures of prices and profits, because ruined men weep and suddenly enriched men dance, the best historian there as elsewhere will look into human psychology and social psychology. Diplomatic history has been revitalized. Social and intellectual history have been deepened. Because, in all this, narrative power is indispensable to the best historical effort, the historian still tells romantic, heroic, and heart-rending stories, and still has his heroes, his villains, and his yet more interesting mixtures of the heroic and the villainous.

No nation, it is pleasant to note, has done more in the last sixty years to add to the amplitude and vitality of its historical record than the United States. Great single names may indeed seem lacking, but for this deficiency our writers have largely atoned by a wealth of books and monographs, some brilliant, more of them searching, and still more impressively thorough. It is seldom realized even by well-read people how much remained to be done at the beginning of the twentieth century—what large areas of the past stood untouched, and what other areas were like raw, new-broken prairie. Our best historians, Prescott, Motley, and Parkman, had not turned to national history at all, George Bancroft had but reached the threshold of that field, and the history of the South, of the West, of manufacturing, transportation and labor, of thought, and of institutions remained to be covered.

Theodore Roosevelt early in the century, in his essay "History as Literature," could speak of the great inviting reaches that beckoned to authors.[6] They could paint anew, he declared, the labors of the colonists to plant civilization in the Indian-haunted forests. They could describe almost for the first time the backwoodsmen with their long rifles and light axes hewing their way to the Mississippi, and the endless caravans of white-topped Conestogas swaying across plain and mountain to the Pacific. "They will show how the land which the pioneers won slowly and with incredible hardship was filled in two generations by the overflow from the countries of western and central Europe. The portentous growth of the cities will be shown, and the change from a nation of farmers to a nation of businessmen and artisans, and all the far-reaching consequences of the rise of the new industrialism. The formation of a new ethnic type in this melting pot of the nation will be told. The hard materialism of our age will appear, and also the strange capacity for lofty idealism which must be reckoned with by all who would understand the American character." Most of this has been done, and part of it with compelling interest. The remainder will rapidly be accomplished. The historical and biographical work of the last generation not only illuminates our past, but suffuses a radiance which more than any other body of books—more than the writings of sociologists, economists, or political experts—casts rays upon our immediate future.

The American who ignores this work has neglected what might be the most vital part of his education.

Were history as nearly static as some branches of learning it would be a drab affair, but it is alive in every aspect. It is most of all alive in that it is constantly being reborn like the phoenix from its own ashes. As mankind lengthens its experience, perspectives change. The lenses through which we look at the past have to be refocused from generation to generation. What seemed wisdom to our fathers is often folly to us, and what is dramatic to our age may seem naïve or banal to the next. While the best history has enduring elements, there is a sense in which every generation has to have history rewritten new for it, and in this fact lies much of the fascination which historical activity will always offer thoughtful men. As the history written in any age bodies forth the form and spirit of that age, a succession of histories is a record of the stages through which thought and feeling have passed. In its protean forms, history touches the realm of ideas at more points than any other study, and in the best of its forms it is compact as much of ideas as of fact. There was a profound and not merely superficial meaning in the last instructions Napoleon left for the King of Rome: "Let my son often read and reflect on history; this is the only true philosophy."[7]

II

The Varieties of History

HISTORY MAKES a claim to universality, taking all human activity for its province. From time to time students are struck by the gaps in its interests, and its failure to keep up with the profound upheavals in the life of nations and the world. To take one example, history as we know it has till lately been far too Western-oriented. As long ago as 1899, Henry Adams wrote that "Europe is done," and that America and Russia would be "the two future centers of power," while soon afterward men like Albert J. Beveridge pointed to the rising importance of Asia. Yet Western writers, including Americans, long paid little attention to Slavonic history, and still less to Oriental backgrounds. Not until Steven Runciman's three volumes appeared did any Western author treat the Crusades with due attention to the standpoint and sacrifices of the Islamic world in the conflict. In the new perspectives of history accommodated to recent world changes, Africa too will require not only a larger but a changed treatment. Other instances of short measure in the historical fabric could be named.

On the whole, however, the variety, catholicity, and comprehensiveness of history are among its more impressive qualities. It is a singularly rich department of letters. Its quantity is tremendous, and its diversities in aim, mood, method, and style offer something for every taste. A tolerant appreciation of this variety is one of the cardinal requirements for the general reader and student alike.

Even the most ascetic student of history can realize that there are "pictures in the fire" and that most readers will look for them. Froude, Theodore Roosevelt, and Henry W. Nevinson, waving their hands toward the library shelves, thought first of such pictures, and of the historians who knew how to paint men and scenes with such color that to people of imagination intervening time melts away between the present-day and long-past events. Roosevelt wished Americans to so catch the magic of far-off times that they would see Queen Maeve playing on her golden harp, thrill to the resonance of Roland's horn, and hear the keels of Norman sea-raiders grating on the pebbles of the Saxon beach. But history has scenes which, touched with imagination, are more actual than these.

What a panorama, indeed, history conjures up! We are still moved by the sight of Nebuchadnezzar, his hair tangled on his shoulders, his uncombed beard hanging down his swarthy chest, his nails sharp as eagle's talons, returning sane at last to the gates of Babylon. We still thrill to the shout of Xenophon's Ten Thousand as, reaching the crest of their final hill, they at last descry the dark line of the Euxine Sea. We catch the crash of brazen impact, the crackling of flames, and the yells of rage and pain as Antony's five hundred ships close with the Octavian fleet, and then we see the purple sails of Cleopatra's ship puff in the breeze as she signals the Egyptian vessels to flee with her. We watch Diocletian, entering the massive amphitheater near his palace at Spalato, take the salute of two bands of doomed criminals before, rushing upon one another with sword and spear, they open the gladiatorial show. We see the thin English line at Crécy halting at Edward's sharp command, planting their pointed stakes in the mud, drawing bow to ear, and suddenly darkening the air with clothyard arrows that crumple the French host in front. And so the story marches down with ever-widening sweep until we see Wolfe reciting the Elegy below Quebec, Lincoln sinking back unconscious in his chair at Ford's Theatre, Bismarck presiding over the Congress of Berlin, the German tide rolling through Brussels in 1914; until, with a start, we face the events of yesterday—Hitler and Stalin invading Poland, and an American airplane exploding a bomb over Hiroshima.

The library shelves contain fare, certainly, for every taste and nutriment for every mind. Students of the borderland between legend and fact can read Herodotus's pages telling how the Arabians collected frankincense from trees guarded by winged serpents, how the Scythians boiled meat without firewood, and how the Carthaginians carried on a dumb commerce with certain African tribes. Lovers of a tense and harrowing narrative can turn to the chapter in which Thucydides relates how the Athenian expedition against Syracuse came to utter ruin under its walls. Anyone who wishes to lay beside recent wars a panoramic picture of an earlier world struggle can follow Livy's story of how Hannibal massed an army in Spain, marched it across the Alps, and bringing it into the plains of Italy, defeated one Roman army after another until he stood at the gates of the desperate capital. Not a few people will say that in sheer enjoyment and human interest Herodotus, Thucydides, and Livy are superior to any recent novel. Other readers may like a picture of a dark age painted in somber colors. If so, they need only turn to Tacitus. Himself an eyewitness of the reign of terror in the last three years of Domitian, he saw the worst side of Roman imperialism; and figuring Tiberius as another tyrant of Domitian stripe, he has retold every exaggerated tale of the emperor's misdeeds.

Those who prefer the quieter aspects of history, avoiding its more violent and melodramatic occurrences, may find it in long shelves from the portraiture of national life and manners in Xenophon's *Education of Cyrus* and in Tacitus's *Germania* down to Elie Halévy's masterly presentation of most departments of English life in his *The English People in 1815* and Karl Lamprecht's thorough volumes on the cultural development of the German people. George Macaulay Trevelyan's *Social History of England* is as entertaining as it is informative. For those concerned with the intellectual and spiritual history of mankind an equal treasury of material exists. They may begin with James H. Breasted's *The Dawn of Conscience*, describing the emergence of a sense of social morality in Egypt five thousand years ago, W. Robertson Smith's *Religion of the Semites*, and Gilbert Murray's *The Rise of the Greek Epic*; and from this they may come down to such historians of the modern mind as Taine, Lecky, Georg Brandes, and Vernon L. Parrington. Some may prefer history of a highly analytical order, with an ample introduction of statistical and sociological data; such history as we encounter in Paul Leroy-Beaulieu on Russian economic changes, or the works of J. B. and Barbara Hammond on the town laborer and rural laborer in England.

To add to the variety of history, whole new fields are from time to time annexed to its domain. The history of political leadership in the United States once meant merely the study of parties, votes, and individual biographies. It has been given a radically changed character by writers who apply to its problems the skills of the sociologist, economist, social psychologist, and anthropologist—so many skills, in fact, that one historian despairingly suggests that "the study of leadership in large, fluid, heterogeneous societies is no job for mere mortals."[1] Modern histories of leadership emphasize the social, governmental, and behavioral situation rather than the individual. The history of law was long written superficially if at all. However, Frederic William Maitland's books on English law, and FitzJames Stephen's three volumes on English criminal law, brought a fresh expertness to the field, followed in the United States by Charles Warren, Richard B. Morris, and others. Administrative history was long an untrodden area. But early in the twentieth century various writers, American, Continental, and British, placed medieval administration in different countries under searching gaze,[2] and Sidney and Beatrice Webb in their eight-volume work on *English Local Government* showed how rich the subject was.

The Spirit of critical inquiry for

The Whole truth = History

I

Because history has been approached from many different points of view, it has received more varied definitions than even the novel. The cynics definition of it as a *mensonge convenu,* a lie agreed upon, may harmonize with the statement attributed to Disraeli that he preferred romances to history because they told more truth, but it is a piece of baseless flippancy. It is precisely the fact that historians are always ready to disagree with each other which makes any persistence of lies in history—that is, true history —unlikely. Carlyle, approaching the subject from his special predilection, which emphasized the role of the individual, termed history the essence of innumerable biographies. But obviously it is a good deal more than that; it takes account of many forces which are not personal at all. John Cotter Morison defined it as "The prose narrative of past events, as probably true as the fallibility of human testimony will allow." Good so far as it goes, that definition is too pedestrian to be wholly satisfactory. Conversely, a familiar modern statement that history is the record of everything in the past which helps explain how the present came to be, is too philosophical and priggish. It emphasizes too much the utilitarian role of history, which we often wish to read without reference to the present—even to get entirely away from the present.

History is any integrated narrative, description or analysis of past events or facts written in a spirit of critical inquiry for the whole truth. A definition which attempts to be more precise than this is certain to be misleading. For above all, it is the historical point of view, the historical method of approach—*that is, the spirit of critical inquiry for the whole truth*—which, applied to the past, makes history. It will not do to lay down a more exclusive formula. There are as many different schools and theories of history as the schools of philosophy, medicine, and painting. But it will be agreed that a newspaper report of some current event, such as a debate in Congress, is not history, because it cannot be written as an inquiry into the *whole* truth. Only superficial sources of information, generally speaking, are open to newspapermen. It will also be agreed that a Democratic or Republican campaign-book reviewing events of the four years just preceding publication is not history, for it is not written as a critical inquiry into the truth. A careful historical novel, like Charles Reade's *The Cloister and the Hearth*, holds many historical values. But certainly this is not history, for it is not written primarily as an inquiry into past *truth* at all, but primarily to entertain and please by an artistic use of the imagination.*

Since the varieties of history are almost as numerous as the eminent writers of history, these writers, having adopted firm convictions and founded schools, have sometimes been deplorably contemptuous of one another. No reader should be misled by their occasional displays of professional narrowness or ill-nature. Macaulay wrote in his diary for December 7, 1849, when his first volumes had just appeared, that he had a more just conception of history and understood its nature more fully than Hume, Voltaire, or Gibbon; though at the same time he admitted that Thucydides wrote better history than he did.[3] But Macaulay's own contemporaries disagreed bitterly as to his merits. Lord Acton records that, conversing at different times with Stubbs and Creighton, and with the German historians Mommsen and Harnack, he found that they agreed that Macaulay was the most gifted historian of modern times. Yet other contemporary historians denied in the strongest terms that he was more than a very second-rate writer. Carlyle, speaking as a moralist, declared his *History of England from the Accession of James II* "a book to which 400 editions could not lend any permanent value, there being no depth of sense in it at all and a very great quantity of rhetorical wind and other ingredients, which are the reverse of sense." A more moderate critic, Frederic Harrison, asserted that Macaulay's conception of history

---

* A definition of the *purpose* of history is clearly a very difficult matter. Perhaps Arnold Toynbee's statement that it is a search for "light on the nature and destiny of man" is the most satisfactory.

was grievously erroneous, for he was a mere painter of lively pictures, whose narrative came closer to romance than fact. Yet Carlyle, sure that his own historical methods were just, fared as badly at other hands. Prescott angrily pronounced his *French Revolution* "perfectly contemptible."

A humorous exaggeration has sometimes crept into these broadsides fired by historians at one another. Carlyle remarked that Henry Hallam's *Literature of Europe in the 15th, 16th, and 17th Centuries* was a mere "valley of dry bones"; and Hallam meanwhile confessed to Tennyson of Carlyle's *French Revolution* that "I have tried to read it but I can't get on, the style is so abominable." American historians, too, have been savagely critical of one another. James Ford Rhodes, attentive to analysis, entertained a low opinion of the historical methods and achievements of John Bach McMaster, primarily a descriptive historian. In turn, Albert J. Beveridge believed that Rhodes's *History of the United States from the Compromise of 1850* was shallow in thought, sectionally biased, unfair to Stephen A. Douglas and the Southern leaders, and ill-written.* Every strongly individual historian sets up his own standards, and few historians of the first rank will admit that a different conception of historical aims is as good as their own. But many of these attacks have no more real validity than Francis Jeffrey's famous verdict on Wordsworth's *Excursion*, "This will never do!" The reader should cultivate a taste for different varieties of history, varying as widely in form and aim as *War and Peace, Humphry Clinker, The Talisman, L'Assomoir, Treasure Island*, and *Swann's Way*, all novels and all good ones.

To limit the variety of history, to crib and cabin it within narrow bounds, would constitute the greatest injury that pedants could do it. If the reader's mood or taste demands brilliant irony, piquant epigram, a style as stately as an army with banners, and the dexterous management

* For an amusing excoriation of one historian by another, see W. A. Dunning's analysis of the defects of James Schouler's volume on the Civil War; *Truth in History and Other Essays*, pp. 173–78.

of a mighty panorama of peoples and empires, Gibbon
waits upon the shelves. If he demands eloquence, enthusiasm, a headlong rush of language, a vivid succession of
scenes lit up as by a succession of lightning flashes, he can
turn to Michelet and Carlyle. If he calls for systematized
erudition, inexorable logic, a scientific attention to the arrangement of facts in neat categories, there are Von Ranke
and Gardiner. If the reader asks for adventure and suspense, he may follow Cortez and Pizarro as Prescott shows
them picking their way amid deadly perils; or, if a broader
setting and mightier issues be demanded, he may read
Hodgkin's careful history of the barbarian invasions of
Italy. If he wishes the gloomy coloring of the forest on
his page, there is Parkman; if the rich sparkle of court
and palace, there are Froude's pictures of Elizabeth at
Hampton Court and Windsor, and Guizot's of the French
monarchs at Fontainebleau and Versailles. If he calls for a
searching narrative of a great political movement, in which
minute research is combined with power of bold generalization, he may turn to Theodor Mommsen's history of
the struggle which felled the Roman Republic and created
the Empire.

History → factual - statistical - interpretive ideas -

II

We have happily all sorts and conditions of history—
factual and interpretive; popular and learned; history as
minutely erudite as H. L. Osgood's of the American colonies, or as lively as Lytton Strachey's; history that presents
an economic interpretation of the past, and history that
gives ideas and acts a more elevated motivation; history
concerned with statistics and history concerned with ideas.
The true lover of history will reject none, but try rather to
take what is good from each. Neither will he, in spite of
definitions, reject fiction and poetry as often having a
legitimate relationship with history—as sometimes almost
falling within its bounds. Gogol's *Taras Bulba* is not formal
history, but no other work in Russian or English will give
the student so vital an impression of the grim Cossack
struggle against Mohammedan Tartars and Catholic Poles

in the sixteenth century—and needless to say, none is written in such beautiful prose. It is safe to say that the general conception of several reigns in English history has been
molded much more powerfully by Shakespeare's historical
dramas than by any historian, and while the poet rear-
ranged many events to suit himself, his genius pierced
nearer the essential character of Richard II and Henry V
than mere students of documents have done. After the
reader has mastered all that Lecky and Trevelyan have to
tell him of the eighteenth century in England, he will still
have to con Fielding's *Tom Jones*, with its crowded stage
of characters disposed about the figures of Allworthy,
Blifil, Jones, and Squire Western, its wealth of observation upon manners, dress, and speech, and its accurate
reproduction of the ideas and ideals of the age. In a sense
it and *Humphry Clinker* are materials for the social historian; in another sense they approach *history*, their pages
containing much that no social historian can redistill into
his own volume.

As variety means wealth, wealth also means a necessity
for selection and organization. The diner at the well-laden
table of history should not forget that while aimless
voracious reading may at first seem profitable, it will end
in dyspepsia. The amateur reader no less than the student
should give plan to his attack on historical literature if it
is to yield mental stimulation and spiritual enrichment
instead of disappointment; and if he has no advisers, he
can easily find handbooks of advice. Nor can we forget
that our reading should always be critical. The general
student may begin his survey of the world's past by reading—for example—Will Durant's *Story of Civilization*, an
illuminating work which has stretched well beyond the five
volumes originally projected. He should realize, however,
that as each of Durant's volumes has been criticized in
detail by specialists in the field it covers, some knowledge
of this criticism will suggest to him both reservations and
additions.

A tolerant view of historical work will make little of
the hoary dispute, inaugurated by George Otto Trevelyan,
whether history is a science or an art. It is essentially futile

because the answer depends upon the definition given the word science, and disputants seldom agree upon that definition. It is futile also because of the profound truth stated by T. H. Huxley in his *Letters:* "Literature and science are not two different things, but two sides of the same thing." As Von Ranke, one of the founders of the so-called scientific school, stated, history is both a science and an art. There is nothing irreconcilable in the two. Darwin's *The Voyage of the Beagle* is sufficiently scientific to please the zoologist who cares nothing about art, and more than sufficiently artistic to please the literary man who cares little for geology or biology. History makes demands upon science in that it must perform every possible office of research and criticism. It makes demands upon art in that if it is to reach many readers or endure for many years, it must have vital attractions of form, style, and spirit. Like Darwin's book, a consummate history, the work of Mommsen or Fustel de Coulanges or Prescott, unites art and science indissolubly.

We can understand this better, and can approach a true comprehension of the word science in this connection, if we note that historical writing involves three elements. One is the element of factual inquiry and sifting—that is, research. This should be strictly scientific in its use of highly exact principles to accumulate, observe, and weigh data; it is scientific, that is, in method. The second element is that of interpretation. Having accumulated his facts, the historian must discover their logical connection with each other, the laws which rule them, and their significance for the period studied and for our own time. In this second element lie possibilities for the establishment of a scientific set of deductions. But here the word science is used in a different sense; a scientific generalization from a large number of historical facts has the same quality as a generalization from a large number of zoological facts. It is an attempt to set up a general law resting on the weight of evidence. Darwin not merely accumulated a mass of data bearing on the differences among species; he tried to establish a law explaining the differences. A scientific historian who studied revolutions would not merely accumulate a mass of data on these human upheavals; he would try to formulate some laws common to all. Finally, the third element in historical writing is presentation—the narration, description, and exposition required to set forth the results of research and interpretation.

A superficial observer might say that the first two elements are scientific, and the third literary. But as a matter of fact, all three are scientific and all three literary. Presentation, while primarily an art, involves the complex and exacting science termed Rhetoric. It must also be scientific in temper; it must not understate or overstate. As for the first two elements, they should have their aesthetic side. If research unites precision and ingenuity as it should, it achieves a beauty as pleasing as a fine mathematical demonstration—and Edna St. Vincent Millay tells us that "Euclid alone had looked on beauty bare." Similarly, the element of interpretation draws upon the imagination, and all exercises of the imagination, even for scientific ends, are aesthetic. It will be generally conceded that Sir Henry Maine's *Ancient Law* is an impressive work of history not for any beauty of imagery or diction, for it lacks that, but because the dexterity and force with which it draws from a tangled array of facts certain well-substantiated laws excite our admiration. A finished intellectual demonstration may excite the aesthetic sense as the powerful, smooth-spinning dynamo excited Henry Adams's. Thus it is that some passages in R. H. Tawney's *The Acquisitive Society* charm by sheer intellectual grasp and power.

The critics who deny history any scientific standing whatever must rest their case upon an excessively narrow definition of the word science. It is obvious that history is not a science in the sense in which physics, chemistry, and astronomy deserve that term. For one reason, these sciences are strictly impersonal, while history is violently personal; molecules have no loves and hates, while men do. For another, these studies aim at the discovery of laws that exist quite out of time, and that repeat themselves consistently with the repetition of a given set of circumstances. It is a law of chemistry that hydrogen and oxygen in fixed proportions will always produce water, a law of physics that every mass tends toward every other mass with a force varying directly as the product of the masses, inversely as the square of their distances apart. History, far from attempting to discover laws that exist out of time, is a more or less generalized description of some segment of a time-process. If the description is not in time it is not history.

Moreover, historical events never precisely duplicate themselves. It is commonly said that history repeats itself (and Max Beerbohm adds that "historians repeat one another") but this is wrong. The historian has no control of phenomena in the blowpipe or test-tube sense. He may be greatly puzzled by Stephen A. Douglas's motives in hastening on the Civil War by introducing the Kansas-Nebraska Act, but he cannot call Douglas before another Congress of 1854 to test his theories. G. K. Chesterton was not quite correct when he wrote that the great lesson of history is that mankind never profits by the lessons of history. The wholehearted acceptance of the United Nations by the American people, for example, showed that they had learned the folly of the rejection of the League of Nations. But in general, Chesterton's statement holds true, and often for the valid reason that the lesson is unclear; mankind can say with truth that its situation at any given moment differs in vital particulars from any previous situation, however parallel in outline. Moreover, human beings change as much as situations, so that pronouncements upon "their instincts immature, their purposes unsure," must always be imprecise—and ours would be a dull world if they were not.*

But science is not confined to physics and chemistry, to the table of the elements and the laws of heat and motion. It includes biology, which is incapable of discovering laws of a purely timeless and mathematical character. When science deals with the motions of leaping tigers, skimming swallows, and diving tadpoles, it must include with the

---

* Students will profit from the treatment of this subject—the limitations of experiment—by John M. Keynes's *The Scope and Method of Political Economy*, and the pages upon "Reason in Social Science" in Morris L. Cohen's *Reason and Nature*.

formulae of dynamics certain new elements. Matter behaves in unpredictable ways because it is alive, and this unpredictability colors the whole subject. And the biologist can no more abolish the time-element than the historian can. Apart from the minor phenomena of individual behavior, he finds himself facing the major phenomena of progression and evolution. A scientist dealing with biological development has to do on a small scale what the historian will try to do with much larger and more complex phenomena—he will formulate conclusions as to tendencies, and lay these down as laws. Some tendencies, both in biology and in history, are more enduring than others, and so come nearer to laws of the timeless kind. Obviously history cannot demonstrate so many uniform and enduring conclusions as biology, but it can substantiate a good many.

Few observers will deny that generation after generation history is becoming more of a science in the broad sense of the word. The steady accumulation of data, together with our increasing ability to classify and analyze facts bearing upon individual psychology, communal psychology, economic changes, and the growth of institutions and mores, enables us to lay down more "laws" and to do so less tentatively. It is true that they are still few and for the most part feeble, but then mankind has a recorded past of only about six thousand years. Historians have discovered, for example, certain uniform tendencies governing movements of religious enthusiasm. They are the same for the rise of Christianity, the rise of Mohammedanism, the rise of Mormonism; for the Crusades and the Great Awakening. On this subject the historian derives much aid from psychologists like William James (see *The Varieties of Religious Experience*) and other scientists. Laws which seem to govern the growth, flowering, and decline of certain forms of capitalism can also be outlined with more clarity than a generation ago. Here economists, as in the treatment of the economic cycle, have helped history to find a way. And in a few fields where the sociologist and historian can ally themselves, the social tendencies of history are being adumbrated if not formulated. One is the before-noted field of the great politico-social revolutions, where historians have made bold to lay down general laws which hold good for the English, American, French, and Russian Revolutions alike. They begin, for example, with the rule that revolutions originate not where populations live in utter wretchedness, but where they live in comparatively good and (though pricked by sharp hardships) progressively better conditions.

It is evident that the biologist holds many advantages over the historian in the accumulation of his facts. He can do much to control environment; he can rule out chance and eliminate abnormal individuals; he can repeat his experiments, using plants, fruit flies, and guinea pigs, with great rapidity. The historian may watch Middletown for a generation, but cannot isolate it under a glass bell or increase the tempo with which it changes. Yet this is a difference in the conditions of work, not in the basic character of the work. Both historian and biologist, dealing with life in time, have to grapple with factors that are a mixture of the scrutable and inscrutable; for this reason history is at bottom almost as much a science as biology. Nor must we push too far the statement that history never repeats itself. While no situation reproduces itself in detail, many reproduce themselves, as we have said, in outline. Any tariff fight brings a body of lobbyists to Washington and a movement for logrolling; every great war in Europe arouses furious partisanship in America; every wave of hard times gives vitality to radicalism. The statesman should be the last person to underrate the scientific element in history, for much of his success will depend upon his proper scrutiny of it.

A skeptical statement on the extent to which history written with sociological aids can attempt prediction is made by Karl Popper in the *Poverty of Historicism* (1957). He utterly rejects the possibility of a theoretical history, ruled by such laws as Henry Adams essayed to find; that is, a historical social science that corresponds even roughly to theoretical physics. He declares that while long-term predictions by the social studies are perhaps not inherently impracticable, they can only be large-scale forecasts. On the other hand, short-term predictions must lack exactness in their treatment of detail, yet since they are confined to short periods must deal wholly with detail; "but a prediction of details which is inexact in its details is pretty useless." The real question, then, is as to the value of the long-term and large-scale forecast, and Popper's verdict is "Dubious." This statement overemphasizes the importance of exactness, for the teachings of history can be real and potent even if they lack detailed precision.

III

If some extremists minimize too much the role of science or law in history, others decidedly exaggerate it. A considerable number of writers swallow unreservedly the mechanistic view which considers history a regular process of evolution, a series of inevitable results proceeding from clear causes. Its principal phenomena seem to them nearly as predictable a growth as the succession of plant forms in a cut-over tract of woodland, for certain great facts and forces bring on other forces as logical, almost inescapable, sequels. These historians exhaust their ingenuity to prove that the establishment of the Norman Empire was bound to occur; all the elements were present in England and Normandy to produce it, and if William the Conqueror had not done it, someone else would. William, they hold, played about as important a part as Rostand's Chantecler, who thought that his crow evoked the sunrise. They maintain that the growth of the medieval papacy was an equally inevitable process. They urge, again, that the Reformation resulted from the evolution of certain economic, social, and intellectual forces, and that it produced Luther— Luther did not produce it; had Luther never lived, someone else much like him would have arisen. They argue that the American Civil War, as a collision between two economies and two cultures, was an evolutionary event, not a cataclysm. Chance played no part in it, and given the principal forces of the day, it was absolutely inescapable.

Holders of this view can point to some striking facts to support their emphasis upon the scientific basis of history.

They assert, for example, that America owed its discovery not to Columbus but to various inventions and forces which would have effected it at that very time had Columbus never lived. Pedro Alvarez Cabral, sailing from Portugal to India in 1500, was blown westward to the coast of Brazil; he might well have taken Columbus's place in history. And had it not been Cabral, the improvements in navigation, the irresistible thrust of commerce, would soon have produced somebody else.

But this view can be pushed to the point at which it becomes demonstrably false. It underrates the powerful role which fortune or accident plays in history. After all, events frequently present themselves not as a logical chain, but a fortuitous string of occurrences, affected by chances of a thousand kinds. A sudden illness; a change in weather; the loss of a document; a man's or woman's whim suggested by a mere accident—these have altered the very face of history. "For want of a shoe the horse was lost," and the battle and the kingdom. It has been said by H. A. L. Fisher that the destiny of Egypt was changed by the fact that in 1884 Sir Evelyn Baring (Lord Cromer) had a severe cold which temporarily cost him his voice, so that at Cairo he could not impress upon Gordon all the instructions he was to follow at Khartoum. Like Shakespeare, we may call the changes of history Providence, which shapes our ends rough-hew them how we may, or, like the Orientals, we may call them Kismet. But President Franklin D. Roosevelt was right when, facing an audience at the Harvard Tercentenary during the great depression, he told them that they ought to wear their worries with a difference, for they knew enough history to realize that misfortune, like fortune, seldom comes from the quarter in which it is apprehended.

The most prominent of the fortuitous chances of history is the intermittent appearance of commanding personalities, of great men. We need not accept the whole view of the school of historians founded by Thomas Carlyle; the school which makes little of the "dull multitude" and much of the "hero," and protests with asperity against the Darwinian view of history as altogether too mechanical. Carlyle was

shocked by the <u>materialism</u> inherent in the doctrine that
the <u>masses stumble upward to a better order by a process
of evolution.</u> He believed that a living spirit guides the
race, and that this spirit is best embodied in the great
leaders—whether the hero as soldier, the hero as saint,
or the hero as man of letters. All wholesome aspiration,
in the opinion of Carlyleans, must look up to the wisdom
of these select archetypes; it is unwholesome to rely upon
"blind laws" as agencies of progress. An opposite view is
expounded by writers like John Richard Green and John
Bach McMaster, who write history in terms of whole peoples, not select leaders. The greater truth is probably with
them, and with their belief that the "hero" is usually important not in himself but as an expression of the *Zeitgeist*.
But into this hoary quarrel we need not at the moment
enter. It is sufficient to say that the Carlylean gospel,
though often pushed too far, has a decided element of
truth in it. As Sir Charles Oman states, it is easier to go
wrong by denying the importance of the hero's role than
by exaggerating it.[4]

For beyond doubt some personalities have been—to use
Oman's word—"cataclysmic." It is easy to conceive that
Philip of Macedon might have left behind him a son as
weak as Oliver Cromwell left in his son Richard. Had he
done so, had there been no Alexander the Great, history
would have recorded no Macedonian conquest of Asia
Minor and Persia, no establishment of Greek kingdoms
as far east as the Oxus, no clearance of the way for the
Roman Empire, and no such annexation of Egypt and Syria
to the Western World as was the fact for eight hundred
years after Alexander's death. The course of all ancient
and medieval history would have been profoundly different. Suppose, on the other hand, that Cromwell's son and
heir had possessed the genius of Alexander. What might
not have been the dominating role of England in Western
Europe in the years following 1658? A still more striking
illustration of the "cataclysmic" personality is afforded by
Mahomet. The founder of Islam profoundly influenced
the course of world history, and he is the only Arabian
who ever did so. What was there in the relatively monoto-

nous and unambitious history of the Arabian tribes in the
fifth and sixth centuries to suggest that they would suddenly become leaders in a great world movement? What
cultural, religious, and political factors existed in the Arabic
peninsula when this son of a poor Mecca trader appeared
which would make his spectacular career an inevitable
response to social law? Almost none; the only general factor
which helps to explain Mahomet was a religious ferment
which, with the advent of Christianity and Judaism, had
seized upon part of Arabia just before his birth. On the
whole, he was as unaccountable a phenomenon of nature
as an earthquake or a tornado. And history presents not
a few such cataclysmic personalities—Peter the Great, Napoleon, Lenin.

The true path is a middle path. By careful research we
can attempt to decide what part of history is due to evolution or law, and what part is explicable in terms of a
natural process—and unquestionably this is a much larger
part than was once supposed. The remainder, we can say,
is due to chance, or at any rate is inexplicable. As we
ascertain more facts about the past, and as we bring various modern sciences, such as psychology, economics, and
sociology, to bear upon them, we are able to assign more
of history to the operation of known principles. That is,
we are able to increase its scientific character. We can
thus analyze the great natural processes of history much
better than Gibbon or Voltaire, and historians a century
hence will be able to analyze them much better than we.
The chief interest of history lies in accounting for past
events by a reasoned array of causes, and in refusing to
admit that mere fortuity produced them until we have
no alternative.

What caused the rapid spread of Christianity after the
sudden conversion of Saul of Tarsus on the road to Damascus in A.D. 34 or 35? Was it sheer bad fortune, as many
pagans thought? Was it Providence acting in ways inscrutable to man, as the church fathers taught? Of course
we know that it was neither. Gibbon gives us a partial list
of the true causes. He enumerates the facilities of communication created by the Roman Empire; the zeal of

many Jews for the new religion; the widespread acquaintance of the ancient world with the doctrine of the immortality of the soul; the virtues of the first Christians;
and the persecutions by Roman officials, making the blood
of the martyrs the seed of the Church. A fuller acquaintance with historical causes has enabled later writers to
elaborate upon Gibbon's list. They enumerate the wide
diffusion of Judaism and Jews, furnishing a ready soil; the
close kinship between Hellenistic syncretism and Christian
doctrine; and the vigorous expansion of Mithraic religion,
whose ceremonies—baptism to remove sins, anointment, a
sacred meal of bread and water, the use of consecrated
wine—strongly resembled some of the rites used by
Christians.

Yet when we have taken account of these and other
logical causes, one non-logical element remains. What if
Saul had never undergone the experience, mystical or
pathological, on the Damascus road? For Saul by his personal force revolutionized the ideas held by the leaders
of the Church upon its future development. He took a
movement that might easily have been restricted to the
reformation of Judaism, and transformed it into a great
new evangel which, as Jesus had apparently intended, was
fitted for worldwide acceptance. But for the "cataclysmic"
personality of Saul, what might Christianity have been
like? No — but the Holy Spirit.

So we may follow various movements through history.
We can today account by logical and orderly causes for
much that formerly seemed mysterious. We can show that
the Saracens were not turned back merely because Charles
Martel was a better soldier than Abd-er-Rahman at Poitiers
in A.D. 732, but for better and far more complex reasons.
We can explain the rise and fall of feudalism without reference to individuals or to accidental events. We can account by logical social causes for the development of Jack-
sonian democracy, and can reduce the credit to be assigned
to its idol and exemplar, Andrew Jackson himself. Scientific history is constantly advancing in its work of making
the past more logical, orderly, and comprehensible. But
when scientific research and interpretation have done their

utmost, we must still give a powerful emphasis to chance and to the "cataclysmic" personality.

To chance, to the hero, and to the unknown or non-analyzable forces that keep a penumbra of twilight about many historical occurrences. Because of these and other factors written history belongs not to the sciences but to the humanities. Its genius is the development of free human beings, the elevation of the spirit of man, and the enrichment of the character of nations. Its highest expression involves qualities of imagination and graces of style which lift it out of the general aridity of scientific writing and place it with literature.

IV

Another attempt to limit the happy variety of history comes from those who would hem in the field of historical presentation by narrow rules of approach. They would have the historian write in a certain way or not at all. The demand most frequently advanced by such writers is that history be kept absolutely impartial and unbiased. In the preface to his detailed life of Lincoln, Albert J. Beveridge states that absolute disinterestedness can and should be secured. "Facts when justly arranged interpret themselves," he remarks. "They tell the story." This is an echo of what Lord Acton said of Von Ranke's emphasis upon absolute impartiality: "He taught us to be critical, *to be colorless*, to be new."

In answer to this it may be confidently affirmed that no important history has yet appeared which did not reveal some bias, and that in the greatest of histories the element of partiality is strong. Even Beveridge did not dare say that "facts interpret themselves"; he wrote that "facts *when justly arranged* interpret themselves." But when the same facts can be arranged in an order tending to prove that Lincoln in 1854–56 was more statesman-like than Douglas (as Lord Charnwood arranges them), or in an order indicating that Douglas was more the states-man (as Beveridge arranges them), who shall say which is the *just* arrangement? Facts cannot be selected without some personal conviction as to what is truth, and cannot be arranged without the same conviction—and this conviction is a bias. In historical writing, as in current politics, what seems to one man a principle may seem to equally honest students a prejudice. Ulrich B. Phillips and Frederic Bancroft were in possession of much the same body of facts regarding slavery; they were both thoroughly honest, and determined to tell the uncolored truth as they saw it; but one arrived at friendly, the other at hostile conclusions upon slavery as an institution.

The best answer to Beveridge's rash statement is his own book. Every true historian has a mind formed by practical experience and observation, and Beveridge's was highly formed. He held likes and dislikes, trusts and distrusts, convictions and disbeliefs; some topics especially interested him, and some bored him. A Westerner, reared in a state which united Northern and Southern blood, of progressive and expansive temperament, he responded more readily to Douglas's desire to throw open the West on a popular-sovereignty basis than to the Free Soil demand for restrictions on Western settlement. The mental thrust and firmness which had made him a political leader carried these predilections over to give a sharp individuality to his history.

Of course it is important that the historian have what the French call all intelligence *délié*, a mind free from conscious prejudices. Some pseudo-historical writers take pleasure in absolutely closed minds. Hilaire Belloc's, for example, was barred and shuttered against any ray of light on matters touching the Catholic Church; he delighted in his prejudices, and wrote for other willfully prejudiced minds. It is impossible to examine Charles A. Beard's historical treatment of America's part in world affairs from 1914 to 1941 conscientiously without feeling that the author did not so much arrange his judgments to fit the data as he arranged the data to fit his preconceived judgments. Fortunately it is seldom impossible to draw a clear line between honest conviction on the one side and prejudice or preconception on the other; for it is not difficult to detect the warping of evidence which the latter involves. Con-

viction rules out absolute impartiality, but nevertheless
aims at truth. An examination of the work of the greatest
historians shows that while essentially honest, it not merely
falls short of absolute objectivity, but owes much of its
greatness to its conviction.

Macaulay would assuredly have penned a history of
England much poorer in color, narrative power, and portraiture had he not written as a Whig, an earnest officer
of a party in whose rapid rise he played his part as member of Parliament and Cabinet Minister. To be sure, he
sometimes carried his adjectives and epigrams too far, giving a certain basis for the criticism that his work is "a huge
Whig pamphlet"; but this was the excess of an honest
quality. George Grote's history of Greece was originally
conceived as an answer to the extreme Tory views expressed by William Mitford in his earlier five-volume history. Whereas Mitford had been a conservative member
of Parliament, the banker Grote held advanced democratic
ideas, he had helped carry the Reform Bill to enactment,
and he wished to right the wrong which he believed Mitford had done to free institutions. No small part of the
warmth and inspiration of his work flows from his close
sympathy with democratic tendencies in Greece and ardent dislike of Greek aristocracy. No reader of Gibbon
needs to be told that he was strongly biased in the sense
of holding intense convictions. The most vital pages of
the *Decline and Fall,* the section most frequently read,
are the famous fifteenth and sixteenth chapters ("Progress
of the Christian Religion" and "Conduct of the Roman
Government Toward the Christians"); where, under the
veil of a grave and deliberate irony, he arraigns Christianity as the principal dissolvent of ancient civilization. An
equally important conviction was his firm belief, which
modern research has shown to be mistaken, that the Byzantine Empire was weak and miserable, and that the de-
generacy, cruelty, and factionalism associated with the
very name Byzantium made the study of events at Constantinople of minor importance. This conviction, which at
points became a prejudice, weakens the whole later part of
Gibbon's history.[5] But who would care to read a Gibbon

who possessed no strong convictions, who aimed at absolute objectivity even if he sacrificed color and drama, and whose personality counted for nothing in his history?

Illustrations of the same truth may be found among our own historians. Parkman held powerful innate convictions of a racial and religious character. He believed English civilization superior to French and the Protestant religion more favorable to free institutions than the Catholic. His *Jesuits of North America* is on the whole a magnificent tribute to the missionaries of that creed, and he brings out all the heroic qualities of La Salle, Frontenac, and Montcalm. But the underlying conviction flows as a strong pulse through all his books. The same national and religious beliefs give color and energy to much of Prescott's work. When we turn to Bancroft, we encounter a different form of bias, for he felt a passionate American nationalism, and an equally powerful devotion to egalitarian democracy. As J. Franklin Jameson has said, all his histories voted for Jackson, just as nearly all recent historical writing in this country votes for Franklin D. Roosevelt.

Similar illustrations might be multiplied by reference to the modern historians of Continental Europe. Heinrich von Treitschke, successor of the "colorless" Von Ranke as Prussian state historian, was an ardent believer in German unity, who resigned his chair at Freiburg when Baden joined Austria in the Austro-German War, and went to Berlin. He held a profound belief in a centralized monarchy, in the Prussian ideal of the state, and in the conquering mission of Germany. These convictions, expressed with sincerity and high ability, colored his *Deutsche Geschichte* more to its advantage than its disadvantage.

Impartial annalists and monograph-writers we may have; but the impartial historian, using the noun in its highest signification, does not exist. If history became impartial in the sense of lacking conviction it would be a poor affair. The only completely unbiased historian is one whose works are not on the shelves of libraries—the Recording Angel; and doubtless he has convictions which to Satan, as Mark Twain irreverently suggested, would seem prejudices. The chief difficulty with history which sacrifices conviction to an exaggerated ideal of impartiality is that it often falls into a cold, colorless, and timid character. Such history is likely to lack large architectural elements, for nothing imparts structure to a book like the attempt to prove a thesis. It is likely to lack fervor; likely to lack proportion. It will frequently fail to distinguish between what is important and what is unimportant because it has no fixed standard of measurement; and it will frequently refuse to pass even elementary moral judgments, though a great historian is always a great moralist.

It was an "objective" historian who wrote the unconsciously humorous sentence: "The Turks sawed the Commandant and his wife in halves, and committed other grave breaches of international law." Perhaps the most striking example of the completely impartial historian in English is Samuel Rawson Gardiner. His work has almost every merit that laborious research, taken alone, can give it, and it treats the most controversial period in English history from an absolutely non-partisan standpoint. But he is so colorless that his readers have dwindled to a handful; his history of England 1603–56 is out of print and for much of the period has been supplanted by Miss C. V. Wedgwood's robust work. What influence has his impartial biography of Cromwell exercised in comparison with Carlyle's book on the same leader, full of the strongest basic opinions? Carlyle's admiring treatment has formed almost the whole modern conception of Cromwell.

Here again, as in writing of scientific history, men will do well to take care with their definitions. While the historian should avoid bias in the sense of prejudice, he should court it in the sense of honest conviction. That conviction should follow, not precede, a study of the evidence, and be formed during and by the historian's researches. In brief, the author should approach his evidence as a judge, but should present it as a guarded and honest advocate. It is his duty to form judgments, but even more his duty to avoid *prejudging* the evidence. Beyond question even Von Ranke, the leading exponent of colorless history, did not succeed in being wholly objective, for much of his work was unconsciously written from the standpoint of the conservative reaction of his time in Prussia. When he criticized George Bancroft's democratic point of view, Bancroft might have retorted in kind. Beyond question no writer can wholly emancipate his mind from the coloring influence of time, environment, education, current ideals, personal ambitions, and national trends. But that does not exempt him from the duty of striving to attain the greatest possible degree of objectivity and impartiality. Truth is promoted by a clash of honest judgment. After Mitford and Grote have had their say, a Bury or a Droysen finds his ground better cleared and his ideas illuminated by their controversy. After the clash of Clarendon and Carlyle on the character of Cromwell, C. H. Firth can draw a more accurate portrait. But the clash of mere prejudice retards the truth.

It is a defeatist gospel which would have the historian, on the ground that he can never wholly purify his mind from preconceptions, abandon the attempt altogether, and commit himself instead to a philosophy in accordance with which he will deliberately write. One eminent historian has urged that American scholars turn to "the task of exploring the assumptions upon which the selection and organization of historical fact proceed," not with the object of reducing the role of assumption, but with that of enlarging and emphasizing it.[6] The implication is that one set of assumptions would be chosen as sounder than another set, and an effort would be made to organize historical writing upon this set of preconceptions. This is the doctrine to which historical writing has bowed under state pressure in Nazi Germany and Fascist Italy; it is a doctrine which regards truth as purely relative and pragmatic. Those who have a higher ideal of truth will, while admitting that their effort to attain it is often doomed to failure, never give up the attempt. Historians have often come close—human frailties considered—to unprejudiced truth in the past, and will often do so in the future.

V

Under the general heading of style the dogmatist has also had his say, chiefly in condemning a highly literary treatment of history. Should the historian cultivate literary art, even artifice? Or is it the business of history simply to be "scientific," "scholarly," and "exhaustive," to disdain ornament in an effort to bring the dry white light of truth to bear upon the past? One would think a decision in favor of literary art might be taken for granted. Yet it has had its enemies, some of them writers of prominence. "If economics is the dismal science," asserted Freeman, "history is and ought to be the dull science." An almost equally sweeping statement has been made by James Harvey Robinson. A large school of plodding research workers in history not merely disdain literary "brilliance," but condemn it as pernicious—as leading to subtle perversions of the truth. Their ideal of history is not Mommsen, Guizot, or Macaulay, but the heavily documented page of William Stubbs, the laborious array of marshaled facts in Herbert L. Osgood, the grim drabness of Heinrich von Sybel's monograph on the Crusades. Their hostility to art or inability to achieve it led Philip Guedalla to speak of the style of modern historians in England and America as an occupational disease; the style of the smooth, monotonous French historians as one long Taine without a turning.

Literary artifice is indeed often carried too far by the more popular historians. It results in invented conversations, particularly frequent in much popular biography; in invented or twisted details, thrown in for color; and in the overdramatization of situations. It must also be remembered that the degree of literary art possible, or legitimate, depends greatly upon the subject. The history of charities in the United States, the financial history of England or France, are not themes which offer scope for stylistic ornament or eloquence. On the other hand, Thierry's subject of the Norman invasion would almost kindle the dullest pen. But even with dull subjects, literary skill adds not merely to readability, but to historical values. It supplies the difference between a clear and murky landscape. A comparison of Von Holst's dull constitutional history of the United States with F. W. Maitland's lucid writings on the legal history of Britain will quickly demonstrate this fact.* Scholarliness and thoroughness are high ideals, but scholarliness combined with literary skill constitutes an ideal far higher. In almost any subject some literary values exist— Gladstone could render a speech on the fiscal affairs of England fascinating; Woodrow Wilson and Walter Bagehot made their semi-historical analyses of Congressional and Parliamentary government almost as interesting as romantic history. The methods by which historical masters develop these values are as interesting as the methods by which they extract the truth from an obscure document, or decide between two contradictory pieces of evidence.

There is a sense in which the highest kind of historical truth cannot be found without literary art, and in which every historical writer must cultivate his artistic faculties as a means of ascertaining truths. It requires imagination to penetrate the past. The historian who best understands Hannibal, as Sidney Smith wrote, is the man who sees the brilliancy of Hannibal's single eye; the best record of his campaigns will be written by the writer who audibly hears the clash and jingle of the rings stripped from Roman dead that Hannibal's messenger emptied on the floor of the Carthaginian Senate after Cannae. The historian who best understands De Soto's exploration of the Southwest is the man who feels with his own hand the warmth of the sluggish Mississippi as De Soto plunges his arm into it over the side of his boat. It requires imagination to fuse the materials of history into a malleable whole, glowing with life. Realities are seldom dull; they seem so simply because some writers bring a dull mind and heart to them.

In this sense we may well quarrel with James Harvey Robinson's harsh statement of the literary restrictions which should hedge in the historian. "Fiction and drama," he declares in *The New History*, "are perfectly free to conceive and adjust detail so as to meet the demands of art, but

* To be sure, the works are very different in character; Von Holst's is primarily political.

the historian should always be conscious of the rigid limitations placed upon him. If he confines himself to an honest and critical statement of a series of events as described in his sources, it is usually too deficient in vivid authentic detail to make a satisfactory story." Certainly if the historian can attain vividness only by inventing statements, he had better leave vividness out. He should not give excuse for such a gibe as Mark Twain's at the reconstructed dinosaur, "three bones and a dozen barrels of plaster." But Mr. Robinson went entirely too far in saying that the sources are "usually" too meager to permit of vivid authentic detail. That is true of much (by no means all) medieval history; it is emphatically not true of later times. Memoirs, letters, diaries, public documents, newspapers, provide for the greater part of modern history a wealth of vivid detail. Moreover, a great deal of vivid detail is usually *inherent* in the situation itself and in the environment, social and physical—detail of the most authentic kind. The truly imaginative historian perceives this authentic detail, his more prosaic fellow does not. A masterly use of such detail may be illustrated by one extract from a historian describing General Braddock's advance upon the French and Indian forces at what is now Pittsburgh:

> It was the tenth of June before the army was well on its march. Three hundred axemen led the way, to cut and clear the road; and the long train of packhorses, wagons, and cannon toiled on behind, over the stumps, roots, and stones of the narrow track, the regulars and provincials marching in the forest close on either side. Squads of men were thrown out on the flanks, and scouts ranged the woods to guard against surprise; for, with all his scorn of Indians and Canadians, Braddock did not neglect reasonable precautions. Thus, foot by foot, they advanced into the waste of lonely mountains that divided the streams flowing to the Atlantic from those flowing to the Gulf of Mexico—a realm of forests ancient as the world. The road was but twelve feet wide, and the line of march often extended four miles.

It was like a thin, long parti-colored snake, red, blue, and brown, trailing slowly through the depth of leaves, creeping round inaccessible heights, crawling over ridges, moving always in dampness and shadow, by rivulets and waterfalls, crags and chasms, gorges and shaggy steeps. In glimpses only, through jagged boughs and flickering leaves, did this wild primeval world reveal itself, with its dark green mountains, flecked with the morning mist, and its distant summits pencilled in dreamy blue. The army passed the main Alleghany, Meadow Mountain, and Great Savage Mountain, and traversed the funereal pine-forest afterwards called the Shades of Death. No attempt was made to interrupt their march, though the commandant of Fort Duquesne had sent out parties for that purpose. A few French and Indians hovered about them, now and then scalping a straggler or inscribing filthy insults on trees; while others fell upon the border settlements which the advance of the troops had left defenceless. Here they were more successful, butchering about thirty persons, chiefly women and children.[7]

No memoir or diary of Braddock's march supplies such details as the stumps, roots, and stones of the narrow track, the parti-colored snakelike column, red, blue, and brown, the omnipresent shade and dampness of the shaggy primeval forest, the glimpses through flickering June leaves of distant summits penciled in dreamy blue. They were inherent in the situation and Parkman's imagination extracted them. They give his paragraph a vitality—a reality —that lift it to a plane of the highest truth. Such writing comes nearer meeting Michelet's demand that history be more than a narrative—that it be a "resurrection." Parkman's work shows how even when sources are meager, the "vivid authentic detail" which Dr. Robinson thought out of reach may often be supplied; and it shows how literary art, with its triple support of imagination, vivid language, and graceful periods, is not merely a valuable ally of history, but is indispensable to its highest attainments.

III

Primitive Materials for History

THERE IS a vivid page in one of James Ford Rhodes's essays which is full of suggestion as to the variety and antiquity of materials for history. He relates how, spending a day at the Pyramids, he first filled his eyes and mind with the novelty of the spectacle; and then, his initial curiosity satisfied, "found nothing so gratifying to the historic sense as to gaze on these most wonderful monuments of human industry, constructed certainly 5000 years ago, and to read at the same time the account that Herodotus gave of his visit there about 2350 years before the date of my own."[1] That evening, going to his modern and garish Cairo hotel, he took up the latest issue of the London *Times*. It contained an account of the annual meeting of the Royal Historical Society, including a report of a carefully prepared address by the president on Herodotus, pointing out the value of the Greek writer as a model to modern historians. This newspaper report was reinforced by an editorial article upon the merits of Herodotus and the lessons he conveyed to current European writers. "I ended the day with the reflection of what a space in the world's history Herodotus filled, himself describing the work of 2600 years before his own time and being dilated upon in 1894 by one of the most modern of nineteenth century newspapers." In this page are mentioned at least four different types of material for history—the great Pyramids, hoary with fifty centuries; the first truly illustrious chronicler of ancient times; the proceedings of a historical society; and a modern newspaper. In addition, Rhodes's own paragraph is a bit of material interesting to the social historian.

The two basic elements in history are a body of more or less trustworthy materials, and a critical method applied to them. History was not born—it could not be born —until both these elements came into existence.

Of the latter, the critical spirit, we shall have much to say later, and it is necessary here only to make a brief general statement. Everyone with much experience of the world knows how difficult is the ascertainment of truth even in matters of immediate record. We are soon taught how hard it is to trust the letter we receive from a real estate agent, a politician, even, alas! some friends. Coming from a public meeting, we are astonished by the garbled account published in the newspapers. If we have passed forty, we find acquaintances writing self-justificatory memoirs over which we shake our heads. It is often difficult to obtain an exact account of even a simple transaction witnessed by a large body of observers; courtroom trials are constantly proving the fact. Ingenious psychologists like Hugo Munsterberg have arranged that some disturbance should occur unexpectedly before the eyes of watchers, have demanded written narratives of it, and have shown that the records differ in an astonishing degree. The happenings in Ford's Theatre just after the shot which killed Lincoln, though observed by a large audience, have been the theme of angry dispute. After the Wall Street bomb explosion of September 1920, several of the nine eyewitnesses testified that numerous vehicles had been in the block, one declaring he had counted nine; three witnesses asserted positively that they had seen a red motor truck carrying the bomb! Yet it was finally proved that only two vehicles were in the block, and that the explosion occurred on a small horse cart. If the truth about what happened under so many eyes in Ford's Theatre and at noonday on Wall Street is difficult to obtain, what about the truth of events in 1775, or 1492, or 55 B.C.?

Hence it is, as Lord Acton declared, that it is far more important to possess the historical spirit—a doubting, critical mind, which demands proofs and verification—than to have a mass of historical learning. The beginning of wisdom in history is doubt. Its votaries should be imbued with the mental toughness of Bret Harte's M'liss, who, told in school that Joshua had bidden the sun stand still and it had obeyed him, shut her text with a loud snap and defiantly asserted: "It's a damn lie. I don't believe it." The true historical scholar is not the man who spills facts out of every pocket, who can tell instantly when Nicholas of Cusa lived and what were the contents of the Constitutions of Clarendon—matters on which an encyclopedia can furnish more precise and interesting information. It is the man who, confronted with facts, assertions, and testimony offered with varying degrees of authority, knows how to test them, discard what seems false, and evaluate what seems true.

True history was impossible until this skeptical attitude had been sufficiently developed for application to myth, tradition, and the firmer materials of history. Although the admiration of James Ford Rhodes and the London *Times* for Herodotus was not misapplied, it must be admitted that the Greek was woefully lacking in this spirit. His work is a storehouse of mingled fact and fable, a strange mixture of intelligent firsthand observation and uncritical credulity. In his rich and fascinating narrative the myths of the Greeks, the hearsay tales of other ancient peoples, are often swallowed whole. He accepts the old legends of Croesus, of Proteus, of Battus, and of Labda in childlike spirit. With unquestioning faith, for example, he describes the reputed visit of the great Athenian sage, Solon, to the court of Croesus at Sardis—a visit which perhaps took place, for the Lydian king was a munificent patron of arts and letters. Herodotus tells how Croesus asked Solon whom he considered the happiest man of his acquaintance, expecting the complimentary answer "Croesus"; but how Solon resolutely abstained from flattery, remarking that no life could be called happy until it ended, and that the best felicity was that of men like Tellus, who had died victoriously in battle. He further narrates that years later, when Croesus had lost his kingdom to Cyrus and was awaiting death, he remembered this conversation with the Athenian, and cried out: "Solon, Solon, Solon!"—which cry, being explained to Cyrus, won him a pardon. It is a pretty tale—but is it true? Herodotus felt an uncritical reverence for all that pertained to religion, and accepted sacred or moralistic stories as easily as medieval historians swallowed the miracles of the saints.

To be sure, even in Herodotus we find beginnings of skepticism and the historical spirit. He presents certain materials for what they are worth. Describing the temple of Jupiter Belus in Babylon, and writing, "In the time of Cyrus there was likewise in this temple the figure of a man, twelve cubits high, entirely of solid gold," he hastily adds: "I myself did not see this figure, but I repeat what the Chaldeans report concerning it." He also takes the legend of Io, and gives us to understand that the Greeks and Phoenicians presented it in two radically different versions. According to the Greeks, Io was vestal or priestess of Hera at Argos. Zeus fell in love with her, and when Hera's jealousies were excited, tried to avoid them by transforming her into a cow. After some complications, Hera sent a gadfly which drove Io into Egypt, where she was restored to her original form, and became the mother of Epaphus—one of a line of heroes. But the Phoenicians told a more realistic story. They declared that Io was simply a wayward young woman of Argos who became the paramour of a Phoenician sea captain; she eloped with him, wishing to conceal her pregnancy, and was carried in his ship to Egypt, where she gave birth to a son. Of course neither story has historical value, and by setting them side by side Herodotus perhaps intended to show this.

But it is in Thucydides, writing a short generation later than Herodotus, that the historical spirit first appears. He made essentially the same critical demands upon history as those which animate modern writers, and pursued much the same objects. His aim, he declared, was to give an accurate narrative of important and interesting events, and to teach lessons of value for the future—to hold the lamp of the past at the stumbling feet of mankind. Approaching the Peloponnesian War in this spirit, his method was one of thorough research, skeptical examination, and patient verification. When dealing with the conflict, in which he had fought and been cashiered, he relied primarily upon personal observation and the questioning of eyewitnesses; but for preceding events he had to use other writers. In his first pages he assails these early compilers and chroniclers for their indolence and credulity. His own ruling principle, as he asserts, was very different, and he has given us a classic statement of the importance of a critical attitude:

> And with reference to the narrative of events, far from permitting myself to derive it from the first sources that came to hand, I did not even trust my own impressions, but it rests partly on what I saw myself, partly on what others saw for me, the accuracy of the report being always tried by the most severe and detailed tests possible. My conclusions have cost me some labor from the want of coincidence between accounts of the same occurrence by different eye-witnesses, arising sometimes from imperfect memory, sometimes from undue partiality for one side or the other. The absence of romance from my history will, I fear, detract somewhat from its interest; but if it be judged useful by those inquirers who desire an exact knowledge of the past as an aid to the interpretation of the future, which in the course of human beings must resemble if it does not reflect it, I shall be content. In fine, I have written my work, not as an essay to win the applause of the moment, but as a possession for all time.[2]

Since Thucydides blazed the way, true history has never deviated from the highroad that follows his thorough and skeptical method.

(handwritten marginalia)
1. Physical remains
2. Ballads - legends
3. Chiseled stones
4. Handwritten materials
5. libraries
6. pub-archives
   priv-collections
7. films &
   records

I

Before critical methods can be applied, we must have the materials for history; and as James Ford Rhodes's paragraph suggests, the earliest of these materials antedated Herodotus by tens of centuries. The accumulation of these materials is one of the great romances of man's activity on the planet. For ages it was an exceedingly slow process, and for many centuries even after written history began the materials grew but slowly and clumsily. In the ancient world it was only for a comparatively brief time and in a few places that really large bodies of material ever existed. Then in the Middle Ages came a long period of poverty and darkness. Only in late modern times have materials become voluminous. Indeed, their first production and preservation in large quantities came near to coinciding with that Age of Enlightenment which has been called the parent of modern history. Lord Acton, in his inaugural lecture at Cambridge in 1895, spoke of the immense change that had occurred even within a century, so that "where Hallam had no diplomatist but Barillon, his successors command the correspondence of ten countries." He spoke of an entirely new era in history—the documentary age.

As a prelude to the examination of the critical tests used in historical study, let us review briefly the romance of which we have spoken—the romance of man's accumulation of data upon his own past. The sources for history, originally confined to few and simple categories, have gradually become more complex in character and will continue to do so. They may now be listed in half a dozen broad groups. One is made up of physical remains, of which James Ford Rhodes's Pyramids are a salient example. Another comprises such orally transmitted material as legends, ballads, sagas, and traditions—material of the type so undiscriminatingly used by Herodotus. A third is the more elementary and durable kinds of representative material, such as chiseled stones, stamped coins, woven tapestries, vases, and sculptures. Then come handwritten materials, including papyri, bricks bearing cuneiform writing, vellum or parchment manuscripts, and modern documents; and after this of course that vast group of materials made up of printed books and papers. The motion picture film and phonograph record may well come to be counted in a sixth category. To these must be added that great primary source of historical material, personal observation—either by the writer, or by people whom he interviews. It is not often realized how many of the great historians have dealt with events which passed in part under their own eyes, in part under those of men they could easily consult. Among them have been not only Herodotus and Thucydides, but such other ancient writers as Polybius, Sallust, and Tacitus; such early modern writers as Guicciardini, Dávila, Grotius, Clarendon, and Burnet; such late modern writers as Hanotaux, Treitschke, Winston Churchill, James Schouler, and James Ford Rhodes. The writing of contemporaneous history has its special difficulties, but also its advantages and rewards.

The picturesque possibilities of the first source listed above, physical remains, are too seldom realized. Their variety is immense—historic sites, roads, aqueducts, pyramids, fortifications, buildings ruined or whole, furniture, pottery, implements, weapons, and museum pieces of a hundred kinds. Usually they throw more light upon social and economic history than upon political history; usually, also, they are more valuable for the descriptive than the analytical elements in history. But even those who write of rulers and generals sometimes owe much to them. Thucydides in his accounts of battles displays a minute acquaintance with the topography of the fields. Even Livy made some slight use of them. He speaks of the breastplate dedicated by Cossus in 428 B.C. which he saw hanging in the temple of Jupiter Feretrius in Rome, much as a modern British historian might draw some significant fact from the armor of the Black Prince still somberly depending in Canterbury Cathedral. A long list could be made of writers who in recent times have found physical remains rich in value. Even Parkman, writing the history of a region still largely wild and unpeopled, visited every battle-site and familiarized himself with every important bit of terrain. But it will suffice to quote what one scholar has written of Edward A. Freeman, the historian of the Norman Conquest:[3]

> He was an accurate observer, not only of the broad features of a country but of its ancient roads and earth-works, its prehistoric monuments, and its earlier and especially its ecclesiastical buildings. No man was bet-ter versed in the distinctive style of Christian architec-ture, or had a better general knowledge of the earth-works from the study of which he might hope to correct or corroborate any written records, and by the aid of which he often infused life and reality into otherwise obscure narrations . . . He visited every spot upon which the Conqueror is recorded to have set his foot, compared many of the strongholds of his followers with those they left behind them in Normandy, and studied the evi-dence of Domesday for their character and possessions. When writing upon Rufus he spent some time in visiting the afforested district of the New Forest, and sought for traces of the villages and churches said to have been depopulated or destroyed . . . When he attended a provincial congress and had listened to the description of some local antiquity, some mound, or divisional earth-bank, or semi-Saxon Church, he at once strove to show the general evidence to be deduced from them, and how it bore upon the boundaries or formation of some Celtic or Saxon province or diocese, if not upon the gen-eral history of the kingdom itself . . . He thus did much to elevate the pursuits of the archaeologist, and to show the relation they bore to the far superior labours of the historian.

The largest single branch of the study of remains is archaeology, and it of course has many subbranches. A discussion of even the outlines of archaeological work in one of these fields—in the archaeology of primitive man, for example, or classical archaeology—would fill a large volume; and it is sufficient to say here that the rise of archaeology has run parallel with the rise of modern history, and that the same scientific spirit animates both. The discovery of Herculaneum in 1720 and Pompeii in 1748 opened the great age of classical archaeology; and during the lifetimes of Voltaire, Hume, and Gibbon the antiquarian spirit which had at first dominated the study was rapidly supplanted by more adequate methods. Two men, the Count de Caylus, whose seven-volume work on antiquities appeared in 1752–54, and J. J. Winckelmann, whose history of ancient art was published a decade later, may be called respectively the prophet and founder of historical archaeology in the classical domain. Winckelmann enunciated the famous theory that the character of artistic creations is always in harmony with the spirit and events of their times. Britons were the first to undertake a well-organized and systematic exploration of ancient sites in Greece and Asia Minor, the achievements of two scholars, Stuart and Revett, who issued a four-volume work on the antiquities of Athens, inspiring the Society of Dilettanti to send out an expedition to continue their work. It was as a result of this early British interest that Lord Elgin at the beginning of the nineteenth century removed the Parthenon sculptures to the British Museum. What Heinrich Schliemann later did for history at Troy, Mycenae, and Tiryns, what Sir Henry Layard did in Asia Minor, and what Sir Flinders Petrie did in Egypt, is common knowledge.*

The romance of such work seems unending. Following the example of Schliemann, the keeper of the Ashmolean Museum at Oxford, Arthur Evans began excavating the site of Cnossus in Crete in 1900, and found a palace not unlike that at Mycenae. It was the dwelling, he decided, of the pre-Greek kings of Crete, bearing the dynastic name of Minos, and ruling in an environment of sumptuous artistry the first maritime empire in the world. To Evans it seemed impossible that so brilliant a civilization as that of Mycenae and Cnossus could have been illiterate. He

* Scientists have used radioactive carbon 14 to ascertain the dates of many ancient and even prehistoric objects, such as the Dead Sea Scrolls and the paintings on the walls of the Lascaur caves near Montignac in France.

was therefore not astonished when he found in the ruined
palace, which had been sacked and burned by mainland
invaders about 1400 B.C., a collection of two thousand inscribed clay tablets. He was able to show that this splendid
library of documents was written in three scripts—the earliest and commonest in hieroglyphics, the second and more
cursive in what he called Linear A, and the third in Linear
B. But how could the tablets be read? No such key as
the Rosetta Stone existed. Similar tablets were found at
other points, but for decades the writing defied those who
tried to identify it as of Sumerian, Basque, Hittite, or other
origin.

Then in 1935 the British School of Archaeology celebrated its half-centenary in London with an exhibition
and an address in which Sir Arthur Evans described the
failure at decipherment. A listening schoolboy named Michael Ventris decided to consecrate his leisure to the task,
and eighteen years later, when he had become an architect, accomplished his purpose. He showed that the Minoan script called Linear B concealed a form of Greek;
and as transcription began, light poured in upon the culture of the Greek Bronze Age, upon ancient economic
life, and upon the writings of Homer, who put King Aga-
memnon in Mycenae, where Schliemann found his palace,
and King Idomeneus in Cnossus, where Evans found his
palace also. The scholars had unearthed the earliest contemporary record of any Indo-European language; they
had found evidence suggesting that some form of bardic
poetry had existed even before the siege of Troy; and they
had discovered a broad bridge between the Mycenean
Bronze Age and the Greek Iron Age, which had once
seemed totally disconnected.

Archaeology is a science in itself, its work to be performed by men who have received long training in that
profession alone. Now and then, as the names of Stéphane
Gsell and James H. Breasted remind us, an eminent historian will appear who is also an eminent archaeologist,
but in general each study is a jealous mistress. The find-
ings of specialists in some branches of archaeology are
adding so rapidly to our knowledge of the past that the

historian must depend upon expert judgment. It used to be held, for example, that the Mayas did all their carving with tools of obsidian, nephrite, and other stone; but recent workers have offered strong evidence that the Mayas had entered the bronze age and used copper implements as well.[4] The feats accomplished in our Southwest in ascertaining the precise time when the beams of the dwellings of prehistoric tribes were hewn and put in place, feats made possible by the new tree-dating method, are very remarkable. And when the expert archaeologist is also an expert ethnologist, he can sometimes do a great deal to penetrate the curtain that separates history from prehistory.

Lewis H. Morgan, for example, the father of American ethnology and an enthusiastic student of archaeology, undertook to reconstruct the extinct society of the Mound Builders from their half-obliterated embankments. His boldness excited the wonder of his contemporaries.[5] "If anyone were to say that, given a mound octagonal in shape, on the banks of a river, constructed in an age long gone by, science would tell us what sort of people had built it, the purpose for which it was built, how these people lived, where they came from, what sort of houses they constructed, how they defended themselves against their enemies, how many of them there were, and what became of them in the end—we should be inclined to imagine that any answers must be reached by guesswork"— so commented the *Nation*.[6] "But these are the questions proposed by Mr. Morgan, and . . . the process by which he resolves them in as strictly scientific as chemical analysis."

Of course Morgan arrived only at what he called approximate solutions. He concluded that the Mound Builders were Indians who had reached the "middle status" of barbarism, like the Indians of the Southwest, Old Mexico, and Central America. They came from beyond the Mississippi to the Northwest. They had practiced communism and dwelt in houses of adobe brick—joint tenements with a ground floor ten to twelve feet high, closed up solidly on the first floor externally for defense. In the Middle

West adobe was out of the question; and hence they built their tenements on huge mounds, ten or twelve feet high, the tenements themselves being of wood, with sloping walls covered with mud or mortar. These made strong fortresses. Since no traditional knowledge of these Mound Builders persisted among tribes east of the Mississippi, they must have been ancient. Because the number of such remains is small, the tribesmen must have been few. The Mound Builders finally perished or withdrew, according to Morgan, because a warm climate is necessary to a vigorous form of Indian communal life. Of course in the sixty-odd years since Morgan wrote, his conclusions have been modified, especially by newer evidence that many mounds are mortuary or sacrificial, but his work was shrewd and illuminating for its time.

The Indians who built mounds, some of which are nearly 2000 years old and some constructed in historic times, were presumably ancestors of the Indians living in the various areas when white men came, possessed no political or tribal connection, and intended their mounds for various uses—defensive, totemic, or burial. Those who wish a fairly complete record of the way in which a series of distinct Indian cultures have been developed over a period of many centuries will find it at the Ocmulgee National Monument in Georgia. And at various museums in the Southwest students may find stone implements associated with Folsom man, who roamed that area not 5000 years ago, the date once assigned to the first appearance of human beings in North America, but more nearly three times that far in the past.

Yet while archaeology is a field for the expert, and for the latest expert at that, this fact does not exempt the historical student from careful labor of his own if he finds a topic which involves archaeological lore. The example of Prescott in writing his chapters on Mexican culture before the Conquest is instructive. The ground in his day had been very imperfectly explored. Casting aside many pretentious writings as moonshine speculation, he found Humboldt almost the only authority of any solid value. After reading all the secondary works, he himself went to the primary sources. That is, he studied the documentary collections of Lord Knaresborough, the volumes of the *Antiquités Mexicaines*, the accounts, manuscript or printed, of the early Spanish chroniclers, and the works of all the keen-eyed travelers in Mexico and Yucatán from Bernal Diaz to moderns like John L. Stephens. As he had given thorough study to the coins of Ferdinand and Isabella's day, so now he spent equal effort upon the astronomy of the Aztecs. We find him writing: "Finished notes on the hieroglyphical part of the chapter—a hard, barren topic. And now on the astronomy—out of the frying-pan into the fire. I find it, however, not so hard to comprehend as I anticipated. Fortunately, the Aztec proficiency does not require a knowledge of the *Principia*. Still it was enough to task all my mathematics, and patience to boot. . . ." After nearly a century Prescott's chapters on Aztec culture yet stand in no great need of revision, and the pains which he took carry a plain lesson.*

To any understanding of the vague twilight beginnings of history, or of ancient times, the study of remains is fundamental; and if for later ages it holds a place subordinate to other materials, it is nevertheless important. The discerning eye will often find in architectural monuments the key to a whole age. Ruskin's *Stones of Venice* effectively illustrates his belief that the buildings and art of a people express their morals, their spiritual emotions, their manners and customs, and their national ideals; Henry Adams's *Mont St.-Michel and Chartres* uses two great shrines to penetrate to the soul of an era. No imaginative student of medieval times can visit Carcassonne or Rothenburg without new illumination, while the spirit of the eighteenth century is preserved forever in the crescents and triangles of Bath. For a critical evaluation of remains, some students will need a knowledge of art, others of costume, others of weapons, and still others simply the ability to distinguish between a telford and a macadam road. A

* Maurice Collis in *Cortés and Montezuma* (1955) supplements Prescott by approaching the conquest through the minds of the Mexican Indians of 1518-21, and their faith in an old prophecy of invasion and downfall.

memorable statement of the way in which history lies written, half blotted, half plain, upon the very face of a great city, occurs in Victor Hugo's *Nôtre Dame de Paris:*

> There is the Paris of Catherine de Medicis at the Tuileries, the Paris of Henry II at the Hôtel-de-Ville—two edifices which are still in fine taste; the palace of Henry IV at the Place Royale—a brick front, faced with stone, and roofed with slate, real tri-colored houses; the Paris of Louis XIII at Val-de-Grace—of architecture crushed and squat, with basket-handled vaults, big-bellied columns, and a humpbacked dome; the Paris of Louis XIV at the Pantheon—St. Peter's at Rome ill-copied, and the building has been awkwardly heightened, which has by no means rectified its lines; the Paris of the [First] Republic at the School of Medicine, a poor Greek and Roman style . . . ; the Paris of Napoleon at the Place Vendôme—something sublime, a brazen column composed of melted cannon; the Palace of the Restoration at the Bourse or Exchange—a colonnade very white, supporting a frieze very smooth; the whole square costing twenty millions of francs.

> To each of these characteristic structures is allied, by similarity of style, manner, and disposition of parts, a certain number of houses scattered over the different quarters of town, which the eye of the connoisseur easily distinguishes and assigns to their respective dates. When a man understands the art of seeing, he can trace the spirit of an age and the features of a king even in the knocker on a door.

Even in a land so young as the United States the study of remains is an invaluable pillar of history. It is a gratifying fact that Americans, who used to let such monuments of the past as John Hancock's splendid house on Beacon Hill, Federal Hall in New York, and the first skyscraper in Chicago (the Home Insurance Building) perish without a qualm, have learned to appreciate the historical—or at least the sentimental—worth of such relics. Today we not only preserve Lincoln's birthplace and Mark Twain's boyhood home with pious care; we have erected skillful reproductions of colonial Williamsburg, the Harrodsburg fort, old Salem on the Sangamon, Sutter's fort at Sacramento, and the log-cabin settlement of Norwegian pioneers at Decorah, Iowa. We have a museum at Doylestown, Pennsylvania, which preserves specimens of agricultural apparatus, another at New Bedford, Massachusetts, devoted to whaling, and even one at Oshkosh, Wisconsin, which specializes in the products of fancywork. Henry Ford, who was by no means indifferent to history although he spoke slightingly of its written forms, brought to his interesting if jumbled Greenfield Village at Dearborn, Michigan, the original laboratory of Thomas A. Edison at Menlo Park, New Jersey, the office in which Luther Burbank worked at Santa Rosa, California, a steam manufacturing plant of the eighties, an old blacksmith shop, an Illinois courthouse in which Lincoln had argued a case, and the birthplace of the compiler of the McGuffey *Readers*. Woodwork, hangings, and furnishings of American domestic interiors for various periods are to be found in numerous museums. One may step into the authentic domestic atmosphere of the seventies as he enters the reproduction of Theodore Roosevelt's birthplace, with much of his parents' furniture intact, in New York City.

II

Folklore and ballads are among the most beautiful and alluring of the sources of history. They have the dewy freshness of the morning of the human race upon them, for they have sprung in the main from times and communities innocent of written literature. The ballad in particular, which often throws a bright prismatic light upon manners, customs, beliefs, and primitive emotions, is the composition rather of a folk than of an individual; it rose from the heart and lips of a whole people. Like the fairy tales or *märchen*, much balladry goes back of historic times to the immemorial past of European peoples. Resemblances of story, incident, tone, and style all unite the Scottish, Provençal, Scandinavian, Italian, German, and Slavic folk song and folk tale and point to an extreme antiquity. Of course, originating in the improvised song of the rustic dance or warriors' feast, and then handed down through long centuries by shepherds, servants, nurses, and other simple folk, the more ancient ballads contain no direct historical facts. But the spirit of the long-gone peasant folk breathes in their measures. As Andrew Lang wrote, they are "a voice from secret places, from silent peoples, and from old times long dead." They bind us to peoples who migrated from Asia to Europe in ages long forgotten; and for this reason as well as for the spirit and eloquence which made Chevy Chase stir Sir Philip Sidney like a trumpet, they hold an unfailing magic.

Even the more recent ballad compositions usually contain little explicit and authentic fact, but they are none the less valuable. Was there really a Sir Patrick Spens? Was he actually wrecked in the Orkneys? How much explicit truth resides in the ballad of Chevy Chase, which obviously contains incidents drawn from the real battle of Otterburn? It appears that this ballad is full of confusion, and indeed is founded upon confusion. Henry Morley writes: "In the warfare against English settlements in France a raid was called by the French allies of Scotland a *chevauchee,* and by a common process, that name was corrupted into Chevy Chase. It lives yet among schoolboys as a 'chivy.' Now, since there are in Northumberland Cheviot Hills, as well as an Otterburn, Chevy Chase was interpreted into the hunting of the Cheviot. The old ballad of the 'Battle of Otterburn,' of 'Chevy Chase'—the battle of the *chevauchee* which was its cause—was therefore recast as 'The Hunting of the Cheviot,' always with some confused sense of identity between one incident and the other. The battle of Otterburn is an incident that arose out of a hunting on the Cheviots." But despite the absence or vagueness of fact, the *spirit* which breathes in the border ballads is highly valuable to the historian.

Legends, in the most technical sense, are a branch of folklore relating to a sacred person, place, or incident.*

* For Henri Bergson's classic distinction between the *fabulatory* function and the *verificatory* function, see R. Klebansky, ed., *Philosophy and History,* pp. 27 ff.

The early Christian church, for example, produced stories of the saints which were sometimes primarily historical and sometimes even at the outset primarily fabulous. Successive tellers altered and expanded them; different priests or clerks embroidered them to suit local ideas and preferences; and finally chroniclers gathered and repolished the whole. The result was a wild though charming medley of facts and inventions. Chief among the early chroniclers was James of Varagium, who late in the thirteenth century compiled his *Golden Legend,* a work still read. He has had many successors, some credulous, and some as scholarly as Sabine Baring-Gould, whose revised *Lives of the Saints* fills sixteen volumes. Analogous legends have grown up in the pagan, Moslem, Jewish, and other faiths.

But in the popular sense "legend" of course has a much broader significance. It refers to any narrative which professes to be historical, but which is actually traditional and imaginative in character. The Talmudic stories, the cycles of Arthur and Roland, the traditional tales of the Catskills which Irving transmuted into the pure gold of *Rip Van Winkle* and *The Legend of Sleepy Hollow,* all the personages of the poetic world which embraces the city of Troy, the Forest of Broceliande, and the Halls of Tara, with such cruder personages as Mike Fink of the Western waters, may be included under the one name.

Sometimes, like the ballads and *märchen,* legends represent a strange survival from the distant past. The story of St. George's rescue of the daughter of the king of Libya obviously derives from the more ancient tale of Perseus the dragon-slayer. At the one extreme a legend may be pure myth, like the tale of the witch under the water in the poem *Beowulf.* At the other extreme it may embody a large percentage of fact, like the legends of Hengist and Horsa, or of the Norse discoverers of America. In still other instances the mixture of fact and fancy may defy analysis and leave savants debating endlessly. Though six centuries before Christ Stesichorus exclaimed that Helen never really came in the beached ships to Pergamum, we know that there was a Troy and that it was besieged. Though such a commanding hero as the Roland of the great Song

never existed, we know there was an obscure Count of
Brittany who three centuries before the Song fell in the
defiles of the Pyrenees at Roncesvalles. On the granite of
hard fact grows the moss of legend, and even pure myth
contains its grains of stony reality. Though *Beowulf* is an
invention, it mentions the historic incident of the raid of
Hygelac's Vikings on the Frisian coast.*

An effort has been made to draw a line between legends
of secular heroes, and legends of sacred persons and places,
and to assign greater historical value to the former. But
this distinction is far from being definite, as anyone may
prove by a little reading on the heroes Theseus or Hercules.
One recent student of comparative folklore, Lord Raglan,
concludes after a survey of both the classical and medieval
bodies of traditional narrative that they are all derived
from dramatic ritual, not from historical fact. The whole
body of popular literature he regards as a detritus of myth-
ical stories connected with religious rites. The rites perished, but the stories remained, repeated endlessly by rote.
This theory, which he ably defends, may really account
for many folk heroes, like those of Thebes and Troy. That
is, the hero of legend may in numerous instances have
originally been an actor in a dramatic ritual, not a leader
in real life.

But this denial of the historical value of all legendary
stories is far too sweeping. Helen as a semi-mythical figure
is nearly as valuable as—and more suggestive than—Cleopatra as a real human being. We know that there was an
actual Cid who fought against the Moors in Valencia;
we know that an actual Marko Kraljevitch fought the
Turks and died in battle in 1394. Both men became heroes
of legend, and the folk tales furnish us unquestionable bits
of fact about them. In legend, indeed, we find values that
become the greater the nearer we approach modern times,
and the farther we leave primitive social conditions behind.
Lord Raglan contends that an illiterate and primitive peo-

---

* Dorothy Whitelocke in *The Audience of Beowulf* (1960)
argues that *Beowulf*, which exists in a single manuscript copy
in the Cotton Collection of the British Museum, was written
after 700 and very possibly in Mercia.

ple cannot preserve the memory of a historical event for more than 150 years. But as inroads are made upon illiteracy and the primitive, legends can preserve fact for much longer periods. It may often be debatable fact, but taken in a body it cannot be spared by history.*

Such works of comparative folklore as Sir J. G. Frazer's *The Golden Bough,* though written chiefly from a religio-sociological standpoint, have suggested many ideas and supplied much valuable material to the student of ancient history. Sabine Baring-Gould's tales of the saints cannot be neglected by the student of medieval culture. Sir James Stephen, in his *Lectures on the History of France,* remarks that even the more absurd legends of the saints, as voluminously compiled by the Benedictine and Bollandist monks, have a deep significance in that they help express the character of the period in which they had their birth. Embellished as they are with grotesque fables of visions, angelic visitations, ecstasies, and miracles, they attest that their authors lived "at a period when the ideal of human existence, the very poetry of life, consisted in meek suffering, in patient endurance, in pouring oil into the bleeding wounds of a groaning world, and in escaping from the prevalent bondage and oppression, its cruelty and lust, into communion with . . . more than angelic purity." The writers of these medieval hagiologies by no means in all instances intended them to be received as literally true. They were rather studies in ideal existence, answering to the requirements which a Greek priest of the ninth or tenth century, Metaphrastus, had laid down in his treatise "On the Art of Writing Holy Romances."

Not even American historians can ignore legends and ballads. The story of the earliest discovery of the continent is unquestionably to be found in Icelandic sagas, which in their first written form were founded on oral tradition. The principal sources are two, the *Saga of Eric the Red,* and the *Tale of the Greenlanders.* The former, written not later than the close of the thirteenth century and possibly in its

* Douglas Bush's *Mythology and the Romantic Tradition in English Poetry* (1937) is a work of impressive erudition which is full of suggestions to students of history.

early years, seems to be founded upon a fairly direct and reliable tradition. The *Tale of the Greenlanders,* known to have been written late in the fourteenth century, is less trustworthy—it plainly represents an oral tradition in process of dissolution. But there are some elements in the *Eric Saga* which are not plausible, while there are bits in the *Tale* which may well be authentic. The task of excluding what is inaccurate and combining and collating what is accurate in the Icelandic Sagas is, like the treatment of most legends, one in which experience and a full knowledge of historical backgrounds count for much. Experts have thus far not agreed, in dealing with Leif's voyages to America, upon the question whether Vinland lay as far south as Cape Cod or as far north as Labrador; or whether the *vinber,* for that matter, were wild grapes or cranberries.*

For both pre-Columbian and post-Columbian times, again, Indian legends possess a historical coloring which gives them genuine utility. Though ordinarily worthless in what they state of heroes or sacred persons, they supply much information upon tribal organization, migrations, and customs. Their full interpretation of course demands the ethnologist's equipment. In our more recent history the legends of pioneer settlements, mining camps, lumbermen, and the cowboys of the Western range, whether in prose or ballad, are by no means devoid of light upon social and cultural history.

Perhaps the clearest illustration of the way in which legend merged with the first important writings upon history is to be seen in Livy. His great work, beginning with the landing of the legendary Aeneas, and coming down to the establishment of the republic, is based primarily upon annalists, who in turn had drawn in large part upon the flimsiest kind of popular legend and upon family traditions. For the regal period of Roman history these annalists had possessed little else upon which to draw. The Gauls who burned Rome in 390 B.C. had destroyed the records of the city, and subsequent chroniclers perforce contented them-

---

* For a valuable treatment of the Leif Ericson story, which places Vinland on Cape Cod, see Frederick Pohl, *Atlantic Crossings before Columbus* (1961).

selves with myths, ballads, oral tales embroidered generation after generation, and treacherous reminiscences. Modern scholars can hardly feel certain of the reality of a single
incident in all this glittering mass of material. They cannot
be positive that such persons as Numa Pompilius, or Ancus
Martius, or Servius Tullius, ever breathed; they *are* positive that the tales of their conquests, reforms, and institutions have but a vague relationship to truth. They can
easily discern the fables which ultra-patriotic Romans invented to lend a spurious grandiosity and splendor to the
petty and checkered beginnings of the republic.

After these beginnings, the filiopietistic myths became
intermixed with more dependable data. The historian finds
in the fragments we possess of the old annals extremely
brief notices, precisely dated and rather archaic in style,
of arresting events—wars, treaties, consecrations of temples, and so on. Obviously these were taken from the first
written records—the notes kept by the pontiffs and
aediles, and by certain families. Such annalists as Quintus
Fabius Pictor, called the father of Roman history, filled
in this bare framework from the many bits of legendary
stuff at hand. The resulting composition, judged by present-day standards, was a weird affair. But it held grains
of wheat among the chaff. Had later annalists only applied critical methods to it, they might have given Rome
the beginnings of true history. But they refused, and a
school of rhetoricians arose who even dressed up the traditions with new exaggerations and interpolations.

Livy's second to fifth books inclusive, embracing Roman
history down to the evacuation of the city by the Gauls,
are not only founded upon the annalists but exemplify the
worst methods of using traditional material. His preface
admits the unsafe character of the early traditions. "Such
things as are reported either before or at the foundation
of the city, more beautified by poet's adornments than
grounded upon faithful records, I mean neither to assert
nor deny," he remarks. He adds that the whole history
previous to the Gallic sack is obscure because of its great
antiquity, the paucity of monuments and writings, "the
only faithful remembrancers of times past," and the de-

struction of the priestly and civic records. But while these
statements are critical, his handling of the annalists' work
is not. He made no effort to go behind their writing even
where other evidence existed; nor did he compare different
annalists, as he should. Moreover, for whole books his history gives no references to authorities, contenting itself with
such phrases as "they say" or "ancient writers declare." The
work is a compilation, in whose later chapters the materials
are so imperfectly fused that inconsistencies and contradictions are by no means rare. In contrast with it, readers
who wish to learn how a scientific treatment of legendary
materials can separate the gold from the dross need only
turn to the first chapters of Mommsen.

III

Our third category, that of representative materials not
written in the ordinary sense, began (if we exclude the
cave paintings of remote prehistoric ages) with inscriptions—inscriptions baked upon clay, chiseled upon stone, or
engraved upon metals. Even in very ancient times it was
seen that such inscriptions were extremely useful for the
study of history. Great Greek orators, like Demosthenes
and Aeschines, cited them as evidence for their arguments.
Herodotus used them repeatedly, and his record of the
battle of Plataea is drawn in part from the inscription on
the bronze base of the golden tripod dedicated at Delphi
after the victory. Thucydides and still more frequently
Polybius used them. Dionysius of Halicarnassus, who wrote
his *Antiquities of Rome* just before the commencement of
the Christian Era, mentions several important inscriptions
as sources, two dating from the regal period and one from
the early years of the republic. It is one of Livy's faults
that when he might have used such sources freely, he ignored them. In Greece the systematic collection of inscriptions was begun by certain scholars at an early date. Philochoros made a compilation of them about 300 B.C., and
Polemon one in the second century B.C.; still others were
made by Aristodemus, Craterus of Macedon, and lesser
men.

When the Revival of Learning dawned upon Europe and renewed man's interest in ancient literature, the study of inscriptions revived also. Early in the fifteenth century an imposing number of them were copied by Cyriac of Ancona, one of the most enthusiastic Renaissance antiquarians, an Italian scholar who devoted his travels in Italy, Greece, Egypt, and Syria not merely to the collection of manuscripts, coins, and works of art, but to the study of inscriptions and the sketching of roads, walls, buildings, and other physical remains. But for him all knowledge of many monuments and inscriptions would have perished utterly. He had contemporaries who did much, and successors who did more. By the beginning of the nineteenth century, thanks to traveling scholars of many lands—Italian, French, German, English—a large stock of Greek and Roman inscriptions had been accumulated. The time was ripe for competent hands to compare, arrange, and edit this information; and the work was undertaken for Greek inscriptions by the eminent German scholar, Augustus Boeckh.

It was Boeckh who raised Greek epigraphy to the position of a science, one of the most useful handmaidens of ancient history. The Royal Academy of Sciences in Berlin made no mistake when in 1818 it chose him to classify and annotate the known inscriptions in one systematic work. The first volume of his monumental *Corpus Inscriptionum Graecarum* appeared in 1828, the second in 1833, and the third and fourth, in which he was aided by other scholars, in 1853 and 1856. These four volumes permanently established the methods of Greek epigraphy. For Boeckh's own time they constituted a masterpiece of lucid arrangement, erudition, scholarly care, and brilliant generalization. In his treatise on the public economy of Athens, Boeckh also gave the world a masterly application of the principles of epigraphy to historical study. But of course his collection was merely a beginning. The liberation of Greece from Turkey and the development of archaeological research resulted in a far more systematic exploration of famous sites, and the exhuming of huge numbers of new inscriptions. Boeckh's four volumes had contained approx-

imately ten thousand. In 1871 the Berlin Academy began
the preparation of a new Corpus, still being published under canons of the highest scholarship. By 1880 the number
of Greek inscriptions known to scholars was estimated at
nearly 30,000, and today we have about 20,000 surviving
inscriptions from Athens alone, ranging from epitaphs with
a single name to financial records of 5000 words.*

The variety, color, and instructiveness of the Greek inscriptions are far greater than the amateur would suppose.
Dating as far back as the middle of the seventh century
B.C., they comprehend not merely political and religious
affairs, but commercial and private relations. Among the
political materials, the decrees of rulers, representative
bodies, and popular assemblies are extremely numerous;
so numerous for the Athenian state in the fifth and fourth
centuries B.C. that a complete compilation "is like turning
over the minutes of the Athenian Parliament." They include also the laws of such statesmen as Draco, and such
bodies as the Amphicytyonic Council; treaties between
the various Greek cities; awards by arbitral authorities in
disputes between states; accounts of public expenditures;
records of the armies and navies; and even royal letters—
such as that which Lysimachus wrote to the Samians,
printed in Boeckh's work. An interesting series of inscriptions deals with the conditions under which colonists were
sent out by the various cities. Among the religious inscriptions are those which decree festivals and prescribe an
elaborate ritual for their observance; which give rules for
the appointment, discipline, duties, and rewards of priests;
which pertain to auguries and sacrifices; which deal with
the lease of sacred lands; and which contain prayers or
imprecations in tombs and temples. Certain Delphian inscriptions illustrate the enfranchisement of slaves under
the form of sale to a god. The innumerable private inscriptions deal with leases, mortgages, athletic competi-
tions, and honors to individuals.

We have long known from literary sources that the

---

* A. G. Woodhead's *The Study of Greek Inscriptions* (1959)
provided the first guide to Greek epigraphy in English published
in more than a half century.

pleasure-loving Alcibiades lived well in the days of his prosperity. It is delightful to find this fact confirmed by the stones which catalogue all his property put up for sale when he fell from power. The list of his furniture includes twelve Milesian beds, one elaborate, takes note of his yellow wool fabrics and overstuffed pillows, and offers a huge accumulation of wine jars. When Dr. Benjamin Jowett made his translation of Thucydides, he spoke contemptuously of the inscription-reading of his day as something like the pastime of looking at autographs; a more recent editor of Thucydides has termed the value of epigraphy "incalculable."

While the earliest Latin inscriptions, with few exceptions, run back only to the first part of the fourth century B.C., for the republic and empire they are quite as important as Greek inscriptions. It is interesting to note that the first man to make extensive use of them in historical study was Cola di Rienzi, the celebrated orator and reformer, who about the middle of the fourteenth century prepared a description of the Eternal City which cited them effectively. Early in the fifteenth century the antiquarian Poggio Bracciolini amassed a collection of inscriptions, and after that date such compilations appeared at frequent intervals. The careless or unscrupulous methods of many students, permitting gross inaccuracies and grosser inventions, made Latin epigraphy an unscientific study until the nineteenth century. Forgers like Pirro Ligorio of Naples palmed off false texts on the world in the most brazen fashion. But in this field as in so many others, the eighteenth century showed itself the parent of a truly scientific method. The critical and systematic handling of Latin inscription began most notably with Marini, who published an epochal work in 1795, and whose principles were followed by his disciple, Conte Bartolommeo Borghesi. The Berlin Academy followed up its success in the field of Greek inscriptions with careful plans for a similar Corpus in Latin; and it found an even greater editor in Theodor Mommsen. He and William Henzen brought out in 1863 the first volume of the *Corpus In-*

scriptionum Latinarum, which is still being continued by German scholars.

Though to a great extent the Roman inscriptions parallel those of Greece, important differences exist. Erectors of public structures of many kinds—bridges, aqueducts, temples, and other buildings—were usually permitted to engrave their names upon them, and these *tituli operum publicorum,* with their dates, supply much information upon the growth of public facilities and the aspect of ancient cities. Boundary stones show political limits. The *Fasti,* or lists of consuls and other leading magistrates, are an interesting source of information. One of the most striking of all inscriptions is the famous Monumentum Ancyranum, the record of his own exploits which Augustus graved in Greek and Latin upon the walls of a temple at Ancyra in Asia Minor. Constitutions, decrees, laws, and documents connected with public worship are numerous. From Pompeii have come many inscriptions painted or drawn on street walls—advertisements, election handbills, and notices of highly diverse and often indecent character. And private documents, incised upon bronze, lead, or ivory tablets, are for obvious reasons more numerous for Rome than for Greece.*

Not only the riches, but the difficulties and problems of inscriptions are greater than the amateur would suppose. The date of inscriptions has first to be determined. This can sometimes be done by internal evidence furnished by the subject, event, or person treated. It can sometimes be fixed, with general accuracy, by the dialect or style. Finally, the approximate date can often be ascertained simply from the form of the letters and the manner of their execution. In Greek inscriptions carved before 450 B.C. the characters have a stiff and angular outline, while for the Periclean Age they possess a graceful though simple form. Inscriptions of this later period, moreover, are usually

---

* Discoveries of Roman inscriptions in Cyrenaica have thrown much illumination upon imperial administration under Augustus; see Francis Cumont, *Journal des Savants,* March 1927, pp. 126 ff.

written in such a fashion that the letters are aligned vertically as well as horizontally.

The Greek alphabet also underwent notable changes. After the archontate of Euclides in 403 B.C., the Athenians used a fuller alphabet than that which Ionia had theretofore employed. In the Macedonian period appeared the use of apices, a stroke or curved line, as an ornament of letters. In the period of the Roman domination, a sharp distinction can be made between the Greek inscriptions of the Augustan Age, which are clear and handsomely designed, and those of the subsequent empire, which rapidly degenerate. Similarly, in dealing with Roman inscriptions it has been possible to lay down clear and detailed rules for supplying dates. The Latin alphabet again varied from age to age—the old Z as the seventh letter was replaced in the fourth century A.U.C. by G; in Cicero's time two new letters were added from the Greek; and the Emperor Claudius unsuccessfully attempted to make still further additions. Changes in the form of letters were numerous, and these paleographical alterations can be given a fairly certain chronology.

Since the alphabet, the outline of the letters, and the style of execution count for so much in the proper interpretation of inscriptions, it is obvious that the utmost care in copying them is indispensable. Many early collectors were more enthusiastic than precise. Others, as we have noted, were thoroughly dishonest. Here, as in every other branch of historical materials, forgers early appeared. The Pirro Ligorios of the fifteenth, sixteenth, and seventeenth centuries did much injury to history until in the nineteenth century the severely critical methods of modern epigraphists and paleographers exposed them. Of course the invention of photography has greatly benefited exact scholarship.

IV

For the purposes of history, coins may be considered almost a branch of inscriptions. They also go far back into the past—in the classical world, to about 700 B.C., gold

apparently having been first coined in Lydia, and silver in
Aegina, from which lands coinage spread with great rapidity throughout the Hellenic part of the Mediterranean
world. For the ancient world coins were issued in fair
profusion, and their varieties were steadily increased during medieval and early modern times. By 1880 the European museums possessed several hundred thousand different varieties of coins and medals, and the number held in
classified collections today can hardly be less than half a
million. So enormous an array of "monuments" of past
times is naturally of value to the study of politics, economics, art, and religion. Their usefulness for history as
well as their aesthetic interest was recognized, indeed, by
those same scholars of the Renaissance who first clearly
perceived the value of inscriptions. Petrarch collected
coins, and made presents of some of his best to the
Emperor Charles V. Many early critics of the classics illustrated their commentaries by reproductions of coins. In
1517 an Italian, Andrea Fulvio, published an album of
portraits of illustrious figures of the ancient world taken
from coins and gems, his *Illustrium Imagines*. Such al-
bums soon became numerous. So did historical or pseudo-
historical works illustrated by reproductions of coins; a
whole series of them produced by Hubert Goltz of Antwerp in the latter half of the sixteenth century is still remembered for its commingling of genuine with fraudulent
coins, for Goltz invented pieces to suit his own purposes,
and even created consuls and generals who never lived.
Fulvio Orsini, a famous collector of antiquities and gems,
issued in Rome in 1577 an epochal work on Roman silver
coins from his own collection; but though he was a man of
profound learning and of stricter rectitude than Goltz,
many spurious or wrongly described coins marred his
pages. Adolph Occo, whose work on imperial Roman coins
appeared at Antwerp in 1577, can be credited with a more
scholarly and reliable treatise.

But the truly scientific study of numismatics goes back
to about the same period as that of inscriptions. It hardly
became possible until great national collections, larger
than any in private hands, had grown up. J. H. Eckhel,

Studies & coins

its first exponent, was curator of the imperial collection in Vienna. He has been called the Father of Numismatics, for his eight-volume work, the *Doctrina Numorum Veterum* (1792–98), gave the study of ancient coins an expert and critical basis. His erudition, judgment, and accuracy were such that even now his writings are valuable to students, his material being regarded as a starting-point in the study of classical coins, and his principle a model for other students. Since his time the study of coins has of course become highly specialized. In our own day the numismatics of nearly every ancient and modern people of importance has been made the subject of a special treatise. There are books on Merovingian coins, Anglo-Saxon coins, Byzantine coins, Russian coins, Chinese coins, Papal coins, and many more—and some contain a surprising amount of historical information.

To political history coins seldom contribute much new information beyond the supplying or correction of dates; their value to such history, in general, lies simply in *illustrating* it. It is true that in a few lands for a few periods we must rely largely upon coins for what little information we possess. The records of the Graeco-Bactrian kingdom established about 256 B.C., and comprising a considerable part of Central Asia, for example, have been pieced out chiefly from coins discovered in Afghanistan and surrounding areas. They furnish a list of names of rulers whose succession can be fixed with general accuracy. But early coins seldom offer much precise information, for they disclose only that certain states or princes issued money at certain dates. Later coins, whose inscriptions and devices present more facts, also deal for the most part with peoples and times for which other sources supply far fuller and clearer information; they corroborate this information, but they rarely alter or extend it. When they do, it is chiefly by fixing details of chronology, or by expanding our knowledge of royal genealogies. The pedigree of more than one royal house has first been traced by a set of coins. In economic history, the *spread* of coins is often significant. Discoveries of Greek coins in the Mediterranean basin, of

Roman coins in India, help fix the extent of ancient trade areas.

But the illustrative value of numismatics, for students of political history alone, is striking. In the vast museum exhibits of coins we possess contemporaneous or almost contemporaneous effigies of most of the great rulers and captains of the world from Alexander the Great down to our own time. Painters did little to supply portraiture to history until the latter part of the Middle Ages; sculptors, though active in both ancient and medieval times, gave the world far fewer portraits than the coinmakers, and often so idealized them that they lack authenticity. "There is no more delightful companion in historical reading," justly writes one student, "than a cabinet of coins and medals. The strength and energy of Alexander, the ferocity of Mithridates, the philosophic calmness of Antoninus, the obstinate ferocity of Nero, and the brutality of Caracalla, are as plain on the coins as in the pages of history." He goes on to say that in the Dark Ages numismatic portraits lost their individuality, but regained it with the revival of art. For the later Middle Ages and modern times "we can form a series of portraits more complete and not less interesting than that of the ancient period." Engraved gems and cameos often afford useful information; and everyone knows that for a century the stamps of the world have carried many admirably engraved portraits.

Religious as well as political history, particularly that of the Greeks, was illuminated by coins. All Greek coins until the death of Alexander, or virtually all, were stamped with sacred subjects alone. In later times the reverse of the coin was usually devoted to sacred images or emblems. But for these representations, modern scholars would have encountered immense difficulty in forming a complete and satisfactory set of the effigies under which the Greek divinities were represented. While ancient statues and reliefs of good workmanship and preservation do not exist in sufficient numbers for this purpose, coins fill all the gaps. Many of them, indeed, supply effigies of divinities which are not merely good, but excellent. The mythology of the Romans is less fully illustrated, but numerous coins nevertheless bear images which refer to the religious traditions of the early decades of the city. And as we should expect, coins also fix many geographical elements in history. They often supply invaluable information as to the position of towns on ocean or streams, as to the race and allegiance of the inhabitants, and as to natural productions—for these last are sometimes represented on ancient money. Finally, coins convey much as to the progress of art and architecture.

Even textiles may have much the same historical values as coins, sculptures, and inscriptions. Something of the history of Oriental lands has been wrought into the traditional designs of their rugs, and experts can tell at a glance whether the pattern reflects the austerity of the Sunni or the freedom of the Shiah branch of the Moslems. The most famous piece of embroidery in history is doubtless the so-called tapestry of Bayeux, which is not a tapestry at all, but a long-stitch embroidery in crewels on a long, narrow strip of linen cloth. Executed late in the eleventh or more probably early in the twelfth century, it represents various episodes in the conquest of England by William the Conqueror. Though tradition ascribed it to no less a personage than Queen Matilda and her maids, it is difficult to believe that they undertook so laborious a work on materials so coarse. It is much more likely that it was done in England by needlewomen employed at the expense of those Normans upon whom William had bestowed rich grants of English lands, and was sent by them as an offering to the Bayeux Cathedral. But whatever its origin, it furnishes almost invaluable illustrations of the arms, modes of fighting, and general customs of the time of the Norman Conquest. Few manuals of English history are so brief as to omit mention of it or reproductions of some of its scenes. Freeman terms it "the highest authority on the Norman side," adding that it presents "hardly any of the inventions, exaggerations, and insinuations of the other Norman authorities."

Primitive materials for history, we have called these various forms of non-literary data; but while they are primitive in the sense of lacking subtlety and detail, in

another sense some of them are far indeed from primitive.
The New Zealander of Macaulay's illustration, taking his
stand to sketch the broken arch of London Bridge, would
find nothing primitive in such physical remains as a loco-
motive or dynamo, such representative materials as an
Aubusson tapestry, a painting by Turner, or a coin by St.
Gaudens. Mr. Dooley, dropping once into historical vein,
closed his catalogue of American progress by a list of the
representative materials which illustrate it. "I have seen
America spread out fr'm th' Atlantic to th' Pacific, with a
branch office iv th' Standard Ile Company in ivry hamlet.
I've seen th' shackles dropped fr'm th' slave, so's he cud
be lynched in Ohio . . . An' Corbett beat Sullivan, an'
Fitz beat Corbett . . . An' th' invintions . . . th' cotton
gin an' th' gin sour an' th' bicycle an' th' flying machine
an' th' nickle-in-th'-slot machine an' th' Croker machine an'
th' sody fountain an'—crownin' wurruk iv our civilization—
th' cash raygister." It would be more correct to say that
these are the broader, simpler materials for history, ad-
umbrating and illustrating it rather than offering means
for presenting it in detail. But they are essential parts of
the mass of evidence upon which historians must rely.
They are important elements in the immense flood system
which drains the past for the benefit of the present, not to
be ignored because they flow apart from what is today the
great central stream of historical evidence, the written or
printed word. To that central stream we must now turn.

IV

Modern Materials for History

IN THE BEGINNING was the written word—so the historian would amend the ancient text. It was the fact of writing that was all-important; and in placing inscriptions in a different category from writings upon more perishable materials, we must not draw any deep line of division between them. Men learned to write on skins, clay, bark, and papyrus quite as early as on stone or metal, and they still write on them all. The adoption of parchment and paper as media for writing is important simply as it made written records far fuller and far more abundant. Browning's lines on Saul are full of historical truth in their expression of the unconquerable desire of mankind to record the past in manifold forms:

> Is Saul dead? In the depth of the vale make his tomb—
> bid arise
> A gray mountain of marble heaped four-square, till,
> built to the skies,
> Let it mark where the great First King slumbers: whose
> fame would ye know?
> Up above see the rock's naked face, where the record
> shall go
> In great characters cut by the scribe,—Such was Saul,
> so he did;

With the sages directing the work, by the populace
    chid,—
For not half, they'll affirm, is comprised there! Which
    fault to amend,
In the grove with his kind grows the cedar, whereon
    they shall spend
(See, in tablets 'tis level before them) their praise, and
    record
With the gold of the graver, Saul's story,—the states-
    man's great word
Side by side with the poet's sweet comment. The river's
    awave
With smooth paper-reeds grazing each other when
    prophet-winds rave:
So the pen gives unborn generations their due and their
    part
In thy being!

I

Far back in neolithic days, primitive man—man a stage
beyond the string-knotting savage—learned to make rude
pictures which would convey simple ideas and record
events. Still earlier, no doubt, the chieftains and rich men
of various tribes had placed distinctive marks upon their
property to identify it: strokes embodying a rough sketch
or emblem. Out of these beginnings grew more flexible
systems for identifying facts and objects by symbols. Gods
came to be represented by their sacred animals; upper
Egypt was represented by a conventional lily; famine by a
picture of an emaciated man with protruding ribs. As culture advanced, men learned to use these pictographs and
ideographs to transmit really complex ideas and considerable bodies of information. But they were long puzzled, no
doubt, by the difficulty of presenting an abstraction, or
even a concrete object for which no comprehensible picture could be made. Easy enough to sketch a man; but
how indicate that he was a father, a son, a husband? In
this difficulty, ingenious minds struck upon the utility of a
punning similarity of sounds. The Egyptian word for "son"

was almost identical in sound with the word for "goose"; what more natural than to indicate the idea of a son by a sketch of a goose? It was as if in English the sketch of an eye served to represent the pronoun I. Having thus begun to make symbols not for objects and ideas but for sound, the ancient scribes drew close to the invention of the alphabet.* Pictographs and ideographs gave way to a *transitional* mode of writing, in which they were mingled with symbols which represented a sound or syllable alone. Half a dozen different peoples developed this transitional system of conveying intelligence: The Egyptians, the Sumerians and Babylonians, the Hittites, the Chinese, the Aztecs, and the Mayas.

Historians of Western civilization have made us most familiar with the transitional scripts of the Egyptians and Babylonians, which go far back into antiquity. In Egypt we find pictographs and ideographs—that is, hieroglyphs —well developed even in the First Dynasty, when annual records of events were kept in them. The hieroglyphs, written rapidly upon papyri sheets, soon became a series of scrawls which followed the original symbol about as closely as the letters in modern cursive handwriting imitate the printed capitals. Such running-hand or "hieratic" writing became well developed under the First Dynasty. In Babylonia the pictographs had to be impressed upon clay tablets, stiffer and more refractory than paper, and for this purpose sharp-pointed writing instruments were employed. The rudely scratched symbols were ranged in vertical columns. As scribes wrote faster and faster, the pictographs and ideographs became more abbreviated, and were soon impressed, not incised, with a three-sided graving tool which left a wedge-shaped or cuneiform mark. This emergence of cuneiform writing paralleled the emergence of the hieratic or cursive writing in Egypt; but in Babylonia the cuneiform marks wholly superseded the pictorial symbols, while in Egypt the hieratic writing did not. By the same process of evolution in both lands the introduction of syl-

* See E. Clodd, *The Story of the Alphabet;* Sir W. Flinders Petrie, *The Formation of the Alphabet.*

labic symbols gradually provided a transitional mode of writing, halfway to the alphabet proper.

The use of papyrus supposedly dates back about as far as 4000 B.C., and we actually possess a historical papyrus which contains an account of the reign of King Assa, 3580–3536 B.C. Of the cuneiform tablets of Babylonia, we possess specimens which were written far back in the third millennium before Christ. As early as 2400 B.C. legal records and public accounts were being systematically kept on such tablets. Large collections of Egyptian papyri, some of them believed to be not less than four thousand years old, have been made by European and American libraries and museums, and are constantly being enlarged. None of the historical books written in hieroglyphics, for such books existed, have survived, but the world possesses an abundance of other hieroglyphic material. It likewise possesses huge collections of Babylonian tablets, commercial, legal, and religious, ranging from 3000 B.C. to the second century of the Christian Era. Our knowledge of very early Babylonian literature—legends, hymns, incantations, epics —is exceptionally full; other tablets give us a very considerable understanding of social conditions, economic and cultural life, and legal procedure; and the annals and the commemorative inscriptions make it possible to trace much of the political history of the country from an early period. The era of modern scientific exploration for historical material in Egypt began with Napoleon's invasion, the discovery of the Rosetta Stone, its acquisition by Britons for transfer to London, and its decipherment by Jean François Champollion. It began in Babylonia with Sir Henry Rawlinson's translation of the inscription on the Behistun Rock in 1834, and his opening of the first Babylonian mound at Birs Nimrud in 1844.

The alphabet proper—our own highly conventional form of writing, with no essential connection between sound and symbol—is of uncertain origin. Some scholars would trace it to the Egyptian or Babylonian systems of transitional writing; some to the Minoan writing in Crete; some to the syllabic system of writing in Cyprus; and some to the Phoenicians. One scholar, Sir Flinders Petrie, holds that it developed from a series of conventional signs employed for commercial purposes throughout the whole Mediterranean area in earliest times.

What is certain is that the beginnings of the alphabet date much farther back than men recently supposed. Inscriptions discovered by Petrie in the Sinai Peninsula in 1916, which appear to be purely alphabetic, go back at least as far as the sixteenth century B.C., long antedating the famous Moabite Stone of the ninth century B.C. which, written in the Semitic alphabet, was once believed the earliest known example of such writing. Over these Sinaitic inscriptions, again, scholars have quarreled. Some hold the writing to be Egyptian in origin; some declare that it is independent of Egypt, and ancestral to the Semitic alphabet. The Greeks may possibly have adapted their alphabet (which in essentials is also ours) at a remote time from some such source, independent of any other. But it is far more probable that they derived it from Semitic origins. We have inscriptions in the Greek alphabet which belong to the eighth—perhaps even to the ninth—century B.C. This carries us as far back as Hesiod, and almost as far as Homer, who is supposed to have composed the *Iliad* about 950 B.C., perhaps himself reducing it to a written text.

No Greek documents exist which have the antiquity of the oldest Egyptian papyri or Babylonian tablets; in fact, none were produced in Greece until much later. Nevertheless, Cretan records have been found which prove the existence of written documents in that island at a date of very respectable antiquity. One record narrates that when an Egyptian envoy visited Byblos about 1080 B.C., but unhappily neglected to bring presents with him, the official documents of Crete were brought out to prove to him that earlier Egyptian deputations had offered valuable gifts. As a result the Egyptians apologized and made amends by sending various presents, including five hundred sheets of papyrus, evidently for writing purposes. Historians would give much for a glance at these first written archives of Crete, far back beyond Homer.

II

But the written word is of little use to students of history until it is collected into systematic repositories; until fact is added to fact, document to document, book to book. The librarian must aid the scribe in preparing the ground for annalist and historians to till. So early was this fact perceived that priests and rulers began to form libraries soon after hieratic and cuneiform writing became important. A few decades ago it was supposed that the two libraries of Rameses II (1300–1236 B.C.) mentioned by Diodorus Siculus were the first institutions deserving the name; if indeed even they were not the stuff that legends are made from. Now we know that they did gloriously exist; papyri have been found which, though of later date than Rameses, came from these collections. We know that they were deservedly the most famous of the early ancient libraries. But we also know that collections of books and documents went back in Egypt to a much earlier time. Egyptian inscriptions refer to the library of Khufu, a monarch of the Fourth Dynasty, and to that of Khafra, Fourth Dynasty builder of the second pyramid. The very spot on which stood the library of Ikhnaton (who died about 1350 B.C.) is now known. In Babylonia, too, rich and extensive libraries had been collected long before Greece became a center of civilization. Just how early they appeared cannot be ascertained, but Assurbanipal, whose reign ended about 625 B.C., made one of the greatest collections known before modern times.

The last of the great Assyrian kings, Assurbanipal, gathered at Nineveh tablets containing not less than ten thousand separate works and documents; this royal library preserving not only the records of his reign, but a collection of Babylonian literature. It was the British archaeologist Layard who found its remains, two large rooms filled with tablets. Later discoveries extended the number of titles. Most of the collection is now housed in the British Museum. Important supplementary discoveries were afterwards made at the sacred city of Nippur, which Assurbanipal had restored, by an American expedition. J. P. Peters, H. V. Hilprecht, and others uncovered a series of rooms where, stored neatly on shelves, lay more than 20,000 clay tablets. Like those at Nineveh, they had been systematically arranged and catalogued, and though this library was at least partly an adjunct to a temple school, they may have been open to the public. In addition to these royal and ecclesiastical libraries, still other Babylonian collections existed. Many of the surviving cuneiform tablets pertain to business affairs, and were as systematically collected and preserved as the records of business corporations today. They show that in Hammurabi's day, more than 2000 B.C., Babylonian production and commerce had been thoroughly organized by that keen business sagacity which has marked the Semitic race ever since.

As the civilizations of the Mediterranean basin developed, papyrus makers, clerks, authors, and libraries increased in number, until long before the Christian Era the written materials for literature and history had become fairly abundant. In Greece we hear, though vaguely, of a library collected by Peisistratus, and prized and increased by the Athenians after his death; a library which, according to the writer Aulus Gellius, was carried off to Persia by Xerxes, and later brought back. We hear also of a library belonging to Polycrates of Samos, and of another at Heraclea Pontica about the beginning of the fourth century B.C. It is certain that Aristotle had an excellent library, which passed through interesting vicissitudes after his death, and was finally carried to Rome by Sulla about 82 B.C. We know also that after Aristotle libraries multiplied so remarkably in Greece that Cicero speaks of an infinite multitude of books there. Book collecting became fashionable. It is said that after the Goths seized Athens in 267 A.D. they threw together a huge pile of books, which they were about to burn as containing dangerous magic, when one aged leader cried: "Let the Greeks have their books. So long as they waste their days with these idle toys, we need never fear that they will give us any trouble in war."

The effulgent center of all critical and historical work in the silver age of Greek literature was Alexandria, where Ptolemy I, the Louis XIV of that era, founded an imposing library. Ptolemy II continued and completed it, and also built a daughter-library, called the Serapeion. Though these were partly displays of royal magnificence, they proved of priceless utility to ancient scholars. No such literary workshops existed anywhere else, for estimates of their contents range from 200,000 to 700,000 volumes. They continued to be the marvel of the learned world during early Christian times. A long-popular tradition assigns the shame of their destruction to the Islamic forces of Amru and the Caliph Omar, who thought them wicked if contrary to the Koran and superfluous if in harmony with it. But Gibbon long ago pointed out that Omar could not have burned them because they did not then exist; the early Christian leaders had been far more destructive than the Moslems! Still other large libraries flourished in Egypt in the time of the Ptolemies. Great quantities of papyri have been dug by modern archaeologists from the mounds covering ancient towns and cities, and from cemeteries. One of the discoveries made in this way was the long-lost work of Aristotle on the Athenian Constitution.

No important libraries, with perhaps one or two exceptions, existed in Rome until the last century of the republic. But by the time of Cicero both public and private libraries were numerous. He owned a much-valued collection, as did his friend Atticus. Well-organized publishing houses, some of which employed numerous copyists, were at work multiplying volumes. These houses—the Sosii in Horace's day, for example—produced hundreds and even thousands of copies of a popular author; and books became so cheap that Juvenal refers to a poor fellow living in a garret who possessed a number. Wealthy Romans prided themselves upon their groaning shelves, or rather drawers. Licinius Lucullus, for example, whose name is still synonymous with luxury, confiscated large numbers of Greek books in his Eastern campaigns (67 B.C.) and housed them magnificently. As Plutarch says, the generosity with which he let men use them redeemed the meanness with which he had acquired them. His reading rooms and grounds were thrown open to all students, and Greeks repaired thither "as to an abode of the Muses." Seneca speaks of the ostentation with which his wealthy contemporaries covered their walls with book presses of ivory or inlaid wood and their tables with expensive volumes. "Nowadays a library takes rank with a bathroom as a necessary ornament of a house," he declared; but he sneered at the men who yawned among their thousand titles, and whose chief delight was in their rich bindings and rubrics.[1]

The public libraries of Rome came in with the empire. Julius Caesar planned to build one, for which the learned Terentius Varro collected and assorted many volumes. Cicero has eulogized the villa which housed this library and which was used by Varro as a place of retired study. "What noble discussions used to take place in that building! What writings were composed there! What ideas were originated there! The laws of the Roman people, the memorials of our ancestors, the consideration of all wisdom and all learning, were the topics dwelt on . . ." But Caesar did not live to complete the undertaking, and Varro's books were scattered by Mark Antony. The first public library in the city was founded soon after Caesar's murder by Asinius Pollio, who had returned from a victorious campaign against the Illyrians (39 B.C.). A little later Augustus opened a more famous library, with two collections of books, one Greek and one Latin, in a structure called the Porticus Octaviae. Later still, to commemorate the victory at Actium, he established another large library of Greek and Latin works on the Palatine Hill, reached by a colonnade leading past the temple on that eminence. The very names of the first librarians of these institutions have come down to us. Horace refers to one collection in a warning to plagiarists:

> Bards should draw inspiration from themselves,
> And not from Palatine Apollo's shelves.

As time passed, the number of Roman libraries increased; and about the end of the first century A.D. we meet a great new landmark in the development of means for historical study—the first true public record office. This was the Library of Ulpius Trajanus, which contained many state records as well as ordinary volumes. The Emperor Trajan deposited in it the ivory tablets and the linen books which held the records of the *senatus consulta* and other official bodies. The collection, removed about two hundred years later to the Baths of Diocletian, remained in use until the storm of the barbarian invasions burst upon Rome in the latter part of the fifth century.

By the decade 360–370 A.D. the city of Rome possessed no fewer than twenty-eight public libraries, while such towns as Milan and Tibur (Tivoli) also had valuable collections. Some of the most important combined the function of library with that of a discussion-club for learned men. A scene in which Aulus Gellius played a part—one that holds an instant appeal for present-day students—has been summarized by a modern writer as follows:

One very hot day he and some friends were outside the Temple of Hercules at Tibur, drinking melted snow. A discussion arose as to the wisdom of the practise. One of the party declares that not only did many of the physicians disapprove of snow-water, but that Aristotle had expressed a like opinion. To prove his case he goes to the temple library for Aristotle's treatise. In imagination we can see him in this room. It is small, evidently designed for the storing of books and not for use as a reading-room. Presses run around the walls, and probably there is an additional press in the middle of the room. He must refer to the catalogue, then to the numbered press, and run his eye over the tickets hanging from the ends of the rolls stored in it—doing, in fact, precisely what a reader in an open-shelf library does today. Finding his Aristotle, he rejoins his friends—because he seems to have been allowed to take books out of the library room—unties the straps, removes the colored envelope, unrolls the manuscript, and triumphantly displays to the disputants the convincing passage. The same writer also mentions a discussion in the Tiberian library, and says that a grammatical difficulty was

settled by consulting a book in the Temple of Peace, in
the Forum of Vespasian.[2]

III

The great black line which closed the history of ancient
libraries was drawn in blood and ashes during the century
450–550 A.D., when nearly all the book collections in the
Italian peninsula, whether public or private, were destroyed. But happily many libraries still survived in the
eastern part of the Roman world. When Constantine transferred the seat of his empire to Byzantium and founded
Constantinople, many Roman bibliophiles and scholars followed him to the East. The spirit of history went with
them. On the Golden Horn they were joined by Greek
scholars. Constantine lost little time in searching for books
both Christian and pagan, and before his death had gathered an imperial library of about 7000 volumes. His son
Constantius and other successors augmented it until it became impressive. Julian the Apostate founded another library, this time non-Christian, and gave it all his books.
Meanwhile, many of the religious institutions of the East
became fairly safe centers for the preservation of books
and documents. The monasteries of Mount Athos bore
throughout medieval and modern times a peculiar fame
for their collections. Early in the nineteenth century a
British traveler, Robert Curzon, who went to Mount Athos
to search for ancient books, found in the twenty monasteries of that single peninsula about 2000 manuscripts on
vellum and 5500 on paper—not to mention more than 20,-
000 printed volumes. These Eastern monasteries were one
of the principal sources from which Italian book collectors of the Renaissance gathered their treasures. And even
after the First World War a writer could declare: "The
Balkan provinces and Russia hold great masses of Greek
and Slavonic manuscripts as yet very incompletely known."

For centuries the world's principal storehouse of written
materials, historical, literary, and scientific, its great nurs-
ery of learning, was the Byzantine Empire. Constantinople
did not fall until 1453, and long before that date the

savants of the Western world were busy studying there, while its collectors were seeking for ancient manuscripts and bringing back whole cargoes of Greek and other books. The transfer had reached sweeping proportions before turban and scimitar stormed the walls. So much had been carried westward that historians like John Addington Symonds deem it unlikely that the works of any of the more important ancients perished in the capture. For that matter, the enmity of the Turks for books has been much exaggerated, and they gladly continued the sale of manuscripts to Frankish infidels.

It is impossible, as Frederic Harrison says, "to see how our knowledge of ancient literature or civilization could have been recovered if Constantinople had not nursed through the Middle Ages the vast accumulations of Greek learning in the schools of Alexandria, Athens, and Asia Minor . . . ; if indefatigable copyists had not toiled in multiplying the texts of ancient Greece." Once carried out of the East, the manuscripts were likely to be safe. It was the great ones of the earth who did most in sending emissaries to rescue them, and these princes and prelates, regarding a Greek manuscript as a rare jewel, locked most of them up in libraries where they were less exposed to dispersion and maltreatment than ever before. Latin manuscripts, though less highly esteemed, were also protected.[3]

A second great channel through which the learning of the ancient world was poured down into late medieval times was the Saracenic power. The speed and energy with which the Arabs conquered much of the East, all of North Africa, and most of Spain, is one of the marvels of the Middle Ages. But almost equally marvelous was the taste for learning displayed by many of the Arabic conquerors. While secular writings were still little valued by Christian folk, and even reprobated, men in Arabia, Syria, and Islamic Egypt read them with avidity. Moreover, the learned Moslems showed a strong predilection for scientific works, which were long neglected even by such Christians as paid attention to pagan history, poetry, and philosophy. It was no accident that the Arabs of Spain gave Western Europe its first knowledge of most of Aristotle's works. A long line of Saracenic book collections can be traced, spanning the medieval world from the far West to the farther East. Haroun-al-Raschid, ruler of Bagdad's shrines of fretted gold, patronized scholars and treasured manuscripts. We hear of libraries at Bassora; at Cairo, where the Fatimids collected ten thousand volumes only to see Saladin scatter them; at Tripoli; and above all, at Cordova.

It seems difficult to believe that Moorish writers did not indulge in a little Oriental magnification in their pictures of the culture of tenth-century Andalusia. They speak of seventy public libraries. They describe the magnificence of the central collection in Cordova, where the sovereign Alhakem founded an academy, sent out agents to scour the East for Greek treasures, and at one time employed three hundred scholars in translating them into Arabic. This library at its height is said to have contained 600,000 titles. But after full allowance for any exaggeration, it is undeniable that Moorish Spain in that century was the chief well-spring of culture in Western Europe.

Meanwhile, in various nooks throughout the Christian West many scattered books and papers survived the tidal wave of barbarian invasion and the storms of local violence. Scholars here and there cherished a few volumes—Boethius more than a few. Some Western monasteries preserved them, for while these institutions often suffered severely from the general lawlessness, they were long the safest of all repositories. When St. Benedict founded the abbey of Monte Cassino in 528, he enjoined the monks to study constantly to save themselves from idleness. This abbey, despite destructive onslaughts by the Lombards and later the Saracens, kept many books intact. In the eleventh century its monks transcribed numerous important works, pagan as well as Christian; in Boccaccio's day it still owned many volumes, though he wept at seeing their neglect; and long afterward Ernest Renan discovered there unpublished manuscripts of value. From St. Benedict in 528 to Renan in 1849 is a far cry, but the abbey had spanned it!

As the Benedictine Order spread over much of Europe, it established libraries and centers of study; in England, for example, at York, Canterbury, Whitby, Glastonbury,

Wearmouth, and Croyland. Another founder of monasteries, Cassiodorus, encouraged his monks to study and transcribe the classics, and thus, as Hodgkin writes, "utilized the vast learning of the convent for the preservation of divine and human learning, and for its transmission to later ages." Ireland of the sixth century, full of monasteries, schools, and other Christian institutions, was also rich in books. In various parts of Western Europe the Franciscans, pledged to poverty, first departed from the strict interpretation of their vow by taking up book-collecting. They and other mendicant orders often showed such creditable energy in building libraries that Richard de Bury, after visiting their convents, speaks of finding "heaped up amidst the utmost poverty the utmost riches of learning." Some monasteries did history and letters an unwitting service. Valuing old manuscripts of classical origin simply as paper for their own writings, they erased the script and used the pages for religious material. These palimpsests can easily be restored by the devices of modern chemistry. Some of them, particularly in Italy, have yielded important materials—"lost" fragments of Cicero's *Republic*, orations by him and others, works of the rhetorician Fronto, and so on. Early in the last century the head of the Vatican Library, exploring what was still an almost untouched field, gave the world some delightful surprises of this sort.

Thus gradually the medieval world acquired the material for secular schools, for research, and for historical writing. The early English churchman Benedict Biscop (628–690), founder of the monastery at Yarrow, labored diligently to collect books, bringing them from Rome on six occasions and at least once making a special trip. Dying, he urgently enjoined his friends to preserve the "most noble and rich library" he had brought together; and his successor Ceolfrid made important additions to it. On this library the Venerable Bede largely founded his *Ecclesiastical History of the English People*, the first great monument of English historical writing. One of Bede's pupils, Egbert, became Archbishop of York, and established on the model of Yarrow a school and library. Ranging among the volumes in this collection, the scholar Alcuin acquired his vast and varied erudition; and in due time he became director of the school at York. Thence he was called to be head of the greater school supported by Charlemagne, who in 782 proclaimed that he had undertaken "the task of reviving, with the utmost zeal, the study of letters well-nigh extinguished through the neglect of our ancestors." The richest phase of the Carolingian Renaissance had begun. It was one of the palace scholars, a close friend of Alcuin's, the versatile Einhard, who wrote in imitation of Suetonius's lives of the Caesars the chief monument of Frankish historiography, his *Life of Charlemagne.* Some critics would credit him also with authorship of part of the Frankish annals.

Before the death of Charlemagne in 814, the means for historical and other literary work had been securely established in his dominions. The light that had been held aloft in Ireland in the sixth century, and that had flared up in England during the seventh and eighth, was now burning brightly on the Continent. During the ninth century, while Britain was being harried by the Danes, a vigorous intellectual life flourished at the Carolingian court and in the great French and German abbeys; a life stimulated by scholars from Ireland, England, and Italy. The author of *The Wanderings and Homes of Manuscripts* has told in a few words what this ninth century accomplished for future students of history:

There is immense activity, literary and artistic, afoot at the Court of Charlemagne and his successors. The German abbeys—e.g., Lorsch, Fulda—and cathedral schools (Mainz, Bamberg, etc.) are full of scribes and teachers. Irishmen who know Greek flock to the Continent, driven from home by Danish invasion; such are Johannus Scotus Erieugena, and Sedulius Scotus. They haunt Liege, Laon, Aix-la-Chapelle, and penetrate to Italy: at Tours the handwriting called the Carolingian minuscule, the parent of our modern "Roman" printing, is developed, though not at Tours alone. At Corbie, Fleury on the Loire, St. Riquier by Abbeville, Rheims, and many another center in Northern and Eastern France, libraries are accumulated and ancient books copied. Of St. Gall and Reichenau the same may be said. The archdeacon Pacificus (d. 846) gave over two hundred books to the cathedral, where many of them still are; and at Monte Cassino, the head house of the Benedictine order, books were written in the difficult "Beneventane" hand.[4]

By the thirteenth century the book trade of Western Europe had become enormous. It still found its center in Paris, where it was passing from the control of monastic scribes into that of tradesmen or stationers; men who made a livelihood by transcribing books, and who sometimes hired a corps of professional copyists. Toward the close of the century the trade took on specialization. Bologna, for example, with the most renowned school of law in Europe, turned out legal texts and commentaries, both ecclesiastical and civil. Picardy and Artois manufactured quantities of illustrated romances, containing such legends as those of Arthur and Lancelot, which families of wealth bought to pass the long winter evenings. Thus we reach the fourteenth century, when old books were copied in far greater number than ever before; when, as we have seen, the East was scoured by emissaries of wealth and scholarship to obtain its manuscripts; and when more new books were written than ever, for this was the century of Petrarch and the dawn of the Renaissance. And just beyond it lay the fifteenth century, when the Age of Manuscripts ended, and the Age of Printed Books began; the century of Gutenberg, Aldus, and Caxton.

IV

The medieval annalist could perform his service to history with such materials as his own memory afforded, aided sometimes by monastic or private archives, sometimes even by an interested court official. But before the more ambitious chronicler of medieval days could accomplish his work, libraries of some scope had to be built up;

and ere the true historian could make his bow, the world had to have at least the rudiments of our great modern libraries and archives. The story of their development is full of significance for all lovers of history.

The annalist, in the strictest meaning of the word, always filled a highly limited function. Perhaps the best examples are supplied by Britain. From about the beginning of the seventh century, the Anglo-Saxon Church was accustomed to draw up formal tables which indicated the date of Easter over certain periods of years; and in these Paschal tables, each annual date was followed by a blank space in which church dignitaries or monastic scribes might briefly note all important events. Early annalists, using oral information and the scanty records at hand, set down in these spaces a concise record. Their practice having obvious value, missionaries carried it from the British Isles to the Continent. Gradually in both areas the record expanded and grew more satisfactory. The Carolingian Renaissance gave us such important works as the *Annals of Einhard,* the *Annals of Lorsch,* and the *Annals of St. Bertini,* officially compiled as a record of the acts of Charlemagne and the rulers who preceded and followed him.

In time the best of such annals became worthy of the name of chronicles. That is, they became much broader in scope. Chronicles, though in general still impersonal, sketchy, and founded upon vaguely indicated sources, are distinguished from annals by their comprehensive character; they relate to a whole nation or a large aspect of history, instead of to one locality, one religious body, one court, or at most one phase of national affairs. *The Anglo-Saxon Chronicles* are thus a general history of the Danish Wars, their most ancient portion having been written in the ninth century, and the whole composed at Canterbury, Evesham, and various other places by various writers. Alfred the Great has been credited with inspiring the composition of this national chronicle as distinguished from local annals, and may even have revised the part describing his own campaigns. Obviously, the chronicler had to search more widely than the annalist for materials and tap a larger range of sources. One of the prime difficulties in dealing with chronicles, indeed, is to ascertain just what were the chief sources, and how much value should be assigned to each. Compelled in this way to find resources outside his own office or monastic hall, the chronicler demanded more books, more papers, more advisers and helpers than the annalist; he demanded the library and the archive, the librarian and archivist.

The development of historical study from the Renaissance onward thus moves *pari passu* with the development of libraries and archives, and the history of these institutions is inextricably intertwined with that of historical scholarship. The first important history of scientific temper written in England was David Hume's. It is significant that in 1752 Hume was appointed head of the Advocates' Library in Edinburgh, a post small in emoluments but rich in opportunities for literary work. By 1753 he was preparing for his great historical endeavor. He wrote his friend Clephane that he felt completely settled in life. He had an income, a house, reputation, and independence; what more could he ask? "A wife? That is not one of the indispensable requisites of life. Books? That is one of them; and I have more than I can use."

Without the Advocates' Library, we should never have had Hume's *History of England*. Gibbon wrote the first three volumes of his *Decline and Fall* amid all the literary accumulations of London, and collected there the materials (including a large private library) for the three final volumes; Voltaire wrote his most ambitious historical works with the aid of the libraries of Paris and Berlin. It was no accident that historical writing in the United States first flourished in the shadow of the libraries at Cambridge (where the Harvard Library was begun in 1638) and in Boston (where the Athenaeum was established in 1807). Nor was it an accident that several distinguished American historians—John Fiske, Justin Winsor, Reuben Gold Thwaites—were also librarians.

Since historical writing in its modern character began only about two centuries ago, we should expect to find the great modern libraries comparatively young; and it can be truly said that none was beyond its infancy five

hundred years ago, and that the best did not attain great
scope or vigor until the eighteenth century.

The Vatican Library, which ranks first in the variety,
antiquity, and value of its manuscript collections, really
began with the return of the Papal Court from Avignon
after the Great Schism—that is, was a creation of the fifteenth century; and it was still a tiny collection of only
2527 volumes when Sixtus IV gave it an ornate abode
and appointed its first librarian in 1475. So well did
Platina, the librarian, exert himself, that only six years
later it counted 3500 volumes. Yet it grew but slowly.
Montaigne has left a description of it just a hundred years
later (1581), when it was contained in five or six rooms.
"I was taken to every part thereof," he writes, "by a gentleman who invited me to make use of it as often as I
might desire." Sixtus V began in 1586 the erection of the
handsome structure in which the Vatican books are still
housed, and thereafter it enjoyed almost uninterrupted
prosperity. Early in the seventeenth century the archives
were separated from the library proper. The one serious
disaster was the seizure of nearly all the early manuscripts
and the finest illuminated books by the French in 1798,
but after Waterloo these treasures were restored. For centuries access to the library was difficult; until 1881 it contributed less toward historical study than any other great
collection. But under Leo XIII commendable advances
were made in opening not only the printed books but the
manuscripts, and, with some severe restrictions, the Vatican archives, to research; while since his time still more
has been done. Within recent years (1927–29) a new
catalogue has been compiled by Vatican officials and
American librarians working together, upon the best principles of American library practice.

The Bibliothèque Nationale, for a long period the largest library in the world, was first established in France as
the king's library, and had no real importance until the
time of Louis XI; indeed, one of the royal collections was
actually bought at the beginning of Charles VII's reign by
the Duke of Bedford, and carried away to England. But
various monarchs took pride in the collection, and by 1500

so many volumes had been acquired by purchase or seizure that it was a really splendid collection—one of the "four marvels of France." At this time it was at Blois. But about 1520 Francis I, desiring a library nearer his court, established one at Fontainebleau, under the charge of one of the best scholars in his realm. He required that one copy of every work printed in France be sent to his collection, and though at first the rule was more often evaded than obeyed, the time came when it was enforced. In 1544 the Fontainebleau collection absorbed the library at Blois, and some twenty years later the whole body of books and manuscripts was removed to Paris.

Here by steady growth it ceased to be the king's private possession and became a general court library. The great Colbert, as superintendent of royal buildings, obtained control of it in 1661, and his wise and energetic administration raised it from about 17,000 to about 50,000 volumes. Historians may remember gratefully that Colbert required provincial officials to search for books and documents illustrating French history and politics, and directed them to copy what they could not buy. It was under Colbert, too, that systematic cataloguing began to make the books more useful to scholars. Before the seventeenth century closed the library was opened to students twice a week, though this generous rule did not long endure. By 1715 the collection amounted to about 70,000 volumes.

Throughout the vicissitudes of the eighteenth century the Bibliothèque continued to grow, until 1790 found it with more than 150,000 volumes, in addition to opuscules and manuscripts. Then the Revolution brought an astonishing expansion. Books poured in from seized estates and dissolved monasteries. Within a few years the collection more than doubled. Now renamed the national instead of royal library, it retained that title under the first and second empires. During the Napoleonic régime appropriations were increased, the Belgian librarian Van Praet labored amain to make his treasures valuable to scholars, and the conquests of the Emperor brought books from all over the Continent. Though most of these had to be returned after the peace of 1815, by that date the Bibliothèque possessed an easy primacy. Its growth thereafter was enormous; in 1927 it boasted of 4,400,000 printed books and more than 120,000 manuscripts. From Van Praet's time onward the library had been open every weekday to students using its historical and literary treasures.

The British Museum, almost as large as the Bibliothèque and so much better classified and administered that French scholars have sometimes crossed the Channel and used it in preference to their own, can also be traced back to a small royal collection. This was formed by Henry VII, and slowly increased by his Tudor and Stuart successors. During the Commonwealth a few friends preserved the puny collection intact, and it was handed over to Charles II unharmed. Under William and Mary it received its first eminent librarian, Richard Bentley. His strict enforcement of a much earlier rule (1662) enabling the library to claim a copy of every work published under the British flag brought in about a thousand volumes. The early Hanoverians took little interest in these printed treasures, and George II presented them to the nation in 1757.

Meanwhile, two other important libraries had grown up in England. One was the Cottonian, especially notable as having been established for historical objects. It was founded by Sir Robert Cotton, a younger contemporary of Shakespeare, who spent money lavishly for historical materials—chronicles, records, charters and other state papers, as well as survivals of the old monastic collections. His array of public documents, many of them priceless originals, was scrutinized with a rather hostile eye by the public authorities; some of them jealous because they needed his papers for official purposes, some fearful lest he sell state secrets. But historical scholars, including Bishop Burnet, used them. The other great English collection was the Harleian Library, founded by Robert Harley, Earl of Oxford, who was roughly a contemporary of Pope's (1661–1724). It included the collections of Stow, the historian of London, and of Fox, whose history of the Martyrs so edified our Puritan forefathers. Harley's son, the second Earl of Oxford, continued the accumulation of manuscripts, charters, rolls, prints, and books. They, like the Cottonian books and papers, were gathered primarily to furnish materials for the study of English history.

Finally, in 1753, the Harleian manuscripts, though not the books, were bought by the government. This was the year in which Sir Hans Sloane bequeathed to the nation his books, manuscripts, and rarities, the nucleus of the British Museum, for the nominal sum of £20,000. The Cottonian, Harleian, and Sloane collections were at once united, and four years later the gift of George II added the royal library to them. At the beginning of 1759, in the midst of one of the greatest periods of victory in the annals of the British Empire, the consolidated collections were thrown open to the public under the name of the British Museum. At once bequests and donations began to enlarge the Museum. Many of them were rich in materials for British history and biography. Though the government was long parsimonious in its appropriations, at Victoria's accession the Museum contained about 240,000 volumes, and by 1865 it held 640,000. This was in the midst of the great era of Victorian historiography, when Froude, Freeman, Stubbs, Carlyle, Milman, and others were most active, and they all relied heavily upon the collection. By 1927 the library contained some 3,200,000 books, a vast array of pamphlets, and about 56,000 manuscripts. Of all the great libraries, it has unquestionably been the most useful to historical scholarship.

The principal American collection, the Congressional Library, is by far the youngest of the major libraries, but the generosity with which the government has supported it has already rendered it in many respects pre-eminent. Founded in 1800, the efforts of Albert Gallatin and Samuel Latham Mitchill had made it a valuable though small collection by 1814, when it was destroyed in the British capture of Washington. After the war, Jefferson's library of some 6700 volumes was bought by the government for $23,000 as the basis for a new collection. By the middle of the century the library held more than 50,000 volumes. Though a fire in 1851 destroyed more than half of it, most of Jefferson's books fortunately survived; and Congress spent such generous sums for replacements that before the Civil War opened it was larger than ever. At the close of this conflict the library of the Smithsonian Institution, about 40,000 volumes, chiefly scientific, was combined with the Congressional Library. Thenceforward its progress was more rapid and sustained than that of any rival. Two able administrators, A. R. Spofford and Herbert Putnam, led in building it up; Congress appropriated funds for purchases on an unprecedented scale; and it became the chief repository for papers of distinguished Americans. Under acts of 1834 and later, it purchased those of Washington; in 1848 those of Jefferson, Madison, and Hamilton; in 1849 those of Monroe; and by purchase or gift it has since acquired those of many other public men.

A great building, the most costly and ornate ever devoted to books, was opened in 1911, and though it was designed to hold 4,000,000 volumes, it became so crowded that in 1938 it was necessary to supplement it with an annex. By 1958 it held nearly forty million pieces of material, the chief components of which were 11,780,000 books and pamphlets, 16,185,000 manuscripts, 2,980,000 photographic views, 2,470,000 maps, and more than 2,000,000 pieces of music. In that year the House of Representatives passed a resolution authorizing plans for a third great building. Strongest in history, politics, and law, the Congressional Library is perhaps better adapted to historical work than to any other purpose, and has for a generation been the chief focal point of research into the American past.

It is impossible to say anything here of other national libraries only less important than those just briefly described—the great State Libraries in Berlin and Munich; the National-bibliothek in Vienna; the State Library at Leningrad, declared by some authorities to be the largest on the globe, with not fewer than 5,000,000 volumes and 240,000 manuscripts; and the Lenin Memorial Library in Moscow, with more than three million volumes. We can merely mention the numerous libraries rich in unique books, like the Laurentian Library in Florence, the Bibliothèque Mazarine in Paris, and the John Rylands Library

in Manchester; the great municipal collections all over
Europe, the Americas, and Australasia, of which the New
York Public Library plainly stands first; the many university libraries, like the Bodleian at Oxford, the Sorbonne,
those of the Universities of Berlin, Vienna, Warsaw, and
Leningrad, and the even more extensive collections at
Harvard, Yale, Columbia, and the University of Illinois;
and such treasuries of manuscript material as the Huntington Library at San Marino, California. It is sufficient to
say that since the invention of printing the fast-increasing
production of books has scattered libraries throughout the
civilized world. In far-off New Zealand, in young lands
like Argentina and California, in what a few generations
ago was the hermit nation of Japan, collections of books
exist far richer than those known to the eighteenth-century
historians of Western Europe. The extent and variety of
the modern collections, in fact, impose upon historical
study one of its chief present-day characteristics—its specialization.

V

But modern historical work rests upon a triple base,
and books, whether manuscript or printed, are but one of
its supports. The other two are public archives, and private collections of papers and pictorial materials. Until the
later decades of the eighteenth century, most historical
works of modern times were based upon book material,
for little else was available. Yet until government documents were made available for study upon a broad scale,
no student could write critically or exhaustively of political
transactions. Until the letters, memoranda, and diaries of
individual leaders were thrown open on a comparable
scale, no man could write expertly of the role of personalities in any movement or conflict. A brief examination
of the steps by which such aids to historical composition
became available will throw much light on the progress
of historiography.

Among modern governments Great Britain's has shown
the most enterprise in collecting, arranging, and throwing

open to search its official records. "Both from an earlier
date and on a larger scale than other nations," according to
competent American authorities,[5] it has displayed a conscientious zeal in protecting, cataloguing, and giving use
to its archives. Few lands have suffered so little from invasion or civil war as England, and her internal tranquil-
lity has done much to keep her papers intact. Yet even
Britain's records remained largely inaccessible to the historian until the beginning of the nineteenth century.

For many centuries every department of the British government, administrative, legislative, and judicial, kept its
own records. They were used, in random and unsystematic
fashion, by a few specially favored historical workers in
the seventeenth and eighteenth centuries, but their contents were unclassified, unexplored, and largely unknown.
At last, in 1800, a Record Commission was appointed by
Parliament, which with other royal commissions and com-
mittees began examining the records, publishing lists of
documents, and even making calendars or abstracts of the
most important. These lists were sufficiently well done to
have permanent usefulness. For example, students of Irish
history will always find of basic importance the three
volumes (1813–25) of "Reports from the committee appointed by His Majesty to execute the measures recommended in an address to the House of Commons respecting the public records of Ireland." The Record Commission
was shortly offering important sources in full, such as
the proceedings of the Privy Council from 1386 to 1542,
which it issued in seven volumes in 1834–37. Altogether,
before it went out of existence in 1869, this single body
published almost a hundred volumes, and did much to
drive highways into the *terra incognita* of official papers.
Meanwhile, as early as 1786 the British Government had
set up a state printing establishment which made possible
a careful supervision of printed documents. This was the
Stationery Office, which still acts as printer, publisher, and
bookseller for government departments, and whose publications have long been divided into two general groups:
parliamentary papers, or "blue books," and non-parliamen-
tary papers.

Then in 1838 the British authorities blazed a path for other nations to follow by establishing the first central repository for archives, competently administered, and open to all students of the past. A law of that year created the Public Record Office, and made the Master of the Rolls its head. From the beginning he was custodian of practically all the judicial records of the realm; while fourteen years later an Order in Council placed all administrative records under his authority. The Public Record Office pushed on with the work begun by the Record Commission in publishing lists, calendars, and complete documents from the archives. For a century its gray stone home, quietly placed between Chancery and Fetter Lane just off roaring Fleet Street, has been a magnet for historical students from all parts of the planet, and especially of the English-speaking world. Americans find here much of their own early history. The records brought from the Colonial Office include the papers of the Committee on Trade and Plantations down to the severance of the thirteen colonies from the Empire. The records brought from the Foreign Office begin with 1782, when it was established, and contain a wealth of material on Anglo-American relations. A great part of the important manuscripts in the British archives have now been printed entire, or calendared so fully that the abstracts relieve the student from the necessity of consulting the originals.

In the year that the Record Commission ceased work (1869), Queen Victoria appointed a Royal Commission on Historical Manuscripts, its chairman being the Master of the Rolls, which has become famous throughout the domain of historical studies. Its duty was to inquire as to the existence of private manuscripts and papers, "a knowledge of which would be of great utility in the illustration of history, constitutional law, science, and general literature." Everyone knew that the older families of the kingdom possessed immense stores of manuscripts. In 1870 the Commission issued the first of its long shelfful of reports, to which it is steadily adding. The calendar of the Cecil manuscripts, owned by the Marquis of Salisbury and more valuable for the time of Elizabeth than any in London, fills fourteen volumes. The papers of the Marquis of Ormonde, at Kilkenny Castle, have been abstracted in ten volumes; the Stuart manuscripts in Windsor Castle, the property of the king, in seven volumes; and the American manuscripts in the Royal Institution, four volumes. Many finds of sensational historical and literary value have been made. At first defective in scholarship, the reports have long since become models of their kind; and they are indispensable to any working library of European, Imperial, or American history. To cite but one of many items interesting to Americans, the diaries of the first Earl of Egmont are full of material on the establishment and development of Georgia —the work of Oglethorpe, the activities of the two Wesleys, Indian relations, immigration, the progress of settlement, and so on. Indeed, American colonial history could not have been properly written without the work of the Commission.

Many of the searches of the Commission were made in the nick of time. Increasing changes in the distribution of wealth in Great Britain have brought about a rapid breakup of estates, and the sale of libraries and muniments. Numerous collections of family papers, especially those containing autographs of value, have been sold piecemeal; others have been bought in bulk and transported abroad. The Commission reported in 1926 that "the number of collections that have actually been reported on and cannot now be traced is no longer inconsiderable, but in these cases our reports supply to some extent their place."

The publication of Parliamentary debates naturally began in the country which was the mother of Parliaments. The first systematic and satisfactory collection made in England was the work not of the government but of an eminent journalist—William Cobbett's *Parliamentary History of England from the Earliest Period to the year 1803*. It supplanted various earlier works by private hands; *D'Ewes's Journals of the Parliaments of Queen Elizabeth*, for example, and *Grey's Debates . . . 1667–1694*, as well as the more ambitious *Parliamentary or Constitutional History of England, 1066–1660*, issued in twenty-four volumes in the middle of the eighteenth century. Cobbett's enterprise was continued from 1803 by Thomas C. Hansard, whose father was government printer, under the title of *Parliamentary Debates;* and the reports continue to be generally called *Hansard's Debates.* The user will quickly discover that the editorial principles used are very different from those employed in the reports of the *Congressional Record.*

French archival practice, unlike British, has been based upon a decentralization of materials, and has been imitated by most nations of continental Europe. As the result of a policy carefully formulated in 1789, the national archives have been preserved in well-classified groups in the Hôtel de Soubise in Paris. Each of the departments has meanwhile guarded its separate archives as scrupulously as have the American States, while municipal and communal records have also been kept separately. In some respects France has led the world in the critical study of official documents—especially medieval documents—as sources for history. The first great textbook in this field (that is, in diplomatics) was the work of the Benedictine scholar Jean Mabillon, whose *De Re Diplomatica* was published in 1681. The best-known institution for cultivating diplomatics, the École des Chartes, founded in Paris in 1821, has ever since been an unapproached center for documentary and paleographical studies. In this way France has been kept fully supplied with archival experts. All the French collections, national, departmental, and local, have been well explored since the Revolution; a part of the material has also been inventoried, though some of this has been done so badly that the lists have been withdrawn from circulation.

Germany has her Reichsarchiv, and long had separate archives for all the states of the country. Italy has seventeen different repositories, one for each of the ancient divisions of the country, the Tuscan archives at Florence being particularly important. Of course the Vatican has its separate archives, impressive in extent and value. Switzerland and the Netherlands possess national archives at Berne and The Hague respectively, and separate cantonal and state archives as well. Both in Germany and

Austria the government has given support to the study of diplomatics, and Italy has not neglected it.

The United States held the unhappy distinction of being one of the last great Powers to provide itself with a central building and administration for its national records. After the Civil War, as wealth and population increased, and as federal functions grew at the expense of the states, the mass of documents in Washington rapidly became prodigious. Yet even in 1900 it remained the general rule that each bureau and office retained all its past records; a rule modified only by a partial concentration into departmental collections, and the deposit of a few groups of papers in the Congressional Library. Thus widely scattered and ever more voluminous, the records were grossly neglected. They were constantly being damaged by dampness, heat, insects, and careless handling, fires repeatedly destroyed valuable files, and many documents were thrown away as valueless. One Cabinet officer sold 400 tons of official records as junk.

As the result of a long agitation, Congress finally appropriated a total of about $12,000,000 for an archives building—a sum sufficient to erect the best structure of its kind in the world. Ground was broken in 1931, the building was completed five years later, and, the office of Archivist of the United States having meanwhile been created, the removal of records to this monumental home began in 1936. The stack space comprised five and a half million cubic feet. Here the papers could be kept in perfect physical condition, protected by elaborate devices from fire, burglary, dust, and sunlight; could be carefully classified; and could be made instantly available to students.

At the outset the Federal Archives were hampered by the reluctance of various departments to surrender their more interesting and valuable records, even when not needed for frequent official reference. But as this reluctance is slowly overcome, the collections promise to grow rapidly. No other government has furnished such complete facilities to historical students—catalogues, inventories, and other finding tools, aid by staff employees, and every mechanical device. As the first Archivist has written:

Filing equipment designed by government architects especially for the National Archives Building, for the purpose of facilitating the filing and handling of government archives, has been installed. Three beautiful "Search Rooms," well-lighted, air-conditioned, and furnished with comfortable desks and chairs—a feature almost unique in buildings of this kind—are provided for the use of students. Around the walls of these rooms is open shelving for approximately 50,000 books, which will place almost within arm's length of the student a carefully selected service library to supplement the archival material. . . . If he wants this material copied by other methods than pen or typewriter, reproductions can be made for him by photostating, photographing, microfilming, or multilithing processes.[6]

The National Archives, the Congressional Library, and the various State Libraries are being supplemented by great Presidential libraries, of which the Roosevelt Library at Hyde Park, New York, and the Truman Library at Independence, Missouri, were the first and second in time. The Hyde Park collections by 1960 included more than 28,000 books, 40,000 other printed titles, Roosevelt's collection of naval prints, 3500 cubic feet of his White House papers, and approximately the same quantity of other papers. The Independence collections are equally important for Truman's years as President, and in 1961 an Eisenhower Library was in process of creation in Abilene, Kansas.

The fact that the Roosevelt Library housed hundreds of film records of important events during his Presidency, sound recordings of his important speeches, and more than 62,000 still photographs suggests the importance of these newer forms of historical material. The Prints and Photographs Division of the Library of Congress constitutes one of its most important elements. The first war photographer of any note, Roger Fenton, had to use the messy collodion wet-plate process in recording the Crimean conflict, preparing the plates in the heat of action, exposing them wet in the heavy camera, and developing them immediately under every disadvantage of peril and confusion. Yet his achievement was classic. He had better-equipped successors in America, so that Civil War scenes were preserved in effective detail by Mathew Brady, Alexander Gardner, and other intrepid Northerners. The first man to attempt photography in the Far West was the explorer Frémont, who after initial failures found an aide who was successful. By the time that the ranchman and the cowboy reached their apogee the trans-Mississippi scene was being expertly photographed in almost every phase. Meanwhile, such painters as H. W. Hansen and such illustrators as J. H. Smith were making a record as important as that left by the more famous Frederic Remington.

VI

For fully a century and a half governmental aid to history has extended in some nations to still another field, from a literary point of view the most interesting of all. This is the publication of historical texts—chronicles, annals, collections of private or public letters, and the like—particularly for the formative periods of national life. To Germany belongs the honor of leading the way. While the Napoleonic Wars were still raging, it occurred to Von Stein that the printing of the principal sources for early German history would be a valuable contribution to patriotism and scholarship alike. His enterprise—the *Monumenta Germaniae Historica*, which by 1925 had attained its 125th volume—thus began as an expression of the new German spirit born from the Napoleonic upheaval. When peace came in 1815 a commission of the ablest German historians was named to edit the known sources, and to search out new ones. The first volume was published in 1826 under private auspices, but the German government soon took the series over and subsidized it. The first two editors were succeeded in 1886 by a board, and nearly all the distinguished medievalists of Germany for a century past have been enlisted in the undertaking. Jacob Grimm and others had initiated in 1849 the publication of a series of German translations of the chief Latin chronicles and histories of the Middle Ages, which has reached more than ninety volumes. Various German states have of course also published sets devoted to the material from their archives.

In France the historian Guizot, while minister of public instruction, planned a collection of unpublished documents on national history, of which the first volume was brought out in 1836. This was carried forward after 1881 by the Comité des Travaux Historiques et Scientifiques, with government encouragement, and not far from 300 volumes have now been published. The Comité has also issued about a hundred volumes of documents upon the economic history of the French Revolution. The French Foreign Office has meanwhile been commendably active in publishing collections of treaties, instructions to ambassadors, and other documents—though the archives of the Ministry are not open to such recent dates as those of the British Foreign Office and the American State Department. It may also be mentioned that the publication of stenographic reports of parliamentary debates began in France under Napoleon III, and is of course still carried on by the state. Meanwhile, a compilation of debates from the beginnings in 1787 down to 1860 has also long been carried forward, and is approaching completion.

Other nations began to publish historical texts soon after the bodies created by Stein and Guizot did so. The labor of the German and French commissions inspired King Charles Albert of Sardinia to establish a similar body in 1833; and its work for Italian history, the *Monumenta Historia Patriae,* has extended down to our own day. The Italian Historical Institute, founded a dozen years after national unification and kept under governmental control, has edited a large collection of sources for the history of Italy, as yet relating to medieval times alone, and has also carried on the publication of a valuable series of Italian chronicles, originally begun by private enterprise. Even Russia, even Spain, early fell in with the general movement. The Czar's government in 1835 created the Archeographical Commission, which in 1841 began to publish the old Muscovite chronicles, since supplemented by a wide variety of narratives and documents. In Madrid, the Royal

Academy of History commenced in 1841 its *Collection of Inedited Documents for the History of Spain;* a publicly supported enterprise which, dealing chiefly with the reigns of Charles V and Philip II, had reached a total of 112 volumes before the Spanish-American War. Belgium, too, established a Royal Historical Commission in 1834, which two years later began issuing a series that has now grown to more than 180 volumes. The Dutch royal family caught the impulse, and in 1834 initiated a series of volumes drawn from the archives of the House of Orange-Nassau.

The individualistic tradition has always been strong in Britain. The state hesitated to trench upon fields which might be occupied by commercial publishers or learned societies. Yet even there, the government finally determined to publish materials upon the early history of the nation. In 1857 the Master of Rolls submitted to the Treasury a project for a series of chronicles, records, and other source works from the Roman invasion to the accession of Henry VIII, which was at once approved. Precedence was to be given to the scarcest and most valuable materials, and they were to be edited by scholars without mutilation or abridgment. Each was to be treated as a first edition, and the most accurate text possible was to be achieved by a collation of manuscripts; while each was to contain a historical and biographical introduction.

The year 1858 thus saw the inception of the so-called Rolls Series (the full title is *Rerum Britannicorum Aevi Scriptores,* or *Chronicles and Memorials of Great Britain and Ireland During the Middle Ages*) with several interesting books. Among them were John Capgrave's chronicle of England to 1417, a volume of lives of Edward the Confessor by various hands, a history of the Gray Friars written in the early thirteenth century, and the only metrical history of early Scotland. These octavo volumes, beautifully printed, carefully edited, their texts superseding all previous editions, were highly useful, while their example was not lost upon individuals and historical societies. When the First World War began, nearly 250 volumes of the Rolls Series had been published. They comprised one of the fullest collections of medieval chronicles issued in any country in the world.

The American government has till lately done singularly little sustained work in publishing materials for history—materials, that is, going beyond the *Congressional Globe* and *Congressional Record* (begun in 1833 and 1873 respectively), and the annual volumes on *Foreign Affairs*. The antiquarian Peter Force, an editor and mayor of Washington, prevailed upon Congress to subsidize his compilation of documents of colonial and Revolutionary eras, called *American Archives*. Later the government supplied money for a series of American State Papers covering approximately the first half century of national activity; for a fairly complete collection of the messages and papers of the Presidents; for an admirable compilation of the military and naval records of the Civil War; for the fullest edition of Washington's writings yet made; and for some less ambitious enterprises, such as a collection of Territorial Papers. Full military and naval histories of the Second World War have been prepared on the basis of monumental collections of materials by the defense departments. Nevertheless, the government's activity has been sporadic and has resulted in no such impressive work as the *Monumenta Germaniae Historica* or the Rolls Series. As our history lengthens, it doubtless will follow a more generous policy.

For more than a century the efforts of governments to promote the study of historical records have been vigorously supplemented by those of learned societies. A few of these bodies may be traced back for more than two centuries. One of the first was the Society of Antiquaries in London, which began its active career in 1717, and later won the patronage of George II. An organization of the same name later sprang up in Edinburgh. But the heyday of the British societies did not come until the nineteenth century. The Bannatyne Club, founded in Edinburgh in 1823, and the Abbotsford Club, established there in 1835, both published important sources for Scottish history. The Camden Society of London began in 1838 to issue volumes chosen from "whatever is valuable, but at present little known, amongst the materials for the civil, ecclesiastical, or literary history of the United Kingdom." When the Rolls Series began, the Camden Society turned to the later centuries; but the Caxton Society Publications, commenced in 1845, pertain to the Middle Ages. Famous throughout the world are the Hakluyt Society Publications, carried on since 1846, and consisting of rare and valuable voyages and travels by men of divers races. The Pipe Rolls Society was founded in 1883 to publish the Great Rolls of the Exchequer and other public documents prior to 1200 A.D.; and the Selden Society was formed in the same decade to present materials for the history of English law. In Ireland the Ossianic Society, established in 1853, has brought out materials upon early Irish history.*

Most of the important historical societies in America bear the names of States or cities. The first, the Massachusetts Historical Society, was modeled upon the London Society of Antiquaries. Founded in 1791 by Jeremy Belknap, John Pintard, and Ebenezer Hazard, it launched the next year upon its long and distinguished work of publication. Such editors as Charles Deane and Worthington C. Ford have given its *Proceedings* and its *Collections*—a long

---

* Similar bodies exist on the Continent. Some are of earlier date than any in England. It is impossible here to make more than passing mention of the work of the Bollandists, the Belgian Jesuits who began in 1643 to publish their great collection of the lives and legends of the saints, arranged chronologically by days. The work was interrupted late in the eighteenth century, but was resumed with the support of the Belgian Government in 1837. The Bollandists also began in 1882 to issue a quarterly review; and they have published valuable catalogues and analyses of the hagiographic manuscripts in the principal libraries of Belgium, France, and Italy. Almost coeval in origin was the great work done by the Maurists, or French Benedictines of St. Maur, who in 1645 began issuing their scholarly series of writings of the church fathers. Their activities soon broadened into the publication of collections of documents, works on French ecclesiastical history, and other learned works, executed with sound scholarship and acute critical sense. On the Continent some great individual scholars, such as Ludovico Antonio Muratori, also carried through remarkable enterprises in documentary publication at an early date. Muratori died in 1750.

array of both—a value surpassed by those of no other society in the world. Fifteen years after its establishment, John Pintard, with the aid of De Witt Clinton, Gouverneur Morris, and James Kent, founded the New York Historical Society, which published its first volume of *Collections* in 1811. A third prominent organization, the American Antiquarian Society, was chartered by the Massachusetts legislature in 1812; but its publications have contained less notable source material than those of the two pioneer bodies, or of the Pennsylvania Historical Society, founded in 1825.

This type of enterprise was soon taken up in the West. As early as 1830 the Indiana Historical Society was organized, less than twenty years after its first president had taken part in the battle of Tippecanoe. Of all the Western societies Wisconsin's, which under Lyman Draper and Reuben G. Thwaites built up unsurpassed pioneer collections at Madison, has been the most influential. A number of historical societies in time formed close relations with neighboring universities. The work of historians at Harvard, for example, has long been facilitated by the libraries of the Massachusetts Historical and the American Antiquarian Societies; McMaster did much of his work in the Pennsylvania Society; and the Wisconsin Society greatly influenced the labors of Frederick J. Turner and other university scholars. In Minnesota and California the State universities and the State historical societies have maintained close relations.

Where the initiative of the privately formed historical societies first blazed the way, State enterprise has followed. The Massachusetts, New York, and Pennsylvania Societies asked for no public aid. But the Wisconsin Society represents a hybrid effort, for though it is a body of private individuals, it has received liberal State grants. And in a number of States public agencies have been set up to collect manuscript materials, publish lists and abstracts, and edit volumes of sources. Among them are the State Historical Library in Illinois, the historical commissions of North Carolina and Indiana, and the departments of archives and history in Iowa, Alabama, and Mississippi. New York has an active State Historian. Four of the Canadian Prov-

inces, Nova Scotia, Quebec, Ontario, and British Columbia,
possess archival departments of real vigor, which have published valuable lists of materials and volumes of sources,
and which cooperate with the extensive Dominion archives
at Ottawa. Several of the Canadian Provinces also have
active historical societies. The *Transactions* of the Literary
and Historical Society of Quebec, for example, go back to
1829, and its important series of historical documents commenced publication in 1838. One of the younger Dominion
bodies, the Champlain Society, has issued since 1907 an
especially graphic series of source publications upon the
period of exploration.

Throughout the world, during the past two centuries,
this labor of providing source materials for historical study
—of collecting official papers, manuscripts, letters, diaries,
broadsides, pamphlets, newspapers, and what not; of publishing lists, calendars, and volumes of documents; of
editing long series of annals and chronicles; of digesting
scattered data into historical magazines and volumes of
transactions—has gone on with accelerating vigor. It has of
course been accompanied by a tremendous increase in the
number of printed books of all kinds. At the close of the
eighteenth century only a few hundred volumes were published each year in the English language, but recent years
have found 16,000 to 17,000 books (not including pamphlets) issued in Great Britain, and 13,000 to 14,000 in
the United States. What was a slender stream in 1800, a
modest river in 1850, a rushing torrent in 1900, has long
since swelled into a mighty sea.

Where the ordinary historian in Hume's day thought of
his sources as comparatively small collections of printed
books, now he thinks of huge collections of papers, printed
and unprinted. So vast are they that one recent historian
speaks of the data on European affairs 1871–1890 as "a
staggering mass . . . rapidly becoming too great for one
human mind to grasp."[7] Where in even Macaulay's and
Guizot's day history was necessarily centered in politics
and government, for three-fourths of the available materials pertained to that, now its interest has become centrifugal and diffused; history deals with a hundred facets of

human life previously neglected. Whereas a century ago
the talents required for writing history were primarily literary, now they are equally literary and scientific; and the
historian cannot understand the evidence upon any era
unless he can apply at least the elementary principles of
economics, geography, sociology, and psychology to it.

It must be added that while two centuries ago the historian could blithely essay tasks on the largest scale, Hume
undertaking the history of England from the earliest times
to his own day, Gibbon that of ten centuries of the Western world, and Bancroft the whole American record, today
the magnitude of the accumulated materials forces the historical writer to accept a more modest view of his capacities. To present from the sources, in thoroughness and
detail, the life of a single generation in any of the great
Powers during the twentieth century, will hereafter be regarded as a staggering task.

VII

Yet it must not be thought that the progress of the
written word has given historical students too much material; far from it. The gaps will remain numerous. More
men become writers every decade; more books, periodicals,
and documents are circulated; thanks to stenographers and
typewriters, far more letters are written, mailed, and filed.
Records of public and private business are preserved in
ever greater detail. Yet not all departments of history
have benefited equally from this increasing articulateness.
Changes have come in communication which leave many
transactions unrecorded. The telephone has annihilated
much of the domain of the written word; railways and air-
planes have made face-to-face conversation easy; the radio
has created intangible newspapers and magazines which,
leaving no files, vanish into thin air. Many important decisions of governments, of business, and of private individuals are made utterly without record. Historians may learn
(with or without enthusiasm) that the Federal Archives
have acquired 35,000 cubic feet of records of inactive
pension claims, 800 cubic feet of records of the Railway

Labor Board 1920–26, and 131 cubic feet of records of the Wickersham Law-Observance Commission. But they know that many of the most important acts under Presidents Coolidge, Hoover, and Franklin D. Roosevelt were planned in unrecorded conferences of a few men or in telephone conversations. They realize that whereas in Washington's day a leader would write a long letter to explain his position, today he will catch an airplane and deliver his views orally.

Nor should we, in facing the vast stores of records accumulated by the modern world, exaggerate the importance of the written word in perpetuating the stuff of history. For history, our understanding of times past, is more than facts and ideas; it is a matter of the spirit as well. And our comprehension of the spirit of bygone ages is given us not through physical remains, inscriptions, manuscripts, and books alone; it is given us in large part through the transmission of personalities. A spiritual force runs down from generation to generation, from father to child, from teacher to teacher. The judge who welcomes a successor to the bench finds means to hand on an understanding of the spirit of the law; some undefinable force descends from Marshall to Story, from Holmes to Cardozo. Our own generation could never understand Christianity if that great molding force of society were perpetuated only through the letter of the New Testament. It has been perpetuated far more through personalities, institutions, and successive generations of believers. An apostolic succession of saintly men, in the broadest sense, has perpetuated it; a succession of churches has perpetuated it; a Christian sentiment, traversing successive generations as a wave traverses the wide ocean, has perpetuated it.

In the same way, our own generation could never fully understand the spirit of Anglo-American liberty were that written only in books, newspapers, and documents. It is written instead in the hearts and minds of more than two hundred million English-speaking people, and were every written word blotted out they would re-create its essence. A comprehension of the spirit of Christianity, the spirit of Anglo-American liberty, the spirit that animates other great social forces, is part of the data of history. It is not stored in archives or libraries, and is not cited in footnotes; but it will not be ignored by any student who realizes that the great perdurable elements of civilization have never been constructed by plumbline and yardstick—that some have not been built by human hands at all.

V

The Cheating Document

MANKIND DEARLY LOVES a good story, and dearly loves to believe it true. Before any tale can greatly please the hearer thereof, it must have some degree of verisimilitude; it must conquer part of our faith. Many of the earliest masters of fiction dressed it as absolute fact, and were credited beyond their expectation. Thus multitudes have accepted Defoe's *Memoirs of a Cavalier* as a true history—Lord Chatham did so; and even astute critics, impressed by the wealth of circumstantial detail in Defoe's *Journal of the Plague Year*, have declared that it must have been based on some work by an actual observer. How much in these books is imagination and how much is fact is really a nice question. In daily social intercourse and in literature, an artistic lie is sooner swallowed than a clumsy truth. Indeed, many people insist through thick and thin on having the artistic lie in place of the bald and unattractive fact. Historians may explain a thousand times that Wellington never exclaimed, "Up, Guards, and at them!" and that C. C. Pinckney never blazed, "Millions for defense but not a cent for tribute." These supposed ejaculations will nevertheless remain immortal. Sober critics have now labored for generations to show that Tacitus's portrait of Tiberius is cruelly unjust, but its vigor and artistic unity render it indestructible. Legends often become a point of faith. At one time the State of North Carolina made it

compulsory for the public schools to teach that Mecklenburg County had adopted a Declaration of Independence
on May 20, 1776—to teach what had been challenged and
largely discredited.*

I

Credulity is pleasant; we all like to be cozened a bit.
We love to cover the harsh gray stone of the everyday
world with the moss and ivy of fancy. And it must be
added that pleasing inventions fly like gossamer before the
wind. Mr. H. L. Mencken early in his career wrote an
article on the bathtub, in which he asserted with plausible
historical detail that it had been invented in the 1840s, that
Millard Fillmore had been the first to install one in the
White House, that the medical profession and public long
regarded it with deep suspicion, and that laws had been
passed against the perilous contraption by Virginia, Pennsylvania, and Massachusetts. He was astonished to find his
jeu d'esprit accepted by most readers at face value. He
was still more astonished to find newspapers and magazines
copying these "facts" in ever-widening circles, so that they
cropped up year after year in the most dignified periodicals. This naïveté of humankind has its humorous side.
But to historians it is not quite so amusing. For one reason,
historians prefer a critical-minded to a simple-minded public. For another, the credulity of the public pays charlatans
so well in money, in applause, or in gratification of the
literary instinct, that history is cursed by the constant invention of stories, letters, speeches, documents, and even
whole books.

Our simple forefathers drank delightedly at many foun-
tains on which modern scholarship long ago pinned up the
harsh placard "Condemned." Take as an example that in-
gratiating old book called Sir John Mandeville's *Travels.*

* V. V. Menitt in *Chain of Error and the Mecklenburg Declaration of Independence* (1960) analyzes the mingled truth and
falsehood in the claims for the bold resolutions passed, amid
"bitter antagonisms and turmoil," by the fiery Ulster Scots of
Mecklenburg.

Sir John saw many wonderful matters in his Eastern journeys, and heard of more—the monarch Prester John; a haunted valley in Armenia; two-headed monsters; the dragon of Cos; the castle of the sparrow-hawks; and miracles aplenty. Long after his marvels began to be taken with large pinches of salt, men still believed him a reality and his travels a fact. But he has melted to nothingness like a ghost in sunshine. Critics now doubt whether there ever was a Mandeville, a knight, or even an Englishman connected with the book's composition. Possibly one Jean d'Outremeuse, masquerading at Liége as one Jehan de Bourgogne, was the author. But author is not the correct word, for the volume is an arrant jackdaw's nest. It was stolen in bits from other writings, among which may be named Brunetto Latini's *Tresor*, Albert of Aix's chronicle of the first crusade, the *Speculum* of Vincent de Beauvais, and works by Jacques de Vitry, Piano Carpini, Petrus Comestor, and Hayton the Arminian. Tracing the origins of this pastiche has furnished no little amusement to scholars.[1]

Or consider the delight with which our forefathers read Parson Weems's *Life of George Washington*, first issued in 1800 and greatly expanded by anecdotal material in successive editions. Mason Locke Weems was part clergyman, part book agent, part schoolmaster in northern Virginia, and probably held occasional services in Pohick Church, where Washington had once worshiped. Upon this he based his title of "formerly rector of Mount Vernon Parish." In its original form the *Life* was a brief, inaccurate, and highly rhetorical record of Washington's military career. Subsequently Weems added many homely stories which, if not true, were at least *ben trovato*. Each carried an ostentatious moral. His immortal tale of George, the hatchet, and the cherry tree was introduced as "too true to be doubted," though his only authority was an "aged lady" who as a "distant relative" had sometimes visited the Washingtons. Like the book's long dialogues and set speeches, it was obviously invented. According to a grandson of Weems, it was probably suggested by the fact that one of his own children had cut down a "Pride of China" tree and frankly confessed his misdeed. But multitudes have believed it:

> One day in the garden where he often amused himself hacking his mother's pea-sticks he unluckily tried the edge of his hatchet on the body of a beautiful young English cherry-tree, which he barked so terribly that I don't believe the tree ever got the better of it. The next morning the old gentleman, finding out what had befallen his tree, which by the way was a great favorite, came into the house; and with much warmth asked for the mischievous author, declaring at the same time that he would not have taken five guineas for his tree. Nobody would tell him anything about it. Presently George and his hatchet made their appearance. "*George,*" said his father, "do you know who killed that beautiful little cherry-tree yonder in the garden?" This was a *tough question;* and George staggered under it for a moment, but quickly recovered himself, and, looking at his father, with the sweet face of youth brightened with the inexpressible charm of all-conquering truth, he bravely cried out: "I can't tell a lie, pa; you know I can't tell a lie. I did cut it with my hatchet."

II

Of course forgery need not ordinarily be feared by students of history working under reasonable safeguards. The contents of most historical libraries are carefully sifted and re-sifted by experts. Custodians of public archives usually take every precaution to exclude spurious documents. Dishonest books, whether forgeries or plagiarisms, are in general soon exposed. Though single letters may be forged, it is practically impossible to forge a whole file of them without detection. Newspapers almost defy forgery, for the practitioners of the art do not have the extensive apparatus required. Many a historian, many a biographer, has worked for years without being tripped by falsified data. Nevertheless, the first duty of every student of the past is to make sure of the authenticity of his materials, for not a little history has been vitiated by the careless acceptance of non-authentic materials. No less a work than Lord Morley's two-volume *Rousseau*, long accepted as standard, has been shown to be profoundly mistaken in its view of Rousseau's personality because it is based in part upon Mme. d'Epinay's *Memoires*, which have been proved false.[2] Las Cases, Napoleon's faithful companion in his last years, wrote a four-volume *Memorial de Ste-Helene* whose documents were for decades taken at face value; until it was shown that he had actually forged a number of Napoleonic letters.[3]

Forgery is in fact one of the oldest and commonest of human offenses. In ancient India grants of land made by rulers for sacerdotal purposes were often defined in inscriptions upon plates of copper. But implicit reliance cannot be placed upon these records. As early as the time of the lawgiver Manu punishments were decreed for the falsification of grants, and copper plates have been found which are barefaced forgeries. A rascal named Schapira long ago asked the British Museum a million pounds for what he represented to be an ancient Moabite Pentateuch containing a special version of the Ten Commandments. The Museum authorities took the work—and shortly discovered that it was an ingenious fraud concocted on ancient Syrian synagogue rolls. In those instances the motive was venal in the lowest sense, and the action untouched by artistry.[4] Forgeries committed by politicians who wish to damage an opponent, such as the famous "Morey letter" falsely attributed to Garfield in 1880—a letter approving the importation of Chinese labor—are equally devoid of dignity.

Much more dangerous are those forgeries in which a skilled hand attempts to supply the market for writings by famous men. One of the first warnings the teacher of Renaissance history must give students of Luther, Erasmus, and numerous other figures is to beware of the stream of manufactured documents attributed to them. The forgery of letters purporting to be by Marie Antoinette has long been a thriving industry, and still continues. In Americana, the New York Public Library maintains a large collection—a veritable museum—of false autographic material. As spurious letters of Franklin, Washington, Jefferson, Lincoln, Poe, and other famous figures come up for sale and are recognized, dealers turn many over to the library. The most notorious of American autograph forgers, Robert Spring,[5] a bookdealer in Philadelphia just before and after the Civil War, turned out hundreds of skillful forgeries to supply the market. His fictitious documents are more plentiful today than his own genuine letters; and grandsons of his original clients are not infrequently astonished to learn that their treasured papers by early American heroes are impostures. Manufactured Lincoln letters have found their way even into printed compilations of his papers.[6]

The most impudent if not famous of all literary forgeries, those of the nineteen-year-old William Ireland at the close of the eighteenth century, offer a study in psychology as well as imposture. They proved again how many people will believe because they *want* to believe, and for no better reason. Ireland, the son of a dealer in antiques, pretended that he had found not only Shakespeare letters, but a missing play by Shakespeare called *Vortigern*. The hero of that name, taken from one of Shakespeare's much-used sources, Holinshed's *Chronicles*, was an early British chieftain vanquished by Hengist and Horsa. A foremost scholar of the period, Samuel Parr, accepted the drama though Ireland had not even troubled to master the Elizabethan fashion of spelling. So, for two years, did Boswell, Pitt, Burke, and the actor John Philip Kemble. Many doubted, however, and when the play was staged it was howled down on the first night.

Portraits are as easily and frequently forged as documents. Sometimes they are deliberately invented, with intent to deceive. More than one painter has been hired by potentates or millionaires to manufacture a line of handsome ancestors, as James De Witt was employed by the Scottish government in 1684 to paint the 110 portraits of kings of Scotland hung in the long gallery of Holyrood Castle. Gilbert Stuart thus once made an ancestral line to order. Very often painted or engraved portraits are misnamed by mistake, or inadequate inquiry; a process rendered easier if the painting is clumsy, or the reproduction unskillful, so that confusion follows. When John Locke had his portrait painted by Sir Godfrey Kneller he directed that his name be inscribed on the back, lest the identification be lost in another generation. All the so-called portraits of William Penn are false, for none was made during his lifetime, and the only head carved from memory was done by an apothecary. "The familiar portrait of Patrick Henry with spectacles upon his forehead," writes an authority, "painted by Sully sixteen years after Henry's death, was founded on Dance's portrait of Captain James Cook." A catalogue of engraved portraits of Washington issued by the Grolier Club in 1904 described no fewer than 147 as fictitious. Errors and frauds find their way into reputable books, so that Paul Leicester Ford's able work on *The True George Washington* presents a portrait of Nellie Custis which is really Lawrence's well-known painting of Mrs. Siddons.[7]

Sometimes the motive in forgery has been a curious compound of venal and artistic instincts. No one today would censure harshly the tragic boy-genius Thomas Chatterton, whose "Rowley Papers," certain invented documents brought forward as authentic remains of medieval Bristol, were touched by an inspiration which made them valuable in their own right. Nor has anyone ever thought severely of the gay Scottish poet Allan Cunningham, who, employed to collect border ballads for an Edinburgh publisher, found it easier to invent some than to discover them in but-and-ben—and easily surpassed the ancient balladists. Sometimes a work temporarily accepted as authentic is rather a hoax than a forgery. Such was the little volume by Cleone Knox entitled *Diary of a Young Lady of Fashion,* which many accepted as a genuine document of the eighteenth century. It was of course simply a pleasant piece of fiction.

Much less innocent was the forgery palmed off upon *The Atlantic Monthly* in 1928 as letters exchanged between Abraham Lincoln and his sweetheart Ann Rutledge. This correspondence purported to be written by the lovers while temporarily parted, chiefly when Lincoln was living in New Salem, Illinois, and Ann attending school in Jacksonville. They deceived not only Ellery Sedgwick, perhaps then the ablest of American editors, but even Carl Sandburg and W. L. Barton, experts upon Lincoln's early career. Yet a little shrewd study by historians conversant with the details of Lincoln's life and with the period sufficed to reveal inaccuracies which proved them fraudulent. One letter spoke of Kansas before that name came into use, and in another letter Lincoln was made to refer to section 40 of a township, though as a surveyor he knew that townships have only 36 sections. The author of this forgery was motivated in part by a desire for monetary gain—the articles based upon the letters bringing a high price—and in part by a desire for reputation.[8]

Among the most horrifying of venal rascalities were those perpetrated by Thomas J. Wise of London, who attained a position of eminence as bibliographer, book collector, scholar, and friend of famous writers. He made a collection of English literature called the Ashley Library which after his death was sold to the British Museum for £60,000. Oxford gave him an honorary degree. In 1934, however, two young booksellers, John Carter and Graham Pollard, in a brilliant piece of detection called "An Enquiry into the Nature of Certain Nineteenth Century Pamphlets," began the work of exposing him. They showed that Wise had forged or pre-dated some fifty first-edition pamphlets containing work by Ruskin, the Brownings, Tennyson, Arnold, Swinburne, Dickens, George Eliot, and others. After a feeble effort to meet the charge of putting his forgeries into the rare book market, Wise died in 1937.

It was soon afterward shown that he had for most of his life secretly dealt in rare books while angrily denying it. Scholars demonstrated that many of his 250 or more private printings of books were piratical. He had deliberately inserted wrong dates in his bibliographies and other works of scholarship to validate his forgeries. More shocking still was the disclosure that while he was acting for nearly a quarter of a century as the trusted friend and agent of John Henry Wrenn, a rich American collector whose library ultimately found lodgment at the University of Texas, he had sold Wrenn a copy of each of his forgeries—and at high prices. But even this was not his worst offense. Like other collectors, he had been wont to improve his defective copies of rare books by inserting leaves taken from other copies; and it was found that he had slyly and ruthlessly torn many of these leaves from the volumes in the British Museum. More than forty copies of Museum books had thus been mutilated. In short, this supposed scholar was "forger, trickster, vandal, and thief"— a subject, doubtless, for the psychoanalysts.[9]

III

The most dangerous and vicious of all forgeries are those committed in behalf of a cause—the cause of a nation, an institution, or a leader—and intended to bring about a permanent falsification of history. Perhaps pre-eminent among such forgeries stands the so-called Donation of Constantine. This was a supposed grant by the Emperor Constantine to Pope Silvester and his successors. In gratitude for his conversion to Christianity, Constantine according to this document not only recognized the spiritual supremacy of the Roman pontiffs over the other patriarchates of the church in all that pertained to faith and worship, but also gave them temporal sovereignty over Rome, parts of Italy, and all provinces and places of "the western regions." This document was forged sometime between 750 and 800 A.D. During the ninth century the ecclesiastical writer now called the pseudo-Isidore included it in the collection known as the False Decretals; and in time, with the authority of Pope Nicholas, it was accepted as part of the canons of the church. Gibbon pointed out that in his own day it was still formally "enrolled among the decrees of the canon law."

Throughout the Middle Ages adherents of both popes and emperors regarded it as genuine. Two early popes, Silvester II and Gregory V, used it to support important territorial claims, and in 1050 Leo IX employed it in his controversy with the Byzantines involving still larger papal

pretensions. During the twelfth century and afterward it
became a powerful engine of the church in its contest with
the political rulers of Europe, the partisans of the Holy
Roman Empire regarding it with dread and hatred, and
the partisans of the Pope somewhat cautiously employing
it. Dante accepted it as genuine, and as a good Guelph
execrated Constantine for the supposed grant as a source
of enormous evils. But Laurentius Valla critically assailed
the Donation in 1440, and though the controversy persisted until the close of the eighteenth century, its fraudulent character was at last completely demonstrated.

In this instance the forgery, which long imposed upon
chroniclers and historians as well as ecclesiastical authorities, which indeed enjoyed almost six centuries of unchal-
lenged vitality, was at last consigned to outer darkness.
Discussion has long since shifted to the question of its authorship, some Catholic writers attempting to prove that
the church had no hand in it. The best evidence is that
it was executed in the papal chancery about 775, partly
as a defense of the papal possessions, and partly as a
means of attacking Byzantine heresy. The wonder is that
it had so stubborn a life. But it must be remembered that
the Middle Ages were poorly equipped to deal with questions of evidence.

Another famous example of a forgery committed in behalf of a special cause is offered by the manuscripts of
the poems *Rukopis Královedvorský* and *Zelenohorský*, two
crude but fervent effusions composed early in the nineteenth century by some Czech patriots who wished to provide the world with works showing that medieval Bohemia
possessed a high degree of literary culture. Many Czechs
eagerly accepted these texts. They appealed to the rising
nationalism of the race. But honest Slav philologists soon
threw doubt upon them. When Thomas G. Masaryk
founded his critical review, the *Athenaeum*, in Prague in
1883, he took up the issue of their authenticity; and while
he analyzed them historically, the philologist Gebauer analyzed them linguistically. These men conclusively proved
them forgeries, and this proof gave full impetus to the
"realist" revolution in Czech culture and politics—an un-

remitting effort to apply the scientific method in these fields. A partial parallel to the work of the Czech bards is offered by the forged Ossianic poems of the Gaelic enthusiast James Macpherson, which many ardent Celts accepted as genuine for more than a century. But Dr. Johnson and others denounced Macpherson's epic of *Fingal* from the moment it was published.

In one striking instance the debate as to whether certain documents represent a political forgery still rages. Men yet take sides heatedly on the question of the "Casket Letters."[10] These letters, together with a sonnet-sequence, Mary Queen of Scots is accused of having written to her lover Bothwell in 1566-67. They have long ago disappeared. Their very disappearance is a mystery, some students believing that Mary's royal son James obtained and destroyed them. But the text remains, and if authentic, offers incontrovertible proof that Mary was an accomplice in the murder of her husband Darnley. If authentic! The controversy revolves chiefly about the second or "Glasgow letter," a long and peculiar epistle. If even the compromising parts of it were genuine, Mary was certainly guilty. But her accusers, the men who first produced the letters and pushed their evidence vigorously, were completely lacking in veracity. The Earl of Morton and the Regent Moray cannot be believed upon oath; they lied, they contradicted themselves, and throughout the episode they behaved most disingenuously.

Nevertheless, the ablest student of the subject, Andrew Lang, concludes that the whole "Glasgow letter" was written by Mary. Some German writers, applying the principles of the higher criticism of Homer and the Bible, conclude that the documents are of composite origin, being partly letters by Mary and partly a diary, combined and edited by other hands. Still other writers attack the letters as wholly or largely false. As Lang writes,[11] "The topic is so perplexing, and possibilities are so delicately balanced, that inquirers may change their views, and modify or reverse their opinions, on the appearance of each fresh document that is brought to light; or even upon a new consideration of existing evidence." In this instance the problem of authenticity is of vital importance to our view of a great historical figure—and yet it is probably insoluble. *

In the same way, controversy long raged over the genuineness of the Kensington Stone, though here the balance has definitely inclined toward a verdict of falsity. This runic inscription was found on a stone unearthed in 1898 at Kensington, Minnesota, by Olaf Ohman, a Swedish-American farmer. It is alleged to contain a record of an expedition which had been sent from Norway to Greenland about 1354 or 1355, and whose survivors reached the present Minnesota in 1362. They had made a camp "fourteen days journey" from the sea (supposedly Hudson's Bay), and carved on the stone a memorial of their heroic journey. The controversy has involved the age of the tree under which the Kensington Stone was found, the language of the inscription, the character of the runic alphabet employed, and the geographic possibilities of such a journey. Much ink has spilled over the issue. One scholar, H. R. Holand, has written a book, *The Kensington Stone,* defending the inscription; others have entered vigorous and on the whole convincing dissent. Of course many Scandinavians would like to believe that the Norsemen reached Minnesota 130 years before Columbus sighted the West Indies. But it is a writer of Scandinavian blood who concludes that the inscription is a fabrication, and adds: "Two choices have been suggested: the forger may have wished to add strength to the belief in the Vinland narratives, which were much in debate in the seventies and eighties, or he may have intended to foist a new sort of hoax on credulous citizens for the enjoyment that the inevitable discussion would bring. The writer prefers the latter alternative as the one that produces the fewer problems."[12]

Even when the falsity of a document has been amply proved it frequently makes so striking an impression upon the public mind that, as we have said, vestiges of belief

---

* The brass plate of Sir Francis Drake found near a small bay north of San Francisco in 1936 and given to the University of California has been certified as genuine by metallurgical engineers, electro-chemical experts, and the historian Herbert Bolton.

in it linger for many years. In 1781 the Reverend Samuel A. Peters, publishing a *General History of Connecticut,* gave it a memorable bit of spice by inserting a table of "Laws made by this independent Dominion, and denominated Blue Laws by the neighboring colonies." His cloth made it seem impossible that he should prevaricate. Indeed, the laws that he quoted had a certain ring of truth, for they chimed with the popular idea of Puritan severity. Other writers began to accept them, and for decades a belief in the inhuman blue laws of The Land of Steady Habits was almost universal. But experts on colonial law and history presently began scrutinizing Peters's list with a suspicious eye. One alleged law made it criminal for a mother to kiss her infant on the Sabbath, and others had a very queer look:

No one shall run on the Sabbath day, or walk in his garden or elsewhere, except reverently to and from meeting.

No one shall travel, cook victuals, make beds, sweep house, cut hair, or shave on the Sabbath or fasting day.

No one shall read Common Prayer, keep Christmas or Saints'-days, make minced pies, dance, play cards, or play on any instrument of music, except the drum, trumpet, and jews'-harp.

Married persons must live together, or be imprisoned.

Peters had attempted to protect himself by stating that this code, which even regulated the style of the hair and the mode of crossing streams, was "never suffered to be printed." Indeed it was not, for it never really existed. Various sets of Connecticut laws were published; and while they do offer some basis for a majority of the forty-five statutes which he cited, they fall far short of the grim picture he drew. The laws of 1650 did not even provide penalties for Sabbath-breaking. Yet a general impression that Connecticut had a frightful code of interferences with personal liberty, based upon or fortified by Peters's inventions, persists in quarters which wish to think ill of Puritanism.

Some minor forgeries, indeed, are impossible to kill. It is

of course a mere misattribution which leads many people, year after year, to declare that Washington warned the country against "entangling alliances"; the truth being that Jefferson expressed that particular warning. But outright invention is responsible for a quotation which American protectionists, decade after decade, have put into the mouth of Abraham Lincoln. "I do not know much about the tariff," Lincoln is quoted as saying, "but I know this much, when we buy manufactured goods abroad, we get the goods and the manufacturer gets the money. When we buy manufactured goods at home, we get both the goods and the money. When an American paid $20 for steel rails to an English manufacturer, America had the steel and England the $20. But when he paid $20 for the steel to an American manufacturer, America had both the steel and the $20." There are three reasons for our certainty that Lincoln was not the author of this quotation: (1) Lincoln was too sagacious to make a statement containing so much economic folly. (2) The most thorough ransacking of Lincoln's speeches and writings reveals no such statement. (3) Lincoln was shot April 14, 1865, and the first steel rail was not rolled in America until May 1865. Yet this barefaced forgery, in behalf of the high-tariff interest, was repeated as Lincoln's by no less a person than Alfred E. Smith so recently as 1934. It is of a piece with another statement not infrequently attributed to Lincoln which represents him as a prohibitionist in advance of his time.

IV

Invention, indeed, runs a strange and wonderful gamut. It may be used to cast discredit upon a whole race, as in the forgery of the so-called Protocols of the Wise Men of Zion, purporting to lay bare a Machiavellian plan for Jewish world dominion. It may originate, on the other hand, in a trifling private jest. "This day," writes Samuel Pepys on August 28, 1661, "I counterfeited a letter to Sir W. Pen, as from the thiefe that stole his tankard lately, only to abuse and laugh at him." Or it may be employed in the

Las Casas style to give verisimilitude to an otherwise bare and unconvincing narrative. Thus A. C. Buell published in 1900 a two-volume life of John Paul Jones which was praised by the *American Historical Review,* accepted as an authority in various universities, and recommended to students of the Naval Academy at Annapolis. It seemed sober history; it was actually a mixture of authentic and manufactured materials. When his sources ran thin, Buell manufactured new ones. He invented a French memoir upon Jones by Adrien de Cappelle, a volume of papers by the North Carolina worthy Joseph Hewes, and a printed French collection of Jones's own papers, drawing "facts" liberally from these imagined storehouses. He invented collections of papers by Robert Morris and Gouverneur Morris in places where they had never existed, and so obtained more "facts." He invented a will by William Jones of North Carolina in order to give John Paul an estate, and had Jones deposit 900 guineas in the Bank of North America in 1776—a wonderful feat, for the Bank was not established until 1781. In short, as Albert Bushnell Hart has written, this inventor of materials recalls Mark Twain's praise of the duckbilled platypus, so versatile and gay. "If he wanted eggs," remarked Mark Twain, "he laid them."

Invention has even been used to gain a few dollars by spurious contributions to a biographical dictionary. A long-standard and still-useful compilation, *Appleton's Cyclopaedia of American Biography,* is disfigured by not less than forty-seven sketches, and probably many more, of men who never existed. The unknown author of these sketches was paid by space, and to obtain a larger remuneration coolly created heroes out of thin air. He gave the world an explorer, Bernhard Hühne, who discovered a good part of the coast of California; a botanist, Oscar Hjorn, whose book on *Les Legumineuses Arborescentes de l'Amerique de Sud* produced a "sensation" when published; an industrialist, Penanster, who in 1755 broke up the Spanish monopoly of the cochineal dye industry; and a French scientist, Henrion, who won fame by combating the Asiastic cholera in South America in 1783, fifty-two years before it first appeared there. It appears that the editorial work on this *Cyclopaedia* was somewhat lax; contributors were free to suggest names not included in the original lists, and their sketches were not verified, and not revised save for literary form. But the large body of excellent material in the compilation has floated the spurious articles, so that many writers have been led astray by the misinformation—the errors being repeated from book to book, even in our own day.

And not least of all, invention has been used as a ready passport to fame. One early volume of English impressions of the United States, Thomas Ashe's *Travels in America, Performed in 1806,* is almost as dubious a production as Mandeville's work. Written with engaging vivacity, portraying with brutal realism such backwoods scenes as a gouging rough-and-tumble fight between a Kentuckian and a Virginian, it was quoted by Henry Adams and reprinted by Reuben Gold Thwaites in his series of Early Western Travels. That it has very considerable historical value is certain. But the available evidence indicates that it was put together out of secondhand materials, and does not represent firsthand observation. It can perhaps better be classified as plagiarism than forgery. Still another famous piece of literary imposture, Father Louis Hennepin's second volume of travels, is not quite forgery and not quite plagiarism, but achieves the object of both by an unblushing piece of literary piracy. Yet as late as the time of John G. Shea, who edited an edition of Hennepin's works, this narrative was treated as trustworthy, save for large "interpolations" by another hand.

There is much in the explorer Hennepin's story to interest students of the problems involved in authenticity.[13] He was a Recollect friar who possessed not a few virtues —an adventurous nature, genuine heroism, and powers of close observation. The Church did well when it sent him out to New France. But he was spiteful and vain, a braggart, and a colossal liar. He cherished a jealous enmity toward La Salle, while he was eager to magnify his own fame as a Western explorer. Under La Salle's instructions, in 1680 he had explored the Illinois and the Upper Mississippi. In 1683, while La Salle was still alive, he published a fairly accurate account of his exploits in *La De-scription de la Louisiane*. But in 1697, after La Salle was dead, he issued a *Nouvelle Découverte*, in which he stated that it was at last safe to make a momentous disclosure; that having nothing to fear from La Salle's terrible enmity, he could now reveal the fact that he had explored the Mississippi as far as its mouth. He had thus anticipated the discovery which La Salle claimed as the crowning glory of his career. Of course such a claim needed proof. Henne-pin realized that if he could present a journal of his pre-tended voyage down the Mississippi, abounding in circum-stantial detail, it would be good evidence. He might have invented such a record as Dr. Cook made in 1910 of his "dash to the Pole." But he lacked a Defoesque imagina-tion. It happened that another Recollect friar, Le Clercq, had published some years earlier a book containing the diary which a companion of La Salle's named Father Membré had kept on the authentic voyage down the Mis-sissippi in 1680. This book had been suppressed by the Jesuits, and Hennepin, who possessed a copy, believed that all others had been destroyed. In concocting his own jour-nal, he therefore copied whole sentences, sometimes even whole pages, from the earlier document. Of course he was undone when stray copies of Le Clercq's volume came to light. But in any event he would have been left in Dr. Cook's predicament as soon as later generations read his weird description of the lower Mississippi:

From the mouth of the river of the Illinois this river . . . is almost a league wide. It is very deep and has no sandbanks, nothing interferes with navigation, and even the largest ships might sail into it without diffi-culty.

All in all, the danger that the student of history will be misled by inauthentic documents is not unreal. Any man using diplomatic collections, or perusing such "White Papers," "Blue Papers," and "Orange Papers" as the chan-celleries of great Powers issue under stress of international crises, will be on his guard against possible invention of interpolation. Any man using the daily press will be on guard against inauthentic interviews, speeches, and even letters. Dickens in his picture of New York journalism about 1840 satirized the impudent mendacity of such papers as James Gordon Bennett's *Herald*. "Pray," said Martin Chuzzlewit to Colonel Diver, "may I venture to ask whether the *Popular Instructor* often deals in—I am at a loss to express it without giving you offence—often deals in forgery?" "Well, sir," replied the Colonel, "it does, now and then." Any student using even the documents published by certain early historians who held loose ideas of the editorial function will be on his guard. Jared Sparks bore an honored name, and is still rightfully esteemed as a great pioneer in American historiography. But he was capable of doctoring papers, and perhaps even of manufacturing a source when he needed one. There is strong suspicion that in his collected edition of Washington's Writings he gives a narrative of Lafayette's escape from France in 1777 to join the American army which may have been concocted by Sparks himself; so completely is it at variance with two firsthand accounts written by Lafayette himself.[14] At every point the student must be watchful.

Readers must be particularly vigilant in studying areas of heated controversy carried on under twilight conditions. Forged "sovietica"—documents on the struggles within Russia and between Russia and the West—have been numberless and vicious. George Kennan in *Russia Leaves the War* had to deal with the papers which the American Edgar Sisson bought and sponsored, purporting to show that Lenin and Trotsky in the closing phase of the First World War were German agents. In time, they were proved beyond all reasonable doubt to be forgeries. The supposed diary notes of Maxim Litvinov, which the English historian E. H. Carr for a time partially accepted, have been completely discredited. A volume purporting to come from a high Soviet officer, Ivan Krylov, on his military career, was accepted by a New York publisher in 1951, and withdrawn when the London *Times* showed that more than twoscore passages of the text issued in France had been lifted from Allen and Muratoff, *The Russian Campaigns of 1941–43*, brought out in 1944. Among other juicy forgeries have been a Stalin Testament, an inside account of secret meetings of Tito and Stalin, and a study of Stalin supposedly emanating from his nephew. Of this last, one of the keenest scholars of Russian history writes: "I must say that I nearly fell for that one myself."[15]

V

But just how is a suspected invention to be detected? In the vast sea of historical materials available for modern students, how shall they pick out the impostures? John Morley read 300,000 documents in writing his life of Gladstone; the principal bibliography of titles bearing upon Napoleon and his times lists more than 125,000 titles of printed works. Most of the labor of detecting fabrications and mystifications can be left to the experts, of whom a large corps is ceaselessly at work. But some general rules should be well understood by even the general reader.

A suspected document, to begin with, can often be tested by certain physical criteria. Is the paper of proper age? Sometimes it has a telltale watermark; sometimes it pretends to belong to a period in which paper was made of silk or linen fiber alone, and yet contains an admixture of cotton; sometimes it purports to be of the linen-and-cotton period, and yet is made of wood pulp. Again, is the ink really that of the supposed period? Old documents will not present any ink containing aniline hues, for such inks were not used prior to 1850. Apart from these physical criteria, does the document have a pedigree?—can it be traced back through a line of reputable, well-authenticated owners? And what, again, of the handwriting? If it is said to be the work of a well-known author, does it tally with the chirography of papers *known* to be by him? Just as paper and ink may be subjected to chemical tests, so handwriting may be measured microscopically. And since criminal bureaus and commercial agencies frequently have to deal with forgeries, experts in graphology and micrography are both numerous and extremely skilled.

If the suspected paper passes the physical tests, its contents may then be subjected to rigorous scrutiny. Does the style of the alleged writer—his use of words and phrases, his sentence structure—resemble that which he exhibits in documents of known authenticity? Do the views and opinions he expresses, if the document be of any scope, tally with those which he has expressed elsewhere? Or if this question cannot be answered, do they harmonize with his general character? Are all the facts stated or implied in the document in accord with *known* facts of the time?—can they be easily reconciled with these facts? And by no means least, are all the statements in the document harmonious with one another? Forgery of documents of any length is a very difficult matter indeed. Even the expert forger is almost certain to slip in some detail which, if his work is examined with hawklike care, betrays him.

A rigorous examination of the Lincoln-Ann Rutledge correspondence, made by Paul Angle, later head of the Chicago Historical Society, showed that the forgery could be detected by a number of the tests mentioned above. The paper, to be sure, was old enough, though it bore the appearance of flyleaves torn from old books. But the ink had a greenish hue, and green ink almost invariably contains aniline dye. The alleged letters had a very weak pedigree, some of the gaps in the past ownership being glaring. The handwriting bore no resemblance to Lincoln's, and defenders of the correspondence had to explain that he had used two different hands! The stylistic differences between the letters and Lincoln's own writings were marked and painful, the letters presenting a weakly sentimental personality. At one point the contents of the letters were distinctly out of harmony with Lincoln's known views on slavery. Finally, the historical inconsistencies were numerous, and several were absolutely inexplicable. Mr. Angle, after noting that Ann Rutledge several times spoke of the New Salem schoolmaster as Newton Graham, when she certainly knew that his name was Mentor Graham, added this clinching statement:

More conclusive, however, than a mistake in a name is the following sentence from one of Ann's letters to Lincoln. "I am greatfull," the writer says, "for the Spencers copy book. I copy frum that every time I can spair." Since Ann Rutledge died on August 25, 1835—the date is recorded in the family Bible—the letter was written prior to that time. But Spencer's first publication on penmanship, under the title of Spencer and Rice's *System of Business and Ladies' Penmanship*, was not used until 1848.

The original manuscript of Hennepin's work is no longer in existence. But in this instance internal evidence is quite sufficient to destroy its pretensions. We may put aside his flimsy excuse for not bringing out his story until years after La Salle's death, that he feared the enmity of La Salle and his followers. We may even put aside the evidence of his thefts from the Membré diary. The proof that he never saw the lower Mississippi lies fair upon the face of what he wrote concerning it—in the simple fact which Reuben Gold Thwaites has pointed out in his introduction to a two-volume edition of Hennepin's *New Discovery of a Vast Country in America:*

> That it was quite impossible for him to have made the alleged trip to the lower waters of the great river, is evident from the dates given by the father himself. In *Louisiane* the party are said to have left the Illinois not earlier than the 12th of March. Upon the 11th of April his party was captured by the Sioux near Lake Pepin. This leaves a scant month for the author to have descended and ascended the Mississippi and reached the place of capture—a journey all told of some 3,260 miles. Hennepin tells us that his canoe was slow, being large and laden heavily; yet to accomplish this feat he must have ascended the river against a strong current at the rate of 60 miles a day, nearly three and a half times the speed attained two years later by La Salle, with better boats.

The cheating document seldom imposes (at least for any length of time) upon any but the ignorant or careless. A combination of scholarly knowledge and common sense can in ninety-nine instances out of a hundred expose it—but they must be reinforced by constant vigilance.

VI

The Dubious Document

WHILE IT IS sometimes troublesome to establish the authenticity of a historical source, that is usually an easy matter compared with making certain of the entire integrity of a source. The authorship of a document or book may be entirely authentic, and yet parts of it may be highly treacherous. Everywhere about the question of historical integrity, pitfalls thicken.

While the forgery is entirely false and dishonest, a far larger body of materials are only partially false, and of these many are not dishonest by intention at all—that is, do not contain any conscious dishonesty. The very fact that a document is entirely and deliberately spurious often makes its character easy to detect. But when truth and misstatements are mingled, both emanating from some writer known to be sincere, discovery becomes difficult. Many a letter, document, or piece of autobiography, originally quite genuine and candid, all its parts possessing the same general value as evidence, has been revised, amended, or otherwise so tampered with that some parts become untrustworthy. In other words, its integrity has been destroyed. Again, students of history must deal with a large class of documents which are frankly composite in character, proceeding from various hands or sources. The task of discriminating among the different parts of these composite documents, and determining which are most valuable and why, requires the use of tests as searching as those which determine the integrity of a document —indeed, even more searching.

I

A simple and picturesque example of a problem in the integrity of documentary sources is offered by a comparison of Captain John Smith's first and second versions of his adventures in Virginia. As the whole world knows, Smith helped to obtain the charter of the London Company, arrived in Virginia with the colonists early in 1607, traded with the Indians for provisions, and when Jamestown fell into grave difficulties, took charge of the colony and by decision and resourcefulness saved it. He restored discipline, set everyone to work and made it self-supporting. In his volume *A True Relation*, written in Virginia and published in England in 1608, he recounted his early exploits and adventures. He told how, making an excursion to the Chickahominy, he was surrounded by two hundred hostile Indians, and after bemiring himself in a swamp, was captured. They carried him before an Indian king. Smith showed this monarch his compass, and so won his favor. Thence taken before the "emperor" Powhatan, he was in danger of being killed by certain Indians whose relatives he had slain, but was saved by his guards. After he had treated Powhatan to a long discourse on the greatness of the British king, the mightiness of his navy, and "the noyes of Trumpets and terrible manner of fighting" in Europe, he was sent back to Jamestown. In this book he barely mentions Pocahontas, then a maiden of perhaps twelve. But in 1616, about the time that John Rolfe brought Pocahontas as a bride to England, he wrote a letter to King James's queen, Anne of Denmark, in which he asserted: "After some six weeks fatting among these salvage countries, at the minute of my execution, she hazarded the beating out of her own brains to save mine." And he soon went still further.

In 1624, in his *General Historie*, Smith rewrote his early narrative of Virginia adventures. This time the two hundred hostile Indians became three hundred. This time he recalled a picturesque detail, the exhibition by the Indians of a bag of gunpowder which they proposed to plant the following spring. Above all, he recounted in more dramatic form the tale of Pocahontas's gallantry. He described the grim and dusky Powhatan in the center of the stage, himself in the foreground, fettered but undaunted, and the lovely Pocahontas suddenly emerging at the climactic instant:

> "A long consultation was held, but the conclusion was two great stones were brought before Powhatan; then as many as could be layd hands on him, dragged him to them, and thereon layd his head, and being ready with their clubs, prepared to beate out his braines. Pocahontas, the King's dearest daughter, when no entreaty could prevaile, got his head in her armes, and layd her own upon his to save him from death; whereat the Emperor was contented he should live."

It is not strange that this story has inspired conflicting views among students. Edward Arber, the most careful editor of Smith's works, accepts it and other remarkable incidents; Alexander Brown, in his scholarly writings on early Virginia, discredits it. John Fiske points out that the printed text of the *True Relation* was incomplete, for Smith had written much which the editor in London omitted as "fit to be private." Perhaps he had really told the full story of Pocahontas in his manuscript of 1608. Henry Adams and Edward Channing assail the story, but Charles M. Andrews accepts it. A pretty question of the integrity of a source is involved.

If John Smith retouched his narrative to make a good story better, he did simply what many raconteurs do. Sir Walter Scott confessed a weakness for dressing up his old anecdotes with new cocked hat and walking stick. His motive was artistic. But that of many a man who renders an old tale more dramatic is vanity. In each new version, oral or printed, the teller's own role becomes a little more witty, heroic, or resourceful. George IV asserted so often (without impolite contradiction) that he had been at the Battle of Waterloo that he at last really believed he had taken an important part there. When the first two volumes of the *Intimate Papers of Colonel House,* edited by Charles Seymour, appeared in 1926, most readers gave them the value of an autobiography buttressed by a huge variety of letters and memoranda. Mr. House had chosen his editor carefully; it was incredible that he had not read every line of the work in manuscript or proof. These volumes claimed for him a decisive part in the shaping of the Federal Reserve Act of 1913. It was not difficult for ex-Secretary Carter Glass, in *An Adventure in Constructive Finance,* to riddle this pretension and show that Mr. House had played no real part whatever. The claim made by him was undoubtedly an instance of self-deception. It was not essentially different from Tartarin of Tarascon's story of his heroic exploits in the repulse of Tartar raids in China, the sole basis for which was that as a young man he had been offered a clerkship in the Orient, which he had refused!

The difficulty of obtaining an accurate knowledge of what occurred in the Constitutional Convention of 1787 has been increased by examples both of the cheating document, and of the garbled document. When in 1818 Congress ordered the official journal of the Convention printed, John Quincy Adams, then Secretary of State, edited it. Undertaking to obtain material from various men, he applied among others to Charles Pinckney of South Carolina. He received what can only be described as a spurious document. Pinckney had been the youngest but one of all the delegates. Taking frequent part in the debates, he had apparently been snubbed by his elders for his boldness. At one stage of the proceedings he had drafted a scheme of government which, in view of the direction already taken by the Convention, had little chance of adoption. It was referred to the Committee on Detail, which took a number of the provisions. Pinckney was not even permitted to deliver a speech which he had prepared. When long afterward Adams asked Pinckney for a copy of his scheme, the South Carolinian sent north a draft of what he "believed" was the paper he had introduced. As published by Adams, it bore a striking resemblance to the adopted Constitution —so striking that it cast great credit upon Pinckney's sagacity, and made him seem one of the most constructive members of the gathering. But it happened that in 1787 Pinckney had printed the essential parts of his scheme in pamphlet form—"Observations on the Plan of Government Submitted to the Federal Convention"! Adams was suspicious of Pinckney's later document, and justly so. It was necessary only to turn to the pamphlet of 1787 to see that the paper Pinckney "believed" he had offered was an imposture—unconscious, no doubt, but nevertheless an imposture.*

The garbled document was left to the world by no less a man than Madison, "father of the Constitution." He had not only played a leading part in the deliberations of the Convention, but had jotted down full and careful notes of the proceedings. In 1840, four years after his death, *The Papers of James Madison* were published in three volumes by order of Congress. Many students supposed that this was a source entirely independent of the official Journal published under J. Q. Adams's editorship in 1819. But it was later shown that Madison had twice revised his notes before his death, using the Journals to correct his record of votes, and to supply new items upon procedure. To distinguish between the original entries and the supplied matter was a task of some nicety. Dr. Max Farrand has described the method employed:

Diff - INK

The ink which was used at the later date has faded quite differently from that of the original notes, so that most of the later revisions stand out from the page almost as clearly as if they had been written in red ink. . . . This is not always the case, for the original manuscript has faded differently in different parts, perhaps because of different exposure or the use of more than one kind of ink. There also seem to have been at least two distinct sets of later corrections, probably made at

* Following the publication of critical studies by J. Franklin Jameson and A. C. McLaughlin, in 1908, C. C. Nott brought out *The Mystery of the Pinckney Draught*.

different times. It is, therefore, sometimes difficult and sometimes impossible to determine whether or not the correction is a later one. A reference to the 'printed Journal' must of course be of later date than 1819, and the ink and writing of these words will frequently make clear all of the corrections of that date. It is also very helpful to know that it was Madison's invariable practise in his original notes to refer to himself as 'M' or 'Mr. M.' In the revision of his manuscript he filled out his own name, so that the ink and writing of 'adison' often furnish the necessary clue.[1]

II

Sometimes a published book bears frank evidence that the text belongs to two or more very different dates. David F. Houston, successively head of the Department of Agriculture and of the Treasury under President Wilson, published in 1926 his valuable *Eight Years with Wilson's Cabinet*. This work is written in two tenses, past and present, which alternate in the most disconcerting fashion. Frequently the two tenses appear on the same page. It is obvious that matter in the present tense was lifted more or less verbatim from Mr. Houston's diary, and that in the past tense was supplied years later. But the line between them is far from clear, while nobody knows just how great were the liberties taken with the text of the diary. To the student of history it is of the utmost importance to learn whether the opinion Mr. Houston gives of Secretary Bryan, of the Federal Reserve Act, or of Wilson's neutrality policies, is his opinion of 1914, his opinion of 1926, or a nondescript combination of the two. The published volume leaves us in the dark. This medley of contemporaneous and reminiscent matter, annoying to the general reader, is maddening to the historian, who never knows whether a statement upon a man or transaction is authentically of the period, or embodies later reflections.

But while Mr. Houston made no effort to conceal his mixture of two different points of view, one during and one after the event, many a personal chronicler has tried to palm off his late-learned wisdom as early sagacity. Most diarists write consciously or subconsciously for publication. They are acutely alive to the impression they will make on posterity. It is difficult to resist the temptation to strike out faulty judgments, or to add new and better strokes to the old picture. A classic instance is furnished by the famous diary which Gideon Welles kept during the Lincoln and Johnson Administrations. Thirty-three years after Welles's death, John T. Morse, Jr., published it in three volumes with a prefatory assurance that the text "has been in no way mutilated or revised." It was true that the editor had not revised it, but Welles himself had done so. Examination of the manuscript, now in the Congressional Library, reveals countless changes, almost all of which have been incorporated in the printed version. Indeed, the ink shows that Welles revised it at least twice. Some changes were made for style, but even they occasionally altered the original sense. Others, made to add color, dramatic force, or picturesqueness, still more clearly distort the picture by unconsciously incorporating impressions formed at a later time, or by adding imagined details. For example, to an interview with Halleck, Welles later appended the comment that he "began to rub his elbows and without thanking me or acknowledgment of any kind said"; to the record of a tense scene with Stanton, he added the clause, "Stanton, in a suppressed voice, trembling with excitement, said." A student who has gone carefully over the manuscript lists still other ways in which the garbling of the document may easily mislead readers:

Another form of revision in which Welles indulged, notably in the case of Seward, Stanton, and Grant, was conscious changing of the text, not to vivify but to add venom commensurate with the growth of his aversion for these men. Thus to an early interview with Halleck he added a comment of several lines: "Strange that this change of military operations should have been made without Cabinet consultation. . . . But Stanton is so absorbed in his scheme to get rid of McClellan that other and more important matters are neglected." To the entry of September 6, 1862, he added: "The war Department is bewildered, knows but little, does nothing, proposes nothing." It was in after years, too, that he injected under June 24, 1866, the comment that "Trumbull and the Senators generally thought Seward too meddlesome and presuming." . . . Similarly, to a later date belong the comments of June 30, 1866, that "Stanton has assumed frankness, but his coarse manner covers a good deal of subtle duplicity," and most of the paragraph of May 31, 1868, in derogation of Grant. Numerous cases massed together paint a picture even worse than the contemporaneous sketch of these men. . . .

Welles also revised portions of his manuscript to satisfy his pride in his powers of judgment or prophecy. One example will suffice. To the call of June 18, 1866, is added, in light of later events, the seeming prophecy: "The call, if not the Convention itself, is, I think, perverted to an intrigue in behalf of the old Whig party, on which Weed and Seward rely."[2] . . .

No memoir or autobiography should be used without an effort to make certain that judgments stated as belonging to a particular date have not actually been colored or wholly shaped by subsequent occurrences. No diary or volume of letters should be used without a watchful eye for intimations that the text has been altered before publication to delete entries that have become absurd, or to insert material which will reflect credit on the writer's shrewdness. In using autobiographical material, the student will note carefully the lapse of time between an event and its record. The prominent Chicago physician and teacher Norman Bridge in his book *The Marching Years* offers reminiscences of a Vermont boyhood written when he was past sixty, and then in an appendix gives memories of the same rural boyhood penned in his early twenties and belatedly discovered. The contrast between the fresh record of young manhood and the dim record of age is illuminating.

One of the most difficult problems in the determination

of textual integrity has been created by the profession of ghost writer. It is an older profession, and has affected more books, than readers usually suppose. In recent years, as industrialists and other men of affairs unused to the pen have turned to autobiography, it has become an increasingly important department of letters. No small proportion of American memoirs are nowadays written less by the noted person whose name appears on the title page than by some journalist or scholar whose help may never be acknowledged. The practice has had its advantages as well as disadvantages. It has given us books which would otherwise never have been born; while a dull autobiography like Winfield Scott's makes us wish that he had been aided by a nimbler mind. But such volumes all too seldom answer the questions: Just what was the extent of the collaboration? How much does the ghost writer put into the mouth of the autobiographer? Which man is responsible for dubious or controversial statements?

Only in recent times has it been learned that a classic of Southwestern history, Josiah Gregg's *Commerce of the Prairies*—a personal narrative of the growth of the Santa Fe trade—was to some extent ghostwritten for him by the New York journalist John Bigelow. Poultney Bigelow, when questioned, said that his father took the field notes of Gregg's ten years' journeys to Santa Fe and Chihuahua, and created therefrom a readable narrative. Had we known nothing more of the collaboration than this, it might have cast doubt on the authoritativeness of Gregg's volume. But fortunately an explicit letter from John Bigelow himself on the matter has been found. He records that Gregg came to New York and carefully prepared his notes. His statements "were so lucid, so realistic, and so unpretendingly honest that they needed little illuminating and refining from his editor." Gregg then critically scanned every word that Bigelow wrote. He refused to tolerate any literary frills. "On the other hand, he was extremely careful about the exactness of every statement that he made, and I do not think that he allowed a word to be printed in that book that he would not have been willing to make oath to." Bigelow's statement makes it evident that historical truth suffered not the slightest loss when he held Gregg's pen. And as a matter of fact, the accuracy of the book is amply attested by much contemporaneous evidence.[3]

But much ghostwriting must be regarded with considerable misgiving. Already a large gallery of American figures, and some Europeans, are represented by ostensible self-portraits really from another hand. S. S. McClure vainly tried to persuade Grover Cleveland to write his autobiography in this easy way. He did prevail upon Charles A. Dana to let Ida M. Tarbell pen his *Recollections of the Civil War*. A trusty author was found for John D. Rockefeller's *Random Recollections of Men and Events*, who of course took much of his information from talks with Rockefeller. In the same way Burton J. Hendrick wrote former-Ambassador Morgenthau's reminiscences of his First World War experiences. Boyden Sparkes has ghostwritten the autobiographies of Frank A. Vanderlip, Evalyn Walsh McLean, and Walter P. Chrysler, his part-authorship being confessed but its extent not defined. In weighing the value of these and like books, not a few questions almost defy answer.

For one, just how authentic is the personal note in such books? It is impossible to believe that Miss Tarbell supplied many ideas and opinions to Charles A. Dana; she would not have felt that course proper, nor would his stubbornly individualistic mind have permitted it. Nevertheless, we feel in the book a milder personality than that exhibited in Dana's capricious, witty, sardonic, disillusioned *Sun*, a softening of Dana's own acerbities. And when we are confronted with such a volume as Henry Ford's *My Life and Opinions*, in which Samuel Crowther was amanuensis and more, we are still more doubtful that this is the real Henry Ford. We find not only a literary style above his reach, but a knowledge of economics so extensive, a set of ideas on modern industry so complex, that we cannot doubt that the opinions of Ford, who did have many original insights of value, were elaborated to their improvement. An anecdotal autobiography like Hudson Maxim's written for him by Clifford Johnson, whose knowledge of mechanics and invention was slight, raises a question of the authority of the facts given. Does Maxim stand squarely behind every one of them? What undertones and overtones have been supplied by his collaborator? Still other questions are raised by a dashing book like Victor G. Heiser's *An American Doctor's Odyssey*. Is the high dramatization his own, or attributable to the skilled woman journalist who took her data from him and helped write that "autobiography"? Ghostwriting ranges from solid, carefully verified work at one extreme to mere publicity, mere presentation of some industrialist, financier, or politician in a highly favorable light, at the other. Its value ranges from an honest historical source to naked propaganda.

Certainly this dual method of composition frequently makes for irresponsibility in treating facts. Certainly it obscures the personality of the protagonist of the autobiography. He appears not as he sees himself, but as another man sees him, or as another man persuades him to pose. Reading a ghostwritten autobiography, the student who wishes to know how much integrity attaches to the text—how much is really Charles A. Dana's, Henry Ford's, or Dr. Heiser's—must severely scrutinize every part. The general public assumes that the book is all Mr. Ford's or Dr. Heiser's. The publisher usually wishes it to do so. But the skeptical student may sometimes glean a few guiding facts from the preface—and reviewers and historians ought to urge that all ghostwritten autobiographies contain prefatory explanations. He will commonly learn more from internal evidence. If he knows something of the personality of the hero, and something of that of the ghost writer, he may disentangle the two. He may find from the mode of narration just which facts are vouched for by the hero, and which come from his literary aide. But unless the contrary evidence is clear, he will have to regard a ghostwritten memoir as lacking the perfect integrity of a book whose author can say that it is written, in Paul's phrase, "by mine own hand."

A peculiarly irritating problem of responsibility is presented by such a book as *MacArthur 1941–1951: His-*

tory in the Pacific, by Major General C. A. Willoughby
and John Chamberlain (1956). Its preface states that it is
"not to be regarded as in the nature of General Mac-
Arthur's memoirs." Yet it is based on material which he
read and annotated, and one of the two authors was Mac-
Arthur's intelligence officer throughout the Pacific fighting,
thereafter his official spokesman, and a close personal
friend. The numerous controversial assertions in the book,
including some which bear harshly on the United States
Navy, 10 Downing Street, and President Truman and his
advisers, would possess values if they came from Mac-
Arthur, very different from those they bear as coming from
Willoughby. It is not clear from whom they *do* come.

III

The document of composite authorship may be garbled
in the harshest sense of that word, or it may be a frank
and innocent document of strict integrity. It may represent a perversion of some original source by materials
drawn from inferior sources—that is, by large interpolations. It may represent an author's honest interweaving of
several sources, perhaps of equal value, into a new record
stamped by his personality. Or it may represent an ordinary collaboration of two or more authors. Though usually
there is nothing reprehensible in composite writings, they
are often perplexing and irritating.

No composite histories are more familiar, and none
more interesting, than the three Synoptic Gospels of Matthew, Mark, and Luke. None has ever been given more
penetrating and exhaustive study than they. It is obvious
to anyone who examines the New Testament in critical
spirit that the value of its different parts to students of the
past is far from uniform. It is a varied collection of narratives, letters, homilies, and prophecies. Some historical inconsistencies of the Gospels have been unfairly exploited
by hostile critics like Thomas Paine and Robert G. Inger-
soll. Matthew and Luke, while giving accounts of the Vir-
gin birth, yet trace the genealogy of Jesus up through
Joseph. Matthew declares that the Holy Family went at

once into Egypt to escape Herod, while Luke states categorically that it stayed in Bethlehem forty days, then went to Jerusalem, and then to Nazareth. We are given more or less discrepant accounts of the Sermon on the Mount, the anointing of Jesus, the betrayal by Judas, the trial scene, and even some details of the Crucifixion; while at many points the narratives are vague. The attempt to wring out of the Gospels their exact historical values is full of interest. How vast an effort has been concentrated into that attempt can be understood only by those who have studied Christian Hermeneutics and what was once termed the higher criticism. It represents, in all probability, the best single illustration of what the historical method can accomplish in a difficult and obscure field. The separation of the Gospels into their component parts has been only one part of that effort.

That they have a composite origin is beyond question. Expert authorities now generally agree that no narrative of Christ's life was written for more than thirty years after his death. The gospel was first preached to people who had seen Jesus, or had heard too much about him to be curious for details of his life, while the disciples looked forward to his second advent at an early date. Since Paul's Epistles, written about 50–60 A.D., make no reference to any of the four Gospels, it is a fair inference that they did not then exist. Tradition indicates that written accounts began to be set down between 60 and 70 A.D. The first of the four was almost certainly the so-called Gospel of St. Mark, and can apparently be dated within a decade of Paul's martyrdom.

For centuries the Church regarded this Gospel as less important than the others, partly because Mark was not an apostle, and partly because Matthew and Luke are much fuller. But it is now believed that a good part of Mark's narrative may have been derived directly from the lips of Simon Peter, and is not merely an earlier story than the other two synoptic Gospels, but in some respects more dependable. They are based largely upon it, or upon another narrative, now lost, which it most faithfully represents. Indeed Matthew and Luke together use almost the

whole body of Mark's narrative. Some authorities believe
that they lean also upon a lost Gospel, which may have run
fairly parallel to Mark, and which has been variously called
the Gospel, and the Urmark or primitive Mark. In numerous instances Matthew and Luke agree together, and
differ from Mark, in reproducing what is clearly Markan
matter—an indication that another version of Mark once
existed.[4] The Gospel of Matthew was perhaps written
last of all, and could certainly not have been penned by
the Apostle Matthew, though it may have been founded in
part upon some of his recollections.

Let us concentrate, for the purposes of illustration,
upon Matthew. It is incontestable, in the view of modern
Biblical scholars, that this Gospel is a composite work,
written from two main sources which the author knew in
Greek, and various minor sources. The two main sources
are Mark, and an unknown work originally written in Aramaic. Scholars have accurately separated the two. For example, the matter from Matthew ix, 27, to the end of Matthew xi is taken from Aramaic document; then comes a
long section from Mark, but with additional data from
some other source; and finally we have the author's own
ending. A peculiar feature of the Gospel is the way in
which the author has welded together a number of discourses, or collections of sayings, by Jesus, taking part of
the material from statements which other sources attribute
to Christ at other times and places. Thus Matthew introduces into the Sermon on the Mount some sayings which
according to Luke were uttered elsewhere. The account
in Matthew x of the address to the twelve disciples contains matter which Luke x, 1–16, states was delivered to a
different group, together with various other sayings of
which the precise occasion is unknown. Altogether, Matthew contains eight distinct discourses or collections of sayings, put together in more or less artificial fashion from
Christ's utterances on various occasions. This artifice does
some violence to history, according to the strict rules of
the present day, but it offers a more effective presentation
of Christ's doctrine.

The Gospel of St. Mark consists of an original text

studded with later interpolations, which scholars have been able to identify with fair certainty, and which stand on a lower plane of credibility than the work in general. Thus from internal evidence it is regarded as probable that the two parables in Mark iv, 26–32, are insertions made in the original, which they do not precisely fit. It is believed also that the collection of Christ's sayings in Mark ix, 41–50, is interpolated; for the author of Mark does not elsewhere make up such discourses. Moreover, some of these particular sayings are given by Luke in different contexts. Such obvious inaccuracies occur in the account of Christ's crossing of the lake after the feeding of the five thousand, inaccuracies the more striking in a book remarkable for precision of topography, that this bit may also be an interpolation. It need not be said that the historical value of St. Mark's Gospel is impaired by these interpolations, and restored when they are struck out.

Similarly, the historical authority of Matthew is compromised at various points by bits which the author apparently derived from untrustworthy traditions. Among them is the story of the setting of the Roman guards at the grave, and their presence at the resurrection; the story of the silencing of this guard by the chief priest; the story of the testimony borne by the guard and the centurion who kept watch at the Cross; and the story of Pilate's effort to throw the guilt of the Crucifixion upon the Jews. Competent scholars regard these episodes, to quote one of them, as "legendary additions which had arisen through the desire to commend the Gospel to the Romans," and which the very late author of Matthew inserted along with his authentic materials.

An excellent example of the kind of composite document which represents a straightforward use of several sources to make a new record—a twisting of several threads into a new cord—is offered by various books of Livy's great history. The prolific Roman was indifferent to original research. Instead, he relied heavily upon other authors. As he uses no footnote references, the identification of these authors and the parts that each contributed to the whole requires much ingenuity. Sometimes he quotes one of the

Roman annalists by name, but more often he insouciantly
remarks, "they say," "the story goes," or "ancient writers
declare." Identification is important in order to judge the
authenticity of the different parts. Patient scholarship,
principally by Germans, has analyzed many of his books in
satisfactory fashion. It has shown that Livy's procedure
was amazingly elementary and even naïve. At rare intervals he would take several writers, and fuse their stories
rather completely and carefully. More often he would follow one writer exclusively for a time, revamping his story
with various embellishments; then, without warning to the
reader, would suddenly turn to another annalist and follow
him. Very frequently, when earlier writers differed, he
would make no effort to correct one by another. The result
is a mosaic, in which materials which possess different
dates, different values, and different points of view, are
awkwardly pieced together, often with an obvious lack of
unity. Only Livy's brio and narrative power saved much of
his history from worthlessness.

Fortunately for modern scholarship, fragments of the
old annalists survive in manuscript collections and can be
compared with Livy's text; while we have six complete
books of Polybius, which in certain parts he followed
closely. Thus it is possible in the third and fourth "decades"
of Livy's works (books 31–45 inclusive) to distinguish between what he drew from Polybius, and what he drew
from such inferior writers as Valerius Antias and Claudius
Quadrigarius. The former contributed the materials upon
Greece and the East, which here are the clearest, fullest,
and most accurate parts of Livy. The latter contributed
materials upon Western Europe, including Italy, some of
which were highly inaccurate, and all of which were cast
in a dry annalistic mold—a mold that Livy indolently followed. The volume in which a German scholar, H. Nissen,
analyzed the sources of these last surviving books of Livy
(*Untersuchungen*, 1863) is a masterly work of analysis.

One of the most striking composite works in the field of
American history is John Marshall's *Life of George Washington*, published in 1804. For more than a century this
biography was extravagantly admired as the product of a

great mind working on a great theme. Jared Sparks thought that after this "able, accurate, and comprehensive work" it would be presumptuous for other hands to touch the subject; Justin Winsor wrote that it gave "the impress of a true historic spirit" to "the most authentic material respecting Washington's life"; and Charles A. Beard declared that it represented long and arduous study and constituted the "classic defense of Federalism." In truth, however, the biography is for the most part a mosaic of borrowings, which Marshall copied almost literally, and then hastily pieced together. It does not represent the application of a critical method to authentic materials, for the materials were drawn from compilers and annalists who preceded Marshall. It is not a memorable Federalist interpretation of history, for there is little of Marshall or any other Federalist in it. The great jurist wrote in an age of successful plagiarism in history, when such authors as William Gordon and David Ramsay copied unblushingly from the British Annual Register and from any other source they could easily pilfer. When a careful analysis of Marshall's work was very belatedly made by a competent scholar, it was found that he stood on the precise level of these men.[5] A book that had been thought to possess great original value had almost none.

In his preliminary volume on the history of the colonies, Marshall levied upon such previous historians as Jeremy Belknap, Thomas Hutchinson, William Stith, George Chalmers, and Robert Beverly. Sometimes he took the matter verbatim, without acknowledgment; sometimes he condensed or skeletonized it; sometimes he paraphrased it— but throughout he was a copyist, and little more. The investigator found examples of unacknowledged copying on 268 of the 488 pages of the original edition, and could have discovered more. The whole second chapter of this volume represents simply a combination of select passages from Stith and Chalmers. In the life of Washington proper, Marshall lifted great sections unaltered or but slightly changed from William Gordon's history of the American Revolution and the *Annual Register*. A twelve-page description of the Battle of Camden, for example, is transcribed almost word for word from Gordon's pages. The description of the affair at Moore's Creek Bridge is a three-page appropriation from the *Annual Register*. When Paul Leicester Ford thought he was quoting Marshall's account of Washington's farewell to his officers at Fraunces's Tavern, he was actually quoting William Gordon's. Anyone who wishes to know the exact historical value of any part of Marshall's book will hereafter find it necessary to make sure of the provenance of that part—a task in which Marshall's rare footnotes lend little assistance. A composite work, it is worth just as much and as little as the brief shelf of books upon which Marshall drew.

As both internal and external evidence may be used to detect the fraudulent document, so both may be employed to analyze a garbled or composite text. Where one fails, the other may succeed. But it should be noted that one kind of internal evidence is extremely risky. Many a critic has gone astray in asserting that a passage belongs to one special author or source, basing his opinion upon character of vocabulary, tricks of style, or trend of thought. Various students of Beaumont and Fletcher have boasted that they could trace with ease the parts which each man contributed to their dramas—Beaumont being the more gifted writer. Yet Coleridge declared that he could find no line of demarcation whatever between them. Part of *Two Noble Kinsmen* is supposedly Shakespeare's and part Fletcher's; yet even here, where the greatest genius of literature mated with a second-rate talent, a complete separation of the two parts seems impossible. Other kinds of internal evidence, if available, offer more certainty. When Livy refers in his text to the annalists Fabius Pictor and Aelius Tubero, the clue is clear. When the Gospels of Luke, Matthew, and Mark can be laid side by side, much can be learned from their differences and resemblances.

Yet sometimes, in dealing with a composite document, a considerable amount of both internal and external evidence may leave students uncertain of source or authorship. One of the most famous of all composite works is *The Federalist*, written by Madison, Hamilton, and Jay. Which of the two former men deserves credit for certain papers in it will always be uncertain. Both left lists of the essays which they claimed, but as these lists conflict, and as it is impossible to say that one man is less accurate than the other, or that either lacked veracity, the question is still open. It has to be decided by the internal evidence offered by the contents of the papers, and the external evidence supplied by Hamilton's and Madison's manuscripts. No prettier exercises in the use of such evidence can be found than the studies which Edward Gaylord Bourne, Henry Cabot Lodge, Jacob Ernest Cooke, and others have made of the authorship of Nos. 49–58, 62, and 63 of *The Federalist,* claimed by Madison and Hamilton alike.[6]

Take, for example, No. 58, which refutes the objection that the House of Representatives may not be properly increased in size as the nation's population grows. Hamilton had met this very objection in New York's ratifying Convention. His argument there—that the large States will control the House, and will favor its augmentation in order to increase their influence—is repeated in No. 58; and this seems to be evidence supporting his claim to authorship of the essay. But after all this is an obvious argument. Anyone would think of it. And a quite different argument is emphasized in No. 58; the assertion that new States will advance in population with peculiar rapidity, and will therefore be interested in frequent reapportionments of representation. It happened that Madison had stated almost precisely this idea in a letter to Jefferson on Federal representation in March 1787. No. 58 also contains one expression which was a favorite with Madison. He remarks that the history of the British Parliament shows a "humble representation of the people gradually enlarging the sphere of its activity and importance." This phrase "enlarging the sphere," occurs at least seven times in Madison's known writings upon the Constitution. It does not occur at all in Hamilton's writings on the subject, and even the metaphor (for he does once speak of "extending the sphere") occurs only twice. Finally, the last paragraph of No. 58 seems to echo the discussion in the Federal Convention on the subject of a proper quorum for the House; and while Madison was present at this discussion, Hamilton was not. On the basis of these arguments, Madison seems the better entitled to the credit of No. 58.

In conclusion, we may note the fact that problems in the cheating document and the garbled document are often wrapped up together. A classic example of the critical examination of a universally known work to weigh first its authenticity, and then its textual integrity is the introductory chapter of Ernest Renan's *Saint Paul*. Present-day Biblical criticism differs from his conclusions at certain points, but his method remains full of illumination. He examines at great length the validity of the original sources for his study, the Epistles of St. Paul; a step the more imperative because Paul himself had spoken of false letters circulating in his name, and had frequently taken precautions against such frauds. Of course Renan had to proceed almost entirely through the use of internal evidence. The earliest surviving manuscripts of Paul's Epistles are of the third century, and rarely indeed do they have any evidential value; though Renan does cite the omission of the words "in Ephesus" in the early manuscript versions of the so-called Epistle to the Ephesians to help prove that this was not written to the Church of Ephesus at all. But by careful attention to phrasing, to ideas, to personal, geographical, and historical allusions or the lack of them, Renan arrives at ingenious and often convincing conclusions. Take, for example, what he writes of the Epistle to the Hebrews, which he regards as by another hand—an anonymous bit of apostolic writing, admitted by error into the Pauline collection. A little of his evidence is external; he notes that early churchmen hesitated over the letter, and early Latin manuscripts showed repugnance to its admission. But most of his data is internal:

> Clement of Alexandria and Origen, good judges in regard to Greek style, do not discover the characteristics of St. Paul's style in this epistle. St. Jerome has the same opinion. The Fathers of the Latin Church, who are unwilling to accept it as an epistle of Paul's, give the reason of their action, *propter styli sermonisque distan-*

tiam. This reason is excellent. The style of the epistle
to the Hebrews is, in truth, different from that of Paul.
It is more oratorical, fuller, the language presents particular words. The basis of the thoughts is not unlike
the opinions of Paul, especially of the captive Paul; but
the exposition and exegesis are entirely different. There
is no personal superscription, contrary to the constant
usage of the apostle. Characteristics always expected to
be met with in an epistle from Paul are wanting in this.
The exegesis is above all allegorical, and resembles that
of Philo much more than Paul's. The author betrays
Alexandrine culture; he only makes use of the so-called
version of the Septuagint; his reasoning concerning the
text of this version shows a complete ignorance of Hebrew; his manner of quoting and analyzing Biblical
texts is not conformable to Paul's method. The author,
on another side, is a Jew; he thinks to exalt the Messiah
by comparing him to the Jewish high priest; Christianity
is for him only a sort of Judaism fulfilled; he is far from
regarding the law as abolished. The passage (ii, 3) in
which the author ranks himself among those who have
only known the mysteries of the life of Christ indirectly
from the lips of Jesus' disciples, in no wise corresponds
to one of Paul's most decided declarations. Finally, let
us add that in writing to Jewish-Christians, Paul would
have neglected his most inflexible resolution, which was
never to perform a pastoral act upon the territory of the
Jewish-Christian churches, so that the apostles of cir-
cumcision should not, on their side, encroach upon the
churches of the uncircumcised.

Taking the whole question of the authenticity of the
thirteen Epistles, Renan concludes that seven are of certain authorship by Paul—the two to the Corinthians, the
two to the Thessalonians, and those to the Galatians,
Romans, and Philippians. He holds that the Epistles to
the Colossians and Philemon are probably authentic. That
to the Ephesians he pronounces probably spurious, and
the two to Timothy and the one to Titus certainly so.
In dealing with the integrity of the text of the valid

Epistles, he furnishes a basis for his criticism by a severe analysis of the Epistle to the Romans, so-called. In this he arrives at what he thinks were the probable methods of the first editors of Paul's Epistles, and explains why these methods resulted in the over-use of salutatory phrases, and other repetitions. The essential part of each Epistle, he believes, was a circular letter addressed primarily to the churches of Ephesus and Thessalonica, but also to some of the Roman churches. To each copy of this general letter might be added special bits of a local or individual interest, which varied according to the destination of the copy. The rule of the editors who finally collected the Epistles, Renan believes, was to add nothing to the text; to avoid repetition as much as possible; but also to omit nothing—so that the local and individual bits have been preserved along with the main letter. They "followed a system of piecing or intercalation, the design of which seems to have been to save writings which otherwise would have perished." It saved these writings—but it sometimes made an Epistle a rather curious document.

IV

The integrity of written documents of all kinds has frequently been vitiated by censorships, political or religious. In many countries and in every century, texts have been mutilated, garbled, or rewritten by some tyrannical authority. No Italian, German, or Russian newspaper under the regimes of Mussolini, Hitler, and Stalin respectively could be regarded by careful students as an authentic presentation of what was originally written for its columns. Still less could it be regarded as what the journalists would have written had they been free! It would be absurd to place the *Corriere della Serra* under Mussolini or *Berliner Tageblatt* of Hitler's day on the same level of integrity as the columns of the *Manchester Guardian* or *The New York Times*. The same rule applies to books and magazines in censor-ridden countries. Not even the greatest of authors have been respected. A student who uses foreign sources of a type exposed to censorship will sometimes save himself from grave error by studying the conditions of bureaucratic or ecclesiastical control for his period. He will then not assume that because a periodical is conservative or obscurantist in tone, its editors and contributors were antagonistic to liberalism or that every paragraph printed is to be taken in its literal sense.

The power of the censorship sometimes manifests itself in curious ways. Eloquent deductions may be made from a bit of reminiscence published by Maxim Gorky upon the relations of Lenin and Trotsky—and published in two forms. The first version, written in 1924 as a magazine article, runs as follows:

Yes, I have often heard him [Lenin] praise his comrades. And he knew how to do justice to the energies of even those with whom he was supposed to be personally unsympathetic.

Surprised by the flattering appreciation he showed for one of them, I remarked that a good many people might be amazed by it.

"Yes, yes, I know. They tell a lot of lies about my relations with him. Yes, they tell a lot of lies—and especially about me and Trotsky."

Pounding on the table, he declared: "Show me another man who could organize in a year an almost model army and win the respect of military experts besides. We've got that man. We've got everything and so we'll do wonders!"

The second version, published in booklet form after Trotsky had been banished and Stalin had come into power, runs as follows:

Yes, he often praised the comrades in my hearing, even those with whom he was not personally in sympathy. Lenin knew how to appreciate their energy. I was very surprised at his high appreciation of L. D. Trotsky's organizing abilities. V. Ilyitch noticed my surprise.

"Yes, I know there are lying rumors about my attitude to him. But what is, is, and what isn't, isn't—that I know also. He was able at any rate to organize the military experts."

And after a pause, he added in a lower tone, and rather sadly: "And yet he isn't one of us. He is ambitious. There is something of Lassalle in him, something which isn't good."[7]

The Stalin censorship was not in effect when the first version was written, and harshly effective when the second appeared. It may be that Gorky voluntarily changed the passage; it may be that he changed it unwillingly in fear of the censorship; it may be that the censor mutilated it. But it is certain that the original passage has integrity and the revision has not. The larger partner of censorship in countries or organizations under dictatorial rule is propaganda, which is equally aimed at the defeat of intelligence. It is as old as history, and has been an active force at least since the Middle Ages, when Pope Urban played up lying stories of atrocities by Saracens to stimulate sentiment for the Crusades. The historian finds it everywhere in his materials, whether presented with the subtlety of a Talleyrand or the crudity of Herr Goebbels, the Nazi Minister of Popular Enlightenment. He cannot avoid it, but he can learn how to grapple with it.

Texts may also, as every reader of general literature knows, be corrupted by bad editing, bad translations, careless printing, and sheer accident. The canons applied to the editing of manuscript sources for publication have become steadily more severe. Of course they are not rigid. According to the nature of the text, the editor may regard his work as primarily literary, intended for the lay public, or primarily historical, intended for general readers. John Evelyn and Philip Hone wrote their diaries with a broad appeal in view; to reproduce every archaic spelling or capitalization in Evelyn, every abbreviation, misspelling, or defect in punctuation in Hone, would repel the general reader, and defeat the main purpose of the diary.

So with volumes of letters expected to have a broad appeal. The editor is not merely permitted, but often required, to spell out awkward abbreviations, make capitalization and punctuation conform to present-day usage, and otherwise, without altering the sense, to render the text readable. The editors of the standard new editions of the writings of Benjamin Franklin, Thomas Jefferson, and the Adams family have all tried to follow a middle course between exact reproduction and complete modernization of the text, preserving the form and spirit of the writings, and at the same time making their work intelligible (and attractive) to the reader. The introductory statements by Leonard W. Labaree and Whitfield J. Bell, Jr., in their first volume of *The Papers of Benjamin Franklin,* by Julian Boyd in the first volume of his edition of *The Papers of Thomas Jefferson,* and by Lyman in the initial volume of *The Adams Family Papers,* all make it clear that accuracy is to be strictly guarded, but pedantry avoided. But where a text is intended primarily for the use of historical students, it should be reproduced precisely as it stands. The *Diary* of Edward Bates, Lincoln's Attorney General, for example, has much value to the historian and no attractions whatever to the general reader; its editor rightly reproduced every letter, every comma, verbatim.

The firm establishment of strict rules for historical editing dates in America from the controversies which attended Jared Sparks's editions of the writings of Washington (1834–37) and Franklin (1836–40). Sparks's methods were loose and irresponsible. He treated historical documents as if they were articles submitted to the *North American Review* (which he once edited), using the blue pencil freely without any indication of his omissions. Justice Bushrod Washington enjoined upon him to avoid giving offense to writers of letters to Washington or their families, and he made editorial changes to do so. Observing that Washington in his old age completely rewrote his early letters, he felt it proper to revise the later letters, of which he had only rough drafts, not the final form, when they seemed to need it. He softened or omitted harsh criticisms of men and policies. Thus when Washington wrote of the "dirty, mercenary spirit" of the Connecticut troops, Sparks left out "dirty"; when Washington wrote of "rascally privateersmen," he deleted "rascally." He changed "Old Put"

into "General Putnam," and Washington's statement that
a certain sum "will be but a fleabite to our demands"
into the statement that it would be "totally inadequate."
In Franklin's writings he similarly paid tribute to Victorian
squeamishness, and dulled the sharp edge of criticism. He
declined to print the famous definition of chastity; when
Franklin spoke of a beer-pitcher with "the coffee cups in
its belly," Sparks omitted the belly. He changed "dung" to
"manure." When Franklin spoke of the "polluted court"
of England, Sparks omitted the sentence, as he omitted
a reference to "George III's character for falsehood and
dissimulation." A subsequent editor of Franklin's works
found that Sparks had sometimes made more than thirty
alterations in a single letter.

In 1851–52 Sparks was called sharply to account by
Lord Mahon in England and John Bigelow in America, the
latter declaring that his edition of Washington's works
must be pronounced absolutely without authority. In reply, Sparks was able to make a partial defense. He had
actually performed great services to scholarship. It was his
misfortune that his methods of editing were those of an
older day, already being supplanted by a careful insistence
upon literal accuracy. After the controversy with Mahon,
it was impossible for any accredited scholar to take such
liberties with a text as he and various other editors had
done. But even since then—even at the present day—absolute accuracy is a goal difficult to reach. Washington's
writings were re-edited by Worthington C. Ford, who
was justly severe upon Sparks's work. But they have since
been edited a third time by John C. Fitzpatrick, whose
work has clearly revealed Mr. Ford's many slips! John
Bigelow published an edition of Franklin's *Autobiography*
—a work which is almost the despair of students of textual
integrity, for it was written in three main parts, separated
by wide intervals of time and space (England, 1771;
France, 1784; Pennsylvania, 1788), exists in two manuscripts, and was published five times in France in five
separate translations, and four times in English in four
separate texts, each differing from the other in almost
every line. Bigelow's edition, based on the original manu-

script in Franklin's hand, contained vitriolic remarks upon all the earlier editions. But when a new editor appeared, Dr. Max Farrand, his careful version demonstrated that Bigelow himself committed numerous inaccuracies!

The present-day tendency is to publish texts in ever-fuller editions, as anyone may see by comparing early versions of Boswell's *Journal of a Tour to the Hebrides* with that produced by F. A. Pottle and C. H. Bennett in 1937 from the original manuscript. But the most courageous editors dare not and perhaps should not publish a complete text of some writings. No useful purpose is served by concessions to mere pruriency, and beyond a certain line, such concessions run afoul of the law. The completest edition of Pepys still omits a small number of passages of outrageous indecency. The editor of the Smyth edition of Franklin remarks: "Unfortunately, it is impossible without offence to quote many of his briefer paragraphs. . . . He out-Smolletts Smollett in his letters to young women at home and experienced matrons abroad. Among the manuscripts in the Library of Congress, and in the columns of his newspaper and the introductions to 'Poor Richard,' are productions of his pen, the printing of which would not be tolerated by the public sentiment of the present age." Though public sentiment grows less squeamish, perhaps a few such productions would really be valueless to history, and their omission, properly indicated, does it no violence. If so, a well-indicated omission is the one allowable course; rewriting, revision, verbal softening, are not for a moment allowable.

Translations may be of all degrees of goodness or badness; as good as the authorized English translation of Mommsen's *Rome* by William P. Dickson, as bad as the current translation of Taine's *English Literature* by H. Van Laun. But it is important to remember that a translation, no matter how excellent, is always a change. It subtly alters the flavor of the original. Not a few historical works have been twice translated. Russian books, for example, have first been rendered into German or French, then into English. At least one important historical book is available to American readers only after passing through the medium of four languages. This is the autobiography of a young Chinese, Tan Shih-hua; dictated in Chinese to Professor S. Tretiakov, written by the latter in Russian, translated into German, and again translated into English! To suppose that the texture of Tan Shih-hua's thought was not transformed in these four processes is to suppose a great deal. One reason why a command of foreign tongues is valuable is that it dispenses with translation, and no man having such a command should be content with less than the original.

The garbling of texts by accident or negligence has sometimes led to grave results far outside the sphere of scholarship. A misplaced comma may cause a diplomatic crisis. In 1912 the misprinting of a single word involved a serious political issue in the United States. The official Democratic Textbook of that year published one plank of the party platform as declaring against "the Aldrich plan for a central bank"—which would have left the way open for another type of central bank. The error was multiplied by many copyings. But party leaders, referring to their records, established the fact that the plank as drafted had condemned "the Aldrich plan or a central bank," binding the party to a sweeping interdiction of all such banks, and President Wilson recognized this reading as valid.

The most interesting work of scholars in the correction of negligent or corrupted texts, however, lies in the field of medieval manuscripts and early printed books.

Particularly remarkable, and full of lessons to the historian, is the immense labor expended upon the establishment of a correct version of Shakespeare's plays. The greatest monument ever erected to the cause of textual integrity is beyond question the New Variorum Edition of Shakespeare begun by Dr. H. H. Furness and carried on by other scholars. The lore of whole libraries, the cunning of the most ingenious minds, the sensibility of the most delicate ears, have been utilized to make straight the thousand crookednesses of the early texts. The early quarto editions of some of the plays were attacked by the printers Heming and Condell in their authorized First Folio as maimed and deformed, and they gave loud assurances of the accuracy of their own versions—assurances that the facts do not support. Some of their plays are less correctly printed than in the quartos they assailed. Beginning with Lewis Theobald and Alexander Pope, a long list of critics in many lands spent patient years to give the world just what Theobald entitled his book, *Shakespeare Restored*.

It was Theobald who suggested the most brilliant conjectural emendation which has ever gained place in the text of an English classic. In Mistress Quickly's description of Falstaff's death, where the line "and a table of greenfield" had long puzzled readers, he substituted the sentence, "and a 'babbled of green fields." He won equally universal acceptance for his recasting of Hermia's line, "Emptying our bosoms of their counsel swelled," into "Emptying our bosoms of their counsels sweet."* He and his successors employed every possible instrument. One German scholar spent a long period studying Elizabethan styles of chirography and ortheopy in the British Museum, and thus constructed an Elizabethan paleography which he applied to the problem. That is, he attempted to conceive what Shakespeare's long-vanished manuscripts, written like other Elizabethan scripts, must have looked like, and tried thus to puzzle out correct readings for some of the printer's misreadings. Still others have labored on the theory that the printers did not set type direct from Shakespeare's manuscript (perhaps much cut up for stage use), but had it read aloud to them.

By the use of varied instruments, Shakespeare's editors have unquestionably done marvels in turning a very corrupt text into one of fair integrity. One typical feat may be cited. By comparing the quarto of *A Midsummer-Night's Dream* with the First Folio, Dr. Furness took a passage which seemed suddenly to turn four fairies into eight—

* A less persuasive suggestion concerning Falstaff's death has been made by Leslie Hotson. Using the fact that the word *table* was sometimes used for *picture* at the time (cf. tableau), and the circumstance that Sir Richard Grenville had lately gained fame by his heroic death, Hotson conjectured that Shakespeare had made Mistress Quickly say that the dying Falstaff's appearance was a picture, or spitten image, of Grenville's.

TITANIA.   And I will purge thy mortall grossnesse so,
           That thou shalt like an aerie spirit go.

*Enter Pease-Blossom, Cobweb, Moth, Mustarde-Seede,
and four fairies.*

FAIRIES.   Ready: And I, and I, and I, where shall we
           go?

and converted this into the piquant and convincing
fragment:

TITANIA.   And I will purge thy mortal grossness so
           That thou shalt like an airy spirit go.
           Pease-Blossom! Cobweb! Moth! Mustard-
           Seed!

           Enter four fairies.

FAIRIES.   Ready; and I, and I, and I. Where shall we
           go?

What has thus been done for great texts of literature can
sometimes equally be done for important historical texts
mutilated by medieval copyists or early printers. For
examples the student need only turn to the Rolls Series or
the *Monumenta Germaniae Historica*.

1. government documents
2. newspapers —
3. letters, memoirs

VII
Pilate on Evidence

THE DIFFICULTY which most frequently daunts the historian, in dealing with evidence, is precisely that which most often disturbs judge and jury: there is not enough of it. Rarely indeed do we encounter a historical event of importance regarding which *all* the pertinent facts are known; all too frequently we are nonplused by transactions whose most vital particulars are missing. History is frequently an attempt to find the correct answer to equations which have been half erased. And in addition to the paucity of evidence, historical students must often lament its bad quality. Even when it exists with a fair degree of technical integrity, it is not unlikely to be evidence of a type which a keen opposing attorney could riddle with holes. Quantitatively and qualitatively, students of the past frequently find their data quite inconclusive.

I

The present age, with its vast equipment for recording events, might be supposed capable of producing sufficient quantities of evidence on every aspect of life. But not merely do indifference, neglect, and mischance constantly do their work. In addition, a widespread and sleepless conspiracy exists against history. A host of men and not a few institutions find it important to their interests—sometimes essential—to destroy the records of their activities. Every European chancellery had its missing documents. How much German evidence on the origins of the First World War might not have perished in flames but for the revolution which gave Karl Kautsky and his associates free access to the records? How many Russian documents might not have been suppressed but for the sudden rise of the Bolshevists to power? Before the United States required publicity for expenditures in Presidential campaigns, national chairmen delighted in conflagrations. Matthew Quay in 1888, for example, when bribery was openly used in New York and Indiana, obliterated all the Republican records. Many a dishonest official has destroyed the evidence of his activities. Tweed's associate Richard Connolly invented the watchword "Addition, division, and silence," but the idea was old long before him. Similar practices are common in business. Collis P. Huntington's order for the disposal of all papers bearing on the construction of the Central Pacific; the destruction of some Standard Oil records during the anti-trust prosecutions— these are typical of many episodes. It may be said of documents as one of Cromwell's men said of a hated opponent, "Stone dead hath no brother."

Not that the destruction of evidence is always dishonest or improper. In highly competitive businesses, corporations may well deem secrecy indispensable. Officers of the law sometimes find it wiser not to trust records to paper, for they may leak out to those who will use them to defeat justice. It was a fearless prosecuting attorney, working to break up a criminal gang in Colorado, who concluded: "Better walk a thousand miles than write a letter."[1] Secretary Benjamin H. Bristow, striving to annihilate the Whiskey Ring in 1874–75, had to carry forward his labors in the dark, with as few letters as possible and most of those written in cipher. Spies in his office would otherwise have defeated all his plans. All secret services are necessarily carried on almost without record. The business of the world, in fact, will always involve a huge amount of confidential activity, public and private, and the interests of the historian are often less important than the proper dispatch of this business. Nor is this greatly to be regretted. The past is the more fascinating for its patches of darkness; our imagination is sometimes better stimulated by what has disappeared into death's dateless night than by what remains in the bright light of noonday. An old letter that lacks the answer may stir the heart more than a complete file of correspondence. Plunging into a long-past period in the diaries of Pepys and Hickey, or the letters of Walpole, we find the experience all the more delightful for the surrounding twilight.

But readers of history should realize that even when the evidence of an event seems fairly satisfactory, it may actually represent no more of it than the fraction of an iceberg seen above water represents of the whole icy mass. Take, for example, a diplomatic exchange in 1938 between Great Britain and the United States. The British proposal perhaps originates at a Cabinet meeting, where only a brief minute (not any record of discussion) is entered. As it affects the Dominion of Canada, Prime Minister Chamberlain asks the Foreign Minister, Anthony Eden, to discuss it with Prime Minister Mackenzie King in Ottawa. To save time, this is done by telephone. The Canadian Prime Minister then discusses the subject with his Cabinet, this again receiving no record whatever. Meanwhile the Cabinet in London has been hearing from important financial interests, which try to reach it by other means than letters. After a final Cabinet discussion in Downing Street, the Foreign Minister communicates with his Ambassador, Sir Ronald Lindsay, in Washington. The latter deputes one of the embassy staff to call on Mr. J. P. Moffat, head of the European Division in the State Department. He and Mr. Moffat are friends, having served together in some European capital. The Englishman outlines the proposal his government has in mind, and asks for advice upon the best way to present it. Mr. Moffat requests a few days to think it over, and then talks with Secretary of State Hull. It at once comes before the American Cabinet, where no record of deliberations is kept. Mr. Moffat then tells Sir Ronald Lindsay what he can. A few days later the British note arrives. It has taken shape as a result of long preliminary discussion in three capitals, and the historian is lucky if he finds a cablegram or two and a casual jotting in somebody's diary to indicate this. If unlucky, he finds nothing.

It is undeniable, however, that a deal of *needless* destruction of valuable historical material steadily goes on. Men of the utmost probity and rectitude may destroy records simply from a sense that they are confidential. Thus Senator George F. Edmunds burned his personal papers before his death, with all their intimate matter on American politics from 1860 to 1890, not because they would damage anyone, but because he thought letters from other public men a sacred trust. Still more frequently men conceal the evidence of others' misdeeds because they believe that oblivion is seemly.* Hamilton Fish told his daughter that he had not entered in his voluminous diary the transactions in the Grant regime most discreditable to Grant. The poet Tom Moore consented, on demand of the publisher Murray and the family of Lord Byron, to destroy the manuscript of Byron's memoirs—for Murray had been told that publication would involve the poet in infamy. We read in the autobiography of Charles Godfrey Leland how he did away with some excessively frank evidence upon various American writers collected by the waspish Rufus Wilmot Griswold:

> Dr. Griswold . . . had got himself into great trouble by his remarks on Edgar A. Poe. . . . Poe's best friends told severe stories of him in those days—*me ipso teste* —and Griswold, naught extenuating, and setting down naught in malice, wrote incautiously more than he should. These are the words of another than I. But when

* Abraham Lincoln's son Robert, according to a story which has been much exaggerated, destroyed some family papers, and was estopped from destroying others only by the intervention of friends, including Dr. Nicholas Murray Butler. A. K. McClure's papers on Lincoln were deliberately destroyed; so were those of Robert Levi Todd, one of Lincoln's intimate associates. Papers and evidence on Lincoln collected by his partner Herndon were suppressed by Jesse W. Weik in writing the Herndon-Weik life, and might easily have been destroyed. See Emanuel Hertz, *The Hidden Lincoln*, pp. 17–19.

Griswold was attacked, then he became savage. One day I found in his desk, which he had committed to me, a great number of further materials collected to Poe's discredit. I burnt it all up at once, and told the doctor what I had done, and scolded him well into the bargain. He took it all very amiably. There was also much matter to other men's discredit—*ascensionem expectans*—awaiting publication, all of which I burned. It was the result of long research, and evidently formed the material for a book. Had it ever been published, it would have made Rome howl! But, as I said, I was angry, and knew that it would injure Dr. Griswold more than anybody.[2]

Tom Moore forgot, Hamilton Fish forgot, that the fame of Byron and Grant was not the only interest to be considered, but that posterity also had its rights—a right to the full truth. After a certain lapse of time, letters such as Senator Edmunds doubtless received from various American statesmen cease to be private property and become affected with a public interest; to destroy them is to injure the public. But historians have learned to take philosophically the inevitable loss of much of the raw material of their calling. Libraries, learned societies, governmental archives, and individual scholars will strive to save what they can. The business of the historical student is to make the most of what evidence he has, not to repine that it is not fuller. But it should be added that more systematic effort to stimulate the writing of contemporaneous records—such a work as H. H. Bancroft did when he sent stenographers to take down the dictated narratives of California pioneers, and the Oral History Office of Columbia University has done more effectively with an apparatus of trained interviewers, tape recorders, and secretaries—is much needed.*

* It is interesting to note how narrowly the Robert Morris Papers escaped destruction. Jared Sparks had access to them; they disappeared; they were discovered by George Meredith Read in a French country town just as they were about to be consigned to a paper mill; he guarded them like a dragon, letting nobody see them; and they finally went to the Library of Congress.

What the honest historian will never do is to use conjecture in piecing out the imperfect evidence of the past; save, of course, as he frankly confesses that it is a guess at truth. It is extraordinary how far pseudo-historians will go in substituting conjecture for fact when symmetry and completeness of narrative are otherwise unobtainable. Hilaire Belloc, in his life of Marie Antoinette, is certain that the friendship of the beautiful queen for Comte de Fersen never passed platonic bounds, for Mr. Belloc had an austere conception of what his Catholic heroine must never allow herself to do. Arnold Zweig, however, in his biography of the queen, is certain that she and De Fersen loved one another with romantic unconstraint, for Herr Zweig's code expected that of a woman in Marie Antoinette's position. The fact is that no evidence exists for a positive statement. Wisdom would have dictated the course which Froude recommends, absolute avoidance of guesses. One of the *obiter dicta* of his stimulating *Short Studies* runs:

> In perusing modern histories, the present writer has been struck dumb with wonder at the facility with which men will fill in chasms in their information with conjecture; will guess at the motives which have prompted actions; will pass their censures, as if all the secrets of the past lay an open scroll before them. He is obliged to say for himself that, whenever he has been fortunate enough to discover authentic explanations of English historical difficulties, it is rare indeed that he has found any conjecture, either of his own or of any other modern writer, confirmed. The true motive has almost invariably been of a kind which no modern experience could have suggested.[3]

But let us turn to the quality of what evidence historians do possess.

II

Those acquainted with legal procedure are aware that jurists use the term evidence in a variety of senses, and direct much of their effort to determining the degree of falsity or truth in any fragment of it. The courts draw an emphatic distinction between direct evidence and circumstantial evidence; that is, between the evidence of witnesses, documents, and material facts, and the evidence of environing circumstance. The latter kind of evidence may be termed presumptive evidence; certain facts are proved from which the existence of a fact vital to the case may logically be inferred. The courts distinguish, again, between original evidence and hearsay evidence. The former means the sworn statements of competent witnesses standing before the judge; the latter refers to a statement by some witness of what he heard another say outside of court. In dealing with documents, the law distinguishes between primary and secondary evidence. The original of a disputed contract is primary evidence, while a sworn copy of that contract is secondary evidence.

Beyond certain obvious limits, no hard and fast rules exist by which courts can distinguish between good and bad evidence. It is clear that except in the most bizarre cases, original evidence is better than hearsay evidence; indeed, the latter is usually excluded altogether. It is equally clear that when some question of documents arises, the originals are better than copies. But there is no sure touchstone for distinguishing between a veracious and an unveracious witness. Some men perjure themselves more plausibly than others tell the truth. And contrary to the popular view, direct evidence is frequently inferior to circumstantial evidence. This is because human beings lie, while material circumstances (if properly observed) do not. Judge Alton B. Parker used to tell jurymen who evinced undue suspicion of circumstantial evidence the story of his first murder case—a case which showed that such evidence may be absolutely conclusive. A man was tried for killing a woman at Cochecton, Sullivan County, New York. Nobody had seen the killing. But it was proved that the defendant had bought powder and shot in the village; had borrowed a shotgun from a resident there; had torn a page from a copy of the *Deaf Mutes' Institute*, a magazine received by this resident, and using one-half for wadding, had put the other half in his pocket; had been seen approaching and returning from the murdered woman's house on the night of the murder; and had tried to spend a $5 bill which was known in the village to be the property of the murdered woman's husband because it had been identified as counterfeit. The wadding had been found near the body. The other half of the page was in the defendant's pocket. The $5 bill was also in his pocket, though he tried to throw it away when the constable arrested him. On this circumstantial evidence the defendant was convicted and executed.

Similarly, no fixed rules exist by which historians can discriminate offhand between good and poor evidence. Historical writers are commonly not so rigid in examining evidence, or at least so bound by rules and precedents, as judges and juries are compelled to be; they should be equally severe in essentials, but their procedure may be marked by greater flexibility. This is because the issues at stake seldom affect life or property, because the verdict can always be reversed, and because the conditions under which evidence is taken are looser, broader, and less obedient to close control. The best historians, however, try to make their evidence meet ultimate tests as severe as those of the courts, and to reach many verdicts that are as compelling and trustworthy. Their regard for the veracity of witnesses and documents must be as close. And in several respects their practice runs precisely parallel with that of the courts. For example, if an accusation is involved, if one character in history denies a charge while others press it, in most instances guilt cannot be held conclusively established save by corroborative evidence from at least one independent source.

Even this parallel, however, must not be pushed too far. One obvious difference between courts and historians in handling evidence is that the former must, at least in all criminal cases, establish substantial certainty, while the latter can be satisfied with establishing high probability. When there is a direct conflict of testimony, the historian can give more weight than the court to the inherent evidence of the situation. A court of law might not have held

Mary Stuart guilty of connivance in the murder of Darnley, or might at least have brought in the Scots verdict of "Not proved," but the historian Andrew Lang could pronounce her probably guilty. No public official can be held guilty in court of taking a bribe simply on the oath of a single witness that he has paid one to the official; canceled checks, marked money, the testimony of an independent witness, or some other distinct and clinching evidence, is required. A Federal Court in St. Louis, lacking such evidence, declared Orville E. Babcock guiltless of complicity in the Whiskey Ring. But several historians, after careful scrutiny of the collateral and inherent evidence, have unhesitatingly declared the probability of Babcock's guilt to be so great as to be conclusive. A neat problem of disputed evidence was presented by the famous interview which James G. Blaine arranged in Washington with Jacob Mulligan in May 1876, just before Mulligan was to appear before a House investigating committee with letters highly damaging to Blaine. The two men met alone in a hotel room. According to Mulligan, Blaine begged on his knees for the letters, saying that they would blast his career forever and ruin his six children. Finally he borrowed the letters, and stubbornly kept them. Blaine, who admitted getting the letters by this trick, denied the remainder of this story. No other evidence as to his pleas for pity was available. A court of law could not have accepted Mulligan's statement. The historian, however, accepts it because Mulligan bore a good reputation, had no incentive whatever to lie, and told a detailed story which bore many inherent marks of truth. Blaine had every motive for lying, and his reputation for veracity was bad.

In short, the tests of evidence, in history as in courts, are principally *ad hoc* tests. They must vary with the witness, the problem, and the circumstances. Students of history may to some extent profit, in developing a method of weighing evidence, by reading such legal works as Thayer's *Preliminary Treatise on Evidence,* or Dean Wigmore's *System of Evidence.* Nevertheless, in the end such students have to devise their own methods to meet each problem, and the success of every historian depends upon his judgment, ingenuity, and honesty. It is possible to give only a few general words of advice. The chief of these must always be the old maxim, "Be skeptical—regard every assertion with doubt."

Deliberate mendacity is common both in the handling and the recording of historical transactions. Vyacheslav M. Molotov, so long Soviet Foreign Minister, wrote in 1913: "A diplomat's words must have no relation to action—otherwise what kind of diplomacy is it? Words are one thing, actions another. Good words are a mask for the concealment of bad deeds. Sincere diplomacy is no more possible than dry water or iron wood." It is not strange that Churchill, after characterizing Molotov as a man of outstanding ability and cold-blooded ruthlessness, added a statement on his "remarkable skill in duplicity." How much validity would any historical statement by Molotov possess?

III

The best evidence is that in which no element of self-interest, no element of ignorance, and no element of bias appears. Among written materials, ordinary government documents in highly civilized lands meet the tests implied more perfectly than anything else. When we use the report of debates in the *Congressional Record,* the British or Canadian *Hansard,* or the official journal of the Chamber of Deputies; when we refer to a law in the officially printed Federal Statutes at Large, or official volumes of State statutes; when we read the text of a Presidential message in one of the executive documents, we are using almost absolutely dependable material. This reliability holds true of court records, treaties, proclamations, and such official correspondence as that published in the annual volumes of *Foreign Relations* and the British Blue Books.

Insofar as such material states matters of record, not of opinion or supposition, it is as authentic as human productions can be. This is because the honor of nations, States, and cities is bound up in the accuracy of their records, and proportionate care is taken to prevent error. It is because while at rare intervals the interest of an individual might be promoted by falsification, in general such vast and overwhelming interests are served by accuracy that unreliability would be regarded as intolerable. It is because governments are able to hire corps of experts animated by strict discipline, and this discipline demands the rigid elimination of ignorance or bias—the instant correction of even the slightest error.

Thus in history, as in courts of law, complete credence is usually to be given records of fact from official government sources. Of course this record must not be used naïvely. A student of the *Congressional Globe* or *Record* is expected to know that, as its pages plainly show, not all speeches printed there have been delivered on the floor of Congress. "Leave to print" accounts for extensions of spoken discourses, and for long discourses of which not a word was ever spoken. Such a student is also expected to know that important speeches delivered in executive sessions of the Senate do not appear in print at all for many years, and perhaps never. He is expected to know that the speeches published in the *Record* are frequently revised by the author, sometimes drastically, while at times rude or profane language is expurgated by the clerk; so that press reports of Congressional speeches may be quite accurate, and yet differ materially from the official report.

Students of diplomacy are supposed to know that some foreign nations make treaties with secret clauses, as even the United States once in its early history did, so that the published version may be incomplete. Everyone should know that proclamations are frequently used for propagandist purposes only, and are not always to be taken at their face value. And we should be constantly alive to the fact that while an officially published statute proves the passage of a law, it may prove nothing whatever as to its vitality. Many statutes, Federal, State, and local, have been dead letters from the moment of their enactment. Many more, like the Fugitive Slave Law of 1850, have been effective in some areas while a nullity in others. Many men who realize that this is true in our own day forget that it has always been true in the past. They are aware that the Eighteenth Amendment and Volstead Act were inoperative for great urban communities before their repeal, but assume that the European laws which once punished trifling offenses with death, or the colonial laws which seemed to bear harshly upon religious minorities, were enforced to the letter. As a matter of fact, the old criminal laws were in practice mitigated by an extraordinary number of expedients. So were the old laws against debtors; King Charles II even took poor folk into his nominal employ as royal servants to save them from debtors' prisons. Though various American colonies had laws restricting Catholics, the general colonial practice was mild. A careful work written by a Catholic

> offers exhaustive evidence that in the general history of religious intolerance the Puritans and other Protestants of the colonies were far from being the worst offenders. After all, no blood was shed; no martyrs were burned at the stake; no confessors were made to suffer and die in dark prisons. . . . Extreme *violence* against the Catholics was more oratorical exercise and display of verbal fireworks than actual practice. It had no counterpart in the use of violent means of repression or bloody persecutions. Even when laws were enacted which, if strictly applied, would have prevented any Catholic from taking up residence in a colony, very seldom do we find a very rigorous enforcement of them. In most cases Catholics, though deprived of special rights, could live in peace.[4]

IV

The newspaper as a form of evidence merits consideration immediately after the official document. For one reason, to students of modern history it is second in importance only to official sources—if not actually equal; for another reason, parts of the modern newspaper have a quasi-official character. It is obvious that the extraordinary expansion of press activities has made the historical value of the newspaper a complex and somewhat baffling subject, on which easy generalizations are impossible. The accuracy of newspapers varies greatly from land to land. In the same country, their reliability and fullness varies greatly from city to city. A newspaper may utterly change its character within a few years, sometimes almost overnight. The Washington *National Intelligencer* was a valuable repository of historical material in the 1840s, less valuable in the 1850s, almost worthless after 1861; *The New York Times* was of mediocre value in 1890, but of steadily increasing usefulness after Adolph S. Ochs assumed ownership in 1895.

One generalization, however, may be ventured. Journalism has reached its highest development in English-speaking lands, and the evidential value of the average newspaper in English is distinctly higher than in most other languages. Many journals in Continental Europe and Hispanic-America must be used with extreme caution. The press of France, as we know from the pages of Balzac, from the Panama and Dreyfus scandals, and from more recent revelations, has in great part been shamelessly venal. Before the First World War, the press of Czarist Russia was rigidly and that of Imperial Germany somewhat less strictly controlled. The rise in postwar years of Hitler in Germany, Mussolini in Italy, and other dictators elsewhere was accompanied by the stifling of all independence in the presentation of both press news and opinion. In contrast, the best American, British, Dominion, Scandinavian, and Swiss newspapers have long occupied a high plane of independence, enterprise, and accuracy in gathering news and in editorial comment.

The largest of these dailies are invaluable to students of nineteenth- and twentieth-century history, and in the broad view have become steadily more useful. At various times and places famous Continental journals—the *Journal des Debats*, the *Berliner Tageblatt*, the *Frankfurter Zeitung*, the *Corriere della Sera*—and a few such South American dailies as *Il Prensa* of Buenos Aires, have had great importance. But the significance of their files to the modern historian does not equal that of the *London Times*, founded in 1785, the *Manchester Guardian*, founded in 1821, the New York *Evening Post*, founded in 1801, the *New York Tribune*, founded in 1841, and *The New York Times*, founded in 1851.

Another generalization may be ventured as to the departments of the press. The modern newspaper is a curious mixture of official, semi-official, and unofficial information. Its weather reports are strictly official; barring misprints, they may be trusted with confidence. The reports of stock markets, produce markets, and merchandise markets are semi-official. They are presented without bias, without self-interest, and by experts working under carefully guarded conditions. Behind their accuracy stands the honor of the newspaper, and the knowledge of its managers that error would mean angry protests, loss of confidence, and a ruinous drop in circulation. News of the results of all kinds of games and contests is likewise semi-official, its accuracy guaranteed by precisely the same considerations. So with news of ship movements, announcements of radio programs, and lists of deaths, births, marriages, bankruptcies, and probated estates. But this almost closes the list. The remainder of the newspaper—and "all the world is in the newspaper," said Thackeray—is a mixture of the reliable and the unreliable, the impartial and the tendentious, the shrewd and the naïve, the superficial and the well-informed. Useful as the news columns and editorials are, their best values can be extracted only by patient winnowing.

Since all newspapers are produced by men working under extreme pressure of time, a small percentage of outright inaccuracy is inevitable. Reporters and correspondents gather facts in a hurry and write with eyes on the clock; copyreaders revise this material hurriedly; headline writers fit it with hurried captions; the proofroom corrects it hurriedly. On such newspapers as the *London Times*, *Manchester Guardian*, and *The New York Times*, gross inaccuracies are infrequent. Substantial errors are punishable by discharge; they are publicly corrected. But inadequacy of news is much more common, and sometimes amounts to inaccuracy. All newspapermen, from editors to reporters, feel a despairing sense that they write from a half-knowledge of affairs. With their limited time and sources of information they simply cannot gain a full knowledge. Samuel Bowles once remarked that no journalist could wait to get his work precisely right, and then publish it just as the last trump sounded. While aiming at the whole truth, good newspapermen must frequently content themselves with half or three quarters of it. Men engaged in any complicated transaction, political, economic, or cultural, often waver, as they read press reports of this transaction, between admiration that the reporter has learned so much and irritation that he has not learned more. They realize that the story is accurate so far as it goes, and yet without challengeable misstatement or conscious dishonesty, sometimes subtly misrepresents a situation. Readers of press files must bear this in mind. Those who can gauge newspaper reports by intimate sources of information, such as letters or diaries, are not likely to forget it.

Nor will any careful student forget that bias enters the news columns of even the best journals. Such journals sometimes go to extreme lengths to prevent any coloring of the news. Thus *The New York Times,* itself antipathetic to Bolshevism, maintained for years in Moscow a correspondent (Mr. Walter Duranty) who was distinctly sympathetic to the Soviet regime, and the *New York Herald Tribune,* sternly opposing Franklin D. Roosevelt in 1936, chose as its correspondent with his Republican opponent a biographer and warm admirer of Roosevelt's. The best English-language journals the world over try to exclude from their news all trace of overt editorializing.

But coloration nevertheless insidiously creeps in. Reporters and correspondents of the *Manchester Guardian* simply cannot forget that its general attitude in labor questions, colonial questions, and issues of international relations is that of the left-wing Liberals; this fact unconsciously affects their observation of events and their mental composition of a news story before it is written down. A writer for the *Guardian,* however honest, will not be so quick to see an outrage by labor as one by capital—because he is looking for the latter; not so quick to see the benefits of imperialist rule overseas as its defects. He has a sub-conscious sensitiveness to one, a subconscious insensitive-ness to the other. This general principle applies still more clearly to American newspapers. Every great journal has its *tone*, and it is remarkable how men of the most salient abilities lose all individuality on such journals, merging with it their own personality. The point at which it ceases to be legitimate for a managing editor to play up that news which supports the editorial attitude, and play down that news which runs counter to it, is a difficult question. Crusading journals like the *New York Tribune* under Greeley in the fifties, and the *New York World* under Pulitzer in the nineties, tended to weld the news and edi-torials together in a seamless fabric. The editors fought these newspapers as a captain fought his battleship. They did good service for one side of the truth, but they were often very one-sided indeed.

During the first three quarters of the nineteenth cen-tury the bias in American newspapers was primarily politi-cal, and could easily be detected. Any reader could see that the news favored Whigs, Democrats, or Republicans, and also favored certain sectional interests allied with parties. But as the nation became an industrial giant the newspaper bias grew more and more largely economic. As such, it was better concealed and more dangerous. Democrats and Republicans long divided the press with some evenness, but by 1890 belief in the *status quo* of the economic system almost monopolized it. The historian finds it difficult to obtain a fair statement of the Free Silver cause in 1896 in the Eastern press; difficult to ob-tain a balanced treatment of labor upheavals like the Colorado coal and iron strike, the Paterson and Lawrence strikes, and the steel strike of 1919; and difficult to obtain a fair-minded treatment of some aspects of the New Deal 1933–40. Issues between business and government in re-cent years have been widely misrepresented by the daily press, which, since even small-city newspapers now re-quire a large investment, has become distinctly an organ of business. Of course those newspapers in which bias is most obvious present the fewest dangers to students of history. Such students will be on their guard in using Bennett's sensational *Herald* in the 1840s, or the still more sensational Hearst press in the period 1895–1920. They will see that the *Chicago Tribune* has been decidedly partisan on economic issues from the time when it assailed the Pullman strikers of 1894 until its latest criticisms of organized labor. It is the journal of but mild and occasional news-coloration that is likely to mislead later students.

A mélange of bias and outright dishonesty in the management of foreign intelligence in particular has at times affected the entire press of the United States—not to speak of other countries. In wartime this is taken for granted. During the First World War news stories of "nationalized women" and "corpse-rendering factories" in Germany were printed broadcast. Many American editors took the same view as the English newspaper manager who rebuked a correspondent for writing an account of exceptional German heroism: "Do not send us any more stories about the dear good Germans; the only good German is a dead German."

Dr. Samuel Johnson had noted the situation long before: "In wartime a people only want to hear two things —good of themselves and evil of the enemy. And I know not what is the more to be feared after a war, streets full of soldiers who have learned to rob, or garrets full of scribblers who have learned to lie." The lying certainly continues after the war. In 1920 Walter Lippmann published a supplement to the *New Republic* (August 4) demonstrating that one of the greatest and fairest of American journals had systematically distorted or falsified the news about Russia. Similar accusations were from time to time leveled against the press, with supporting evidence, throughout the tense period leading to the Second World War, the conflict itself, the ensuing cold war, and the troubles with the Castro regime in Cuba.

Prejudice and mendacity in reporting domestic news is especially common in election years or other times of heated political battle. A journalist serving as copy editor for the *Boston Traveler* made a thorough examination of the treatment which thirty-one major newspapers throughout the country gave in 1952 to the disclosure that Nixon and Stevenson had handled political funds, the charges against Nixon being much the graver. He found that with one possible exception, "all papers, both Republican and Democratic, showed evidence of favoritism in their news columns," and that "almost every example of news favoritism in the news columns coincided with the paper's editorial feelings."[5] It was flagrant coloring of the news fed to millions, not editorial-page policies, that gave Hearst's press its bad reputation, his slanting of intelligence being particularly flagrant at one time of strained relations with Mexico, where he owned huge properties. What misled the public in 1913 might mislead the student of history later.*

Many files may also mislead uncritical readers by habitual and natural magnification of the news. Reporters usually desire to give their accounts an air of importance, and to do this resort to various formulas, the principal being the substitution of general for particular statements. Thus several policemen are ordered to search for a certain criminal. Newspapers next day may report, "Police were ordered today to begin a dragnet hunt for so-and-so," the implication being that most of the city force is so engaged. We even see, "Police of three states were hunting today," etc., the truth being that half a dozen detectives were at work. So when a flood threatens a city, a reporter interviews several barge captains or fishermen, with the resulting statement, "Fears of rivermen were increasing today," or even, "River experts agreed today in predicting . . ." A factory superintendent makes a statement to a reporter, and next day the public reads, "Officials of the Blup Manufacturing Corporation declare . . ." Or a correspondent goes downtown in New York and sees a half-dozen brokers and bankers. Next day: "Wall Street

---

* The question of the honesty of editorial comment sometimes has historical importance. Murat Halstead told the Wisconsin Press Association in 1889 that he saw no objection if readers should "find out that the advertiser occasionally dictates the editorials." "No objection at all to that," retorted E. L. Godkin; "the objection is when they don't find it out."

circles viewed with apprehension the news that the Administration . . ." This is shortly countered by a dispatch from the Washington correspondent, who has seen several bureau heads and Congressmen: "Circles close to the President today met with grave resentment the Wall Street view . . ." Of course the more reputable journals avoid this exaggeration.

Students of bound newspaper volumes should be suspicious of vague and general statements. "Informed Washington quarters" may be only a minor civil service employee; "medical experts" may mean a young doctor; "Pennsylvania authorities" may cloak the identity of a few justices of the peace. Particularly in the foreign news is this tendency toward a vague magnification often given absurd rein. A London correspondent sees an under-secretary at the Foreign Office, and cables home: "Downing Street evinced great irritation when told today of news from Cairo that . . ." In certain journals the hurried headline-writer plays this up as "British Suspicion of Egypt Grows," and the reader is left to picture 55,000,000 Britons and 25,000,000 Egyptians glowering angrily at one another. Winston Churchill said in a speech July 29, 1941:

> We are often told that "the House of Commons thinks this," or "feels that." Newspapers write: "The general feeling was of grave uneasiness . . ." All this is telegraphed all over the world, and produces evil effects. No one has a right to say what is the opinion of the House of Commons. We suffer now from not having divisions. We have debates, to which a very small minority of members are able to contribute, because of the time available. . . . These members do not represent the opinion of the House of Commons or the nation, nor do their statements give a true picture of the prodigious war effort of the British people.

Still another danger to history lurks in the steady efforts of press agents and propagandists to reach the columns of the press; efforts against which editors wage a sleepless but not always successful warfare. Two generations ago not a few newspapers still published the paid reading-notice—a puff or advertisement barely distinguishable from ordinary news. That is dead. But no little part of the news for many years from Washington and state capitals has originated in press releases by government departments or bureaus ("handouts"), often decidedly biased in character. Recent years have witnessed an alarming increase in the use of press agents by different branches of the Federal government. Good Washington correspondents still obtain their information by hard work, and the initial exposure of many a scandal from Teapot Dome to the corruption of public officials by Teamsters' Union leaders has come from their earnest digging. Lazy reporters, however, may collect news—of a sort—without effort. The diggers, however, develop a sullen suspicion of press releases. "It doesn't make any difference whether it is the State Department, the Internal Revenue Service, or Justice Department," Clark Mollenhoff of the *Des Moines Register and Tribune* said in 1960. "If we rely on what they put into their handouts, we will be peddling a phony bill of goods, because they are going to put the best possible blush on it. What we have to do is to take what they give us, inquire into it, dig into it."

Government agencies plant news for unconfessed purposes, doctor news, and frequently endeavor to deny access to legitimate news. Secrecy in government is an old complaint of journalists. "The reporter tries to get the news," Edwin A. Lahey of the *Akron Beacon-Journal* has said; "the bureaucrat tries to conceal it."* Late in the Eisenhower Administration a Congressional committee under Representative John E. Moss tried to break down improper executive secrecy. But the departments are far from the only offenders. A thousand pressure groups in Washington and other capitals try to feed their special versions of the

---

* In the Second World War President Roosevelt created the Office of War Information by executive order, and appointed Elmer Davis as head. The bitter struggle he waged with Cabinet officers, generals, admirals, and members of Congress who labored to suppress news while he strove to give the public an accurate picture of the war is narrated in Roger Burlingame's *Don't Let Them Scare You: The Life and Times of Elmer Davis* (1961).

truth to the public by the press or other media. It is largely because the shrewdest business corporations do not believe what they read on national affairs in the newspapers, or do not consider it adequate, that they maintain their own news gatherers to verify statements of fact before they base important action upon them. Historians who evaluate press reports as a type of evidence must remember that much of the published matter is born in an atmosphere of ballyhoo.[6]

Thus any intensive use of the files of a given newspaper for historical purposes should be preceded or accompanied by an effort to determine its *tone*, and how much that counts in its treatment of events; the degree to which its editors permit coloration of the news; its canons of accuracy; and its special sources of information. Important staff members should as far as possible be identified. It may be of value to know that the Washington correspondent whom Theodore Roosevelt most trusted for years was Francis E. Leupp of the New York *Evening Post*, that President Hoover made a similar confidant of Mark Sullivan of the *New York Herald Tribune*, and that Arthur Krock of the *Times* was a favorite of Secretary Cordell Hull.

V

Beyond the field of the government document, beyond the newspaper, lies that vaster field presented by personal source materials—letters, diaries, memoirs, and autobiographies. A government is largely impersonal and a newspaper often tries to be; but when we come to records made by individuals in their private capacity, new difficulties appear. Each personal witness must be regarded by the student much as judge and jury regard witnesses on the stand. Testimony must be evaluated as firsthand or hearsay, fresh or stale, prejudiced or unprejudiced, corroborated or uncorroborated, vague or definite. All this should be obvious, but to many students and writers it is not. Theodore Roosevelt includes in his *Winning of the West* some amusing paragraphs on the importance of edu-

cating American writers to treat personal narratives of the
frontier critically. He found it necessary to point out "the
very obvious truths that with the best intentions in the
world the average backwoodsman often has difficulty in
describing a confused chain of events exactly as they took
place; that when the events are described after a long
lapse of years many errors are apt to creep in; and that
when they are reported from tradition it is the rarest thing
imaginable for the report to be correct."

We can illustrate the means of testing personal evidence
by examples. Take as one a letter that became famous for
its direct bearing on disputed questions in the career of
Joan of Arc. It was written July 21, 1429, when Joan had
raised the siege of Orléans and set out for Rheims to attend the coronation of Charles. Its author, Perceval de
Boulainvilliers, chamberlain to Charles, addressed it to the
Duke of Milan. After some preliminary words, he thus
took the witness stand:

> Already, I am sure, news has reached your ears of a
> certain Maid, sent to us, as we devoutly believe, by God,
> and in order that I may briefly set forth her life, deeds,
> station, and character, [I] shall first tell of her origin.
> She was born in the small village of Domrémy, in the
> country of Bar, within the confines of Kingdom of
> France, on the river Meuse, near Lorraine, of upright
> and simple parents. During the night of the Epiphany
> of our Lord, when the nations are wont most joyfully
> to recall the acts of Christ, she entered upon mortal
> life, and all the people of the place were wondrously
> moved by a great rejoicing, and though ignorant of the
> birth of the Maid, they rushed hither and thither in
> search of what might be the new event. The hearts of
> some were conscious of a new gladness. More: the cocks
> as heralds of a new joy, against their wont, burst forth
> in songs not heard before, and with flapping wings for
> more than two hours appeared to foretell the coming of
> a new thing.
>
> The child is reared, and when she had reached the
> age of seven years, after the custom of peasants she was

placed by her parents in charge of the lambs, during which time no lamb is known to have died, nor was anyone killed by wild beasts, and while she was under her father's roof so great was the security she afforded the whole household that they suffered not the least injury from enemy, deceit of barbarians, or other ill. Finally when she had reached the age of twelve years, the first revelation was made to her in the following manner:

When she and other maidens were guarding the sheep of their parents, they were wandering about the field. Those round about approached, and they asked her whether she would like to enter a race for a handful of flowers, or the like. She consented, and the conditions being agreed upon, she moved during the second and third circuits with such speed that they did not think she touched the ground at all, so that one of the children cried out:

"Joan," for that was her name, "I see you flying close to the ground."[7]

Thus far the witness is not in the least credible. He is giving us hearsay, and a poor quality of hearsay at that— the popular fables of the time. It is probable enough that the villagers of Domremy rushed gaily about the streets on Twelfth Night, perhaps causing the cocks to crow, but the rest of this farrago is worthless. But the letter writer continues, more soberly:

The Maid is of a satisfying grace, of a manly bearing, and in her conversation displays wondrous good sense. Her voice has wondrous charm. She eats little, partakes even more sparingly of wine. She delights in beautiful horses and armor and greatly admires armed and noble men; avoids contacts and converse with the many, sheds tears freely, her expression is cheerful, and she has great capacity for work. Of such endurance is she in the handling and bearing of arms that she remained for six days and nights in full armor.

She declared that the English have no rights in France, and that she herself was sent by God to overcome them, and that God had so declared to her. For the King she has the greatest reverence. She declares that he was chosen by God, and was and will continue to be under her special protection. She further declares that the Duke of Orleans, your grandson, will be set free by a miracle, a warning having first been given to the English who are holding him in custody, to set him free.

Here the witness begins to be of value, for he is no longer writing hearsay, but giving facts on his own authority. As he was chamberlain of the French monarch and constantly at court, he had ample opportunity to observe Joan; he was certainly at Chinon during part of the time she was there. His portrait thus carries conviction. At one point he drops into hearsay again, writing that Joan remained six days and nights in her armor. This is doubtless a wild exaggeration, for she was never six days and nights in the field at one time. But when he says that her voice is charming, that she is cheerful of mien, and that she is emotional of temperament, he is speaking from his own knowledge. Moreover, corroborative testimony exists. Another contemporary, Gui de Laval, speaks of her pleasing voice, and still another, Louis de Contes, of her sparing appetite, while her whole career proves her emotional warmth. Altogether, the letter of Perceval de Boulainvilliers offers a perfect illustration of the weakness of hearsay evidence, the strength of original evidence.

It is equally easy to demonstrate the general superiority of direct evidence over circumstantial evidence. American historical literature presents a singularly striking instance of a blunder, committed through reliance upon circumstantial evidence alone, by a practiced scholar who was also a highly experienced man of the world. Charles Francis Adams, Civil War minister to England, and the biographer of his grandfather John Adams, published soon after the war (1873) a brochure on William H. Seward. He made therein the rash assertion that the success of Lincoln's Administration was traceable primarily to the keenness and wisdom of Seward. For this statement he marshaled circumstantial evidence. Lincoln was uneducated, Seward a graduate of Union College, deeply read and widely traveled. Lincoln possessed little experience of public office when chosen President, having been merely an inconspicuous Congressman for two years; Seward's public experience had begun with his election as Governor of New York, and in 1861 included twelve years of leadership in the Senate. Lincoln had been reared in a frontier state, Seward trained in the richest and most populous part of the nation. Lincoln had only lately taken that determined stand on questions of the day which Seward had long taken and which had led him in 1850 to refer to "a higher law than the Constitution." Lincoln had made Seward his Secretary of State, obviously meaning to lean heavily upon him—to make him Prime Minister. Lincoln had been given the benefit of Seward's advice at every step, consulting him not only in the Cabinet but in frequent private meetings. It was clear, declared Adams, that the enduring work of the administration had been done by Seward.

"It is the duty of history," he wrote, "in dealing with all human events, to do strict justice in discriminating between persons, and by no means to award to one honors that clearly belong to another. I must then affirm, without hesitation, that in the history of our government, no experiment so rash has ever been made as that of elevating to the head of affairs a man with so little previous preparation for his task as Mr. Lincoln. . . . Mr. Lincoln could not fail soon to perceive that whatever estimate he might put on his own natural judgment, he had to deal with a superior in native intellectual power, in extent of acquirement, in breadth of philosophic experience, and in the force of moral discipline. On the other hand, Mr. Seward could not have been long blind to the deficiencies of his chief in these respects." In brief, all the circumstances rendered it inevitable that Seward should lead, Lincoln follow. Adams pointed to circumstantial evidence that he had done so. Seward wished the emancipation of the slaves treated cautiously, and emancipation was effected at just the time and in just the way that Seward would have wished it done. Seward wished the administration to defy the more radical and impetuous leaders of Congress, and Lincoln had defied Thaddeus Stevens and Zachariah Chandler. The evidence seemed overwhelming.

But one blow at the weakest point of circumstantial evidence founded on the mere outward aspect of affairs brings it toppling down. So it was with Adams's array of arguments. Gideon Welles, Secretary of the Navy under Lincoln, stepped forward with a small volume called *Lincoln and Seward* which proved conclusively that Lincoln had always been master of his administration—that he had led and others had followed. By direct evidence drawn from his own unpublished diary, and buttressed by other data, he showed that as between the two groups in his Cabinet, the radicals headed by Chase and the moderates by Seward, Lincoln had acted with masterly independence. He proved that all of the President's decisive acts had been stamped with his own sagacity. Sixteen years later Nicolay and Hay, in their ten-volume life of Lincoln based on the Lincoln papers, demonstrated just how fatal any reliance upon Seward would have been. They staggered admirers of the New Yorker by showing that on April 1, 1861, he had proposed that the United States should provoke a war with France and Spain as a means of reuniting the American people, suggesting that he be permitted to carry out this and other policies. They showed how magnanimously Lincoln, while rejecting this folly and putting Seward into his proper place, had suppressed all public notice of the proposal, and how quickly he had brought Seward to recognize his superior wisdom and firmness. Later research has revealed so much evidence of Lincoln's complete control of his administration, including at times the State Department, that it seems almost incredible that C. F. Adams should ever have made his reckless statements. His circumstantial evidence was worthless.

The most difficult form of evidence to test is that given by the single witness, who may be affected by a hundred forms of personal bias, self-interest, or party, national, or other feeling. The complexities of bias are almost endless, and they are frequently compatible with the utmost sincerity. Of course the simpler types of prejudice are easy to detect—but how seldom we meet the simpler types! The primary rule, in historical study as in the courts, is to cross-examine the witness in an effort to ascertain how many varieties of bias he expresses, and to what degree; for it is a safe rule that everyone has some bias, conscious or unconscious. Suppose, for example, the student of Jefferson turns to the well-known passage in John Quincy Adams's *Memoirs* in which that shrewd observer expresses his conclusions upon the Virginian:

Washington, January 11, 1831.—I read about fifty pages of the first volume of Jefferson's *Memoirs*. [J.Q.A. means the *Anas*.] He states that he began his autobiography on the 6th of January, 1821. . . . He tells nothing but what redounds to his own credit. He is like the French lady who told her sister she did not know how it happened, "but I am the only person in the world who is always right." Jefferson, by his own narrative, is always in the right. That is not uncommon to writers of their own lives. Dr. Franklin was more candid. Mr. Jefferson names the teachers from whom he learnt Greek, Latin, and French, and speaks gratefully of William Small, a Scotchman, professor of mathematics at William and Mary College, who became attached to him and probably fixed the destinies of his life. . . . Loose morals necessarily followed. If not an absolute atheist, he had no belief in a future existence. All his ideas of obligation or retribution were bounded by the present life. His duties to his neighbor were under no stronger guarantee than the laws of the land and the opinions of the world. The tendency of this condition upon a mind of great compass and powerful resources is to produce insincerity and duplicity, which were his besetting sins through life . . .

[From 1790 to 1809] all the good and all the evil parts of his character were brought into action. His ardent passion for liberty and the rights of man; his patriotism; the depth and compass of his understanding; . . . the perpetual watchfulness of public opinion, and the pliability of principle and temper with which he accommodated it to his own designs and opinions:—all these were in ceaseless operation during these twenty years; and with them were combined a rare mixture of infidel philosophy and epicurean morals, of burning ambition and of stoical self-control, of deep duplicity and of generous sensibility, between which two qualities, and a treacherous and inventive memory, his conduct toward his rivals and opponents appears one tissue of inconsistency. His treatment of Washington, of Knox, of my father, of Hamilton, of Bayard, who made him President of the United States, and lastly of me, is marked with features of perfidy worthy of Tiberius Caesar or Louis XI of France. This double-dealing character was often imputed of him during his life and was sometimes exposed. His letter to Mazzei and the agonizing efforts which he afterwards made to explain it away; his most insidious attack upon my father with his never-ceasing professions of respect and affection for his person and character; and his letter to Giles concerning me, in which there is scarcely a single word of truth—indicate a memory so pandering to the will that in deceiving others he seems to have begun by deceiving himself.

Here we find Jefferson accused by one who knew him well of loose morals; of being a freethinker, irreligious and probably atheistic; of having no principle; and of displaying utter selfishness in trying to gratify an inordinate ambition. We find him accused of duplicity, of treachery to superiors and friends, and of deliberate falsehood. It is a staggering indictment, drawn by a statesman famous for both astuteness and probity. But if we summon Adams for cross-examination, what do we find? We learn that he is now sixty-three, with a memory not always accurate. We learn that Jefferson defeated his father for the presidency, and that this event terminated J. Q. Adams's service as Minister to Prussia, a comfortable post—for John Adams recalled him, in order not to embarrass Jefferson. We learn that during Jefferson's administration Adams was a political independent, distrusted by both parties, and frequently piqued because neither was friendly toward him. We learn that as a Massachusetts man he was constitutionally incapable of liking Virginians. As he mentions religion, we find that he is one of the devoutest of Congregationalists, distrusting Episcopalianism and detesting Deism, and that his ideas of what constitutes irreligion are narrow and dogmatic. As he mentions morals, a little inquiry elicits the fact that he regards card-playing, horse-racing, and any waste of time on mere amusement as immoral. And finally, we learn that a multitude of witnesses will testify that Adams, however great and good, was the most censorious and cantankerous of mortals, whose diary has been called "a graveyard of slaughtered reputations."

Though in this instance bias stands revealed at a glance, usually it is far better concealed. Adams and Jefferson spent much of their lives in opposite political parties, while they usually held antagonistic sectional views. But take an equally well-known passage, that in which President James K. Polk in his diary excoriates John C. Calhoun; is any such obvious bias present? Polk and Calhoun were both staunch Democrats. Both were Southerners, reared in neighboring states. Both were slaveholders. Yet Polk writes under date of April 6, 1847, that he has no use for either Martin Van Buren or Calhoun:

> The people of the United States, I hope, will cast off all such intriguers, and make their own selection for the Presidency, and this if they are wise they will do. I now entertain a worse opinion of Mr. Calhoun than I have ever done before. He is wholly selfish, and I am satisfied has no patriotism. A few years ago he was the author of Nullification and threatened to dissolve the Union on account of the tariff. During my administration the reduction of duties which he desired has been obtained, and he can no longer complain. No sooner is this done than he selects slavery upon which to agitate the country, and blindly mounts that topic as a hobby. . . . I am utterly disgusted at such intriguing of men in high place, and hope they will be rebuked by the people.

Here is another withering indictment of one of our most eminent statesmen. Calhoun is accused of utter selfishness, base intriguing, and an entire lack of patriotism and party spirit. But a cross-examination of Polk reveals that two years earlier, when he was pressing for hostilities against Mexico, Calhoun spoke and voted against war to the last. It reveals that one year earlier, when Polk was reluctant to settle the Oregon boundary on the 49th parallel, Calhoun vigorously advocated that compromise. It reveals the fact that Polk in 1847 wished to annex a large part of present-day Mexico to the United States—indeed, he ultimately favored annexing it all, but that Calhoun strongly opposed unlimited annexation, and wished to carry the line no farther south than it now stands. In brief, the men had been in constant collision ever since Polk took office, and Polk, smarting under Calhoun's blows, was far from a good witness as to his character and motives.[8]

But the commonest form of bias in memoirs, autobiographies, letters, and travels is that which requires only a slight discount, and determination of the proper degree of reserve is often a nice task. Take a passage from the graphic memoirs of Henry Villard—part of his description of how, as a journalist, he reported the Lincoln-Douglas debates of 1858. He writes:

> I was introduced to Lincoln at Freeport, and met him frequently afterwards in the course of the campaign. I must say frankly that, although I found him most approachable, good-natured, and full of wit and humor, I could not take a real personal liking to the man, owning to an inborn weakness for which he was even then notorious, and so remained during his great public career. He was inordinately fond of jokes, anecdotes, and stories. He loved to hear them, and still more to tell them himself out of the inexhaustible supply provided by his good memory and his fertile fancy. There would have been no harm in this but for the fact that the coarser the joke, the lower the anecdote, and the more risky the story, the more he enjoyed them, especially when they were of his own invention. He pos-

sessed moreover, a singular ingenuity in bringing about occasions in conversation for indulgences of this kind.[9]

How much weight is to be attached to this unfavorable judgment of Lincoln? Unquestionably it offers valid evidence of one of Lincoln's small weaknesses. It is sufficient in itself to destroy Mrs. Honoré Willsie Morrow's statement that Lincoln's stories, while somewhat broad, never held an evil suggestiveness. (Mrs. Morrow asserts that she is sure Lincoln never repeated bawdy anecdotes because she asked various men, experts on Lincoln's humor, to tell her the worst, and they never told her one that was really offensive!) But is the condemnation of Lincoln's vulgarity to be taken at full face value? An examination of Villard discloses some significant facts. Was he a man of mature judgment in 1858? He was twenty-three, when rash estimates are often founded upon surface impressions. Was he well acquainted with America and its robust Western life? He was a Bavarian who had spent but five years in the United States, chiefly in the East. Had his surroundings made him tolerant of the broad if not ribald humor of Boccaccio or Ben Jonson? Reared in the home of an eminent German jurist, he had moved in the most refined circles of Speyer, Munich, New York, and Boston, and had known few but cultivated gentlefolk. He was of a literary and artistic bent. Moreover, he was hostile to Lincoln's politics and wished to see Douglas re-elected Senator. Altogether, Villard's evidence is insufficient to convict Lincoln of innate vulgarity—to disprove Lord Charnwood's judgment that what delighted him in a rough anecdote was the wit and not the roughness. Villard's paragraph showed a natural bias.

The varieties of bias growing out of a general subjective state of the witness, like that given to John Quincy Adams by his Yankee-Congregationalist-Federalist training, that given to Polk by Expansionist Democracy, and that given to Villard by nurture in a refined Bavarian home, are obviously endless. No greater error can be made in historical study than to regard man as primarily a rational being; he is primarily an emotional being, and even when he is

most rational his thinking processes are insensibly colored
by subjective feeling. Everyone recognizes the five or six
principal sentiments which dominate men: racial feeling,
national feeling, local feeling, political feeling, religious or
sectarian feeling, class feeling, professional or vocational
feeling, and the feeling of attachment to particular codes
of morals. These are universally recognized because everyone responds to one or more of them, and because everyone perceives that their intensity frequently amounts to
passion. But less prominent emotions, less important
sources of bias, must also be considered. The ordinary person who looks critically into his own tenets, or scrutinizes
closely those of his associates, will find that they arise not
so much from a cold examination of facts as from aggre-
gates of sympathy and antipathy. Few men even try systematically to prevent the growth of irrational likes or
dislikes of certain doctrines, institutions, ideas, and organizations, while those who do try never quite succeed. A
set of convictions, which many will even call principles, is
gradually evolved in harmony with these sympathies and
antagonisms; and almost every man who looks into his
own bosom must admit that his attitude toward every new
public and private issue is determined by the mass of these
convictions. It is the resultant, that is, of an immense number of forces, some rational, some emotional, but as a
whole shot through with bias. It is because of the multitudinous biases of environment that men vary so widely—
that

> . . . the wildest dreams of Kew
> Are the facts of far Peru
> And the crimes of Clapham chaste in Martaban.

One of the ablest treatments of bias in relation to historical evidence is still that given in Herbert Spencer's
Study of Sociology. He shows how profound a bias is imparted to all civilized mankind by education; an education, he remarks, still curiously divided between those who
teach doctrines of amity as exemplified by the New Testament, and doctrines of enmity as illustrated by the Greek
and Latin epics and the nationalistic histories. It is the

bias given by this latter education which makes men over-
estimate belligerency, "pluck," and "personal honor," a bias
evident in a thousand bits of historical material. He shows
just how deep is the bias inculcated also by patriotic teachings, leading even to such silly extremes as the American
assertion, "Our country, right or wrong." This bias is a
form of egoism, and though emancipation from personal
and national interests is essential to a balanced judgment
of current transactions and events, it is almost impossible to
attain. There exists also an anti-patriotic bias. This may
originate in an honest reaction against chauvinism and
exaggerated patriotism, or it may spring from a desire to
be thought original and emancipated. The man who is
sure that all our American wars were just and noble, and
the man who is certain that our dominant motives for entering the Mexican, Spanish, and World Wars were mean,
selfish, and materialistic, are equally guilty of bias—or, if
the element of insincerity enters, of cant. As a super-patri-
otic bias informs much of whatever evidence the Hearst
papers and the *Chicago Tribune* may present on recent
American history, an anti-nationalistic bias equally informs much of the evidence presented by the *New Republic* and *Nation*. It is valuable as a corrective, but it is
bias none the less.[10]

Class bias and professional bias are also far more pervasive than their victims like to admit. They too are essentially a reflex egoism; they possess their uses as well as
abuses, but they must be allowed for in any judicial estimate of historical evidence. The economist David A.
Wells, who in the generation after the Civil War was employed by great corporations and died worth $600,000,
held that the income tax was beautiful in theory but would
never work in practice in the United States. Was his testimony on the subject unconsciously biased? The great
majority of American businessmen from 1870 to 1933 held
that no abuses existed which really demanded Federal
regulation of business; while large bodies of American
farmers and workingmen held during this period that
grave and widespread abuses required firm intervention,
and even such drastic measures as government acquisition

of railroads and telegraphs. Again, in Herbert Hoover's record of his own administration, what allowance would have to be made for the professional bias given him by his long career as engineer? Since that training had made him definitely hostile to governmental action in the field of industry, a large allowance would be imperative. Still again, the class bias, almost a caste bias, evident in Henry Adams's autobiography and Emma Goldman's memoirs, no one could mistake; but there is a definite bias also in much middle-class writing which cannot be weighed save with delicate balances.

The racial bias is equally evident and is familiar to all Americans. No one can examine the various eulogistic histories of what the Germans, Irish, Scandinavians, Italians, Czechs, and other races have contributed to American life without feeling that the sum of the parts far exceeds the whole. No student would accept Cole Blease's estimate of Negro achievement, or W. E. B. Du Bois's estimate of poor-white achievement. Theological bias is even more conspicuously an ingredient of everyday life and its records; while almost equally potent is the anti-theological bias of many individuals—their reaction against extreme religious dogmatism. The bias of a Catholic may foster ideas hostile to Protestant morality and Protestant institutions. An equal injustice characterizes many Protestant records bearing upon Catholic institutions and practices; while there are many written records which illustrate the tendency of agnostics and Marxians to depreciate the service done by all creeds and churches to society.

In dealing with all the innumerable kinds of biased evidence, the student must discipline himself to a scientific attitude. To do this he must not merely be on his guard against crass misstatements, obvious prejudices, and witnesses of the any-stigma-to-beat-a-dogma school. He must above all form an analytical habit of mind. He must realize that the causation of social phenomena in past history, as in present-day affairs, is not simple but complex, and is not merely complex but marked by continuity and contingency. Realizing this, he will be prepared to discard or discount all partial views of causation.

The clearest mark of the biased witness is his desire to oversimplify historical events; to distort them by giving excessive emphasis to some single factor. The Pennsylvania protectionists long shouted that the agitation for a low tariff was financed by British interests eager to sell their goods, and that Cobden Club gold flowed steadily into the United States. The Populists declared that Cleveland defended the gold standard because he was controlled by Wall Street. A host of radicals have proclaimed that the United States went to war in 1917 to save its munitions trade, its loans to the Allies, and the commissions paid to J. P. Morgan & Co.—though the munitions trade had flourished under neutrality, though practically all the Anglo-French borrowings were secured by American and other neutral securities with a market value one-fifth greater than the loans, and though one of the first results of American entry into the war was Morgan's withdrawal from the Allied agency. Herbert Spencer writes, with some force, that nothing conduces more clearly to a comprehension of the fact that causation in this world has almost never been simple, but multiple and complex, than a study of the natural sciences:

Every organism, if we read the lesson it gives, shows us continuity of causation and complexity of causation. The ordinary facts of inheritance illustrate continuity of causation—very conspicuously where varieties so distinct as the Negro and white are united, and where traces of the Negro come out generation after generation; and still better among domestic animals, where traits of remote ancestry show the persistent working of causes which date far back. Organic phenomena make us familiar with complexity of causation, both by showing the cooperation of many antecedents to one consequent, and by showing the multiplicity of results which each influence works out. If we observe how a given weight of a given drug produces on no two persons exactly like effects, and produces even on the same person different effects in different constitutional states, we see at once how involved is the combination of factors by which the changes in an organism are brought about, and how extremely contingent, therefore, is each particular change.[11]

VI

In short, the scrutiny of all types of historical evidence should be conducted as critically and searchingly as the scrutiny of evidence in the best courts; with these vital differences, that not being bound by legal rules, we may search much more widely for relevant facts, and our combination of analysis and synthesis in weighing them can be more scientific in temper than the deliberations of most judges and juries. A few general maxims may be laid down. All the witnesses available must be summoned. Mere hearsay testimony must be given a low valuation—the word of one observer who was on the spot is worth that of ten who talked with somebody who was there. The freshness of evidence should always be considered; a witness who testifies at seventy-seven to what happened when he was twenty, as Jefferson did in his *Anas,* must be heard with doubt. All witnesses should be cross-examined for evidence of bias, and even the most honest witnesses must often be heard with reservations on this score. Circumstantial evidence of a purely superficial character must be counted inferior to direct evidence, and its deceptive possibilities explored—for it is only in very limited situations that circumstantial evidence can be conclusive.

Above all, the student of historical evidence will find an ark of safety in the collection of all possible scraps of relevant testimony. He should hunt in every nook and cranny for corroboration—or, what is equally valuable, contradiction. He should lay documents side by side in an effort to find discrepancies and disparities. It is amazing how often the whole truth can be disengaged only from two half-truths. In any complicated transaction, one witness is likely to see but one side of the event, another witness the opposite side. A brief reading of Congressional or Parliamentary debates will impress upon the student the fact that the half-truth may be extremely plausible. The Con-

servative will present an argument, involving a long train
of facts, which seems utterly convincing. A moment later
the Liberal will rise, and treating precisely the same facts,
present them in an entirely different light which nevertheless also seems momentarily convincing. It is frequently
only by a direct conflict that the truth can be established.

Even in simple historical events, where observation as
distinguished from interpretation is alone important, it is
often vital to find corroboration. If a witness testifies that
General Joseph Hooker was drunk at Chancellorsville, and
Hooker denies it, asserting that he was merely stunned by
a cannonball which struck the house-pillar against which
he was leaning, judgment must be suspended until fuller
evidence is found. (In this instance Hooker has been ex-
onerated.) A few documents, a few extracts from memoirs,
letters, and newspapers knitted adroitly together do not
constitute history; history is the measure of sound grain
sifted by rigorous criticism from the straw and chaff of
good, bad, and indifferent testimony.

VIII

Problems in History

THE AMATEUR FASHION of looking at history is to regard
it as a simple array of generally undisputed facts. Many
readers do not understand why a historical expert, who
presumably has the means of ascertaining these facts, cannot present them in a treatise which defies criticism. The
ordinary inquirer wishes an absolutely impregnable account of the causes of the Crimean War, for example, or
the character of Bismarck, or the Battle of Jutland, and
expects the historian to furnish it much as industry will
furnish five pounds of sugar on demand. In this spirit naïve
people are constantly demanding of librarians: "Give me
a book that contains the precise truth about Henry VIII's
struggle with the Pope," or "Find me a volume that explains just why we got into the Mexican War." In their
opinion, the whole truth about Henry VIII and the dissolution of the monasteries, or about Polk and the declaration
of war upon Mexico, are substances which the historian
may search out, put up in neat packages, and sell to the
public. The history of any definite part of the past is a
bundle of scientific facts which can be packed into a
standard work.

Of course many historical facts are sufficiently indisputable to be the property of standard books of reference,
but amateurs are usually shocked when told that these are
merely the skeleton of history. Any reader satisfied with

them is satisfied with a valley of dry bones. The entire vitality and interest of history depend upon the fact that universally acceptable summaries are impossible. The general reader who hastily inquires, "What were the real causes of the American Revolution?" must be told that apart from certain obvious factors, students have not yet agreed upon the subject, that great doubt envelops it, and that historians can only present a number of varying theories, each supported by more or less plausible evidence. If the amateur persists, he learns that it is only on the most limited and precise topics that a "definitive" history is possible.

Someone may produce a standard history of the land-system of medieval Yorkshire, or the tax-budgets of Chicago. But any subject of genuine scope and complexity, interwoven with the growth of society, defies final treatment. When readers ask for the definitive history of the French Revolution, they find that such a work is impossible; that we shall never have anything but a violently controversial literature upon that upheaval. They may be told by a Democratic free-trader that Dr. F. W. Taussig's history of the tariff is a standard treatise, but a Republican protectionist will immediately declare that it is a bundle of lies and that Edward Stanwood's tariff history is alone dependable. They will learn that it is almost impossible to write a thorough history of the Protestant Reformation, the Italian struggle for national unity, or the origins of the First World War, which does not make half of the scholars boil while it pleases the other half.[1]

Hereupon the disgusted amateur may give up history in chagrin, declaring that historians are charlatans and incompetents, or he may conclude that since it is useless to try to ascertain the final truth, he will read only the type of history that pleases him. It would be as reasonable to give up the study of current affairs because men disagree violently upon the truth of important issues. In this sense Freeman was right in asserting an identity between past history and present politics. As for reading only what history pleases our prejudices, it is the surest means of confirming ourselves in error. Catholics should read Protestant history, and Protestants read Catholic history; radicals would do well to read conservative history, and vice versa. But it is best of all to read writers who are sufficiently objective to point out errors by every historical group, Catholic or Protestant, conservative or radical.

I

The most important part of history is clearly a series of problems, and more than half of the historian's work is to make a statement of attempted solutions. Obviously a great part of these problems can never be settled. Some are insoluble because they are too vast and complex—the problem of the causes of the fall of the Roman Empire, for example. Others are insoluble because of the loss or suppression of historical evidence. We shall never know whether the visit of the high Jesuit official Francis Borgia to the French court just before St. Bartholomew's had any connection with the massacre, for the evidence has been destroyed. We shall never penetrate many another secret for the same reason. Still other problems are insoluble because they involve psychological motives of extreme difficulty. What was the nature of Burr's conspiracy? Was it a conspiracy against the United States or against Spain? Claude G. Bowers and Thomas Perkins Abernethy declare that it was treason, but Walter F. McCaleb has written a monograph to prove that it was not. In the last analysis, the answer rests upon what was in Burr's mind in 1804–6. How much real danger existed in August 1862, that the British Ministry would recognize the Confederacy? In the last analysis, the answer rests upon what was in Palmerston's mind. Still more completely insoluble are those problems which involve the psychology of whole peoples. Why did the people of the Lower South determine upon secession in 1861? It is always difficult to say what public opinion is, and it is certainly impossible to produce any clear determinant of social psychology—to say what was dominant in the mind of millions of people at a given hour.

The array of unsolved if not insoluble problems is innumerable; and indeed it is their endless variety, their constant challenge to fresh research, their changing aspects as time throws them into new perspective, which makes history so fascinating. We meet problems of time: What are the true dates for those of semi-mythical character in the Anglo-Saxon calendar? When did the desire for independence take firm root in the American colonies? We have problems of identity: Are present-day Armenians the descendants of the ancient Hittites? Who was King Arthur? There are problems of character and personality, like that met by Paul Van Dyke's study of Catherine de' Medici, or Garrett Mattingly's fascinating book on Katherine of Aragon. There are problems of motive: for example, the analysis by George Otto Trevelyan of General Howe's reasons for not going to the aid of Burgoyne, or the sifting by M. Coquelle of Napoleon's reasons for breaking up the Peace of Amiens. There are problems in the origin of ideas —such as Charles A. Beard's argument upon the economic roots of ideas written into the American Constitution, and John N. Figgis's discussion of the divine right of kings. There are problems of place: Where is the battlefield of Bannockburn? Just how far east did Alexander the Great penetrate toward India? We encounter problems of specific cause: Compare Tenney Frank's view of the reasons why Carthage entered upon the First Punic War with Ferrero's view. We face problems as minute as the unanswered question whether Swift married Stella, and as broad as the inquiry into the effect of the moving frontier upon the mind of the American people.

The solution of highly limited problems being usually assigned to monographs or articles, historical periodicals specialize in them; anyone who examines the reviews now devoted to history in most important countries will see that they are largely devoted not to portraits, descriptions, or narratives, but to resolving old problems. They publish fresh material to furnish a new solution, or fresh interpretations of old material. A student of history cannot better learn how single problems are attacked, elucidated, and at least provisionally solved than by reading those reviews which most interest him. He can choose from the *American*

Historical Review, the *Journal of Modern History*, *Speculum*, the *Mississippi Valley Historical Review*, *Southern History*, the *English Historical Review*, *History*, the *Scottish Historical Review*, the *Canadian Historical Review*, and many in foreign languages. In *History*, the organ of the English Historical Association, there long appeared a series called "Historical Revisions," dealing with topics which demanded a fresh attack. It must be said that most monographic literature is lacking in literary quality, and a good deal of it neglects the pluralism of historical causation. Nevertheless, brilliant exceptions can be found. No less striking a work than Parkman's *Conspiracy of Pontiac* is a monograph written to solve a single problem of American history.[2]

In extended histories the solution of problems is necessarily, and properly, combined with much general and noncontroversial matter; with descriptions of places, miniatures of persons, and accounts of occurrences accepted by all. A flowing narrative like Macaulay's or Froude's thus merges the solution of successive problems, almost imperceptively, with the whole graphic tale. Yet some comprehensive histories resolve themselves, upon close examination, into a clear succession of problems freshly restated, freshly attacked, and freshly resettled.

Conspicuous in the list is Edward Channing's six-volume history of the United States, written largely as a product of his seminars. If we examine his sixth volume, covering the years 1850–65, we perceive that, making no attempt at a full narrative, it omits much that ordinary readers expect to find in a history of these crowded fifteen years, but that what it does contain is largely novel. Leaving out the familiar story of Congressional battles, foreign difficulties, and Civil War campaigns, it attacks distinct questions as if no historian had ever dealt with them before. Was slavery a profitable institution? What was its real strength, its real weakness? Was it true that the South had no manufacturing and no immigration? What effect had the low price of cotton in 1848–50 upon the Compromise of 1850? How many advocates of that Compromise saw that if secession could be postponed, the North would soon outstrip the South in manpower and material resources and so attain control of the situation? How many fugitive slaves actually crossed the border? What were the true reasons of the South for secession? How many Northerners wished to resist secession by force of arms? During the war, what was the relative importance of Southern cotton and Northern wheat to Great Britain? What changes were effected in Northern commerce by the closing of the Mississippi and the Southern railways? Why did the Confederacy gain such a start on the North in organizing and equipping its armies? How did conscription actually work in the South?

It is plain that in writing his history, Channing put to himself one searching interrogation after another. He avoided a rehearsal of the firing on Fort Sumter, the Trent affair, Pickett's charge at Gettysburg, and other oft-told tales; he was searching for new light, and found it by treating the period as a series of great new problems. No critic would call Channing's history an ideal work. It is addressed too much to the specialist and too little to the lay reader; it lacks continuity, symmetry, and completeness; and the succession of problems gives it a jerkiness that is inimical to literary finish. At the same time, it illustrates the means by which the best historians attain penetration and originality. The ability of the writer to ask himself the most important and revealing questions, and to ask them constantly, is indispensable to the attainment of reach or depth in his work.

As the spirit of doubt, of scientific criticism, is the beginning of wisdom in historical study, nothing must be taken for granted and everything subjected to strict rules of evidence. It is a simple further step to say that in the practical study of history, the primary requirement is that it be dealt with as a set of problems. If it is treated merely as an entertaining story, a theme for picturesque narrative or well-colored description, the student slips over its surface. The way to penetrate beneath the pretty superficialities and come to grips with historical realities is to propound one incisive question after another, until the past ceases to look like a smooth record and becomes instead a rough and puzzling set of difficulties. It would be too much to say that a good course of historical study is a series of headaches, but that element certainly enters into all true history. When the puzzling problems have been identified and correctly stated, then and then only can profitable study be begun. Obviously, the march of historical writing thus becomes more and more a march of specialization. In some recent periods of history as yet little treated, a broad narrative can have freshness and originality; in the more thoroughly searched epochs of the past, originality can be attained only by bold new generalizations, or by the minute re-examination of monographic topics. It was possible for Frederick Lewis Allen to write *Only Yesterday* on the history of the preceding decade (1920–30) without taking up a single problem. But he who wishes to produce a fresh work on the Civil War period will have to do it in different terms.

In what terms? Only, as we have said, by the use of searching new generalizations or by minute re-examination of special topics, or a combination of both. The history of the French Revolution was first written from a political standpoint, by writers who were immersed in the politics of their own time and treated the revolutionary events in a way which harmonized with their views of contemporaneous affairs. Thus Thiers, Mignet, Lamartine, Louis Blanc, and Taine dealt with the Revolution. Then came François V. A. Aulard, who discussed the subject from an austerely scientific point of view, emphasizing the careful use of original sources, and thus lifted the examination of the great convulsion to a new plane. Before he retired from the Sorbonne in 1922 a vast library of historical work on the Revolution had accumulated, and apparently little new remained to be said on it. Nevertheless, two men, Jean Jaurés and Albert Mathiez, did succeed in saying something quite new. Under the partial inspiration of Tocqueville and Taine, they set a fresh new wind blowing through the record of developments 1785–95: the wind of socioeconomic inquiry and interpretation. The result was refreshing and salutary. Old problems appeared in a new light under their sweeping generalizations, and new tools could be used for their solution.

Meanwhile, more limited studies executed with new ideas and minute care showed that the solution of special problems could invigorate the whole field of study. Georges Lebfevre, for example, carried out a thorough study of the peasant life in a single area near Paris, and M. Labrousse ably analyzed economic conditions in France just before the storm broke.[3]

Problems Solved

II

But once a problem is isolated and stated, what is the best method of bringing evidence to bear upon it? Suppose a historian to have set himself the task of writing upon the Franco-Prussian War. He intends to make it something more than a mere narrative of what everyone already knows about the Spanish succession, the Ems telegram, Gravelotte, Sedan, and the siege of Paris; he means to bring out fresh ideas, and facts marshaled from original points of view. He may attack the problem: Was Napoleon III really afraid of a revolutionary movement in France, and convinced he must re-establish his prestige by a successful war? Or the problem: How much did Eugénie and her religious advisers have to do with precipitating the conflict? Or the problem: Was French unpreparedness due to defective administration, to overconfidence, or to corruption?

The method of dealing with such problems involves distinct rules. These, broadly stated, are three. The writer must collect all the evidence that he can find; he must make sure that he has every pertinent fact available, not merely part of the pertinent facts. He must then classify the evidence and examine it according to the inductive method—which for this stage is the only method open to the historian, and was indeed called by John Stuart Mill the historical method. In other words, as men would say in looser terms, he must analyze it. Next, in this inductive scrutiny the writer will often find that the facts point to one or several hypotheses as likely to afford a solution. He will then formulate the most satisfactory hypothesis, examine all the evidence anew in the light it offers, and test it carefully. Thus he should proceed until he finds a hypothesis, or a combination of several hypotheses, which fits the facts and explains the historical result. Finally, having established his grand cause (or, as in nine instances out of ten, his multiple causation), he will state his proof in the strongest manner possible, or if he is reluctant to load his pages with proofs, at least indicate where they may be found.[4]

The importance of assembling *all* the pertinent facts upon a given situation is not often fully realized by the amateur student of history. It means a tiresome multiplication of details, he will say; some process of selection is necessary anyhow; why not be content with enough facts to support a previously determined formula? We decide by a rapid preliminary survey that Roosevelt broke with Taft in 1911 because he wanted a third term in 1912; how much easier just to pick out enough facts to prove it! A vast deal of so-called history is indeed written in that fashion. It is always easier to write, usually easier to read, and open to only one objection—it generally misses the truth. By a one-sided choice of details almost anything can be proved. But the dangers of partisan selection have been forcibly stated by Froude in his essay on the dissolution of the English monasteries:

> We can conceive a description of England during the year which has just passed over us [1856], true in all its details, containing no one statement which can be challenged, no single exaggeration which can be proved; and this description, if given without the correcting traits, shall make ages to come marvel why the Cities of the Plain were destroyed, and England was allowed to survive. The frauds of trusted men, high in power and high in supposed religion; the wholesale poisonings; the robberies; the adulteration of foods—nay, of almost everything exposed for sale; the cruel usage of women; children murdered for the burial fees; life and property insecure in open day in the open streets; splendor such as the world never saw before upon earth, with vice and squalor crouching under its walls;—let all this be

written down by an enemy, or let it be ascertained hereafter by the investigation of a posterity which desires to judge us as we generally have judged our forefathers, and few years will show darker in the English annals than the year which we have just left behind us. Yet we know, in the honesty of our hearts, how unjust such a picture would be. Our future advocate, if we are so happy as to find one, may not be able to disprove a single article in the indictment; and yet we know that, as the world goes, he will be right if he marks the year with a white stone—as one in which, on the whole, the moral harvest was better than the average.[5]

To go into the technicalities of logic—of induction and deduction—in reference to history would be a barren labor. It is sufficient to say that historians generally accept the statement that the cause of any occurrence lies in one or more preceding events without which the occurrence would not have taken place. Both causes and effects in history are always events; not brute static things, but things in action. To find the complete cause of a given event we should have to ascertain all the indispensable previous events, running back to pre-history. But since human inquiry has to be confined within limits, it is sufficient to attempt to catalogue all those events which may have a clearly demonstrable and significant connection with the occurrence under discussion. Having made a comprehensive enumeration of what seem the significant factors, the writer must choose between those which are important and those which are unimportant. He is in the position, to use a rough analogy, of a mathematician who is given the number 15 and told that it is the sum of four other numbers, of which one is 3. By assembling his data the mathematician knows that the other three may be 1, 7, and 4; or 2, 5, and 5; or 3, 5, and 4; or various other combinations. But if he can find proof somewhere that the second number is 6, that at once limits the number of unknown elements. If he can find additional proof that the third number is 2, then he can at once state what is the fourth number.

For the purposes of history, the laws of induction as long ago formulated by John Stuart Mill really have some utility. Suppose the problem is the cause of the extreme savagery of the Reign of Terror in France. Suppose the writer has collected all the data bearing on the role of violence in the English, American, French, and Russian Revolutions. It is not difficult then to discover the value of Mill's five rules for scientific inferences by induction. The first canon reads: "If two or more instances of the phenomenon under investigation have only one circumstance in common, the circumstance in which alone all the instances agree is the cause of the given phenomenon." The second asserts: "If an instance in which the phenomenon under investigation occurs, and an instance in which it does not occur, have every circumstance in common save one, that one occurring only in the former, the circumstance in which alone the two instances differ is the cause, or an indispensable part of the cause, of the phenomenon." The third canon continues: "If two or more instances in which the phenomenon occurs have only one circumstance in common, while two or more instances in which it does not occur have nothing in common save the absence of that circumstance, the circumstance in which alone the two sets of instances differ is the cause, or an indispensable part of the cause, of the phenomenon." We proceed to the fourth canon, the most useful of all to historians: "Subduct from any phenomenon such part as is known by previous inductions to be the effect of certain antecedents, and the residue of the phenomenon is the effect of the remaining antecedents." But the fifth canon is almost as important: "Whatever phenomenon varies in any manner wherever another phenomenon varies in some particular manner is . . . . connected with that phenomenon through some fact of causation."

Many brilliant examples of inductive reasoning have been furnished by the exact sciences. We may take, for example, the memorable discovery of the planet Neptune without a telescope. Certain perturbations had been observed in the orbit of the planet Uranus, constituting an effect which puzzled astronomers. All the facts bearing on the subject—that is, all the actions of the other known bodies upon Uranus—were collected and weighed. They left it certain that some additional cause was required to explain Uranus's eccentricities. J. C. Adams in England and U. J. J. Leverrier in France made the inference that this was some hitherto unobserved planet, and mathematically determined its position and pull. Other astronomers, turning their telescopes to the quarter indicated, then found Neptune within one degree of the spot indicated. Just so, in history, many a brilliant surmise—an inductive inference—from known facts which seem only partially to account for a cause, has been proved valid by fuller investigation. The surmise that Cleveland's rash action in the Pullman strike of 1894, so unlike his usual deliberation and balance, was due to Olney's misrepresentation of the situation, has been amply proved from Cleveland's and Olney's papers.

III

But historical problems never present themselves as neat logical exercises. Almost every historical puzzle has to be solved in part, and often wholly, by methods peculiar to itself. In determining antecedence and consequence, most historians proceed by plain common sense, not by the rules of logic. However, one general method, the use of the working hypothesis to select what is pertinent and reject what is irrelevant in explaining an historical event, is of overriding importance. The hypothesis is a key that "may" fit a complicated lock; a pattern that "may" assemble in their just relations the scattered parts of a jigsaw puzzle. No sound historical work has ever been written which does not employ hypotheses liberally to arrive at the explanation of complex occurrences. Ordinarily this use is carefully concealed, but sometimes it is exhibited to impress the reader, or to cut off objections.

An illuminating illustration is afforded by some pages late in Channing's treatment of the Civil War. In his sixth

volume he attacks the question, Why did the Confederacy
collapse in April 1865?—a problem interesting in its analogy
with the German collapse in 1918. The Southern organization broke down, he remarks, with a speed and completeness that were entirely unexpected, and that are not easy
to understand. Having assembled all the available evidence upon this collapse, he has subjected it to inductive
examination to reach the proper inference. After classifying his evidence, he has formulated various hypotheses
and tested each one exhaustively. Did the breakdown result from the military defeat of the Confederacy? This
hypothesis was long accepted as satisfactory, but he rejects it as untrue. The Confederacy in April 1865 was not
yet beaten in the field. Lee still had some 30,000 men,
Joseph E. Johnston nearly 30,000, and Kirby Smith, west
of the Mississippi, about 25,000; while scattered throughout the Lower South were smaller commands. All in all,
when Lee evacuated Richmond, between 150,000 and
200,000 Confederate soldiers were still under arms and
ready to fight. Such a force, says Channing, might have
kept up a guerrilla warfare for years. Breaking into small
detachments like the Revolutionary partisans under Mar-
ion and Sumter, or like the Boers in 1900, they might
have fought on until the North was worn out; Texas alone
might have resisted indefinitely. President Jefferson Davis
held this opinion. At a conference with Breckinridge and
Johnston at Greensboro, North Carolina, in April 1865, he
urged them to keep up the struggle, as a little later he
urged Breckinridge and Bragg at Abbeville, South Carolina. "Judging from the history of other wars and other
revolutions," writes Channing, "the end had not come and
was not even in sight had the Southern people, or the mass
of the people of the seceded States, wished to continue
the fight for Southern independence."

A second hypothesis is that the collapse was caused
by a dearth of military supplies. According to this view,
the blockade so completely stopped imports, and invasion
so completely paralyzed various centers of supply, that
the Southern armies were without essential equipment and
fighting became hopeless. Until the end of 1863 the Con-

federacy had relied almost wholly upon French and British arms, and now these were cut off. But after examining this hypothesis, Channing asserts that it is empty. The Southern ordnance service, directed by General Josiah Gorgas, had established a number of effective manufactories of war material. Large arsenals had been organized, a superb powder mill had been established, a cannon foundry had been set up at Macon, and other works were scattered throughout the South. Many English mechanics of ability had been imported. Gorgas wrote in 1864 that he had succeeded beyond his brightest expectations in accelerating the production of powder and arms. "If anyone has doubts," writes Dr. Channing, "as to the capacity of the South to continue warfare in April 1865, so far as war materials are concerned, he has only to read Gorgas's accounts to satisfy himself that it was not any dearth of material that brought about the ending in the spring of 1865."

A third hypothesis would explain the defeat of the Confederacy by the starving condition of the Confederate soldiers and people in April 1865. "Those twin monsters, hunger and malnutrition," Southerners have said, "forced our gates." But Channing attempts to show that the high prices which people in Richmond and other cities seemed to pay for provisions in the spring of 1865 were not really high; that measured in gold instead of the superabundant paper, flour was actually cheaper in Richmond than in New York. The Southern food crops of 1863 and 1864 had been excellent, cereals being abundant, while bacon was run through the blockade in quantity until the latter part of 1864. Official reports on April 1, 1865, showed in Richmond 300,000 rations of bread and meat; at Danville, Virginia, 500,000 rations of bread and 1,500,000 of meat; at Lynchburg, Virginia, and Greensboro, North Carolina, 1,680,000 more rations of bread and meat. In February 1865, Joseph E. Johnston held stored between Weldon and Danville sufficient rations to supply 60,000 men for more than four months. A Confederate leader, J. L. M. Curry, states that at the close of the war enough corn was available along the transportation routes between

Jackson, Mississippi, and Montgomery, Alabama, to furnish the Confederate forces with breadstuffs for a year or more.

There remains another hypothesis to account for the Confederate collapse: the disintegration of Southern morale, the seizure of the people by a despair which sapped their energies. Dr. Channing, after weighing all the evidence, adopts this as the hypothesis which best fits the facts. "It is evident to the under-surface seeker," he writes, "that by the summer of 1864, and even more so by December of that year, the will to fight had gone from large sections of the Southern people." What is his evidence? He quotes from the diaries or letters of such representative Southerners as Howell Cobb, Benjamin H. Hill, and Secretary of War James A. Seddon. He points to the alarming number of resignations of officers from Lee's own army, indicating a loss of hope; on January 18, 1865, and again on March 9, the Confederate Adjutant General issued a list of 1200 officers whose resignations had been accepted by President Davis. As additional evidence, he notes the enormous amount of absenteeism and desertion from the ranks. In September 1864, President Davis wrote despondently that two thirds of the troops were absent; some sick, some wounded, some on leave, but most of them gone without leave. On December 31, 1864, field records for Hagood's brigade of South Carolinians showed 1592 present for duty, and 2011 absent. General Hardee had marched out of Charleston in 1864 with more than 10,000 troops, and had reached the North Carolina line with only 4000, straggling and desertion accounting for the remainder. Many Southern communities were filled with deserters and fugitives. The Confederate authorities in the winter of 1864–65 complained that they were intercepting many letters from families urging soldiers to desert. Finally, as telling evidence, Channing notes the way in which the South recoiled from its terrible losses in the Wilderness and other battles late in 1864. The conclusion Channing reaches is not satisfactory; it evades the question, Why did morale collapse? But the method is interesting.

Channing's treatment of this problem differs from most

historical expositions in that he places his rejected hypotheses as well as accepted explanations upon paper. In general, the historian is content, having found what he believes the correct key to an historical event, to state it and assemble his facts in support of it. History would become intolerably prolix and confusing if the rejected planks, shavings, and splinters of the historian's workshop were not carted out of sight, leaving only the finished product. The more literary polish, in general, the greater the economy, and the less the evidence of labor. E. P. Cheyney, in his long scholarly account of the relations of Queen Elizabeth, the Earl of Essex, and Francis Bacon, includes hypotheses, arguments, and details of a kind which Lytton Strachey in his work *Elizabeth and Essex* thought it wisest to omit, with the result that Strachey's account, while nearly as good history as Cheyney's, is immeasurably superior as literature. But, though concealed, in all ambitious historical works hypotheses have been used; they have been fully examined, all but one or several rejected, and the latter alone presented to the reader.

IV

The principal dangers in the use of hypothesis are three. The first and most frequent is the temptation to let bias, or prejudice, or what we fondly call "conviction," supply a ready hypothesis which we abstain from testing rigorously. Such is the "devil theory" of war. War is made by militarists and autocrats—so millions of Americans believed in 1914. War is made by wicked munitions interests allied with greedy bankers—so a group of radical writers upon America's entry into the First World War later wished men to believe. The hypothesis that American prosperity had been caused by a high protective tariff was asserted by some Republican historians in the eighties and nineties, and Senator Watson declared just before the Smoot-Hawley Tariff passed in 1930 that this law would restore our impaired prosperity within a month. The cold fact was that the Smoot-Hawley Tariff signalized (no true historian would say it caused) the most complete collapse of prosperity in American annals. For these biased hypotheses it is always possible to supply some evidence, though never enough to satisfy scientific minds. Herbert Spencer touches on this common misuse of hypothesis. He writes that a striking example of the effect of a too cherished hypothesis in vitiating evidence was once unconsciously yielded to him by an enthusiast for sanitary laws:

> Producing his papers, he pointed out the great contrast between the number of deaths per annum in the small town near London where he lived, and the number of deaths per annum in a low district of London—Bermondsey, or Lambeth, or some region on the Surrey side. On this great contrast he triumphantly dilated, as proving how much could be done by good drainage, ventilation, and so on. On the one hand, he passed over the fact that his suburban place was, in large measure, inhabited by a picked population—people of means, well fed and clothed, able to secure all appliances for comfort, leading regular lives, free from overwork and anxiety. On the other hand, he passed over the fact that this low region of London was, by virtue of its lowness, one out of which all citizens pecuniarily able to take care of themselves escaped if they could, and into which were thrust great numbers whose poverty excluded them from better regions—the ill-fed, the drunken, the dissolute, and others on the highway to death. Though, in the first place, the healthiness of the locality obviously drew to it an excess of persons likely to live long; and though, in the second case, the unhealthiness of the locality made it one in which an excess of those not likely to live long were left to dwell, or to hide themselves to die; yet the whole difference was put down to direct effects of pure air and impure air respectively.[6]

A second danger in the use of hypothesis lies in the temptation toward oversimplification. Channing's explanation of the sudden collapse of the Confederacy as attributable to loss of morale is beyond question an oversimplification. He overlooks the fact that it may have been, and probably was, a conjunction of all the elements he has

named—dispersion and defeat of armies, scarcity of munitions, shortage of food, and weariness of the long butch-
ery—which brought about the surrender. He underempha-
sizes the fact, pointed out by Charles Francis Adams in
Lee at Appomattox and Other Essays, that the alternative
of prolonged guerrilla warfare, which he thinks was not
considered because of the breakdown of morale, was
weighed by the Confederate high command and rejected
for humanitarian and patriotic reasons. He entirely overlooks one highly important element, the collapse of transportation. Altogether Channing attributes too much to a
single factor in a complex situation.

Various writers who are more fertile in brilliant ideas
than inclined to the drudgery of testing them thoroughly
offer many examples of this oversimplification. Thus James
Truslow Adams's stimulating volume, *The Epic of America,*
which states many problems admirably, and gives many
penetrating answers, sometimes falls short of the "entire"
truth. What was the central motive of European emigration to America? asks Mr. Adams. It was not religious, not
political, but economic and social—to establish better
homes, and gain a better living. But was this all? What
was the origin of American lawlessness? he asks again. It
was the fact that the colonists had to obey laws made
3000 miles away; that the regulations of a distant overseas power governed their use of land, forest, minerals,
the development of their manufactures, trade, and marine,
and even their church relations. Once more, was this all?
Were they not lawless as to the statutes of their own assemblies and even the sentiment of their own communities?
Did the Scotch-Irish of the Pennsylvania frontier obey the
Quaker legislature? Again, Mr. Adams asks why Americans are so self-confident and optimistic. He explains their
attitude by two hypotheses. It was because the simplicity
of life on the frontier, without complications, bred an un-
worried outlook; and because success in the new American environment demanded optimism and courage, so that
the quality naturally developed. But, we may ask, were
there not other factors? Selection by emigration? Wealth
of natural resources? Absence of chilling traditions? Even

the influence of climate? Mr. Adams deals with the problem of the inferiority of post-Revolutionary culture to pre-Revolutionary culture. He offers two hypotheses: the cultivated Loyalists fled elsewhere, and America moved over the mountains. But this neglects the immense war-wastage, while the second part of the answer is properly no answer at all.

As an absurdly extreme example of the assertion of a single cause against a multitude of suggested causes, we may take the statement of two collaborators, Drs. Warren and Pearson, upon the origin of the great depression of 1929–37:

> The present depression is not an act of God for the purification of men's souls. It is not a business cycle. It is not due to extravagant living. It is not due to unsound business practices. It is not due to overproduction. It is not due to too great efficiency. It is not due to lack of confidence, but it is the cause of lack of confidence.
>
> It is due to a high demand for gold following a period of low demand for gold. It teaches the devastating effect of deflation, but teaches no other lesson that is good for society.[7]

This is obviously an overstatement; to ascribe the panic and depression to the one factor of the automatic fall of the price level is as erroneous as President Roosevelt's ascription of it to the stubbornness and incompetence of "the rulers of the exchange of mankind's goods." (And Roosevelt was prudent enough to insert the word "primarily.") Presumably the paragraph written by Warren and Pearson was not meant to be taken literally, but was rather a rhetorical overstatement, designed to point out the cardinal importance of that factor.

The third danger is the tendency of excessively clever writers to reject the obvious hypothesis merely because it is obvious, and to present instead some explanation which will give them a reputation for independence, ingenuity, and subtlety. Highly original minds dislike the obvious, and realize that history which merely states it is dull and unstimulating. Hence some men continually fly to the bizarre. They explain the heroes of history by hypotheses drawn from Freudian psychology. Harvey J. O'Higgins, for example, suggested that Lincoln's place as a great humanitarian and emancipator was due in large part to the inferiority complex which he formed in early life, to his sense of belonging to a humble stratum of society. Such a perverse book as A. J. P. Taylor's *The Origins of the Second World War* (1961) is a prime example of the violence that may be done to history by a writer intent on challenging accepted views at almost any cost—at the cost of marshaling facts in a preposterously bizarre pattern.

It is illuminating to take, as an extreme instance, the treatment of one of the great facts in cultural history, the appearance of Shakespeare's plays. The old hypothesis which accounted for them was simple: William Shakespeare of Stratford and London wrote them. Most people in Shakespeare's time believed that. Ben Jonson, next in eminence among the Elizabethan dramatists, a man for whom Shakespeare obtained a first stage hearing in 1598, believed it. Edmund Spenser believed it, as his references to Shakespeare in *Colin Clout's Come Home Again* prove. The next generation in England universally believed it. John Milton, who was eight years old when Shakespeare died, did so. Indeed, for two hundred years the whole world accepted this hypothesis. Then arose Delia Bacon, a friend of Hawthorne and a woman of brilliant but eccentric parts—who finally died mad—and she found the hypothesis too obvious. She hit upon a rival explanation, that the plays had been written by a coterie numbering Lord Bacon, Sir Walter Raleigh, and one or two other distinguished men. Various students took up this preposterous hypothesis, and a whole school has arisen, numbering such sane men as Mark Twain and Carter Glass, which ascribes the plays not to Shakespeare but to Bacon, or to Edward de Vere, seventeenth Earl of Oxford, or someone else.

Just so, it is a bizarre hypothesis which attributes the fall of the Roman Empire to the spread of malaria in Italy, but it is an explanation that has been seriously advanced. It is a bizarre hypothesis which would explain

Lincoln's assassination as the result of a plot by Secretary of War Stanton, acting to ensure drastic treatment of the conquered South, but it too has been seriously advanced. (As a matter of fact, the assassins had plotted the murder of the supposedly radical Johnson as well as Lincoln.) It is a misleading hypothesis for the Protestant Reformation that it was fundamentally economic in motive, but various commentators have defended that thesis.

V

Since in nine instances out of ten, any important historical transactions should be treated as of multiple causation, its roots as numerous and far-ramifying as its consequences, the office of the historian is not to select one or two explanations, excluding or minimizing all others, but to ascertain *all* the factors and assign each its proportionate weight. Channing's explanation of the collapse of the Confederacy would have been stronger had he done that. It is clear, however, that a slight shift in the emphasis given to various factors may greatly alter the assessment of results, and that all complex events in history contain an irreducible area of uncertainty in which differences of emphasis and interpretation are unavoidable. Different minds will legitimately differ in judgment.

One of the enduring problems of modern history, beyond doubt, will be the reasons for the cancellation of Hitler's projected invasion of England in 1941. The ablest study of the subject from the German point of view is the book of Rear-Admiral Walter Ansel, USN, *Hitler Confronts England*, pronounced by the *London Times Literary Supplement* one of the most impressive of all works on the Second World War. Admiral Ansel shows in convincing detail that Hitler's Sea Lion operation, as it was mounted, would have been a disastrous failure if really launched. He shows that both Hitler's preconceptions, and those of all other high German officers, ruled out any other type of approach. The author's general conclusion, that Hitler's difficulties in this undertaking, as in some other great military thrusts, arose from his habit of confusing political

programs with strategic programs, is forcibly stated and
unquestionably true. The reviewer, however, presents certain demurs which illustrate the fact that in the apportion-
ment of emphasis on the various elements in a complicated,
mutable, hazy—and in this instance uncompleted—situation, any agreement on answers is practically impossible:

> With Sea Lion the uncertainty surrounds the problem
> of Hitler's aims and intentions. Why had he given no
> thought to the invasion project before the collapse of
> France? Why did he then decide on it? Why did he
> call it off? Why did he delay so long in doing so? Ad-
> miral Ansel's answers to these questions are founded on
> a sure assessment of Hitler's mind and on a careful
> weighing of all the factors involved; but inevitably there
> are slightly different answers available.
>
> In answer to the first question he possibly overesti-
> mates the influence of Hitler's expectations of an alliance
> with England (as he certainly does in his treatment of
> the associated problem of why Hitler halted the tanks
> that might otherwise have cut off the retreat of the
> B.E.F. from Dunkirk) and underestimates the impor-
> tance of the fact that he had no plans of any kind, in
> any direction, that looked beyond the defeat of France,
> which came about far more rapidly and completely than
> he had imagined in his wildest dreams. In answer to the
> third he possibly overestimates the influence of Hitler's
> determination to turn on Russia, while underestimating
> the extent to which Hitler probably realized from the
> beginning that Sea Lion was impracticable. . . .
>
> The problem about the decision to turn on Russia is
> not why Hitler decided to do so—it is unquestionable
> that he always intended to do so—but why he decided
> to do so when he did; and it is more likely that his
> realization that he would not get over the Channel led
> him to turn east so soon than that his wish to turn east
> took his mind and his will away from Sea Lion.[8]

Sometimes enthusiastic students of social and economic
history tend to harden a single hypothesis of broad scope
into a deterministic theory that approaches the character

of a law. For generations historians have disputed upon the causes of the rise of the medieval town in Western Europe. Various theories have been advanced. Some men have taken the view that the medieval town developed out of the free village community of the Germans. Some hold that it emerged from the manor by the conversion of manorial institutions into town institutions—that it was of servile rather than free origin. The "market law" theory suggests that the "peace" of the markets created a protected area which was detached from local feudal tribunals, and inhabited chiefly by merchants and artisans; the administration of the town gradually growing out of the administration of the market. The "immunity theory," applying principally to episcopal towns, holds that the immunity of the bishops over neighboring territory created boroughs which finally grew strong enough to establish self-government. The "garrison theory" is based on the view that a population grew up in proximity to fortified military posts which brought trade and industry in its wake and became the nucleus of the future town. Some students have traced the growth of the civil magistracy of the towns back to supposed origins in Carolingian civil administration; others regard the German guilds or fellowships as offering a possible origin for the towns.

But in late years, a large group of scholars, represented in Europe by Henri Pirenne and in the United States by Carl Stephenson, have adopted the "mercatorial" or "faubourg" hypothesis. They believe that in the ninth and tenth centuries new burghs or faubourgs came into existence outside the feudal castles or abbeys, and especially at crossroads, river fords, or other commercially advantageous places. This new burgh was essentially different from the old burghs or seats of important officials. Beyond question, the weight of opinion among recent scholars upon this important question of town origins has favored the "mercatorial" theory. But some adherents have erected it into a sweeping dogma, and overlook the fact that no absolute proof exists that the other theories are not also sound, at least for certain areas and times.

Multiple causation is obviously less dramatic than monis-

tic causation. It is always arresting to point the finger at
one cause and say, "This did it!" Moreover, when a multiplicity of causes are admitted, it is often difficult to assign
the correct weight to each, and the labors of the historian
are thus enhanced. (Of course not all the complexities
need be stated—some should be merely hinted. The best
history is like a painting by Rembrandt, casting a brilliant
light upon certain select causes, and leaving others in semi-
darkness.) Henry Adams in his *Education* has described
some of the difficulties of dealing with the tangled web of
causation. He writes that he published a dozen volumes
of history to ascertain whether, by the severest process of
stating, with the least possible comment, such facts as
seemed sure in such order as seemed strictly consequent,
he could fix a necessary sequence of human movement
during a brief period. The result disillusioned him. "Where
he saw sequence, other men saw something different, and
no one saw the same unit of measure." Nevertheless, it
will be observed that the more scientific the historian is,
the more he will lean to a multiple explanation of events,
and the deeper he goes into the subject, the surer he will
find such a course imperative. Parkman does not give a
monistic explanation of the French failure in North America, nor does James G. Randall confine himself to a few
causes for the Civil War. Since much history has recently
been rewritten by the use of new economic interpretations,
perhaps the most common fault of present-day historians
is an excessive emphasis upon economic hypotheses, and
insufficient emphasis on emotion, sentiment, and other im-
ponderables as factors in events.

In some historical situations it can be held that a rule
of human nature or a principle of sociology or economics
has almost invariable application, and can hence be given
special emphasis in interpreting events. Test oaths or
loyalty oaths have been employed so often and in so many
countries with no result but to create confusion, harass
patriotic people, and give a cloak to traitorous perjurers
that these results may be regarded as well-nigh inevitable.
Governments which fix prices at arbitrary levels, as Diocletian did in Rome, England did after the Black Death,

the military authorities in Richmond did during the Civil War, and various regimes in Europe did during the First World War, find that disobedience becomes irrepressible; economic necessities rule. When a fat lethargic society lies alongside an active hungry society, invasion becomes pretty nearly a certainty. Such broad principles of causation are the main agent in furnishing whatever pattern men can find in the past. They offer the only clear exception to the assertion by H. A. L. Fisher, in his three volumes upon Europe, that history possesses no plot, no rhythm, no predetermined design—that there can be "only one safe rule for the historian: that he should recognize in the development of human destinies the play of the contingent and unforeseen."[9] He can certainly recognize a good deal more than *that*.

It is of course evident that many historical problems are too simple in form to require use of the working hypothesis. Their answer is sometimes a flat yes or no; if not that, it is at any rate supplied directly by research. Take the problem: Were American labor trends in the nineteenth century affected by any considerable participation of wage-earners, especially during periods of discontent, in the westward movement to free lands? It is a very pretty problem. Frederick J. Turner, without thoroughly investigating the facts, assumed that the answer was "yes." He wrote in his essay on "The Significance of the Frontier": "Whenever social conditions tended to crystallize in the East, whenever capital tended to press upon labor . . . there was this gate of escape to the free conditions of the frontier. These free lands promoted individualism, economic equality, freedom to rise, democracy. Men would not accept inferior wages and a permanent position of social subordination when this promised land of freedom and equality was theirs for the taking."

But two recent students, after careful investigation, tentatively assert that the answer is "no"—that actual wage-earners made little use of the frontier as a safety-gate.[10] They qualify this conclusion by adding that so many *potential* wage-earners settled upon western land that the movement did tend "to hold up the level of industrial wages." Whichever view is right, the answer will clearly be found simply by getting at a sufficient body of facts. Indeed, a multitude of problems have to be stated in terms which show that but one, two, or at most three alternatives is possible. Was it Justice Shiras, Justice Gray, or Justice Brewer who changed his vote in the unfortunate decision of 1895 against the validity of the income tax law? We know that it could not have been another Justice. And a multitude of problems are stated in terms, again, which call simply for an assignment of special weight to one of several factors, all being recognized as present. Was the German submarine defeated in 1917 chiefly by the new British convoy system, by the depth charge and other anti-submarine devices, or by American aid in warships and merchant tonnage?

But the fact remains that just as the ability to ask the right questions, thereby raising problems, is the mark of the original historian, so the ability to suggest new hypotheses in answering them is often the mark of penetration and insight. Indeed, it is evident that the qualities chiefly required in solving historical problems are (1) industry, (2) penetration or ingenuity, (3) sound judgment, and (4) intellectual honesty. Industry is needed to assemble all the evidence, to dig out the multitude of significant facts bearing upon the problem. Penetration or ingenuity is needed to supply all the possible interpretations of the material. A commonplace mind will make but an obvious, commonplace combination of facts; a subtle and original mind, full of ideas, will make new and stimulating combinations of facts. Sound judgment is required to bar out eccentric or spurious hypotheses. And intellectual honesty is more frequently needed to enable a scholar to face the facts unflinchingly than the novice would suppose. Nothing is easier than to become enamored of a cherished hypothesis for a historical problem. But if in the end the student finds that the facts run counter to it, what then? The only honest course is to confess error, no matter how publicly he may have committed himself to his pet theory, and bend to the evidence. But that is often more easily said than done. We need only think of the reputable

American writer on the origins of the First World War who once placed himself in an untenable position by stubbornly cleaving to the story of a Potsdam conference of German leaders in July 1914, to plot the conflict, long after it was exploded.

VI

It remains to mention one special difficulty in using historical evidence and solving historical problems—the difficulty of evaluating events and figures of the far-distant past by the standards and atmosphere of their own time, not of ours. The essence of truth often depends upon giving the correct setting, material and more especially moral, to an occurrence.[11] Yet the *nunc pro tunc* fallacy crops up repeatedly in even the best writers. Though it is probably impossible ever to see events of a past age precisely as men living in that age regarded them, we can at least avoid the grosser errors of perspective.

Winston Churchill has pointed out in *The Aftermath* how natural it is to misjudge Britain's policy toward Ireland in the time of William Pitt by applying to it the canons of a later day. At present Great Britain is one of the great Powers, flanked by a firm ally in the French Republic; Ireland is a weak island of four million people divided into two states. Looking at powerful Britain and helpless Ireland, we pronounce Pitt's policy in 1798 brutal. But we forget that in 1798 England was a country of only 12,000,000 people; that on one side lay a hostile France of 20,000,000 people, and on the other a half-hostile Ireland of 6,000,000; that sandwiched between them, Britain felt her very existence menaced. If we recall this, the harsh repressive measures adopted by Pitt become more understandable and excusable. Again, it is usual and beyond doubt just to condemn the Inquisition in scathing terms, for no one defends its many excesses. But critics should measure its cruelties against the practices of the Middle Ages, not of the twentieth century. As a Protestant, Williston Walker, remarks in his work on *The Reformation:* "There is some reason to believe that the methods of the Inquisition, cruel as they seem from a modern standpoint, were milder than those of contemporaneous civil law." While we must condemn cruelty, we should not forget that ideas of what constitute cruelty have changed.

It is particularly hard to recapture past modes of thought; and frequently the *nunc pro tunc* fallacy throws an entirely false atmosphere about some event that involves them. John Fiske, in his *Discovery of America,* notes that Washington Irving (whose work he greatly admires) was guilty of amusing lapses of this kind in his life of Columbus. Irving, in describing Columbus's second voyage, relates that while coasting along Cuba the explorer encountered evidences (as he supposed) that he was coasting India or China. As Fiske comments:

> Mr. Irving . . . could not quite rid himself of the feeling that there was something strange or peculiar in the Admiral's method of interpreting such information. "Animated by one of the pleasing illusions of his ardent imagination, Columbus pursued his voyage, with a prosperous breeze, along the supposed continent of Asia." This lends a false color to the picture, which the general reader is pretty sure to make still falser. To suppose the southern coast of Cuba to be the southern coast of Toscanelli's Mangi required no illusion of an "ardent imagination." It was simply a plain common sense conclusion reached by sober reasoning from such data as were then accessible (i.e., the Toscanelli map, amended by information such as was understood to be given by the natives); it was more probable than any other theory of the situation likely to be devised from these data; and it seems fanciful to us today only because knowledge acquired since the time of Columbus has shown us how far from correct it was. Modern historians abound in unconscious turns of expression—as in this quotation from Irving—which project modern knowledge back into the past, and thus destroy the historical perspective.[12]

Sometimes the error of judging the past from the pres-

ent is displayed by an effort of twenty-twenty hindsight to
describe a bridge which does not really exist; an effort perhaps laudable in intention, for if the bridge could be demonstrated it would give more meaning to the picture.
Howard K. Beale in *Theodore Roosevelt and the Rise of
America to World Power* writes that at the beginning of
the twentieth century Roosevelt, John Hay, and others
shaped an American policy toward China which "was ultimately to throw China into the arms of Russia." That
statement seems on its face to give a richer historical significance to Open Door diplomacy; richer and darker. It
is totally misleading, and quite unjust to Roosevelt and
Hay. No real bridge can be found between the kind of
China that existed in 1900–5 and the China of 1950, and
no bridge between the Russian government of 1905 and
that of 1950. Both countries were profoundly revolutionized, and the conditions of American diplomacy were completely changed. The facts of history are distorted, not
illumined, by a statement that Roosevelt could and should
have foreseen the kind of world that would emerge by
the time of the Russo-Chinese alliance. For that matter, it
was Japanese policy, not American, that did most to throw
China into the arms of Russia.

Time is not the only distorting element, for sometimes
distance in space, and alien standards and conventions,
play precisely the same role. No one could properly write
the history of present-day Tibetans by applying to them
the psychology of the Western world. No one should
judge of Japanese music which has qualities all its own, by
the conventions of European music, which simply do not
apply. And sometimes alien times and alien conventions
combine to test severely the ability of the historian to get
outside his own skin. A good example is afforded by the
scornful way in which many modern writers have written
of Egyptian pictorial art, which at first glance seems somewhat naïve and ludicrous because it totally lacks perspective. The fact is that Egyptian artists responded to a set
of rules which to the Egyptian mind seemed just as admirable as the rules of Rembrandt and Turner seem to us.
Twenty centuries from now the world of art may have

passed under a totally new set of rules, which will make
the classical painters of today appear incredibly quaint
and absurd; and indeed, the art of the modernists or sur-
realists is already poles apart from that of the classicists.
But the fact that it is quaint and absurd to the people of
4000 A.D. will not justify them in adjudging us quaintly
absurd. We find an acute critic very properly defending
Egyptian art from one of the historians who committed this
nunc pro tunc error:

> Vigorous exception must be taken to Mr. Hall's opin-
> ion that Egyptian art is "absurd" in its convention of
> drawing, which disregards perspective and shows dif-
> ferent parts of the human body now in profile, now in
> full front view. The conventions of drawing familiar to
> the modern world are still merely conventions, and not
> necessarily the best that might be devised. Ancient
> Egyptian artists used a different idiom of expression, no
> more illogical than our own. As realists they sought to
> give both plan and elevation in the same drawing, to
> "see around" the figure represented. When we under-
> stand their aim and have taught our eyes to apprehend
> their vocabulary, we shall unhesitatingly accord to the
> great artists of ancient Egypt the supreme credit which
> is their due as masters of line, of composition and de-
> sign, and of surpassing technique in the manipulation
> of materials.[13]

Because of the rapid material progress of the past few
generations, one common present-day form of this fallacy
is a tendency to underrate the difficulties which men of
recent periods faced. People who take the plane from New
York to Los Angeles find it difficult to comprehend the
perils and obstacles that the companions of Daniel Boone
met in blazing the Wilderness Trail. From the deck of the
Queen Mary the most timid man thinks of the fears of
Columbus's sailors with a condescending smile. Only in
recent years has history been able to show that Braddock,
long assumed to be a blunderer, was an intelligent and
efficient as well as brave officer, who took due precautions,

and whose enormous difficulties had not been clearly understood.

Frequently this underestimation of difficulties is carried over from the material to the intellectual sphere. It is easy for historical students to be wise after the event; it is a besetting temptation to clever writers to prove their superior sagacity by demonstrating that the statesmen of grandfather's time were simple-minded, and grandfather rather silly for believing in them. Lytton Strachey exhibited great brilliancy in setting a dunce-cap on the head of Arnold of Rugby; by emphasizing his "slightly puzzled look" as a key to his career, he made him seem decidedly stupid. The truth is that there was never anything puzzled about Thomas Arnold's look or mind. He was a manly, resolute leader, decisive in action and untiring in industry; a great progressive force in nineteenth-century education; a historian of acuteness and diligence; and altogether a man whose numerous activities deserved his son's poetical wreath, and the more modern tribute of H. A. L. Fisher. Full biographical studies have appeared, since the publication of Strachey's *Eminent Victorians*, of three of the figures he treated most harshly, Arnold, "Chinese" Gordon, and Florence Nightingale, and they have all proved that his caustic denigration was often mistaken in points of fact as well as unfair in tone. One book, Cecil Woodham-Smith's on Miss Nightingale, was especially penetrating. Various writers on American history 1870–90 have expressed the view that national problems of the period were much simpler than those of a generation later, and that the leaders who dealt with them were smaller men; a statement with more validity in its second part than the first. Anyone who has earnestly studied the Reconstruction problem, the currency and financial problem, and the problem of bringing railroads and great industrial aggregations under public control, knows that they had endless complexities and bristled with difficulties. To underrate their complications and pitfalls is to do violence to our understanding of history.

A similar fallacy was concealed in the stereotyped denunciation of the "Old Diplomacy" of Europe and America which became fashionable after the First World War. One of the most thorough students of that diplomacy calls the denunciation cheap and ignorant, and adds that as his researches progressed "I have become less and less willing to believe that men in that day were more wicked, more unscrupulous, and more evil minded than in our own or any other day."[14]

VII

Any discussion of the *nunc pro tunc* fallacy involves the relativity of morals. The ancient Greeks, when a crime was committed, used torture on whole households of slaves before taking their testimony; by what standards should the torturers be judged? Few subjects have inspired so much controversial writing as the position which students of history should take as moralists. A fundamentalist position was stated by Lord Acton, who remarked that one tendency against which his moral sense revolted grew out of the laudable wish of historians to be sympathetic to men of distant ages and alien modes of thought—a wish that was pushed into indiscriminate tolerance of past abuses. He saw with dismay that "the general growth of historical methods of thinking supplied a sense of the relativity of moral principles, and led to a desire to condone if not commend the crimes of other ages. It became almost a trick of style to talk of judging men by the standard of their day, and to allege the spirit of the age in excuse for the Albigensian Crusade or the burning of Huss."

Acton felt that this was to destroy the very bases of moral judgment and open the way to a boundless skepticism. Anxious as he was to uphold the doctrine of growth in theology, he made no allowance for changing standards in the realm of basic morals, at any rate in Christian lands, since the thirteenth century. He demanded a code of moral judgment independent of time and place, and not relative to a particular civilization; murder is murder, robbery is robbery. It is not surprising to learn that Acton decided that practically all the great men of history were bad men.

A different view has been stated by other historians, who would not exclude moral judgments from history, but would not ignore relativism either. Neutralism is impossible. Yet since ethical codes and atmospheres change, since all men are sinners, and since infallibility of judgment is given to nobody, these historians hold that great caution is desirable. One writer observes that "the kind of ethical judgments which historians like Lord Acton have been so anxious to achieve are possible only to God."[15] Students of history will continue to differ upon the degree to which present-day people can impose their standards upon the past. No doubt a thoroughly evil man like Nero, Pope Alexander VI, or Hitler, must be unsparingly condemned. No judicious reader of history, however, should indulge in such moral license as that which just after the Civil War pronounced the Confederate cause immoral, or which pronounced Queen Elizabeth a murderess for ordering the execution of Mary Queen of Scots. Prescott's moderate treatment of Philip II and his policy in the Netherlands has long been preferred to Motley's intolerant treatment.

What is important is not to denounce Abdul Hamid for his crimes, but to understand what gave birth to Abdul Hamid and his policies.

One distinction respecting past transactions, moreover, should always be kept in mind: the distinction between private morality and public morality. Nations and their leaders often have to obey a code very different from that proper to individuals. Private war and private atrocities have been morally outlawed, but public war and the public bombing of populous cities have not. Moral judgment condemns men for firing on each other, but it does not condemn a government, in certain circumstances, for firing on a mob. In dealing with individuals, too, we judge actions primarily by motive, but in dealing with governmental acts we judge primarily by results. The historian more frequently pronounces on errors than sins, recalling Fouché's epigram that Napoleon's execution of the Duc d'Enghien was worse than a crime, it was a blunder. These above facts indicate the many difficulties which, surrounding the subject, will always make it controversial.

VIII

Great art is the product of inspiration as much as of rules of thumb, though the inspiration must usually be combined with arduous labor; great skill is the product of long experience. A Macaulay or Parkman masters the principles of evidence partly by intuition and partly by long practice. In his mature work he will apply them to the solution of problems as unconsciously as an artist of genius employs the rules of drawing and composition. It is this subconscious mastery that the student of history should strive to attain. He will then detect instantly a dubious piece of evidence, he will classify and organize his data without much thought of first principles, and he will think out his various hypotheses without troubling to put them on paper. By long practice in examining masses of historical material, his judgment and power of inference may be developed to a high proficiency.

He enters the same realm that the expert in any art or profession rules and enjoys, the realm that William James has described: "Saturated with experience of a particular class of materials, an expert intuitively knows whether a newly-reported fact is probable or not, whether a proposed hypothesis is worthless or the reverse. He instinctively knows that, in a novel case, this and not that will be the promising course of action. The well-known story of the old judge advising the new one never to give reasons for his decisions, 'the decisions probably will be right, the reasons surely will be wrong,' illustrates this. The doctor will feel that the patient is doomed, the dentist will have a premonition that the tooth will break, though neither can articulate a reason for his foreboding. The reason lies imbedded, but not yet laid bare, in all the countless previous cases dimly suggested by the actual one, all calling up the same conclusions, which the adept thus finds himself swept on to, he knows not how or why."[16]

IX
Ideas in History

It HAS OFTEN been remarked that the world is ruled by ideas, or as Napoleon put it with the same meaning, by imagination. The ideas that so frequently control society may be divided into two groups, the practical and the philosophical. By the former we mean those concepts which, expressing immediate mundane aims, can actually be realized by an expression of the human will. As we scan the dark backward and abysm of time we can descry a long list of such ideas which have exercised the most powerful sway over human affairs. Among them are the idea of the ecclesiastical or papal supremacy over temporal powers; the idea of the divine right of kings; the idea of nationalism; the idea of toleration; the idea of self-determination, which ruled events so potently during and after the First World War; the idea of rugged individualism; the idea of State Socialism; and the idea of collectivism or the abolition of private property. These are practical ideas because they depend primarily upon man's will; because they can usually be made to work if most men agree to promote them; and because they are tested by the question whether they are useful or useless, not true or false. Mussolini's idea of the totalitarian state depended for its validity on the readiness of most Italians to employ it, and that readiness endured just as long as most Italians believed that its advantages offset its disadvantages.

But mankind is also powerfully swayed at times by philosophical ideas. Theoretical rather than practical, they are judged not by pragmatic tests but by men's conviction of what is valid and invalid. Society accepts or rejects them not as beneficial or injurious, but as true or false. Such is the idea of personal immortality—and few people realize how profoundly human institutions would be altered if that concept were abandoned by mankind. Such also is the Greek idea of fate, or the Calvinist idea of predestination, with other religious ideas. Such is the idea of Progress, in modern times probably the most important of all human concepts of a philosophical nature.

All historical work which pretends to elevation or importance is written under the influence of ideas. Much historical work, though by no means all of it, is important by virtue of its ideas; that is, its interpretations. Consciously or unconsciously, all significant historians are affected by their intellectual environment, whether they evince hostility to some phase of the prevalent thought of the time, or espouse and defend it. And if the historian is a man of intellectual vigor, he assuredly views his task not as the mere recital of a series of facts and events, but as their arrangement in a pattern which illustrates some underlying truth. The effect of this impulse upon the history of ideas has been very great, but we are here concerned primarily with its effect upon the course of historical writing.

While the analysis of historical evidence is an important process in the study or writing of history, it is not the most important. In the highest type of history the synthesis or interpretation is a much more vital element. The task of analysis involves the discovery of the truth about various events by a combination of industry, ingenuity, judgment, and honesty. It is essentially a piece of anatomical work. But to arrive at an interpretation, the historian takes a considerable body of problems and events, and so arranges them as to illustrate some dominant idea. That is, he synthesizes his material about some concept which governs the whole of it; he utilizes a series of analyses, which at first may have seemed chaotic and jumbled, and produces a general conclusion which throws them into perspective.

This is not anatomy, it is physiology. It breathes the spark of life into dead materials and makes them move as living bodies. Or to change the figure, it lifts the reader above the immediate thicket he is exploring, and shows him the trend of the terrain—the significance of the valley, or the mountain range, of which the thickets are a part.

Thus the *Cambridge Modern History*, or the *Histoire Générale* of Lavisse, offers a huge body of facts upon human events since 1500, caught together merely in a long series of highly factual—and badly related—monographs. But Oswald Spengler, in *The Decline of the West*, offered an interpretation of this long period. Discarding the simple optimistic view of linear evolution or endless progress, he substituted an interpretation of history as a recurring cycle, a Foucault pendulum swing, placing our own unhappy time in the bleakest part of a spring-summer-autumn-winter succession. To take more limited examples, Channing's book on the Civil War offered a score of analyses of problems, consistently declining to draw them together upon any interpretive thread. But in *The Rise of American Civilization* Charles and Mary Beard synthesized the Civil War according to an economic pattern. They viewed it as essentially a conflict between the old rural culture and the new industrial culture of America. Discarding the concepts of slavery and State Rights as dominating the Civil War period, the Beards made their concept of a sharp collision between a business civilization and an agrarian civilization the vehicle of a freshly stimulating, though not necessarily sound, interpretation of the events of 1860–69.

I

At the outset it is important to enforce a firm distinction between a general philosophy of history, and a specific interpretation of historical materials. While the distinction is mainly one of scope, it is also related to the distinction which we have just drawn between philosophical ideas, tested by our faith in what is true, and practical ideas, tested by our experience of their workability. General philosophical concepts of history will not bend to pragmatic tests. The dominant idea of Spengler's book is obviously of this nature. As no one will ever know—at least for hundreds of centuries to come—whether history does move in regular cycles or not, to read and write history in that way is simply an act of faith. So is the philosophy of history built on the doctrine of evolutionary progress, a creed so popular in the nineteenth century. So is the philosophy, toward which Pareto leaned, of history as a pendulum alternating between liberty and authority. But an interpretation like that which the Beards gave the Civil War can be subjected to practical tests, for the facts within a limited domain either sustain or destroy it—when we learn them. The interpretation may provoke a discussion which drags on through the decades, but each student will decide upon its merits by consulting the facts. A philosophy of history springs from a writer's whole view of human destiny, and thus embodies his philosophy of life; an interpretation of historical material is merely a writer's explanation of the significance of a series of events, an epoch, or a movement. The one usually bears a close relation to the thought of the age; the other is usually more personal in origin.

All the principal philosophies of history save two have originated within the past three centuries—a fact which speaks volumes for the close alliance between rationalism and modern history. Greek and Roman writers of history knew but one philosophy, that of Fate. To them the work held a far richer theological significance than it has to us, and from Thucydides to Appian it sufficed to cover their view of human destiny. They made varying allowances for the interposition of the gods, but they never formulated any view of a grand final goal, some far-off, divine event, toward which the gods guided mankind.

Early in the Christian Era, however, there arose a very different philosophy of history, stamped by the fervors of the new faith, and it held almost undisputed sway for more than thirteen centuries. First enunciated by St. Augustine in the *City of God*, it asserted that the whole record of the world turned upon the overwhelming fact of divine concern for mankind. The decisive event of history was the life of Christ, before which all mankind had been doomed, and after which all of the elect were saved. St. Augustine, donning the mantle of seer, described the birth, growth, and destiny of two cities, one of this world and one of God, culminating in the triumph of the latter. His followers continued to regard the earth simply as the footstool of history; the story of humankind as simply part of the divine comedy. That view, which often had Neo-Platonist elements and could be given compelling grandeur, swayed medieval chroniclers no less than Dante and Milton.[1]

This Christian philosophy of history indeed continued to possess the field down to the time of Bossuet's eloquent book, the *Histoire Universelle*, which largely summed it up. His volume, written from the standpoint of dogmatic theology and the official Catholic hierarchy, was imbued with a belief that the pivotal event of time was the Crucifixion, and that the one all-powerful force in human affairs was God's benevolent interposition. He conceived of the changes in history as all slowly tending toward the progress and universality of the true religion—not merely Christianity, but the papal form of Christianity. The book naturally passed Moslem civilization by, and treated Greece and Rome only as part of the Preparatio Evangelicum. Voltaire, remarking caustically that "It seems to have been written solely to suggest that everything in the world was made for the Jews," was stung by it and similar productions into an angry reply. His *Essai sur les Moeurs* a generation later wholly rejected the miraculous interposition of Providence in history, asserting a rationalistic interpretation of the past. In Voltaire's opinion, the events of history were attributable not to design but to chance or fortuity. His brilliant though vague exposition helped to open the way for other rationalistic philosophies. Nevertheless, the Christian synthesis long persisted, and even in America had its followers. Benjamin Trumbull's *General History of the United States*, of which only one of three proposed volumes appeared (1810), attempted to point out the special interpositions of Providence in behalf of the American people.

Since the time of Hegel, whose *Philosophy of History* appeared in 1830–31, metaphysical analyses of the whole range of human events have become numerous, for it is a poor sociologist, economist, or philosopher—not to mention historian—who does not present one. Hegel, whose doctrines created a whole school, attempted to show that every epoch was inspired and dominated by some specific idea; for example, he regarded Napoleon, the new Caesar, as "die Weltseele" of his time. He taught that each idea, affirmed as truth, brings with it the idea that is its negation; they do battle, and a new idea emerges; then the cycle repeats itself. This concept of thesis, antithesis, and synthesis—the dialectic method—has long been discredited as a tool for understanding the past. In conjunction with his glorification of the national state, however, it had a profound and pernicious influence upon European thought. Such more recent historians as Kuno Fischer likewise lay emphasis on the "Einheitstendenz" of every period, which permeates all aspects of its life, and by which alone it is to be understood.

A quarter century after Hegel's book the Darwinian theory of natural selection as a key of evolution seized history in its powerful grasp, which has not yet greatly relaxed; for most historians of the non-esoteric schools still believe in progress, and believe it is attained by evolutionary processes. Indeed, evolutionary ideas long preceded Darwin, who gave them simply a special form and force. Such writers as Lecky, Freeman, Parkman, and McMaster were unconsciously pervaded by the evolutionary philosophy, while Froude, Bagehot, John Fiske, and Rhodes were very consciously pervaded by it. Challenged by few save the Marxian group, the evolutionary writers for decades ruled history with autocratic sway, and even yet dominate the field. An increasing band of dissenters, a vigorous group of advanced intellectuals, have nevertheless from time to time asserted that simple evolution is nearly as absurd as the old theological view of history.

Two of the ablest statements of the evolutionary philosophy of history are to be found in Walter Bagehot's stimulating *Physics and Politics* and John Fiske's *Outlines of*

Cosmic Philosophy, both the more typical for having been written in the heart of the Victorian era. Of Fiske's views we shall say something later. Bagehot significantly gave his work the subtitle, "Thoughts on the application of the principles of natural selection and inheritance to political science." His book did more than state a theory of history, for in its influence upon such future leaders as Woodrow Wilson it made history. Essentially, it was an attempt to show that in social institutions as well as in the animal kingdom the rule of the survival of the fittest applies, and that as an acquired faculty of the parent animal is sometimes distinctly transmitted to its progeny (or so Bagehot believed), acquired characteristics of society are inherited by succeeding generations. "The continuous force which binds age to age," writes Bagehot, "enables each to begin with some improvement on the last, if the last did not itself improve." This implies a general though not uninterrupted continuity of progress in the world, under which weak and erroneous institutions are gradually eliminated. Upon this view, if valid, a grand systematization of history can be built, and Bagehot asserts as much. "We thus perceive that a science of history is possible—a science to teach the law of tendencies, created by the mind and transmitted by the body—which act upon and incline the mind of man from age to age."

In developing his thesis, Bagehot begins with a "Preliminary Stage" of civilization in which progress was achieved by the triumph of the strong over the weak. Powerful tribes, nations, or peoples always tend to prevail over the feeble, and while Bagehot does not believe that might makes right, he does assert that "in certain marked peculiarities, the strongest tend to be the best." In his section on "Nation Making" he accounts by evolutionary theory for the development of national traits. It has been an innate propensity of man to imitate what is before him; thus the primitive savages imitated their leaders and copied their most striking characteristics, "preserving them as they did their favorite animals." These traits gradually tinged the whole community. "Ages are required, but at last a national character is formed." National character is but the name for a collection of habits, more or less universal, which in the course of long generations have produced vast mental and physical effects.

Bagehot continues his evolutionary exposition by showing how primitive and simple nations have given way to modern and complex nations. In the former "fixity was the invariable ingredient," the cake of custom holding peoples in a mold that was sometimes as viciously static as the old-time framework of Chinese society. Then as the Middle Ages ended, various tendencies broke the cake of fixed custom and ushered in the "age of discussion," which is progressive inasmuch as it gives a premium to intelligence. Though Bagehot saw certain dangers in even the modern age of discussion, notably a tendency toward hasty political action which he calls "a hereditary barbaric impulse," and though like Malthus he feared "a diminished reserve for race maintenance," his outlook upon the future was fundamentally hopeful. All evolutionists are meliorists if not optimists. While the conclusions which flow from his evolutionary concept appear naïve to many present-day students, even they admit that he elucidates many secondary truths with memorable eloquence and force.

The "Marxian interpretation" of history is really a Marxian philosophy, as imposing in scope, despite its materialistic temper, as any other philosophy. It has to be carefully distinguished from the writings of many of Marx's followers, who in his own lifetime so perverted some of his doctrines that he mordantly remarked, "Je ne suis pas un Marxiste." Briefly stated, his thesis is that the mode of production in economic life primarily determines the general character of social, political, and cultural processes. With every change in the economic foundation brought about by changes in relationship between man and productive forces, the entire superstructure is more or less rapidly transformed. Marx thus became the first to formulate, in explicit fashion, the economic interpretation of history. Unlike some disciples, he and Engels never gave this interpretation so narrow a form as to exclude all non-economic factors as contributing causes of events; they merely declared the mode of production to be the dominant factor.

Indeed, Marx clearly perceived that society is molded by spirit and thought as well as material environment, and did not believe that history could be explained by a monistic materialism. Rather, he regarded society as an interacting whole of environment and thought, of objective and subjective conditions, and of activity and its practical goals, in which mode of production was the most important single element. It should also be noted that Marx's general conception of history does not have, for students of historical writing, any connection with his belief that society would be remade by passing through a dictatorship of the proletariat into a classless world. As Dr. E. R. A. Seligman says, "there is nothing in common between the economic interpretation of history and the doctrine of Socialism, except the accidental fact that the originator of both theories happened to be the same man."

This philosophy has been under intensive fire ever since Marx briefly presented it in his *Critique of Political Economy*—for he never gave it an elaborate statement. The attack upon those of his followers who take an extremely narrow and dogmatic view of the economic interpretation has of course been more effective than the attack upon Marx himself. German Socialists like Kautsky and Hilferding compressed the Marxian theory of history into preposterously strict limits, making human thought and action not so much derivatives as by-products of economic processes. The Russian Communists have gone to equal extremes in their treatment of history. Lenin's reductive materialism in his *Materialism and Empirio-Criticism*, Bukharin's emphasis upon a technological interpretation of history, which he falsely ascribed to Marx, and Pokrovsky's monistic materialism, which completely excluded either chance or great men as real determinants of events, were all vulnerable.

But the true Marxian philosophy in no way excludes ethical or spiritual forces from history. It simply asserts that the concept of morality is a social product, varying with the state of civilization or with the social class, and as such largely determined, in the last analysis, by economic forces. It does not deny that great men have sometimes exercised a controlling influence upon history. It merely affirms that in general they would never have been great had it not been for certain social conditions which made their rise possible, and that these conditions are in turn governed chiefly by economic factors. It must be added that Marx's own brevity and partial obscurity in stating his philosophy left some of its implications vague, and opened the way for such assaults upon it as those of Dr. M. M. Bober and F. R. Salter.

II

The convulsion of the First World War and its aftermath, which convinced tens of millions of men that social progress is an empty word, and that an "evolution" which marched whole nations to death or ruin offered no hope to mankind, could not but have a profound effect upon popular interest in the philosophy of history. New scientific theories of the universe formulated during the same period exercised an almost equal influence. The universe, which Newton had conceived as infinite in extent and subject to fixed physical laws, was transformed by Einstein into a finite universe governed by relative laws. It was perhaps a universe, as Jeans, Eddington, and others suggested, in which a ceaseless process of destruction and construction went on without assignable object, energy being dissipated into remote space, and there gradually reconstructing new galaxies to dissipate themselves again. The fashion in historical philosophies swung abruptly to exercises in cosmic rhythm. Since H. G. Wells strongly believed in evolution, his *Outline of History* pointed the way to a perfection of society through science and education. But a number of writers explained that history was a series of pulsations; was a swing and counterswing of the pendulum; was a cycle of summer-fall-winter-spring seasons endlessly repeating themselves; was in fact something quite different from the magnificent upward climb toward a higher and better life which Bossuet had believed to be directed by God, and the Victorians to be directed by Evolution (which after all, in Tennyson's if not in Huxley's view, was little else than another name for God).

Of the principal recent treatises offering one or another rhythm-philosophy of history, Spengler's *Decline of the West*, Arnold Toynbee's *A Study of History*, Pareto's *Mind and Society*, and Pitirim Sorokin's *Culture and Cultural Dynamics*, Toynbee's has been by far the most arresting and influential. Unique in sweep and scope, it is a true world history, presenting a study of the total recorded experience of all the noteworthy societies in human civilization. It is unique also in the fervor with which the author insists on certain great truths or lessons. One is that the culture which ordinarily circumscribes our view, that of the white industrialized areas of Europe and the Americas, is relatively a recent, precarious, and perhaps temporary phenomenon; it may be overswept and relegated to the rear in the march of mankind as Athens was overswept by Macedon and Rome. In his first six volumes Toynbee listed twenty-odd civilizations which had run their course and were dead or dying; ours, one of the survivors, might have as tragic a fate, for he finds in it "authentic symptoms of breakdown and disintegration."

Another cardinal lesson which he draws from his world view of history is that the national state is an obsolete, mistaken, and even criminal entity. To him the offenses committed in the name of nationalism are intolerable, and the militarism and despotism which it breeds are a threat to the whole future of man. (From this detestation of nationalism stems his condemnation of Zionism.) By failing to stop making war, he holds, Western civilization is in imminent danger of destroying itself. A world government he thinks eventually inevitable, but its creation will have to be accompanied by a change of heart amounting to a revolution. A still larger lesson eloquently enforced in his twelve volumes is that more interesting than the rise, decline, and fall of twenty civilizations, and more important by far than the evolution, death and resurrection of their political ideas, is the growth of the great religions. Four of them, Hinduism, Buddhism, Christianity, and Islamism, have survived and spread, and give mankind what essential hope it has; but a still higher and better religion may emerge in the future.

In the course of his impressive work, Toynbee throws out a long succession of stimulating generalizations, of which his theories of challenge and response, his explanations of the cause of arrested civilizations, and his idea of the nemesis of creativity—"history shows that the group which successfully responds to one challenge is rarely the successful respondent to the next"—are the most familiar. In laying down his generalizations he expounds a doctrine which if not determinism comes close to it. A demonstration that history is governed by inexorable laws and throws itself into universal patterns, and that omnipotent impersonal forces govern the course of nations, destroys the role of personal choice and responsibility. Toynbee assails "the professional scribes and Pharisees" among historians for denying that his effort at writing universal history is practicable, on the ground that no single human mind can master the detailed study of so many diverse elements; and for questioning the validity of his generalizations, on the ground that twenty-odd civilizations are an inadequate number for testing hypotheses by the empirical method of trial and error.

His most searching critics, however, present a different set of contradictions. They declare that his conclusions are difficult to test, and uncertain in value, because his use of historical evidence is inconsistent, arbitrary, and spotty. The inevitability of a single world government, for example, is not a deduction from empirical observation. They also object vehemently to his determinism as both unhistorical and pernicious.

Isaiah Berlin, for one, has argued in his small book *Historical Inevitability* that it is impossible to apply determinism to history in any exact way, and that the notion that the past has a single patterned structure which explains and resolves the chaotic diversity of the human story is really a kind of myth which distorts the record. Moreover, it is a myth unfortunate in its social and political effects. It is "one of the great alibis pleaded by those who cannot and do not wish to face the facts of human responsibility, the existence of a limited but nevertheless real area of human freedom. . . ."

Others, like Geoffrey Barraclough, have pointed to a "manipulation" of historic fact by Toynbee in making the histories of ancient Egypt, Islam, and Russia conform to his theorems. The Dutch historian Pieter Geyl levels an especially comprehensive indictment. Examined in detail, he declares, Toynbee's pattern does not conform to his evidence, and his evidence is often twisted. To the unschooled, the Toynbee system seems exact, tightly constructed, and shinily polished; but when it and all the historic facts are expertly compared, Toynbee looks like Alice playing croquet in her Wonderland—the ball is a hedghog which runs off, the hoops are bowed soldiers who straighten themselves and march away, and the mallet is a flamingo which twists its neck just as Alice strikes. He, too, attacks deterministic theories, saying they have no place in the writing of history. Theologians may debate predestination and free will abstractly, but in historical work we must—and properly always do—assume the control of human will over human acts.

These criticisms of Toynbee, however devastating, do not deny the prodigious range of his learning or his fascinating fertility of illustration. Nor do the critics of determinist writings from August Comte onward deny that we have learned from economics, sociology, and psychology that the scope of human free will is much more restricted than we once supposed. Geyl rightly states that man is both free and in chains; free because he must always move on and use his will in so doing, chained because he cannot use his will in making uninhibited choices. He is incessantly liberating himself from parts of his past while other parts maintain their sway over him. The determinist views adopted by Toynbee are far less rigid than those accepted by Russia, Nazi Germany, or Fascist Italy.

Oswald Spengler's writings lent themselves to the early development of Nazi ideas, though he sternly rejected the Nazi doctrine of race superiority. His description of the succession of four seasonal phases in the historical cycle, and his conviction that Western civilization has entered a long winter of decay, to culminate in Asiatic domination, harmonized when published in 1918 with the pessimism of defeated Germany. Vilfredo Pareto, who tried to distinguish between rational and non-rational elements in human activity, and on this basis to explain the cyclical development and fall of governing elites, gave Italian Fascism part of its ideology (he died in 1923). He was less inclined than Spengler and Toynbee to play the prophet, and offered more economic and sociological evidence for his generalizations. To him history represented past sociology as to Freeman it represented retrospective politics. He saw in history a repetitive alternation of liberty and authority, the foxes and the lions, and he believed that his own mature period clearly witnessed the swing toward authority. Sorokin, who had been banished by the Soviet Government for his services to the Kerensky regime, was also much more an exponent of social processes than a historian. His *Social and Cultural Dynamics* presented a cycle of history which in rough terms ran from the individualist extreme to the collectivist extreme, and back again.[2]

In direct applications, these cyclical philosophies are of limited help to writers or readers of history. While they offer stimulating suggestions and flashes of insight into historical problems—in Toynbee especially—their grandiose concepts seem of little practical value. The utility of these ambitious philosophies is indirect. They foster a healthy discontent with existing approaches to history, which leads to an effort to obtain a deeper understanding of it. They predispose students to utilize new formulae in an experimental search for truth. They lead to an impatience with shallower forms of history and a demand for more profound treatments. Scornful as we may be of the weakness and vagueness of some of these philosophies, we must agree with Henry Adams—who himself tentatively entered the field—that the impulse behind them is natural. Writes Adams:

You may be sure that four out of five serious students

of history who are living today have, in the course of their work, felt that they stood on the brink of a great generalization that would reduce history under a law as clear as the laws which govern the material world. As the great writers of our time have touched one by one the separate fragments of admitted law by which society betrays its character as a subject for science, not one of them can have failed to feel an instant's hope that he might find the secret which would transform these odds and ends of philosophy into one self-evident, harmonious, and complete system. He has seemed to have it, as the Spanish say, in his inkstand. Scores of times he must have dropped his pen to think how one short step, one sudden inspiration, would show all human knowledge; how, in these thickset forests of history, one corner turned, one faint trail struck would bring him on the highroad of science.[3]

Yet it should be added that general agreement upon any philosophy of history is as undesirable as it is impossible. The great unifying law of which Henry Adams speaks will never be found. If men assented to any such law, it would bind history in fetters as adamantine as the old theological formula of Bossuet, and would ultimately render historical scholarship as monotonous and sterile as the work of the monkish chroniclers.

III

But the ordinary reader of history needs to have little concern with the grandiose conceptions of philosophy. His interest in the application of ideas to history will be confined to the more modest, practical, and personal form which we term the historical interpretation. One of the distinguishing hallmarks of modern historical writing is its powerful interpretive tendency. While the best ancient and medieval historians had a distinct point of view, only a few of them—among the ancients, Thucydides, Polybius, and their disciples—were possessed by that intense desire to revise history ever nearer the truth by arranging it in ever subtler patterns which masters most present-day historians. The element of intellectual *originality* in historical work has become steadily larger since 1750. While the forces which brought this interpretive tendency to its modern vigor are numerous, four may be singled out as particularly important.

The growth of rationalism was as indispensable to the unfettered use of ideas in history as to their unfettered use in science. It was no accident that the Age of Enlightenment coincided with the first great flowering of modern history. Originally in France, and later in England, the eighteenth century produced a special and extraordinary activity in historical work. And it is significant that this activity was promoted by the very men who were doing most in other spheres to emancipate humanity from the trammels of authority. Montesquieu's *Spirit of the Laws*, perhaps the greatest book of eighteenth-century France, is largely historical in content, as the subtitle indicates: "Du Rapport que les Lois doivent avoir avec la Constitution du Chaque Gouvernement, les Moeurs, le Climat, la Religion, du Commerce, etc." Its third part, consisting of six books which treat at length of the dependence of manners and customs upon climatic conditions, has been especially interesting to historical students. Montesquieu was the first writer to emphasize this relationship as it deserved. But the work should be considered as a whole; so taken, it is one of the foundation stones of comparative politics, and its brilliant generalizations in this field at once suggested a number of new ways of interpreting history.

With it should be considered the work of Voltaire. He realized that when he and other rationalists loosed the grip of the old supernatural versions of history, when they proved that men really made their own world, a new significance instantly enveloped the past. Historians must make use of these thousand new *aperçus*. Casting aside the murky lanterns of the religious chroniclers, they must reconstruct the past under the brilliant light of reason. The same conviction animated Hume and Gibbon, two mighty assailants of reigning superstitions across the Channel. It was no accident that the best secular histories of the period were written by the greatest of the rationalists.

Voltaire has left a record of the circumstances under which he embarked upon his rationalist interpretations of history. His active-minded friend, Mme. du Châtelet, whose special talent was for mathematics and philosophy, disliked history.[4] "What does it matter to me," she asked, "a Frenchwoman living on my estate, that Egil succeeded Haquin in Sweden, and that Ottoman was the son of Ortogrul? I read with pleasure Greek and Roman history, which offers great pictures which attract me. But I have never yet been able to finish any long history of our modern nations. There seems nothing in them but confusion, a host of minute events without connection or sequence, a thousand battles which settled nothing. I renounced a study which overwhelmed my mind without illuminating it." Voltaire replied that what was needed was simply a rational interpretation of history, utilizing the ideas forbidden to previous generations. If all the tedious and untrustworthy details of wars, all the pointless negotiations of diplomacy, all the minute incidents which obscured the grand tendencies of history, were shorn away, then a general and well-arranged picture could be made of the significant factors. It would be worth Mme. du Châtelet's time to read that.

The history of the human mind, continued Voltaire, was the truly important part of the human record. His word "mind," of course, embraced a great deal—law, arts, manners, literature, ideas—which he would make the chief concern of history. But every fact that the historian recorded should lead to something else. "Details which lead to nothing are in history what baggage is to an army, impedimenta, for we must look at things in the large, for the simple reason that the human mind is limited and sinks under the weight of minutiae."[5] Unconnected minutiae he would leave to annalists and encyclopedia-makers. These conceptions Voltaire illustrated in his *Charles XII* and *Age of Louis XIV*.

The new scientific attitude toward history was strikingly exhibited by Voltaire in his refusal to accept Tacitus at face value. He did not have the evidence which later scholars have found for believing Tacitus prejudiced and inaccurate. But relying on internal evidence, he pointed out the improbability of much that Tacitus had written upon Tiberius, Nero, Caligula, and other emperors. Could we accept the word of a man born long after Tiberius's death for the sensational story of how the emperor, after living to nearly eighty with unblemished name and a reputation for austerity, thereafter passed his time in monstrous debaucheries? Voltaire applied this same scientific incredulity to other fables of so-called history, demanding more sensible interpretations. Still another new principle which he helped bring into history was his insistence that persons and personal interests are of secondary importance; that it is the community, not the individual, which counts for most. This in itself was a basis for many new interpretations of the past. As Lord Morley says in his essay on Voltaire:

> Voltaire was always conscious, though not so clearly as writers are now, of the great historical principle that besides the prominent men of a generation there is something at work underneath, a moving current on whose flood they are borne. He never fixed this current by any of the names which now fall so glibly from our lips,—tendency of the times, tenor of public opinion, spirit of the age, and the like, by which we give a collective name to groups of sentiments and forces, all making in what seems to be a single direction. But although unnamed, this singular and invisible concurrence of circumstances was yet a reality to him. The age was something besides its heroes, and something besides its noisiest and most resounding occurrences. His divisions of the great epochs of humanity are undoubtedly open to much criticism, because the principles on which he drew the dividing line have lost their force in new generations . . . Nevertheless, we are bound to recognize that a new way of regarding human action, as well as a new way of composing history, was being introduced by a writer whose first paragraph declared that he proposed to himself a greater object than an account of the

life of Louis XIV; that he designed to paint for the instruction of posterity, not the actions of a single man, but the spirit of men; and that while all periods must be alike to one who only desires to fill his memory with facts, discrimination among them cannot be dispensed with for one who thinks.[6]

The temper of the Enlightenment appears quite as clearly in David Hume's *Essays, Moral, Political, and Literary,* as in Voltaire's works. His famous disquisition upon miracles, a masterpiece of irony, was a blow at the very padlock of the old fetters upon history. His essay upon the population of ancient cities, highly skeptical in temper, was one of the first suggestions of the importance of statistics in interpreting history. His views on money, trade, and government, marked by intellectual impartiality and critical acuteness in points of detail, carried many historical illustrations and had a clear applicability to history. Despite his allegiance to the Tory party, they pointed a clear road forward to what in the next century was called Liberalism. They had a profound influence in England and France, and it has been said that but for the conservative reaction following the French Revolution they might even have resulted in the parliamentary adoption of free trade and electoral reform before 1800. But Hume's *History of England,* which followed the *Essays,* was his greatest work. He was the first eminent Briton, as Voltaire was the first eminent Frenchman, to see clearly that history should not be a mere record of war and political intrigue, but should concern itself primarily with the mode of life, the morals, the manners, and the mind of the people. Far more than any previous writer, he had an insight into the complex social forces of history. After his six-volume work (1754–61), no Englishman could write history as it had been written before.

In Gibbon's *Decline and Fall* the Age of Enlightenment produced its principal historical monument. That work still seems, to some acute judges, the greatest piece of interpretive history yet written. To be sure, the interpretation is simple; it is largely summed up in Gibbon's famous sentence, "I have traced the triumph of Christianity and of barbarism." He was animated by a glowing admiration for the empire of Augustus and Trajan as embodying a "solid fabric of human greatness" unmatchable elsewhere; an empire which to him came nearer giving the earth its golden age than had any other regime. Imbued with this admiration, he felt little but distaste for the Christian religion which had done so much to help overthrow the Roman civilization—which had given him in the eighteenth century the sight of barefooted, superstitious friars chanting vespers in the temple of Jupiter beside the ruins of the Capitol. That so great a work should be written upon a theme so antagonistic to all the tenets of theological historiography was, whatever we think of the validity of his interpretation, the blow of an irresistible battering ram against the old narrow citadels. Their walls collapsed in ruin.

IV

The second great constructive influence upon historical interpretation came with the rise of economic science, and was ushered in by Adam Smith's *Wealth of Nations* in the same year that witnessed the Declaration of Independence and the publication of Gibbon's first volume. Smith had taken not a few of his views from the *Political Discourses* of his close friend Hume. His classic book, usually regarded as the main foundation of economics, was also one of the foundation-stones of modern historical writing. The Rationalists had dealt a shattering blow at the theory that history revolved about the facts of Christianity; Adam Smith now dealt a shattering blow at the whole aristocratic theory of history.

Up to that time nearly all chroniclers of the past had held a hierarchal conception of history, regarding the upper ranks of society as those alone worthy of a large place in the record. The king, noble, soldier, priest, and statesman had been the personalities with whom history was concerned; battles, dynastic changes, treaties, and other elements of the contest for power had been the salient events of history. But Adam Smith's ideas let in a new blaze of light. He and other writers showed that the great central currents in the life of any modern nation were economic; that the principal forces which governed that life were those of production, markets, transportation, labor supply, prices, and raw materials. These, like an irresistible current, bore national affairs forward while kings, priests, and soldiers—with some few exceptions—were tossed like flotsam and jetsam on the surface. Important though wars and battles were, they held their importance, in general, because they grew out of economic forces or interrupted these forces; much as treaties often counted, it was usually because they were the visible outcome of greater factors beneath the surface. It was impossible for well-read men, after *The Wealth of Nations*, to write of nations without proper attention to all that built up wealth. A great new interpretive highway had been driven into the wilderness that bordered the old-fashioned history, and colonists were soon making that wilderness rich with fruitful crops.

One of the first and most influential of these explorers was Arnold H. L. Heeren, long professor at Göttingen, who was sixteen when Adam Smith's book appeared, and who lived until 1842, becoming George Bancroft's inspirer in the art of history. Heeren's service was that he first fully applied the new interpretive apparatus to the ancient field. In his *Ideen über Politik, den Verkehr und den Handel der vornehmsten Völker der alten Welt*, and in other works, he presented an altogether fresh point of view. He examined ancient agriculture, manufactures, commerce, finance, and in short, the whole economic system of the early world, together with its politics, laws, and constitutions, and was thus enabled to throw a flood of light on the development of the civilizations of antiquity. His varied learning, calm impartiality, and insight helped to make his works notable. Unfortunately Bancroft, while learning much from Heeren in scholarly method and zeal, never acquired his peculiar interest in the economic aspects of history. In England the Benthamite or utilitarian school of historians, like Jeremy Bentham himself, were originally inspired by Adam Smith.

As a third vivifying influence, novel political ideas also

contributed to the transformation of history by supplying
a number of fresh interpretations; and it need not be said
that the most striking of these ideas came with the French
Revolution. That event was to half of mankind as the
rising of a golden sun. "Bliss was it in that dawn to be
alive"—to be a young historian, no less than poet, very
heaven. Through the lurid flame and smoke of the overwhelming convulsion, the masses of the people came into
view. These masses, unknown to the old-time chroniclers
of royalty, military glory, and the church, had been neglected as unimportant, but they now made history with
unforgettable vigor. They lifted to power one of their own
number, and Napoleon took charge of the destinies of Europe for fifteen years. Thenceforth no historian could slight
them. And when the era of the Napoleonic wars ended, it
was also seen that history must henceforth be interpreted
in terms not merely of the common man, but of a rampant
nationalism. Once the monarch had been thought more
important than the state—often, as Louis XIV boasted of
himself, he *was* the state. But now the people were the
state; and the force of national sentiment diffused throughout the people brought a new Germany, a new Spain, in
one sense a new Russia, into existence. In the course of
another long generation, the growth of nationalism among
the masses gave birth to a new Italy and a newer Germany.

Altogether, by 1830 the age of multiform historical interpretations of the past had opened. The presentation of
the human record had been broadened in a fashion that
would have been inconceivable to pious readers of Bossuet.
It no longer took account of divine providence at all—or
at least not in the ablest writers. Instead, it took account
of all that the rationalism of that era had to suggest, for
Montesquieu's enlistment of geography had been only
one of various utilizations of scientific knowledge; it took
account of the cultural and moral history which Voltaire
had pointed out to Mme. du Chatelet as central to all
understanding of man's past; it took account of economic
factors; of democratic factors; and of nationalistic and patriotic factors. A series of radically new outlooks, within

seventy-five years, had come in. Every student was at liberty to use one or several of them in his synthesis, his interpretation.

Yet although much had been done, fertile fields of speculation remained to be entered. The fourth great element in the modern growth of history lay in its acquisition of the new scientific tendencies of the nineteenth century. In such writers as Macaulay, Guizot, and Prescott the interpretation is what we nowadays term old-fashioned. Why? Because while they reflected the ideas which had been imported into history by Montesquieu and Voltaire, Hume and Gibbon, Adam Smith and Heeren, the Industrial Revolution and the French Revolution, still other ideas arose during and after their lifetimes which have profoundly impressed all subsequent historians. History had in particular to keep up with the march of the sciences, and some were marching fast. In addition to the development of geography, economics, and biology, wholly new sciences were born—first sociology, and later psychology, both useful in historical interpretation. Professional historians are justly suspicious of sweeping sociological theories as likely to be unsound and useless. But the more exact sciences are of indubitable value.

One important book which partly revealed a shift in the trend of historical interpretation, and which partly caused it, was H. T. Buckle's unfinished *History of Civilization in England,* published in 1857. This huge fragment—broken off by his untimely death—is part of an introduction in which he intended, first, to state the general laws governing human progress, and second, to exemplify these laws by the history of certain strongly individualized nations—Spain, Scotland, the United States, and Germany. His most important contentions are as follows: (1) Inasmuch as historians have been shortsighted and unreflective, and as the social phenomena of the modern world are extremely complex, little has yet been done to establish a science of history. (2) It is nevertheless proved by scientific inquiry, and particularly by sociological statistics, that human action is controlled by fixed and predictable rules. (3) It is a basic fact of history that the chief causes of intellectual progress are climate, soil, and food, which govern it indirectly by determining the accumulation and distribution of wealth, and the aspect of nature, which influences the cast and vigor of thought—for peoples reared in sublime scenery are more imaginative than their fellows, people reared in harsh surroundings are tougher-minded, and so on. (4) The distinction between European and non-European civilization rests primarily upon the fact that in Europe man has been stronger than nature, subduing it to his objects, while outside Europe nature has been stronger than man and has largely subdued him. (5) The advance of European civilization is characterized by a steady growth in the importance of intellectual laws, and a diminution in the influence of physical laws.

Though none of his ideas is wholly true, Buckle's work was nevertheless extremely influential everywhere from Russia to the United States. Particularly was one central thesis of his work important. He taught that written history had been too much a record of individuals or select groups, and not enough of whole nations; he believed that the action of great human masses ought to be traced, especially with the aid of statistical law. He also held that in the natural surroundings of every people—its command of necessary raw materials and luxuries, its conditions of soil and climate—lie the chief molding influences of its career, and that parliaments have nearly as little as kings and heroes to do with that molding. In short, Buckle was one of the forerunners of a history built upon sociology, social statistics, and economic geography. His emphasis upon the life of the whole people appears in transmuted form in John Richard Green's *Short History of the English People*, and John Bach McMaster's *History of the People of the United States*. Both writers attempt to trace the life of a whole nation, and to deal with the people as an organic body; as they lived, worked, prospered, suffered, as they developed moral codes, manners, and arts in city and country. Both writers had to fall back upon description much more heavily than Buckle would have approved, for statistics and other sociological data did not exist in any volume. But both were obviously influenced by his doctrines, while he had helped to prepare a reading public for them. The impression made by his insistence upon laws of progress was of course heightened by the publication of Darwin's *Origin of Species* only two years after his book.

V

Only less important than the scientific contribution made to historical interpretation by Buckle and the evolutionists was the quasi-scientific contribution by the founders of sociology. One, August Comte, preceded these men; another, Herbert Spencer, followed them. Neither wrote at any length upon history in itself, but the works of both contain much incidental material upon history. Spencer was of course one of the chief apostles of evolution, who attempted to make universal the principle of evolutionary development and to formulate its law. Comte, whose *Positive Philosophy* was completed in 1843, seventeen years before Darwin's *Origin of Species,* had no connection with evolutionary theory. Nor had he the least sympathy with the desire of Buckle and others to study history by discovering the scientific laws governing society. On the contrary, he maintained that no such laws exist; that while human knowledge has as its objects phenomena in their reciprocal relations, nothing absolute lies at the base of these phenomena. With one exception stated below, the only absolute law is, All is relative. His views represented a development of the rationalistic and skeptical doctrines of Hume and Condillac.

For the interpretive historian, the part of Comte's encyclopedic system which holds the richest interest is the Law of the Three States laid down at the beginning of his *Positive Philosophy,* and always treated by both disciples and opponents its key. He declared that each branch of human knowledge passes successively through three phases in which men explain the phenomena they observe. The first phase is the Theological, in which credulous observers refer phenomena to a supernatural principle, the immediate volition of the object itself or of some supernatural being. The second phase is the Metaphysical, the phenomena being viewed not as an act of volition, but as due to an abstract force residing in, yet apart from, the object. The third is the Positive phase, when phenomena are referred by way of succession or resemblance to some other fact, and so studied. All this has been aptly illustrated by an English follower of Comte: "Take the phenomenon of the sleep produced by opium. The Arabs are content to attribute it to the 'will of God.' Molière's medical student accounts for it by a soporific principle contained in the opium. The modern physiologist knows that he cannot account for it at all. He can simply observe, analyze, and experiment upon the phenomena attending the action of the drug, and classify it with other agents analogous in character." The principal object of Comte's Positivistic teachings was to carry the study of social phenomena into the third stage—to remove them from the sphere of theology and metaphysics, and see that they be given the same scientific examination of their relations and classifications as had already been given to physical and chemical phenomena. To use John Morley's summary:

> While men's minds were in the theological state, political events, for example, were explained by the will of the gods, and political authority based on divine right. In the metaphysical state of mind . . . political authority was based on the will of the people, and social facts were explained by the figment of the falling away from a state of nature. When the positive method has been fully extended to society, as it has been to chemistry and physiology, these social facts will be resolved, as their ultimate analysis, into relations with one another, and instead of seeking causes in the old sense of the word, men will only examine the conditions of social existence. When that stage has been reached . . . the whole of our knowledge will be impressed with one character, the character, namely, of positivity or scientificalness; and all our conceptions in every part of knowledge will be thoroughly homogeneous. The gains of such a change are enormous.[7]

In addition to this emphasis upon the necessity for a

science of society, an emphasis which could not but affect historical work in proportion as Comte's views were accepted and diffused, the *Positive Philosophy* had another important object. This was to show that the sciences are all branches from a single trunk, parts of one great whole. Comte's special aim was the promotion of sociology, a science never formulated until his advent; but while promoting it he tried to assign it a clear relation to other branches of knowledge. He arranged a hierarchy of sciences, each in his view more specialized than the member just before it, and dependent upon all the preceding sciences: (1) mathematics, (2) astronomy, (3) physics, (4) chemistry, (5) biology, and (6) sociology. If we remember that not a few writers now view history as retrospective sociology, it is at once plain that this doctrine also has had its effect upon historical interpretation.

We have spoken of evolution as giving the world a new philosophy of history; but it also supplied various new interpretations of history, practical and immediate in nature. Until the doctrine was fully introduced by Darwin, Spencer, and others, historians had talked of development rather than evolution. During the Age of Enlightenment advanced thinkers had taken a keen interest in the origin and development of language, of philology, of law, of pictorial art, of legendary and written literature. It was natural that this should be enlarged to include an inquiry into the origin and development of animal life. This investigation, in the hands of men like Darwin, Spencer, and Huxley, soon included an inquiry into the source and means of progress of humankind, and soon also brought forth a revolutionary conception of development. In the eighteenth century the animal world had been looked upon as a series of species or types, but it had never been supposed that the types evolved into one another; each was regarded as independent. Now investigation proved that species or types did change into others. In short, development had become evolution. Though Darwin was by far the greatest scientist to investigate the supposed laws of evolution, Herbert Spencer made the most ambitious effort to apply evolution as a universal interpretive principle, using it to explain the development of human society as well as of the animal kingdom. His doctrine of integration followed by differentiation remains highly suggestive to the historian even today.

Holders of the old view of the factors involved in the development of organic life had naïvely fallen back upon a series of cosmic cataclysms to explain what was otherwise inexplicable. Darwin declared that the true factors were increasing complexity, infinite differentiation, adaptation to environment, natural selection by the survival of the fittest, and the transmission of acquired characteristics. Previously an apparently unbridgeable gap had existed between men and dumb animals; now this chasm was filled. Previously no clear alternative had been offered to the theological doctrine of creation; now one was formulated. Previously a huge body of historical facts had seemed trivial and without sequence or relationship; now relationships could be suggested and the significance of nearly all facts demonstrated. A large number of biological analogies suggested themselves to students of history. It is hardly too much to say that most departments of human thought re-oriented themselves after the publication *On the Origin of Species*, and history was one.

Within a single generation the range of evolutionary interpretations became extremely wide. It ran from Freeman's work on the evolution of the English Constitution, and Sir Henry Maine's on the evolution of law, both scientific in character, to such a book as Winwood Reade's summary of world history called *The Martyrdom of Man*— a book which, first published in 1872, has gone through a score of British and American editions. Reade pictures the past of mankind in colors of repellent darkness, and hints at a future of dazzling brightness, finding the bridge between the two in the process of evolutionary betterment. In America the Spencerian interpretation was best applied to history by John Fiske. He interpreted the rise of democracy in this country by analogy from biological evolution, and explained it as analogous to the growth of British democracy from the ancient Teutonic folk moot. The word evolution soon crept into book titles, and has become so firmly established there that no conceivable force could dislodge it; men write on the Evolution of Congress, the Evolution of Fashions, the Evolution of the Novel, the evolution of every force or social element that has a history. The biological analogy is seldom encountered, and even when met is seldom pushed far. But it is safe to assert that more than half the historians now writing bring to their interpretation of the facts at least a few fragmentary ideas of the mutation of species or types, of adaptation to environment, and of natural selection by survival of the fittest. Their minds have consciously or unconsciously taken much of the Darwinian mold.

VI

It is impossible to pursue further the various interpretations brought in by new scientific knowledge or theories. Psychology has resulted in the rewriting of a vast deal of history; not merely by furnishing new concepts of great leaders, but by throwing fresh light on mass-emotion, mass-thinking, the behavior of special groups, and the growth and decay of certain states of mind. The newer medical knowledge, as everyone can see by reading Dr. Hans Zinsser's *Rats, Lice and History* or Dr. C. MacLaurin's works on the pathological record of eminent men and women, has affected the treatment of the past.* The progress of economic geography has made possible searching new interpretations of history. And this scientific advance goes on along an ever-widening front. Many old views are slowly discarded; few present-day historians would think of citing Buckle or Comte to buttress an interpretation and many do not even know what they taught. But even the exploded and outmoded theories have helped to generate a spirit of unfettered inquiry and discussion, to stimulate men to use

---

* In *Post Mortem* Dr. MacLaurin deals with the medical history of Joan of Arc, Charles V, Anne Boleyn, Napoleon I, and Cellini; in *Mere Mortals* with the medical record of Ivan the Terrible, Henry VIII, Frederick the Great, James I, and others. He thinks that the true reason for Charles V's retirement lay in arteriosclerosis.

new tools fearlessly, and to give historical study a pervading atmosphere of alertness and energy. Believers in history realize that it must be kept in touch with other branches of knowledge, and abreast of them. As a result of the successive injections of new ideas, today we have numerous large schools of historical interpretation, and a great many minor schools or sub-schools.

The oldest school is the still-surviving group of religious-minded historians. While the theological philosophy of history has decayed in the sense that few men would think of making Christianity the central pattern of world-history, nevertheless many writers believe that certain phases of history illuminate God's workings in the world. Sometimes the belief is explicit, more often sub-conscious. Thomas Carlyle wrote of the French Revolution as a gigantic object-lesson in the penalty that quackery, greed, and evil bring upon themselves, a tremendous illustration of God's determination to make crooked ways straight. With theological dogmas Carlyle had no patience whatever; he condemned them as "Hebrew old-clothes," talked of priests as apes chattering by the banks of the Dead Sea, and remarked that Newman had the brains of a moderate-sized rabbit. But he was highly religious in a deeper, more mystical sense, and his histories are the utterances of a religious prophet preaching by pictures of the past—flaming and unforgettable pictures. Often accused of holding that Might makes Right, he protested sternly that he believed the precise opposite; that Right and Might are in the long run identical because Right alone is enduring. His belief that Right is the expression of the divine will he wrought into every texture of his histories. It was of course a very different type of religious history that John Henry Newman wrote, but it had more force than Carlyle believed.

And many later historians have had theological preconceptions. The shallower kind of religious history receives—and deserves—general disregard. We have little patience today with George Bancroft remarking in his eulogy of Lincoln: "That God rules in the affairs of men is as certain as any truth of physical science . . . Kings are lifted up and thrown down, nations come and go . . . but nothing is by chance, though men, in their ignorance of causes, may think so. The deeds of time are governed, as well as judged, by the decrees of eternity." We have little patience with Hilaire Belloc's twaddle about the figure of an Ultramontane and very Bellocian God in all human affairs.* But history that discloses a deep pervasive undercurrent of religious conviction may often merit the utmost respect. As Woodrow Wilson declared, the record of nations possesses a spiritual quality, and is fundamentally a product "not of institutions, but of the heart."

An almost equally venerable school of writers still interprets history largely by the lamp of political science. They hold that the most significant aspect of the human past lies in the effort of men to give objective form to the principles of governmental theory. Of this school Von Ranke remains the great exemplar, for even his studies in church history were essentially studies in statecraft and state-organization. To it belong such English historians as Gardiner and Froude; such French historians as Guizot and Michelet; such American historians as Schouler and Rhodes. It remains strong despite all the inroads of newer history, and it will continue to persist and to show strength. In the hands of this group history is a definite and dignified entity, explaining much that is undeniably of first importance in the past, and offering a fixed and solid discipline to the mind. Its history of statesmen, soldiers, and churchmen is narrow and at times a bit arid, but it possesses form and significance. While the record of mankind has become much more than the history of states, state-history remains no mean part of it.

One of the most vigorous schools of all, the school which

---

* A passage in Newman's *Apologia Pro Vita Sua* (Chapter V) shows that even he sometimes lost faith in a divine pattern. He speaks of the unhappy lot of mankind—"their aimless courses, their random achievements and acquirements, the impotent conclusions of long-standing facts, the tokens so faint and broken of a superintending design, the blind evolution of what turn out to be great powers or truths, the progress of things as if from unreasoning elements, not towards final causes . . . all this . . . inflicts upon the mind the sense of a profound mystery, which is utterly beyond human solution."

expounds one form or another of the economic interpretation of history, now boasts of so many departments that it has become difficult to treat it under a single rubric. It has been an extremely fertile school, producing within a century a vast sea of historical literature. For example, Labriola calls the Reformation an economic rebellion of the German nation, and R. H. Tawney has placed some aspects of religion in an economic light. Emile Durkheim (a sociologist rather than historian) asserts that history is essentially the progress of the principle of division of labor.[8] Marxian or pseudo-Marxian historians have interpreted the record of many communities and nations as primarily a history of the division and antagonism of classes —the class conflict. Some historians of the economic school, like Guglielmo Ferrero, have taken a highly pessimistic view of the course of the human race. Some, like H. G. Wells, who has also been greatly influenced by evolutionary doctrine and Marxian ideas, are highly optimistic; they look forward to the rise of society from level to level until it attains a millennial state. One of the compendious histories of the American people, Charles and Mary Beard's *Rise of American Civilization*, is primarily an economic interpretation. Anyone who looks at a critical bibliography of American history must be struck by the sweeping extent of the present-day movement for rewriting the history of American colonization, expansion, the Revolutionary and Civil Wars, and party conflicts, in terms of their economic springs. But this tendency toward economic reinterpretation has gained equal vigor in almost all Western lands.

The school which presents a geographical interpretation of history is by no means a mere subdivision of the preceding school, but maintains a place of its own. It holds that the degree of a people's civilization is determined primarily by its physical surroundings and climatic influences. One of the more prominent exponents of this theory, Ellsworth Huntington, made particularly notable studies of the influence of climate upon history. To the stimulating effect of certain climates, conjoined with the possession of rich natural resources and other factors, he attributes the rise of great civilizations in a few favored lands—the western part of the European continent, the British Isles, eastern North America. To the lack of such stimulation he attributes the cultural barrenness of other lands, and to changes in the climate he would trace much of the decay of earlier civilizations in western Asia and the Mediterranean basin. More modest and conventional uses of geography are to be found in the writings of such Americans as Ellen C. Semple and R. H. Brigham. But the whole relation of geography and history must be reserved for fuller treatment.

Social history, cultural history, intellectual history—these names are applied to the work of various interpretive groups between which it is hard to draw clear boundary lines; groups which all unite, however, in giving history a wide and loose significance. Cultural history can perhaps be set in a special category. In the strictest sense it is a history of cultural institutions related to underlying currents of national or community life. Leslie Stephen in *English Literature and Society in the Eighteenth Century* (1904), an admirable example, not merely furnishes a satisfactory history of English letters from Addison to Walter Scott. He goes further and shows how the content of this literature arose from the social conditions of the time. Not only this, but he goes still further and demonstrates that literary form itself has a vital unity with these social conditions. That is, the lines along which this form—the drama, the epic, the essay, the novel—develop, depend upon the character, origin, and tastes of the literary class which uses it as a vehicle for its ideas and impulses; upon the constitution of the reading class which offers a market for these ideas; and upon the correspondence between these ideas and the most powerful intellectual tendencies of the time. W. J. Courthope's comprehensive *History of English Poetry* places the development of prosody upon a foundation in the developing social conditions of English history. Such a striking little masterpiece of interpretation as Taine's *Art of the Netherlands* does the same. So, also, do the learned and beautifully written volumes of John Addington Symonds on the Renaissance, and Burckhardt's single volume on the subject; Georg Brandes's *Main Currents in*

Nineteenth Century Literature; and Vernon L. Parrington's work. Samuel Eliot Morison's history of Harvard in the seventeenth and eighteenth centuries presents a highly satisfactory cultural history of all early New England.

Sociological and social history of course constitute a much larger and vaguer department of scholarship and letters. At the one extreme we find a group which would base history upon the dictum of Franklin H. Giddings: "Sociology is an attempt to account for the origin, growth, structure, and activities of society by the operation of physical, vital, and psychological causes working together in the process of evolution." This group has given us books like Kidd's *Social Evolution,* which is a thoughtful interpretation of the function of religion in history, and J. Donald Forrest's *Development of Western Society.* At the other extreme we find a group devoted to what the Germans called *kulturgeschichte*—that is, writers who attempt to describe the life of a people during a certain period in all its phases. An early example is offered by Karl Biedermann's *Germany in the 18th Century.* Good recent examples are offered by the best volumes of *The History of American Life,* edited by Arthur M. Schlesinger and Dixon Ryan Fox, and inspired in part by H. D. Traill's co-operative work, *Social England.*

The principal weakness of this type of history is that in undisciplined hands it easily grows into an encyclopedia of unrelated details, a mountain of petty facts piled loosely together. These facts may be departmentalized by labeling one part of them The Changing Church, another part The Educational Revival, another Home Life, another The Deepening of Culture, another Professions and Business; but an encyclopedia is not converted into history by departmentalizing it. Carefully pondered principles of selection—principles of high and permanent significance—are necessary before the facts of social history can be properly assayed; and even when this is done, effective presentation of the facts requires an insight that approaches genius. The best specimens of social history in English remain the third chapter of Macaulay's *History of England,* and the first six chapters of Henry Adams's *History of the United States* under Jefferson and Madison.*

VII

As from philosophy we descend to interpretation, so from the latter we descend to thesis or synthesis. Perhaps few works of history are directly touched by philosophy. Many of the best are also quite untouched by any special interpretation; Macaulay and Parkman, for example, rather wrote history according to their individual bent than according to any school of thought, though accepting to some extent the idea of the superior significance of the state. But few histories of any distinction lack a thesis, or if that word is too strong, at least a definite principle of synthesis; the author wishing to demonstrate some view. It may be a commonplace and obvious view. It may be marked by great originality and insight, and in the most brilliant histories it is. But history which lacks a thesis is a body lacking a skeleton—it is invertebrate. It may contain exhaustive research, may be striking in detail, may throw new light into dark places, but its total effect will be limp. Channing's volumes on the colonial period contain no thesis worth mentioning, while those of George Louis Beer contain a sharp-cut, novel, and emphatic thesis. The result is that while nobody ever speaks of Channing's ideas, Beer's ideas have been a staple of discussion ever since they were propounded; while we try to remember Channing's facts, we distinctly remember Beer's views.

More than once a volume enforcing a thesis has changed the views of millions and itself made history. Thus it was with Treitschke's insistence upon the importance of national unity and a powerful central government; his histories altered the attitude of a multitude of Germans toward their national destiny. Some have traced Germany's plunge into the First World War to his works, as a generation earlier some students ascribed the War of 1870 to the histories of Thiers. Frederick J. Turner's thesis of the effect of the

* G. M. Trevelyan's *Social History of England* may be given nearly equal rank.

frontier upon American life and character has colored not
only all historical thought in this country, but literary
thought, social thought, and political thought. Alfred T.
Mahan, by the vigorous thesis of his *Influence of Seapower
upon History, 1660–1783*, followed by his *Influence of
Seapower upon the French Revolution, 1783–1812*, affected the governmental policy of all the great maritime
powers. His interpretation threw an entirely new light upon
one department of the past, and read from it arresting and
convincing lessons for the future. Japan, Germany, Great
Britain, and the United States applied these lessons to their
naval programs and strategy.

Sometimes a historical thesis may be non-controversial.
Students could hardly quarrel over the central thesis of
Parkman's Jesuits in North America, for example, which is
simply that the Jesuits failed because they built their hopes
of an American empire on the Hurons and their kindred
tribes, and these were ultimately conquered by the hostile
Iroquois. Parkman himself spoke of this thesis as "obvious,"
and drew from it only an elementary inference: "Liberty
may thank the Iroquois that, by their insensate fury, the
plans of her adversary were brought to nought and a peril
and a woe averted from her future." More commonly,
however, the thesis is avowedly controversial. Take, for example, any one of the half dozen principal works upon the
authorship of Homer. After Friedrich A. Wolf's epochal
Prolegomena to Homer (an astonishing piece of work for
its early date, 1795), which contended that the *Iliad* and
Odyssey in their present-day form have been materially
changed from the originals, and are made up of separate
poems composed at different times by various authors, it
was impossible to write on that subject without some highly
argumentative thesis. Andrew Lang in *Homer and His
Age* sounded a counterblast to the disintegrationists. He
held that the *Iliad*, far from being the work of four or five
centuries, a score of bards, and a medley of old and new
ideas, was the product of a single age and a single state
of culture, the poet describing his own environment. It was
an age which had given up burial and adopted cremation,
substituted iron tools for bronze while still retaining bronze

weapons, and learned the art of writing, so that it preserved Homer's work on palm leaves, papyrus, or parchment, now perished. Or as examples of differing opinions,
we may cite the numerous theses applied to the history of
the Tudors by the schools of A. F. Pollard, of Sir John
Neale, of A. P. Newton, of R. H. Tawney, and of Conyers
Read.

Sometimes a thesis rests upon striking new evidence
which really puts an entirely different face upon an old
problem. The series of volumes which the Brookings Institute has sponsored on the Presidential conventions and
campaigns of 1952, 1956, and 1960, written by groups
which include professional political scientists, United States
Senators, journalists, and research specialists, draw largely
upon novel sources. These vary from polls, mass media,
and campaign propaganda to expert studies of political
strategy; and they put the whole election process in the
American democracy in a new perspective. Sometimes the
thesis represents rather a stimulating new study of old material. Henry Osborn Taylor's *The Medieval Mind* affords
an example. Most of the evidence he examined was familiar
to everybody. But he took the unusual view that the true
key to the medieval mind lay not in the vernacular writings, English, French, Spanish, and so on, but in the Latin
writings of the period, which he held incomparably more
valuable for the study of medieval thought—even Dante
being in a sense but a byroad from the main highway of
medieval culture. He amplified his thesis by stating that
the supreme medieval achievement in thought was "the
vital appropriation and emotional humanizing of patristic
Christianity," represented by such thinkers as Albertus
Magnus and Thomas Aquinas.

Or a thesis may combine interesting new material with
a novel reworking of old data, as in some of Henri Pirenne's
books—his *Economic and Social History of Medieval Europe*, for example, which contends that it was not the
collapse of the Roman Empire but the swift rise of the
Moslem power in the eighth century which cut off Western Europe from its Eastern connections, or his *History of
Belgium*, in seven volumes, which emphasizes the economic

and traditional forces which drew Flemings and Walloons together down the centuries.

Sometimes the thesis of a book carries almost instant conviction. Julius W. Pratt's *Expansionists of 1812* made so clear the role of Western land-hunger in provoking the second war against Great Britain that at once every student stood ready to accord that factor much greater emphasis. Gilbert H. Barnes's *The Antislavery Impulse 1830–44* emphasized so successfully the relation of evangelical religion to the rise of the anti-slavery movement, and the prominence of New York and Western leaders—Theodore Dwight Weld, Charles G. Finney, Lewis Tappan, Joshua R. Giddings, and others—in a cause previously connected chiefly with Garrison and other New Englanders that its influence was immediate. One part of Frank L. Owsley's otherwise controversial *King Cotton Diplomacy* was persuasive: his demonstration that the wartime boom 1861–65 enjoyed by British interests engaged in woolens, munitions, shipping, and the iron trade was a powerful factor in keeping Britain neutral. Owsley's *Plain Folk of the Old South,* based on "sampling" studies of manuscript census reports, county records, church archives, and other local materials showed that the yeoman farmers had greater numbers, thrift and energy, and a more humane system of slavery, than the picture given by Frederick Law Olmsted and others had suggested.

Sometimes, however, the extravagance of a thesis soon puts its maker out of court. The various forms of overstatement in Sydney George Fisher's provocative *Struggle for American Independence* offer an instance. He correctly asserts that the struggle did not arise from British misrule, but from the British effort to reorganize the colonial system, and by using the sovereignty recognized as belonging to their government, to modernize it. He goes on to say that this assertion of sovereignty was an absolute necessity after the expulsion of the French from North America— that it was imperative that it be carried through if Great Britain were to retain her control. It was not, he further argues, a policy begun carelessly and stupidly by a corrupt government and arrogant king; it was launched after long deliberation and investigation by capable statesmen who were asserting the only principles upon which, at that time, colonies could be retained and governed. On the part of the Americans, independence was the object in view from the opening hour of the quarrel, and with many even before sharp friction began. The way for it had been paved by economic interests and political ideas which had long made an attempt at independence inevitable. These last assertions all contain some truth—but they also contain a great deal of error.

VIII

It is the special glory of history that it touches the realm of ideas at more points than almost any other study. Long regarded as rather arid in original thought (and with some reason in view of the multitude of mere factual compilations miscalled history), its greatest productions are actually shot through with intellectual elements. Written history is in the deepest sense the world of our epistomological construction of reality; as such it draws from and contributes to the profoundest metaphysical thought of the ages. In a more prosaic sense, it responds to every great new current of ideas that flows through the Western world; it has so responded from the time of St. Augustine to that of Darwin, Bergson, and Einstein, and it will continue to respond. In still more practical fashion, it has vital connections with every other social science—economics, sociology, public law, jurisprudence, social psychology, human geography—and relations of importance with the chief physical sciences, from biology to geophysics. As they grow and change, the content and outlook of history, the range of its ideas, grow and change also. Finally, history challenges its disciples to arrange the ever-growing mass of facts in ever-better patterns, and thus offers scope for the keenest insight and the most subtle ingenuity. All in all, success in history is proportioned as exactly to intellectual power as success in pure literature or in pure science. Behind every really great history stands a great man:

Not from a vein of shallow thought
His awful Jove young Phidias brought.

With the special glory of its many-sided relation to
ideas, history has also a special responsibility. The intellectual element is but one part of history, and its ideas
must never be given too loose a rein. As the bounds of
history widen, as its outer territories become vague and
shadowy, the importance of maintaining precise standards
of factual accuracy and a high level of significance increases. History pushed too far toward sociology, like sociology pushed too far toward history, falls into a limbo
in which it lacks form and value. Interpretation should
be the leaven of the lump; but the result of applying a
pound of interpretation to an ounce of fact is disappoint-
ing. A balance must be maintained between history as a
body of facts, based solidly upon research, and history as
an exercise in analysis, interpretation, and generalization.

X

Man's Home and His History

THE FIRST SCIENCE which men perceived to have a helpful or auxiliary relation to History was Geography, for the connection between them is so intimate that it could not escape the most elementary observers. At least as early as the time of the Greek philosopher Parmenides, whose ideas were later elaborated by Aristotle, thinkers conceived of both physical geography and climate as having an influence upon human action. Parmenides, like Aristotle after him, believed that the earth was a sphere; and he described it as containing a torrid zone in which man could not act effectively because of heat, two frigid zones in which they could not act effectively because of cold, and two temperate zones placed intermediately in which they could live with comfort and progress successfully. The Greek writer Strabo, who came much later, in the time of Julius Caesar, was both geographer and historian, and combined the two equipments in a study of historical geography. To be sure, his conception of the relation between the two branches of knowledge was rudimentary, but he at least knew that a relation existed, and his great work on geography was so planned as to include mathematical geography, physical geography, political geography, and geography in relation to human history. He, like Parmenides, accepted the theory of a spherical earth, and of its division into five zones, whose conditions of life largely controlled human action. His descriptive writings contain numerous historical notices, often of high value.

When the Age of Exploration fully dawned in the fifteenth century, and men's ideas of the earth were first broadened to attain general accuracy, scholars began to perceive with greater force than ever before the truth which the Greeks had merely adumbrated. They gradually realized that however striking are man's conquests over nature, nevertheless the physical environment of man largely inspires and limits his activities. They perceived that the entire process of life upon the planet is a process of adaptation—that this principle applies as fundamentally to the civilized German or Englishman as to bird, beast, or fish. Hakluyt, in introducing his *Voyages*, declared: "Geography and Chronology I may call the sun and the moon, the right eye and the left, of all history"—thus assigning geography a higher rank than chronology. Another early British writer on geography, Peter Heylyn, declared in his *Microcosmus* in 1625 that while geography could possess a certain vitality without history, the converse was not true. "History without geography, like a dead carcass, hath neither life nor motion at all, but moves at best but slowly on the understanding." Francis Bacon also showed that the Elizabethan Age possessed some very modern notions of the interrelation of history and geography.

As knowledge in both domains grew, men of course became able to demonstrate this relationship more completely. By the last decades of the eighteenth century, the greater part of the world had been roughly mapped, while Voltaire, Hume, Gibbon, and other writers had introduced the critical age in historical writing. In fine, the scientific temper had been applied to both subjects; myth and tradition were being fast eradicated from cartography and historiography alike. It is not surprising, therefore, to find the philosopher Kant by this time giving a systematic statement of the interdependence of history and geography.

A genuine understanding of this many-sided interdependence, indeed, was perhaps first exhibited in Kant's lectures on geography at the University of Königsberg beginning in 1765. He taught that history and geography

were two parts of a whole: one being a description of the
world and its inhabitants in the order of time, the other a
description of them in the order of space. He taught also
that physical geography was the primary basis of history,
for it was the great determinant of various branches of
geography which obviously affected and controlled history.
That is, it was the determinant of (1) moral geography,
which has reference to the different characters and customs of peoples, varying according to the lands they occupy; (2) of political geography, which has reference to
the governmental divisions of mankind; (3) of mercantile
geography, or as we should now say, economic geography,
which refers to the various occupations of mankind; and
(4) of theological geography, which has reference to the
distribution of religions.

It is clear that an epochal forward step had been taken
in relating the human past to the human environment
when students began to be taught, for example, that the
history of religions has been largely determined by soil,
climate, natural resources, physical communications, and
like factors. That teaching effectively began with Kant.

Alexander von Humboldt was strictly a geographer; a
geographer who, beginning with his voyage to South America in 1799, and ending with his trip to the Urals and
Yenisei in 1829, traveled over almost the whole known
world to make his observations, and gathered and classified a huge body of facts upon physical geography. His
Cosmos was published between 1845 and 1858. He was
not greatly interested in history, for what absorbed most
of his attention was simply the forms of the land's surface. But he had an encyclopedic range of observation;
he made interesting studies of the languages, architecture,
and customs of ancient peoples in Central and South
America; and he demonstrated that land forms exercise a
determining influence not only upon climate, plant life, and
animal life, but upon man himself. For this great principle
he offered a multitude of interesting illustrations. His eminent contemporary Carl Ritter (1779–1859), who was less
strictly a geographer, expanded and disseminated the
same views. He became far more interested than Humboldt

was in the influence of climate and terrestrial relief upon human history. He was thus led deeper and deeper into a study of archaeology and history; and his voluminous work on geography, *Die Erdkunde*, an encyclopedia of geographical lore as to Asia and Africa, gives great space to the effect of the earth's surface upon man, and is thus largely historical in content. He asserts that certain parts of the world were predestined for the historical role which they actually played. It has been complained that some of his followers look upon geography rather as an auxiliary of history than an independent study.

I

By the time of Ritter's and Humboldt's deaths, the relationship between geography and history was occupying numerous other able pens. Buckle, in the first volume of his *History of Civilization in England*, laid down the great geographical laws which he believed contributed so powerfully to the governance of history. He agreed with John Stuart Mill that the most crude, vulgar, and irritating of all means of evading the effect of physical and social influences upon the human mind was "that of attributing the diversities of conduct and character to inherent natural differences." He classified under four heads the physical agencies exerting the most powerful influence upon the human race—climate; food; soil; and the general aspect of nature. The first three, as he explained, must be studied together, for each is largely dependent on the others. These three influence mankind, he declared, primarily because they govern the accumulation of wealth, and the amount of wealth in turn governs the culture of peoples. Under the rubric of soils, he called attention to the roving Tartars who forsook the barren steppes of Asia, and betook themselves to the fertile plains and valleys of China, Asia, and Russia, there developing great empires and civilizations; to the Arabs who left their stony deserts, and developed brilliant civilizations at Baghdad and Cordova.

Buckle also pointed out that physical causes governed not only the accumulation but the distribution of wealth.

In dealing with this topic, he presents some suggestive pages upon the relation of cheap foods to the growth, standards, and general culture of different populations—rice to India; the date to Egypt; the potato to Ireland; and maize and potatoes to the natives of Peru—showing how such cheap food for the laboring masses may be a national handicap rather than a benefit. In this connection, he hints at the familiar fact that temperate climates, with alternating seasons of plenty and scarcity, develop provident characteristics in a nation. Turning to the general aspects of nature, Buckle attempts to show that it does much in different lands (1) to stir the imagination (2) to affect the understanding. He ascribes to scenery, for example, much of the difference between the ancient civilizations of India, where nature shows itself in forms of "startling magnitude," and of Greece, where it manifests itself in forms more suave, beautiful, and "less threatening to man." Buckle's geographic interpretation of history is impressive not so much by reason of any novelty—for his general ideas are not new—as through its systematic, closely reasoned character, and its many pregnant and thought-provoking observations.

His contemporary Michelet, in the second volume of his *History of France*, showed the influence of the general ideas of the times by giving much space to a treatment of the physical geography of the country. "History is first of all geography," he wrote, and added: "Without a geographical basis, the people, the actors of history, seem to be walking in air, as in Chinese paintings . . . Ground or soil is not only the theatre of the action. Through food, climate, etc., its influence is felt in a hundred ways. As the nest, so the bird, and as the country, so the man." Indeed, few European historians writing on a broad scale after 1850 failed to take note of geographic factors. We may instance, as a not untypical figure, John Richard Green. Geography is sketched in, briefly to be sure, at every stage of his *Short History of the English People*. And in another book, *The Making of England* (1882), geography is almost the chief actor in the drama. Green of course introduces us to Roman and Dane, Jute and Saxon.

But the physical state of the country—with the fens, the downs, the forests, the chalk areas, the mountain fastnesses —is shown on almost every page as determining the conduct of the piratical raiders, the defenders, and the new colonists. Note, for example, the passage in which he describes why London became London:

LONDON

> The commercial greatness of London has made men forget its military importance, but from the first moment of history until late in the Middle Ages London was one of the strongest of our fortresses. Its site, indeed, must have been dictated, like that of most early cities, by the advantages which it presented as well for defence as for trade. It stood at the one point at which either merchant or invader could penetrate from the estuary into the valley of the Thames; and in its earlier days, before the great changes wrought by the embankment of the Romans, this was also the first point at which any rising ground for the site of such a town presented itself on either shore of the river. Nowhere has the hand of man moulded ground into shapes more strangely contrasted with its natural form than on the site of London. Even as late as the time of Caesar, the soil which a large part of it covers can have been little but a vast morass. Below Fulham the river stretched at high tide over the ground that lies on either side of its present channel from the rises of Kensington and Hyde Park to the opposite shores of Peckham and Camberwell. All Pimlico and Westminster to the north, to the south all Battersea and Lambeth, all Newington and Kennington, all Bermondsey and Rotherhithe, formed a vast lagoon, broken only by little rises which became the "eyes" and "hithes," the "islands" and "landing-rises," of later settlements. Still lower down to the eastward the swamp widened as the Lea poured its waters into the Thames in an estuary of its own—an estuary which ran far to the north over as wide an expanse of marsh and fen, while at its mouth it stretched its tidal waters over the mud flats . . . Near the point where the two rivers meet, a traveller who was mounting the Thames from the sea

saw the first dry land to which his bark could steer. The spot was, in fact, the extremity of the low line of rising ground which was thrown out from the heights of Hampstead that border the river-valley to the north, and which passed over the sites of our Hyde Park and Holborn to thrust itself on the east into the great morass. This eastern portion of it, however, was severed from the rest of the rise by the deep gorge of a stream which fell from the northern hills, the stream of the Fleet, whose waters, long since lost in the London sewers, ran in earlier days between steep banks to the Thames at Blackfriars.

The rise or "dun" that stretched from this tidal channel of the Fleet to the spot now marked by the Tower, and which was destined to become the site of London, rose at its highest some fifty feet above the level of the tide . . . Such a position was admirably adapted for defence. It was, indeed, almost impregnable. Sheltered to east and south by lagoons of the Lea and the Thames, guarded to westward by the deep cleft of the Fleet, it saw stretching along its northern border the broad fen whose name has survived in our modern Moorgate. Nor, as the first point at which merchants could land from the great river, was the spot less adapted for trade. But it was long before the trader found dwelling on its soil. Old as it is, London is far from being one of the oldest of English cities; till the coming of the Romans, indeed, the loneliness of its site seems to have been unbroken by any settlement whatever. The "dun" was in fact the center of a great wilderness. Beyond the marshes to the east lay the forest track of Southern Essex. Across the lagoon to the south rose . . . woodlands . . . To the north the heights of Highgate and Hampstead were crowned with forest masses through which the boar and the wild ox wandered without fear of man down to the days of the Plantagenets.

With the coming of the Romans, however, this solitude passed away. We know nothing of the settlement of the town; but its advantages as the first landing-place along the Thames secured for it at once the command of all trading intercourse with Gaul, and through Gaul with the empire at large.[1]

II

But much as had been done by 1880 to relate geography and history, a more advanced set of principles remained to be discovered. In the latter part of the nineteenth century arose the eminent founder of human geography, or anthropogeography, as Friedrich Ratzel called it. The first volume of his *Anthropo-Geographie* appeared in 1882, and the second in 1891. It is not unfair to say that Ratzel, with such enthusiastic pupils as the Frenchman Jean Brunhes, have attempted to reverse the concept held by Carl Ritter, that geography is an appanage of history, and substitute a concept in which no true historian will acquiesce—that history is an appanage of geography. Anthropogeography has been defined as the science of the expansion and distribution of mankind over the earth. To Brunhes we owe the best brief explanation of the objects which Ratzel sought in his published works. "He considers the human race and human peoples in a constant state of displacement, ferment, expansion, and retreat, and from his point of view history is merely the sum of population-movements. But he also treats of peoples and societies as developing in natural domains, occupying a definite area and requiring a certain amount of territory for subsistence and growth. He attaches great importance not only to immediate environment, but to the relation of peoples to the position of the continents, the seas, and the islands, to the zones, to vegetation-belts, to accidents of relief, and to the great pathways of land and sea commerce."

One of Ratzel's principal doctrines is that the relation between man and his environment is not the hostility of two contending forces, but is a process in which man develops himself as part of the earth's equipment. Man has been changed by terrestrial transformations—by glacial ages, warm ages, changes in plant and animal life, changes in rivers, lakes, and seas; man today is a product not only of social development, but of the planet's development, and is inseparably linked with his mother-earth. A second of Ratzel's doctrines, and a very weak one, is that nations and societies are actual organisms responding to nature as an animal does to its physical environment. He emphasizes the distribution of population (which depends upon geographical factors) as one of the key-elements in all history. Civilization and political superiority, he maintains, have always flourished in the thickly populated districts; and the whole of human development has been a progression from small populations dwelling in extensive regions to large populations concentrated in more limited areas.

Among the principal followers of Ratzel have been Ellen C. Semple in America, Elisée Réclus in France, and Halford J. Mackinder in England—though they of course do not accept all of Ratzel's teachings. They agree upon the fundamental postulate that a great part of history must be treated as the result of geographical factors; that looking back of every historical event, we will nearly always find a geographical fact expressed in it. "Back of Massachusetts's passionate abolition movement," writes Miss Semple, "it [human geography] sees the granite soil and boulder-strewn fields of New England; back of the South's long fight for the maintenance of slavery, it sees the rich plantations of tidewater Virginia and the teeming fertility of the Mississippi bottomlands. This is the geographical significance of Herder's saying that 'history is geography set in motion.' What is today a fact of geography becomes tomorrow a factor of history." Miss Semple's theories are set forth in her book *The Influence of Geographical Environment*. She differentiates four great classes of geographical influence: (1) direct physical effect; (2) psychical effects; (3) economic and social effects; and (4) effects on the movements of populations. Like Réclus, she emphasizes the necessity of distinguishing between the static aspects of the geographic environment, and the dynamic aspects, changed oftenest by man's own inventions. Seas, oceans, rivers, were once great barriers; but later man's hand made them the avenues of civilization. Miss Semple's ideas are to some extent applied in her earlier volume *American His-*

tory and Its Geographic Conditions—a book which describes first the effect of the geography of Western Europe upon American history; then the part played by the great coastal rivers; then that of the Appalachian mountain barrier; and then that of the interior rivers and plains. She explains, for example, precisely why it was that Kentucky was settled by a trail that led across the headwaters of the Tennessee.

The effort to formulate novel laws regarding the influence of geography upon history, and to strike out fertile new generalizations, has by no means ceased and will not do so. The most daring recent theorem has been the attempt of Dr. Ellsworth Huntington to establish a direct and invariable connection between a stimulating climate and a high degree of civilization. "Whatever the motive power of history may be," he writes, "one of the chief factors in determining its course has been geography; and among geographical forces, changes of climate have been the most potent for good or bad." A stimulating climate, in his opinion, is one which, though generally temperate—neither excessively hot nor excessively cold for long periods—nevertheless fluctuates constantly in temperature and humidity, so that the body is kept in a perpetual state of readjustment. Such a climate exists today in the Eastern United States, in the British Isles, in Northern Europe, in Argentina, and in New Zealand; it does not exist in India, Brazil, or Southern California. He believes that it existed not only in ancient Greece and Rome, but in ancient Egypt, Assyria, and Babylonia; that is, he attacks the conventional notion that civilization first developed in warm climates, and later was transferred to the temperate zone. Instead, he contends that all the successive centers of civilization had about the same climate at the time their cultures reached an apex—the inference being that the climate north of the equator has been slowly growing warmer. But while asserting that "prolonged study of past and present climatic variations suggests that the location of some of the most stimulating conditions varies from century to century, and that when the great centers of antiquity rose to eminence they enjoyed a climatic stimulus comparable with that existing today where the leading nations now dwell," he carefully safeguards the implied generalization:

> Today a certain type of climate prevails wherever civilization is high. In the past, the same type seems to have prevailed wherever a great civilization arose. Therefore, such a climate seems to be a necessary condition for great progress. This is not the cause of civilization, for that lies infinitely deeper. Nor is it the only, or the most important, condition. It is merely one of several, just as an abundant supply of pure water is one of the primary conditions of health. Good water will not make people healthy, nor will a favorable climate cause a stupid and degenerate race to rise to a high level.

Many of Dr. Huntington's conclusions seem open to question. We may well hesitate over his attempted correlation of periods of Roman expansion with eras of stimulating climate, periods of Roman decline with depressing climatic conditions; did the Italian climate change when Mussolini came in? He explains Germany's remarkable First World War effort as due to the fact that "no other nation in the world has so many people who live under a highly stimulating climate"; but why did Germany remain politically and economically retarded during two thousand years of substantially the same climate? Some observers believe that admirable civilizations may hereafter flourish in lands of heat and of uniform climate. The Australians hope that they may develop energetic and cultured communities in their equatorial zone, and are trying the experiment under almost ideal conditions. The human stock is one of the best in the world; natural resources are great; nothing need be feared from the native races; tropical diseases are few and science can control them; the Australian government is as good as any on the globe, and better than most. North Queensland, as Dr. Huntington admits in *West of the Pacific*, may yet disprove his generalization that a stimulating climate is a necessary condition for a splendid civilization.

One reason for a skeptical attitude toward Dr. Huntington's generalization lies in the fact that bad climates—i.e., climates bad for civilization—have so often been disease-ridden climates, and that the fall of some civilizations, the retardation of others, have been with little doubt traceable in part to epidemic or endemic ailments. Malaria has been a powerful factor in all recorded history. It is quite possible that the decline of civilization in the Tigris-Euphrates basin has been due much more largely to the conquest of that area by malaria than to changes in climate. For centuries malaria affected a great part of Greece; for centuries it made the Roman Campagna one of the notorious fever-holes of the world. Students have seriously argued that, brought in from conquered lands, it was an important factor in the decline of Greek and Roman civilization. The effect of the hookworm upon the cultural level of society in our Southern States had undeniably been heavy; but Dr. Charles Stiles showed how it could be combated, and that brake upon progress has been removed. In recent times, bilharzia—a disease rife in Egypt for thousands of years, for the examination of mummies has shown its ancient prevalence—has also been brought under control. Transmitted by a fast-breeding micro-organism, it penetrates the skin of any person who touches infected water, and causes debility, inanition, and death. It may well have cost civilization in Egypt much more than did any changes in the climate, for we possess no real evidence that the climate altered substantially in the centuries in which civilization was sinking from a high to a low level. During the First World War competent pathologists accompanied the British troops to Egypt, set to work to discover why so many English soldiers died of bilharzia, isolated the micro-organism, and perfected preventive measures. There again a brake upon progress was removed.

III

But while the influence of geography (including climate) upon history may be overstated, beyond question the influence is great, and its principal lines can be defined, though this is a complex matter. The dominion exercised over mankind by geography has not only taken exceedingly numerous forms, but has also varied in the most complicated fashion from age to age, according to the amount and kind of knowledge which man has been able to accumulate. The geographical controls effective in the dawn of history, when civilization first arose in the basins of the Nile, the Tigris, and the Euphrates, were very different from the controls effective some centuries later, when the Egyptians and Cretans, later followed by the Phoenicians and Greeks, learned what the Babylonians never did—to master the inland seas. China until recent times has remained in the Babylonian stage of mastery over its physical surroundings; that is, it has been a river nation instead of a maritime nation. But the Egyptians, Phoenicians, and Greeks learned to convert the Mediterranean from its troublesome status of a barrier into the highly serviceable status of a highway.

Another revolution in man's relation to geography occurred some centuries later, when the Romans perfected the art of road-building, and erected an empire which was held together partly by the old sea-roads, and partly by the new land-roads. Later still man's mastery of environment was enlarged by the discovery of improvements in shipbuilding and the art of navigation, which enabled him to convert the great oceans as well as the inland seas into highways. A new road to India was discovered; the new world of the Americas; Australia and the new world of the South. Thus a novel set of geographical controls was brought into existence, while the old set sank into desuetude. The seat of empire rapidly shifted from the Mediterranean to northwestern Europe, because this became as much the center of the new planet as Italy had been of the old *orbis terrarum*. Most geographical factors in this shift are familiar, but one of them may escape everybody save the specialist. This lies in the fact that northwestern Europe, and especially Great Britain, is a region of heavy tidal energy. These tides prevent the rivers from silting up; rising, they carry vessels far inland, against river currents and adverse winds; ebbing, they carry ships out to sea and around difficult headlands. Still later, when man's knowledge extended to the use of coal and steam, and the Industrial Revolution was born, yet another set of geographical controls achieved prominence. The lands endowed with a great deposit of stored energy in the form of coal were those which physical geography now favored. It is evident to everyone that the mastery of the air by mankind is doing away with certain former geographical controls, and substituting fresh and until recently unforeseen factors. Thus man and environment act and react upon one another, and every advance in science, invention, and technology affects the force and pattern of the interaction. The subtle and often arresting ways in which geographical controls are established, broken down, and reshifted by man's capacity to seek out many inventions, present a challenge to the imagination and penetration of the historian. An arresting example of this form of study is to be found in Walter P. Webb's *The Great Plains*. The author shows how the broad section of the United States between the Missouri and the Rockies was too refractory for hand tools, and could be conquered only when the Industrial Revolution had attained full maturity, and had been brought into the heart of the area by railroad-building. The plains country was level, windy, arid, hot in summer, cold in winter, and practically devoid of timber; it was roamed by especially vigorous and warlike Indian tribes, mounted on horses that had descended from the stock of the Spanish explorers, and well armed with bows and arrows. The natural resources of the region could not be exploited until special tools were invented and used to overcome the obstacles. The introduction of the Colt revolver gave the mounted Westerner superiority over the mounted Indian; fixed ammunition assisted in the extermination of the buffalo. The cattle kingdom sprang up as railways spread fanwise to an increasing number of "cowtowns."

Then the invention of barbed wire just after the Civil War sharply reduced the costs of stock-growing and crop protection in an area where no wood existed for fences. The windmill gave the stockman and farmer a means of reaching water. Power machinery, culminating in the wheat-combine, made low-cost grain crops possible; while after disastrous experiences in periods of drought, methods of dry-farming were introduced to aid settlers in the semi-arid belt. Altogether, there are few sections in which human invention and industry have altered the old geographical controls with more striking results within a half century than in the Great Plains.[2]

One broad generalization may thus be laid down regarding the effect of geography upon history. On the material side, history is the story of man's increasing ability to control energy. The progress of humanity in practical fields may fairly be summed up as the history of its endeavor to acquire and use as much energy as possible, and to waste as little of it as could be avoided. While man's knowledge remained small, available energy was most abundant in warm fertile lands like Egypt and Mesopotamia, where life was sustained easily. At the same time, seasonal changes there required a provision against the future, and so inculcated forethought and the advantages of accumulation; people lived for the year, and not, as in Central Africa with its unfailing plenty, for the day. Another advantage was that, since desert and sea protected the community, no costly expenditure of energy for defense was needed. Step by step we may follow the pursuit of energy throughout world history to the present day, when the great coal, iron, and petroleum nations dominate the world. Whenever man learns a practical method of utilizing the energy of the tides, the radiation of the sun, or atomic forces, the geographic controls will again be revolutionized.

This single generalization permits the student of history to take reasoned account of all the complex conditions of climate, communications, natural resources, and salubrity which govern the physical use of energy; it likewise permits us to take account of the jerky but irresistible increase in human knowledge which governs the use of energy on the technological side. It presents us with the two halves of that whole which constitutes the material element in history. Beyond this single broad generalization it is hardly profitable for students of history to go.

The applications and elaborations of this law, however,

are endlessly instructive, and may of course be studied in various ways. For example, the complementary roles of the plain, the mountain range, the desert, and the sea in the history of various nations is a subject full of illumination. Some students of geology assert that it was a subsidence of the flat Baltic plain early in the Christian Era which caused the first large migration of Goths to the Black Sea area and the Danubian basin. Beyond question, the great invasions of the Roman Empire by the Huns and Goths in the fourth, fifth, and sixth centuries were made possible by the flatness of the Russian plain and the central European plain. An epigrammatist has remarked that Rome fell because the Chinese built a wall to keep out the Tartars. The statement is as unsatisfactory as most such sweeping dicta; but it is true that when the nomadic peoples of central Asia could no longer prey successfully upon the wide Chinese plain, they turned hungrily westward to the wide European plain. "Had Europe been ruled off from Asia by a great mountain range, there would have been no need for Constantine to build another capital on the Bosporus, nor perhaps for Gibbon to write his history." On the southwestern sector, fortunately, the central European plains did have protection by a mountain wall. When the Saracens poured northward through Spain and crossed the Pyrenees, their numbers diminishing in the process, Charles Martel smashed them at Tours; and they did not dare to repeat the experiment.

We may see the importance of the relation of mountain to plain in the sharp contrast between the happy history of Switzerland as a nation and the tragic history of Poland. The political explanation of the downfall of Poland in the eighteenth century emphasizes her vicious constitution, and the want of character in her governing class. But the geographical explanation emphasizes the fact that Poland was a flat country with no natural barriers to defend her, and so offered an irresistible temptation to the three great military powers surrounding her. They could thrust armies into Poland with ease. But Switzerland, though smaller and weaker, is protected by tremendous mountain ramparts. They have enabled a people of three races, three languages, and two religions to maintain their national unity and independence. One good reason for doubting the stability of the Czechoslovak Republic is that a glance at the map shows that its indefinite continuance in its present form is well-nigh a geographical impossibility. China is of course a great plain, but it is well protected on two sides by the Tibetan mountains and Gobi Desert. The broader aspects of its history have been well summed up by James Fairgrieve in a passage which indicates its complete dependence upon geographical factors. He writes that:

CHINA

owing to the existence of three rivers, themselves the product of the more remote geographical conditions of relief and climate, China has produced a homogeneous people, whose essential unity has been strengthened by the existence on the west of a plateau of enormous breadth [Tibet]. These two sets of features, the river system and the plateau, are the chief controls of Chinese history.

Other geographical conditions have had a like result; the position of China fronting the open ocean, on the road to nowhere by sea, and the absence of any Mediterranean Sea, are great, silent, negative controls, which have to an incalculable degree tended to confirm the Chinese in their habits as landsmen, and to prevent their becoming seamen. Nor were the Chinese forced to take to the sea, as were the Norsemen, by the poverty of a cold, sterile land. There was no effective pressure behind, as was the case with the Saxon. China is vast enough to allow such pressures as did come from the plateau or Manchuria to dissipate themselves ere the seaboard was reached, and there was always the southern land where these pressures were less felt. No way reached the sea, as was the case with the Phoenicians. The coast of China is a great round curve with no peninsulas to tempt men seawards, as was the case with the Greeks. China has never been a seapower, because nothing has ever induced her peoples to be otherwise than landsmen, and landsmen dependent on agriculture, with the same habits and ways of thinking drilled into them through forty centuries; so that even when tribes from the plateau have broken in and seized the reins of power, even when millions of inhabitants have been massacred, China has not broken up into numberless units, as did the Roman Empire. The homogeneity of her people, the result to a very large extent of geographical conditions, has always asserted itself.

Some students have attempted, with no little success, to trace the influence of landscape upon national character. Various theories as to this influence have etched themselves upon literature: "When Freedom from her mountain height—" Buckle, as we have seen, tried to lay down generalizations on the subject, and his principles may well possess more validity than the offhand student of the subject would think. Lord Bryce, in his *Memories of Travel*, remarks that he had once intended to give some account of the effect of North American scenery upon the American people, "finding in it a feature of the country which will continue through all the ages to affect the minds of its inhabitants." Beyond doubt this is true, though our country is too young and our population has been too mobile for this influence yet to exhibit itself strongly. But visitors to Southern California have already discerned there a regional character which exhibits a gay Mediterranean tinge, and which differs decidedly from the old-time Puritanism of rocky New England, or the dogged and somewhat unimaginative industriousness of the Middle West.*

* Cf. Clarence Cason, *90° in the Shade*, pp. 45, 46: "I once was lead to believe that I could interpret the Middle Western peoples in terms of my own impressions of their prairie lands. It seemed to me that my personal emotional reactions had given me the key to the restless urge of the Middle Western pioneers: the pent-up nervousness of their bodies, their determination to push their acres farther and farther toward the horizon . . . As the mariner of the sea—so I reasoned with perhaps some injustice to such characters as those portrayed by Joseph Conrad and John Masefield—has but one ultimate pattern, which he constantly repeats from voyage to voyage, that of working with all his strength to pass beyond the monotony of the waves, so

Ruskin believed that the scenery of the gray-sandstone country between Fribourg and Berne in Switzerland was ideal for the development of character and mind. André Siegfried, in a stimulating essay in human geography, maintains that the whole history of France since 1789 proves that the parts of the nation where limestone predominates have had a radical culture, while the portions where granite rocks have been predominant have had a conservative character! Moreover, he has furnished elaborate maps to help sustain this contention.

IV

An interesting but more detailed and less significant part of the application of geography to history lies in the study of the effects of weather upon events. In its month-to-month aspects, weather must of course be rated among the accidents of history. If there had not been a thick fog on the night when Washington withdrew his defeated army from Long Island to Manhattan, the American Revolution might easily have been crushed in its incipient stages. The battle of Valmy was won not alone by the strategy of Dumoriez, but in part also by the weather. The Prussian troops, marching through the heavy clay mud of the Argonne, were exhausted when they reached the French positions, and had to plow up steep and muddy hillsides under the French fire. The great British offensive on the Somme in the First World War, which might have succeeded had fair weather continued, was bemired by heavy and constant rains. And when we try to rise above details and take a larger view, we can only say that weather is so constant and important a factor in history that both statesman and student must always take account of its haphazard possibilities. In England weather played a part in the momentous repudiation of protection and acceptance of free trade in the middle forties. Sir Robert Peel and Cobden still faced the prospect of heavy

the prairie-dweller of the Middle West toiled single-mindedly at his plough, work being his only recourse, his only means of accomplishment."

fighting in their endeavor to repeal the Corn Laws, when the rains of 1845, the wettest English summer in memory, ruined the harvest; and Lord Morley trenchantly remarks in his biography of Cobden that "it was the rain that rained away the Corn Laws." In America the work of the AAA in restoring farm prices during the first administration of Franklin D. Roosevelt was enormously aided by two droughts, and the rapidity of the restoration was a large factor in Roosevelt's re-election. A writer has attempted an interesting study of "Rainfall and the Populist Party in Nebraska":

> To suggest that the farmer held the politician responsible for the shortage of rainfall would be an unwarranted exaggeration of the thoughtlessness of the voters. But it is quite another matter to suggest that the drought in Nebraska made a bad set of agricultural conditions worse, and that the politicians were held responsible for some of the conditions. Perhaps some held them responsible for most of them. The situation of many farmers forced them to think about the things that had brought about that situation. This contemplation resulted in a determination to remedy such matters as lay within their power. They could not make it rain, but they thought they could lower railroad rates . . . Altogether, in estimating the factors which produced Populism the item of rainfall must not be omitted.[3]

In conclusion, we may point out that geography is valuable for the historian only if it is studied in its most comprehensive aspects. If we are to evaluate it properly as an element in history, we must scrutinize not merely physical geography, not merely climate, but the entire situation of a community or a nation—strategic, industrial, commercial, climatic, and in terms of its natural resources. Any geographical study that is narrower than this is likely to be misleading. We may also point out that even when used in this inclusive way, geography is of much more use in helping to elucidate the broad outlines of history than its narrow episodes or phases. It throws a bright illumination on the career of China, or Great Britain, or the United States from the beginnings to the present day, but it does not help much to explain the administration of Martin Van Buren. And finally, we may note that it is often dangerous to try to explain very much of even the sweeping lines of history by this single science. Those who have mastered one key to the past tend to ignore the fact that it has many doors, and that other keys are of equal importance. After all, viewing man not merely as a biological phenomenon but as a thinking entity, geography explains only part of his accomplishments. Highly important factors of a psychological and sociological nature are also involved. An example of geographical history at its best is supplied by Rupert B. Vance's compendious *Human Geography of the South,* which relates geography, economics, and history in well-balanced fashion. He asserts that the climate is not responsible for Southern indolence; he holds that the so-called poor whites possess no inherent defects; and he shows just what factors have made for Southern backwardness and Southern progress. The pages on the Southern diet and its historical consequences, for example, are illuminating.

An animated debate which bears upon this subject was presented more than fifty years ago in two thoughtful papers written by William James and John Fiske. The essay of the former, "Great Men, Great Thoughts, and the Environment," appeared in the *Atlantic Monthly* for October 1880; that by Fiske, "Sociology and Hero Worship," may be found in his *Excursions of an Evolutionist.* Both writers fell afoul of the extravagant statements of such geographical theorists as Grant Allen, who had said that if the people who went to Hamburg had migrated instead to Timbuctoo they would now be indistinguishable from the semi-barbaric Negroes of Central Africa, while if the race which went to Timbuctoo had migrated to Hamburg they would now be white-skinned merchants maintaining a great commercial city. To this rash assertion James replied by asking the question, What was it that made the England of Queen Anne so different from the England of Queen Elizabeth? The difference was not due to environment—that had remained constant. It was due chiefly to "the accumulated influences of individuals, of their examples, their initiatives, and their decisions." But while William James and Fiske agreed in rejecting the exaggerated statements of the geographer, they came into violent collision upon the value to be attached to other elements operative in man's past. And this brings us to the extremely important question of the relations of economics, sociology, and history.

XI
Sociologist, Economist, and Historian

OLD STYLE HISTORY, the history of the great masters writing a century ago, dealt for the most part with the grand pageantry of human action. Its authors were concerned chiefly with political and military affairs, and found their synthesis in the fortunes of the state. Von Ranke and Macaulay, Prescott and Motley, wrote primarily of royal courts and parliamentary chambers, of diplomatic duels and tented fields. Such history lent itself to a dramatic emphasis upon the achievements of powerful individuals. It became a stage on which picturesque figures could strut and fret their little hour. "Universal history," wrote Carlyle in rationalizing this approach, "is at bottom the history of the great men who have worked here." And in another connection he asserted: "Yes, from Norse Odin to English Samuel Johnson, from the divine founder of Christianity to the withered Pontiff of Encyclopaedism, in all times and places the Hero has been worshipped. It will ever be so. We all love great men, love venerate, and bow down submissive before great men; nay, can we honestly bow down before anything else?" Carlyle's longest work is a record of the hero (for so he thought him) Frederick the Great; his most effective single work historically was his *Cromwell*, wherein he forever overthrew the widespread view that the Great Protector had been a canting, insincere, and sly usurper, and demonstrated instead his true stature.

But in one of his books, *The French Revolution*, even Carlyle significantly failed to demonstrate his thesis that the great man dominates all history. That volume contains vigorous portraits of the arresting personalities of the time—Voltaire with face shriveled to nothing and eyes glittering like carbuncles; the "swart, burly-headed Mirabeau," with Samson-locks; the sea-green incorruptible Robespierre; Marat with his cruel soul looking out from his "bleared, dull-acrid, woe-stricken face." But until the last paragraphs of the long volume no dominating Hero emerges. The reason is unescapable. The French Revolution, as a vast social movement, tumultuous and mutable as a stormy tide, represented a multitudinous complex of emotions, economic forces, social aspirations, ideas, and philosophies. All the people of France were the actors, and if any central figure existed, it was an abstraction—the Spirit of Revolution. Indeed, in one of his memorable pages Carlyle pictures the era as a conflict between the Spirit of Imposture and the Spirit of Reformation. The movement comprised a sequence of revolutions, rather than a single convulsive overturn; it had a hundred facets, and only a few of its phases can be attributed to any single leader. Knowing that if he attempted to sum up the French Revolution in the career of one or a few Heroes, he would give his readers an entirely false perspective, Carlyle was too wise and honest to try. Instead, he described it as a tremendous social conflagration:

> Higher, higher yet flames the Fire-Sea; crackling with new dislocated timber; hissing with leather and prunella. The metal Images are molten; the marble Images become mortar-lime; the stone Mountains sulkily explode. RESPECTABILITY, with all her collected Gigs inflamed for funeral pyre, wailing, leaves the Earth: not to return save under new Avatar. Imposture how it burns, through generations: how it is burnt up; for a time. The World is black ashes;—which, ah when will they grow green? The Images all run into amorphous

Corinthian brass; all Dwellings of men destroyed; the very mountains peeled and riven, the valleys black and dead: it is an empty World! Woe to them that shall be born then! ——a King, a Queen (ah me!) were hurled in; did rustle once; flew aloft, crackling, like a paper scroll. Iscariot Egalité was hurled in; thou grim De Launay, with thy grim Bastile; whole kindreds and peoples; five millions of mutually destroying men.

I

As democratic institutions advanced during the nineteenth century and their spirit pervaded historical writing, the individual was more and more frequently left for biography to celebrate, while history concerned itself with the people. Moreover, when a new world was created by the spread of the Industrial Revolution, the growth of dense populations, the advance of science and technology, and the rise of a myriad of interrelated corporations and associations, it became impossible to write history in the old terms. They were too obviously superficial. The most striking characteristic of society in the Western world being its complexity, the modern historian was expected to deal with the multiform aspects of this ever-richer complex. By the middle of the nineteenth century political history clearly represented but one of the many departments which made up history in its entirety. It became the duty of historians to concern themselves with numerous forces quite apart from politics—economic forces, constitutional forces, cultural forces, educational forces, moral forces, religious forces, artistic forces, and so on.

At first writers tended to deal with these facets of history in serial fashion. Neat watertight compartments were built, and to some extent still exist. One writer gave us the economic history of a nation or of a period, another the ecclesiastical history, and still another the literary history. The result was decidedly burdensome, and not a little confusing. Taken together, all these works showed that human history had been the resultant of many factors operating simultaneously, and that none could be neglected if a complete picture were desired. But it did not explain how these factors collaborated with one another, or just what their interrelations were. The students who read a constitutional history of the United States, then a literary history, and then economic and political histories, had felt the trunk, the legs, the ears, and the sides of the elephant, without quite realizing how they were all combined in one animal. Men began to ask whether there was not, after all, some way of integrating all these separate departments of history?

From one quarter came firm and confident "Yes" to this question—the quarter occupied by the sociologists. Sociology was one of the youngest of the sciences; it is roughly accurate to say that it originated with Comte and came of age with the volumes of Herbert Spencer, not earlier than 1860. In the generation after 1875 various sociologists began declaring that their so-called science offered the only true means of integrating the diverse aspects of human society in either the past or the present. Given time, they asserted, they could measure, analyze, and define the exact nature of the social processes which produced historical results; but much time would be necessary to permit them to collect sufficient data in a scientific fashion. Human history, the bolder sociologists argued, is primarily a record of social evolution. Certain laws which govern this evolution could gradually be established, and they would reduce to order the chaos of political history, cultural history, economic history, and so on. Franklin H. Giddings in 1903 set forth to the American Historical Association his doctrine that human development might thus be synthesized, entitling his paper "A Theory of Social Causation." Much later, in a volume called *The Scientific Study of Human Society,* Giddings went on to describe part of the scientific technique—the methods of social measurement—that would be necessary to create a sociological explanation of history.

Still other writers, such as Benjamin Kidd, Karl Pearson, and Albion W. Small, have asserted the possibility of finding a sociological key to history. The first-named made bold in *Social Evolution* (1894) to state what he regarded as the central feature of human history. This was the inherent and irreconcilable conflict between the interests of the individual, and those of the social organism; a conflict that has existed since men first formed communities, and that has steadily grown more intense. On the one hand the self-assertive reason of the individual is more and more developed by evolutionary forces. On the other hand, the immensely wider interests of the social organism demand an absolute subordination of this ever-increasing self-assertiveness of the individual. "In the conflict which results, we have the seat of a vast series of phenomena constituting the absolutely characteristic feature of our social evolution. It is impossible to fully understand the spectacle presented by human history in the past, or the main features of the social phenomena now presenting themselves throughout our Western civilization, without getting to the heart of this conflict. It is the pivot upon which the whole drama of human history and human development turns." Kidd devotes about a hundred pages to a brief survey of human history from the days of the Roman Republic to our own time as illuminated by this general idea.

Carlyle would beyond doubt have been horrified by the way in which sociologists attempted to sweep away the theory that great men offer the best key to history. Not that they swept away the great men—for sociology frankly admitted that they constantly appeared, and that their work had high significance. Even the Hero, however, was reduced to a unit obeying immutable sociological law. William James, for example, pointed out in the before-mentioned essay on "Great Men, Great Thoughts, and the Environment," that there is a striking analogy between geniuses in human history, and "spontaneous variation" in bringing about progress in the biological world. Just so, James believed that geniuses were "sports" who produced a kindred result in the human world. Both represented a marked deviation from the average or norm. If we take a million specimens of a particular species of moth, we shall find that the proboscis of the great majority varies in but the slightest degree from the average length. But perhaps

ten or a dozen moths out of the million may each possess
a proboscis that is a half-inch longer, or a half-inch shorter;
they are extreme instances of the "spontaneous variation."
So with man's intellectual capacity. Among the eight million people in New York City, seven million, nine hundred
thousand come somewhere near the average in intellect.
Most of the remaining hundred thousand fall decidedly
below the average. But a few may rise far above it—there
may be a Byron, a Pasteur, a Newton, even a Beethoven
or Shakespeare, among them. He is the impressive *sociological variation,* and every age produces a few such variations.

Of course nobody can explain their appearance. All the
teachings of Mendel and his fellow biologists cannot tell
us precisely why a moth suddenly appears with a proboscis twice the usual length; still less can anyone tell us
whence comes a genius like Shakespeare or Goethe. William James justly remarked that "the causes of production
of great men lie in a sphere wholly inaccessible to the
social philosopher. He must simply accept geniuses as data,
just as Darwin accepts his spontaneous variations." But
does it follow that the sociologist, attempting to subordinate parts of the historical process to a law, is daunted
by this fact? Not in the least.

For William James at once lays down a sociological
law upon the way in which great men affect the pattern
of history; a law which makes society as important to the
hero as the latter is to society. The relation of the social
environment to the genius, he declares, is strictly parallel
to the relation of the physical environment to the variation
in biology. "It chiefly adapts or rejects, preserves or destroys, in short *selects* him." In the insect world, if the
environment is such as to make an additional half-inch
of proboscis advantageous to moths, then the moths with
more than an average length will tend to survive; moths
with less than an average length will tend to die out; and
the miraculous moth with an extra half-inch may found an
entirely new breed. Those moths which have varied in the
right direction have changed the character of all moth

society. So, according to James, the great man acts as a powerful releaser of energy, a ferment; he unlocks huge reservoirs of force, and sets in motion powerful new social currents. He alters the constitution of society much as the advent of a new biological species changes the balance of animal and vegetable life in the region in which it suddenly appears. Most people are familiar with Darwin's remark as to the influence of cats upon the growth of clover. We introduce some cats near a large field; they kill the field-mice; the field-mice cease their destruction of bumblebee nests; and clover then flourishes in that field. We introduce a great man named Robert Clive into India; and for generations afterward, the hundreds of millions of people in India lead lives that are transformed or at least perceptibly altered.

In short, the stimulating influence of geniuses, whose advent is incalculable, upon social evolution, is strictly comparable to the stimulating influence of spontaneous variation, whose advent is also incalculable, upon biological evolution. But sociologists like Herbert Spencer emphasize even more strongly than William James the thesis that the great man is largely dependent upon his environment. They would insist upon the importance of the following passage from James's essay:

Not every "man" fits every "hour." Some incompatibilities there are. A given genius may come either too early or too late. Peter the Hermit would now be sent to an insane asylum. John Mill in the tenth century would have lived and died unknown. Cromwell and Napoleon need their revolutions, Grant his Civil War. An Ajax gets no fame in the day of telescopic sighted rifles; and to express differently an instance which Spencer uses, what could a Watt have effected in a tribe which no precursive genius had taught to smelt iron or turn a lathe?

The important thing to notice is that what makes a certain genius now incompatible with his surroundings is usually the fact that some previous genius of a different strain has warped the community from the sphere of his possible effectiveness. After Voltaire, no Peter the Hermit; after Charles IX and Louis XIV, no general protestantization of France; after a Manchester school, a Disraeli's success is transient; after a Philip II, a Caesar makes little headway; and so on. Each bifurcation cuts off certain sides of the field altogether, and limits the future possible angles of deflection.

Thus social evolution is a resultant of the action of two wholly distinct factors: the individual, deriving his peculiar gifts from the play of physiological and infrasocial forces, but bearing all the powers of initiative and origination in his hands; and second, the social environment, with its power of adopting or rejecting both him and his gifts. Both factors are essential to change. The community stagnates without the impulse of the individual. The impulse dies away without the sympathy of the community.

Carlyle had seen little besides the great man; William James saw both the great man and his social environment; and, with greater emphasis upon the latter, so did Herbert Spencer, John Fiske, and all the sociologists who have followed them. All these writers have agreed upon one point: That the influence of geography or physical environment upon the history of mankind may readily be exaggerated. All would scoff at Grant Allen's rash statement about the effects of transposing the Negroes of Timbuctoo and the white merchants of Hamburg. A geographical environment cannot produce a given type of mind, but can only foster and further certain types, thwart and frustrate still others.

John Fiske even declared, in his *Outlines of Cosmic Philosophy,* that the ecclesiastical reforms of Gregory VII had (of course in their remote results) wielded more influence upon American history than the direction of the Rocky Mountains or the position of the Great Lakes. Rebutting Buckle's theory that the difference in Arabic civilization before and after Mohammed was due to the difference between the physical geography of Arabia and that of Spain, Persia, and India, he had remarked that the utter superficiality of this explanation could be demonstrated by asking two questions: First, if the Arabs had become highly civilized only because they gave up their native deserts for Spain, India, and Persia, why did not the Turks become equally civilized when they exchanged their barren plateau for the rich empire under Constantinople? And second, what was the impulse which led the Arabs to leave their ancestral deserts and conquer the vast region from the Ganges to the Pyrenees? The answer to these queries would have seemed equally clear to the historian Carlyle, the psychologist James, and the sociologist Herbert Spencer. They would have replied that the principal explanation of the Arabian transformation was psychological, not physical. Carlyle would have ascribed it to the genius of Mohammed; modern sociologists would ascribe it to Mohammed and the social conditions which made Mohammed's work possible.

But while the sociologists admit the striking role of the genius, they unanimously believe that for the general development of society, the social environment, the general human milieu, is more important than the commanding individual. They believe that the slow progress of this average society should hold the primary attention of historians. "If it be true," writes Fiske (here echoing Spencer), "that a genius of a given kind can appear under certain social conditions, and not under others, as a Newton among civilized Englishmen but not among Hottentots; or if it be true that a given genius can work its results under certain social conditions, and not under others, as a Mill in the nineteenth century but not in the tenth; then it follows that in order to understand the course of history from age to age the mere study of the personal characteristics and achievements of great men is not sufficient. Carlyle's method of dealing with history, making it a mere series of prose epics, has many merits; but . . . it does not *explain* the course of events. History is something more than biography . . . One might learn all of Plutarch's lives by heart, and still have made very little progress toward comprehending why the Greek states were never able to form a coherent aggregate, or why the establishment of despotism at Rome was involved in the conquest of the Mediterranean world. The true way to appreciate such historical problems as these . . . is to consider the popular assemblies of the Greeks and Romans in their points of likeness and unlikeness to the folkmoots and parliaments of England and the meetings of Massachusetts." In short, Fiske would place his emphasis upon comparative history, resting upon a sociological foundation.

II

It must be admitted that, traceable as largely to sociology as to economics and geography, an impressive revolution overtook historical writing in the century which followed Freeman and Motley. The difference in method between Macaulay and his grandnephew George Macaulay Trevelyan or Elie Halévy was hardly less than the differences which separate a scientist of 1830 from a scientist of 1930. The new auxiliary sciences, of which sociology, economics, and psychology were the chief, had done most to produce this change. A simple illustration of the change in emphasis is offered by the books of Froude and Mommsen upon Julius Caesar. Both treat Caesar as one of the greatest military heroes of all history. But Froude, who came to maturity before he could profit by the new scientific analysis of social phenomena, lifted Caesar out of his social environment and presented it only as a shadowy background. Mommsen, on the other hand, thoroughly schooled in socio-economic ideas, the comparative method, and the study of institutions, gave careful attention to Caesar in relation to his complex social environment. He thus did better justice not only to Roman history, but to Caesar himself, than Froude. We cannot really understand Caesar's rise to power without the rich social history included in the chapter on "The Joint Rule of Pompeius and Caesar"; we cannot fully understand the use he made of this power without the profound examination of Roman institutions in the subsequent chapter on "The Old Republic and the New Monarchy."*

Yet most historians have always been intensely hostile to the claim that sociology can offer any master key to the historical past; and rightly so. Even if fuller and more scientifically exact data were available on the social aspects of past ages—even if trained experts had been collecting statistics according to Dr. Giddings's formula in the midst of the Renaissance, the Reformation, the Wars of Religion, and the French Revolution—it would be impossible for the sociologist to fix an indisputable pattern upon any part of history. The reasons for this are numerous. The overwhelming complexity of the facts of history stands in grimly majestic contrast to the puny weapons of the sociologist for measuring and classifying these facts; a Himalaya of iron and granite defying a few feeble pick-axes. Then too, as no less a sociologist than Pareto recognizes, the irrational element in all human activity is so enormous, and the unpredictable or fortuitous elements are so much vaster still, that no conceivable formulae can ever deal with past or present in any spirit of certainty.†

---

* Mommsen, writing in the Bismarckian period of blood and iron, undoubtedly overemphasized the genius of Caesar; his interest in Roman society is all the more remarkable.

† A single illustration of the interacting roles of human plan and fortuity in history will suffice. At dawn of June 5, 1944, Eisenhower faced the question whether he should send the Anglo-American forces storming across the Normandy beaches just one day later. If he said yes, the air, ground, and sea elements must start moving in a few hours, and once started, recall would be impossible. He knew that a variety of factors outside his control were needed to ensure success. They included a low tide, to allow destruction of undersea obstacles; a tide early enough to permit a second low-tide wave of invading divisions, and late enough to permit a preliminary hour of daylight close-bombing; a nearly full moon for parachute dropping; a fairly smooth sea and fair visibility to make the ships controllable. No tolerable combination could come again for a fortnight. Yet on June 5 the weather was bad. Eisenhower heard all the arguments pro and con, weighed them for five silent minutes, and commanded "Go!" Had he held off for a fortnight, the assault would have been hit by the worst Channel storm in years, and would have failed. (Walter Bedell Smith, *Eisenhower's Six Great Decisions, Europe 1944–45* [1956].)

Historian and sociologist alike, despairing of any demonstrable relationship between cause and effect in many phases of life, must turn to such ideas as that of the interdependence of variables for a vague clue—and that conception has little practical helpfulness. The true historian is still suspicious of any but elementary laws, though he admits that the area of law has grown and is still growing. Finally, many historians insist that their special field of interest must always lie quite apart from the special field of the sociologist; indeed, that it lies in an entirely different direction.

Summed up in a single sentence, the distinction which such men would make is this: Sociology is concerned with the constant and repetitive element in human affairs, past and present, while history is concerned not only with the constant element, but still more largely with the unique and individual element; with the elements which can never repeat themselves or be arranged in a neat pattern. When Dr. Giddings read his "Theory of Social Causation" to the American Historical Association, three historical writers, Ephraim Emerton, George L. Burr, and Willis M. West, replied to it. All three struck the same note. They asserted that history is rather a branch of literature than of science, though it has relations with both. While the historian, they declared, may busy himself in part with repetitive patterns in social evolution—patterns traceable for him by sociology—he must be concerned much more largely with fortuitous, individual, and unique elements in the record of the past. It is true that certain elements are common to the Puritan, American, French, and Russian revolutions and that historians should touch upon them. But what is of paramount interest to the historian, and what chiefly makes history worth reading, are the elements peculiar to each of these revolutions. When we study the Russian Revolution, we wish first and foremost to learn in what ways it differed from the French Revolution, and why; because the differences are innumerable, and the reasons for them complex, the exposition of them may be fascinating. We cannot appreciate its significance without understanding its unique elements.

From this point of view, sociology may even be envisaged as inimical to history. Certain writers have asserted that, with its flair for all-comprehending syntheses and its demand for generalization on a broad scale, it is merely that age-old siren, the philosophy of history. This philosophy of history, they add, is always a will-of-the-wisp, which changes with every period and simply leads to a distortion of facts. In Fred Morrow Fling's *The Writing of History* we find an extreme statement of this view that sociology and history are at bottom antagonistic:

> The historian is concerned with tracing the unique evolution of man in his activities as a social being, the unique life-record of humanity. If this be history, then history cannot repeat itself; there cannot be historical laws, for law is a generalization and generalization assumes repetition . . .
> History deals with past social facts, but it is important to note that all social facts are not necessarily historical facts. A past social fact becomes an historical fact when it has been made part of an historical synthesis . . . When our attention is directed toward the *uniqueness*, the *individuality*, of past social facts, when they interest because of their importance for the *unique evolution of man in his activities as a social being*, in selecting the facts and in grouping them into a complex, evolving whole, we employ the historical method; the result of our work is history.
> If, on the contrary, we are interested in *what past social facts have in common*, in the way in which *social facts repeat themselves*, if our purpose is to form *generalizations or laws* concerning human activities, we employ another logical method, the method of the social sciences. We select our facts not for their individuality or for the importance of their individuality for a complex whole, but for what each fact has in common with others, and the synthesis is *not a complex unique whole, but a generalization in which no trace of the individuality of the past social fact remains*. The result of our work is sociology, not history. Thus the work of

the historian supplements that of the sociologist. The historian is interested in quality, individuality, uniqueness; the sociologist in quantity, in generalization, in repetition.

Within limits and properly qualified, the distinction made by Dr. Fling is sound. Indeed, sociologists admit its validity, granting that they are interested chiefly in the repetitive elements of the human past, while the historian must be interested principally in the non-repetitive elements. But Dr. Fling goes too far and throws out the baby with the bath. While it is true that historians must be occupied primarily with the unique and individual features of any historical situation, Dr. Fling writes that he must be *exclusively* interested in them. Why? Why should historians not be interested also in the elements common to different situations, different societies, and different periods? Can a historian of the Russian Revolution exclude those parts of it which run parallel with the French Revolution? Comparative history may be made an exceedingly stimulating and fruitful study, even if it does come close to sociology. The examination of slavery in the United States will gain much from an inquiry into slavery in ancient Greece and Rome, in Russia and the Barbary States, and in South America; the student of our own Western frontier, will find a great deal of illumination in a scrutiny of the history of the Canadian frontier, the South African frontier, and the Siberian frontier.

It is fairly obvious, in fact, that in some branches of history the constant or repetitive element offers by far the largest part of the subject matter. The study of comparative history is possible only because so much human action is repetitive. Dealing even with peoples far removed from one another, we can study comparative folklore, comparative religions, comparative literature, comparative jurisprudence, and comparative politics with a certainty of discovering some fairly clear patterns. In these comparative studies, the sociologist may be of distinct use to the historian. He will not offer any all-inclusive synthesis of master key, but he can furnish a number of minor keys. The fact that the two studies are at many points complementary to one another has been vigorously pointed out by C. A. Ellwood in his book *Sociology in Its Psychological Aspects*:

> Although written history furnishes but a part of the facts with which the sociologist deals, nevertheless the cooperation between the sociologist and the scientific historian . . . should be of the closest sort. They are working in the same field and to a large extent have the same aim. The sociologist needs scientific history. He cannot complete his inventory of the social world without its aid. Moreover, sociology cannot content itself, as one author has well remarked, with being merely illustrated psychology; it must also be, at least in its final development, analyzed and compared history . . .
>
> On the other hand, the scientific historian has need of sociology. Without some knowledge of the principles of social organization and evolution he can scarcely obtain a proper perspective of his facts; nor can he rightly interpret his facts or explain the causes of social change without reference to such principles. The scientific historian could do his work more scientifically if he had critical knowledge of sociological laws and principles. We conclude, then, both that scientific history is necessary to the sociologist, and that sociology is equally necessary to the scientific historian.

Necessary in just what way? The question is not difficult to answer. It is possible to discern, after reading a dozen pages of any modern writer who treats of non-political subjects, whether he knows anything of sociological thought or not. If he has really steeped himself in the knowledge which sociology has accumulated since Spencer, and the generalizations which it has based upon this knowledge, his work will have a richness of texture, a depth of penetration, and a sureness of touch exceeding that of any historian of equivalent talents who knows nothing about sociology. How could a writer on American civilization since 1890 neglect the two books on Middletown by Robert and Helen Lynd, not merely for their

facts but still more for their interpretation—a purely sociological interpretation? Glance into Elie Halévy's *History
of the English People in 1815,* and we find three sentences in the introduction which fix the key for the whole
book. "Divided one from another by strong passions,"
Halévy writes of the European nations, "they are nevertheless in many respects internationalized by common interests, by a common outlook on life, and by a common
literary and scientific culture. The institutions or ideas
which one nation has neither borrowed from nor imparted
to their neighbours will be found, on analysis, to be few
indeed. The difference between the nations of Europe consists, after all, not so much in the elements which compose
their national character, as in the different proportions in
which are combined, in each nation, elements common to
most or all." These three sentences, striking the sociological keynote, show that an interest in comparative institutions will dominate the book. It would be possible to quote
passages from the historical work of Henry Adams showing that he had familiarized himself with sociological
writers, and it would be equally easy to quote passages
from Macaulay betraying that he knew as little about
sociology as about radioactivity.

Speaking concretely, it can be said—despite James Harvey Robinson's denials—that sociology can be of the greatest usefulness to students of intellectual and cultural history. Burckhardt approached history through art; Taine
approached history through literature—both regarding
these as expressions of social consciousness. Vernon L. Parrington could never have written his *Main Currents in
American Thought* without a grounding in sociology, and
especially in social psychology. From period to period, his
work shows how American ideas, sentiments, and convictions grew out of the social and economic conditions in
various sections. In writing each part of his work, he first
devotes great labor to the socio-economic foundations and
then takes up each writer or school of writers, and demonstrates how he or they naturally flowered from this milieu.
Thus in the first chapter of all, entitled "English Backgrounds," readers will have no difficulty in discovering

how deftly Parrington applies certain sociological principles to the English scene from which the first colonists migrated. The first chapter of Book II, again, called "Colonial Backgrounds," is an equally deft analysis of the society of America in the first half of the eighteenth century. He begins his study of the literature of the Gilded Age by a long (and lopsidedly unfair) chapter on the social and economic scene of 1870.

Parrington's approach had been molded, as he always admitted, by two principal influences. One was Taine's elaborate study of English literature as an outgrowth of the national character, the environment, and the changing spirit of the people. The other was the writings of his associate J. Allen Smith, who looked below the theories of government to find the material forces that underlay and shaped them. Neither of these men was able to carry his method to a point where it really became scientific, but both gave greater unity and realism to the interpretation of the past. With more partisanship than Taine, more depth than Smith, Parrington exhibited American thought as a product of social and economic groupings.

III

One of the greatest of intellectual historians, the German Karl Lamprecht, whom J. B. Bury calls "the ablest product of the sociological school of historians," issued his *Deutsche Geschichte* in the years 1891–1909. Far transcending the bounds of intellectual history, it treats comprehensively all German activities, cultural, economic, political, constitutional, and literary. But Lamprecht, anxious to give his work integration and symmetry, avoided an encyclopedic range of details, and tried instead to present a highly analytical study of society in each epoch of German life. He did this by attempting to disengage from the movements and events of a given period the soul of society, the social psyche or *geistleben*. Dividing German history into five main periods, he attempted to show that each of them had its social intellectual character, its spirit of the age or social mind.

His method in taking up each period was to dissect its social life with care; then to list the psychological traits or forces generated by these social conditions; and finally to explain a thousand definite events or special activities as the product of these socio-psychological impulses. Thus, treating of the early Middle Ages, he finds an underlying connection between the early Gothic architecture, the form of the popular ballad, the design of furniture, the Donations of Charlemagne, the crude heraldic designs, and the weapons of the soldiers. Burckhardt, from whom Lamprecht had learned a great deal, had tried in similar fashion to describe the social psyche or *geistleben* of the Italian Renaissance. But Lamprecht's task was far more difficult; for he dealt with a succession of epochs, not merely one, and he had to explain how the social psyche of one period was gradually transformed into the psyche of the next. His work is really a study of the evolution of the social mind of Germany. It is a tribute to its quality that both historians and sociologists regard it with admiration, and both would be glad to claim it.

If carried too far, or used without careful judgment, Lamprecht's method gives absurd results. The historian, abandoning the objective world of history and plunging into a subjective sphere, gropes at moonlight and cobwebs. He takes the vast, dynamic complexity of events and forces that make up history, and interprets them in terms of a few simple and static categories—usually quite arbitrary, often eccentric. The *Volks*-psyche which he coolly presents may not have any real substratum of fact at all and may never have existed. A valid sociological framework into which we can fit historical facts has not yet been devised. Perhaps that will come in some areas, and then a powerful, practical, and rigidly honest mind may produce a convincing result. Carl Becker writes: "It is quite possible to deal with the various sets of particular activities in any period—the political, economic, religious, and intellectual activities—as illustrating or as related to certain mental or psychic characteristics common to the social group or nation. These common characteristics thus become a unifying principle around which facts or events, political or other, may be grouped." But the hand of a master is required.

Anyone who reads the social history written by Americans in recent years must be impressed by the extent to which it is merely descriptive. The writings of McMaster and E. P. Oberholtzer, like some of the volumes of the excellent series "A History of American Life," are deficient in integration and unification. They present a serial description of economic phenomena, cultural phenomena, religious phenomena, and legal phenomena; a mass of facts upon dress, foods, important books, colleges, theaters, popular songs, railroads, manufacturing plants, amusements, inventions, and so on; a good deal of information upon popular ideas and prejudices—all with but an elementary amount of system and arrangement. Lamprecht, holding up his hands at such books, would have demanded, Where is the *geistleben*, the social psyche? Historians of the future will not go as far as he did in trying to find a unifying state of mind for each period, for that leads to oversimplification. Nevertheless, they will undoubtedly turn to sociology for aid in analyzing the immense mass of facts upon the life and mind of the people more acutely; its principles may help them understand the morphology of nations. And along with sociology they will levy upon economics.

The phrase "economic interpretation of history" has two senses which need clear differentiation. One is associated with the father of Communism. The radical leader of the First International, Michael Bakunin, wrote in 1870: "As a thinker, Marx is on the right road. He has established the principle that all religious, political, juridical developments in history are not the causes but the effects of economic developments. This great and fruitful thought was not excogitated by him; it was foreseen, partly even expressed, by many others. But at bottom it is his merit to have given it a solid foundation and to have made it the basis of his whole economic system."

His interpretation included, first, the doctrine that the stage of economic development in any land is the major element in determining its social institutions, laws, governmental institutions, and mental attitudes. His interpretation involved, in the second place, a doctrine of the inevitability of class struggle, steadily growing more intense; of an increasing concentration of capital in rich and greedy nations, bringing on economic crises of rising intensity; and of an ultimate revolution by the proletariat, effecting the destruction of capitalism and the establishment of a classless society. The Communist Manifesto put Marx's view of the past into two sentences:

> The history of all hitherto existing society is the history of class struggles. Freeman and slave, patrician and plebeian, lord and serf, guildmaster and journeyman, in a word, oppressor and oppressed, stood in constant opposition to one another, and carried on an uninterrupted fight, now hidden, now open, that always ended either in a revolutionary reconstitution of society at large, or in the common ruin of the contending classes.

As Marx's predictions of the future have not been realized (for a vigorous social-minded capitalism has replaced the old exploitive type, the condition of labor has vastly improved, class lines have grown dimmer, class conflict has diminished, and the severity of depressions has lessened), so history written according to Marxian theory has proved completely unsatisfactory. Pleasing followers of the party line, it repels all objective students of the past, for it distorts fact and falsifies essential realities. It achieves the same kind of "truth" that Sidney and Beatrice Webb served up in *Soviet Communism: A New Civilization?* when they asserted that the Communists had never established a dictatorship in Russia, for the Stalin regime was the purest form of democracy!

The economic interpretation that historians must take seriously is very different. It is simply an assertion that, as the economist E. R. A. Seligman put it, men must in the final instance trace to economic causes "those transformations in the structure of society which themselves condition the relation of the social classes and the various manifestations of social life." That is, students of history should look beneath the clash of parties, the debates of parliaments, the texts of laws, the fashions in ideas, to see what economic forces projected them. J. Allen Smith, using the tools of a political scientist, applied this principle in an examination of the Constitution designed to prove that it was planned and carefully written to frustrate democracy. R. H. Tawney with a richer fund of knowledge and ideas, applied it to various phases of European history in *The Acquisitive Society, Religion and the Rise of Capitalism,* and *The Agrarian Problem in the Sixteenth Century.* Charles A. Beard applied it to our early national history in his *Economic Interpretation of the Constitution,* and his less famous but better-founded *Economic Interpretation of Jeffersonian Democracy.*

This type of economic interpretation expands the bounds and increases the depth of historical study. It expands the limits not only because economics is a huge and complex subject in itself, but because it properly includes technology, and technology more than touches science.[1] It increases the depth because it suggests that a great deal of historical writing has been superficial, treating surface matters when it should dig to root causes, and because economists bring to their study of the past a point of view, and a large number of topical interests, which wrest history into new shapes, and sometimes make it more penetrating. The conventional historian is ready to describe the movement of prices; the economist tells him that to understand this movement he must analyze the supply of bullion, the trend of population, the fluctuations of export-import trade, and the activities of manipulators.

Both history and economics lie embedded in a social framework, and both use special tools, those of the economist being more and more difficult to master. Specialists in each discipline are likely to view the other with lifted eyebrows. The economic interpretation of history in the Seligman sense has unfairly gotten a disrepute in historical eyes for three main reasons. First, some initial experiments in writing it have proved untrustworthy. Beard's *Economic Interpretation of the Constitution* has been largely discredited as inadequate in research, inaccurate in much of the data offered, and hasty in conclusions. Second, a materialist interpretation of any transaction tempts many writers into unfounded conjectures upon the motives of the participants. Why did a certain body of Congressmen vote for or against a tariff bill? According to the ordinary school of economic interpreters, because they had a pocket interest in passing or defeating it. But it is a poor student of human nature who does not know that men often perform actions from principle, party allegiance, or personal ties that gravely injure, even ruin them; it is a still weaker student who does not know that practically all human motivation is mixed, and much of it inscrutable. Yet Beard essayed to read it, in groups, by the dollar mark. And in the third place, enthusiasts for economic interpretation have all too often given it complete precedence in historical causation; they forget that causation is never single, always plural.

The question whether economics controls history, or history controls economics, may be a good deal like the old chicken vs. egg question. It is at any rate certain that each largely controls the other, and writers of economic interpretation should not forget the fact. Nor should they forget that most men belong in several basic economic categories at once—we are nearly all both debtors and creditors; that motive is risky ground; and that visible results are often worth more attention than obscure causation. The cardinal interest of the Constitution, assuredly, lies not in its relation to class lines—for the nation in 1789 was 98 per cent middle class, with few very rich and fewer very poor, and hence with little class feeling—but in the effectiveness with which it served the entire country and summed up an era of political development.

If intricate subjects like industrialization, the movements of population, means and effects of capital accumulation, and urban patterns are to be perceptively treated, followers of all the social studies will have to join hands. It may take them long to solve the problem of their proper relations, but they should attempt it without jealous prejudice. The possibility described by Carl Becker in relating political, economic, religious, and intellectual activities to the psychic characteristics of a society or nation was well illustrated, before Tawney, by Max Weber (whom G. P. Gooch well terms "the most fertile and encyclopaedic mind of his time in the German academic world"[2]) in his *The Protestant Ethic and the Spirit of Capitalism* (1904–5). With subtle analysis and massive erudition he demonstrated the profound influence of Calvinist ideas of industry, enterprise, and thrift in supplying to the spirit of the time one of the essential ingredients that launched economic growth upon its modern development. Then Weber turned to the social and religious history of the Orient for additional illumination on the identification of the special spiritual attitudes in the West responsible for the swift rise of the capitalist system.

As Weber was a sociologist, so students of politics have shown that a new path driven into history from their area can sometimes be surprisingly profitable. Leonard D. White, for example, in his functional studies *The Federalists, The Jeffersonians,* and *The Jacksonians* showed that government, society, and history could all obtain fresh light from a thorough exploration of administrative policy, law, and practice. A student of public law, he gave the kindred disciplines new facts and ideas on the role of the common man, on leadership, on the rise and fall of standards of administration, and even on such stale subjects as office-seeking and the spoils system. What he supplied, like Weber and Tawney on a larger scale, was a fresh point of view and new tools.

XII
Biography and History

THE BIOGRAPHER appeared on the stage of letters hand in hand with the historian, and hand in hand they walk there still. Biography may be termed a form of history—a form applied not to nations or groups of people, but to the single man or woman; history is certainly from one point of view a compound of innumerable biographies. All study of the past, whether for pleasure, instruction, or moral growth, must be based upon a reading of both history and biography, and it is a poor literary prescription which demands one at the expense of the other. While some men have a preference for life in general, and some for *the* life of the individual, each so illustrates the other that neither can be put aside. The commemorative instinct of mankind found expression in biography as early as in history, and very nearly as vigorously. In the Bible, the story of Noah, the story of Abraham, the story of Isaac, and above all the story of Joseph (its length considered, almost a model biography), belong to the category of lives rather than history. Xenophon's *Memoirs of Socrates* is not in strict form a biography, being a defense of the philosopher against his defamers, but in its effect it is a brief biographical masterpiece. During the first century of the Christian Era, Plutarch produced a book which has ever since been "a pasturage of great minds," his parallel lives of forty-six Greek and Roman heroes; and in the second century Suetonius wrote his untrustworthy but unforgettable *Lives of the Twelve Caesars.* Since the birth of modern memoir-writing in France and Britain, since Rohan and De Retz, Walton's *Lives* and Fuller's *Worthies,* biography has been an even more fecund mother of books than history, and has yielded as many masterpieces.

Like history, biography has its overtones and under-tones. It is more than a literary recreation, more than a portrait-gallery of striking faces, more than a study which makes the past vivid with personalities. As H. H. Asquith said: "It brings comfort, it enlarges sympathy, it expels selfishness, it quickens aspiration." But the principal reason for its fascination to many readers may be stated in a sentence: It humanizes the past, while at the same time it enriches the present by showing us life with a vividness and completeness that few men experience in life itself. Particularly in recent decades the biographical approach to history has become the principal highroad in that field. For every man who reads a history of the Civil War, there are probably ten who read lives of Lincoln, Jefferson Davis, Grant, or Lee; for every man who reads a history of the Tudors, there are probably ten who read lives of Queen Elizabeth or Henry VIII. In English and American literature the greatest publishing successes of the first third of the twentieth century, apart from fiction, lay in biography and autobiography. Now and then a volume of history, such as H. G. Wells's *Outline,* rose to a mass-circulation, but far more frequently the vogue lay with a work like Strachey's *Queen Victoria,* Beveridge's life of John Marshall, Emil Ludwig's *Napoleon,* the autobiography of Henry Adams, the memoirs of Lloyd George. Many of the historical works which did attain a wide circulation had been cast in a form closely akin to biography, one or two personalities dominating such books as Maurois's *The Edwardian Era* and Claude G. Bowers's *Jefferson and Hamilton.* To men who lack imagination, history is difficult to visualize, while biography brings them the past in concrete, real, and vivid terms. To men who have known little of life or dwelt in narrow environments, history is often a meaningless confusion, while the reading of a series of biographies holds out all the richness that human existence can present.

Because biography humanizes the past and enriches personal experience of the present in a way that history can seldom do, its continued popularity is certain. It is perfectly valid to argue that the personal element in the past is less important than the communal element; that the cultural tendencies of any period, its great economic forces, its governmental forms and traditions, its social fabric, are in general more potent than the actions of any single man or coterie. The ordinary reader will readily admit this. But he will assert that what he most readily understands, and what interests him most strongly, is the play of personality in history; that he likes to view the past as a swift drama, with the principal figures of the dramatis personae strongly lighted up. Those economic forces, those governmental institutions, those cultural traditions and ideas, he will say, are interesting to me chiefly as elements against which the figures of the drama contend or which they use to achieve their victories. I prefer to select some eminent person as protagonist, and observe how he wrestles with these elements; to learn whether his talents and energy are more than a match for them, or whether he allows himself to be conquered by rival men and adverse social forces. Having said this, the lay reader (not, we hope, the student) respectfully lays aside the history of England in the nineteenth century, and opens Morley's life of Gladstone.

It is a defensible position for the general reader; and, in answering the chief objections to it, three arguments may be offered for biography as an approach to history. It may be objected that biography tends to oversimplify the past; that it invites us to scrutinize the Reformation, the Napoleonic era, or the American Civil War with reference to the ideas and acts of a single man. But the lay student of history will reply that, since the full history of the Reformation, the Napoleonic era, or the Civil War is too vast and complex to be comprehended without great effort —since it overloads the memory and fatigues the attention —a certain amount of simplification is a virtue. It is better to take a well-laid road through a rough and diversified country than to explore every square mile. Again, it may be objected that the biographical approach to history is always subjective and frequently biased; that instead of trying to view events impartially, the biographer of necessity presents them as colored by the ideas, emotions, and interests of his hero.

But the reader may reply that biography at its best is hardly more biased than history at its best; that he can make allowance for any natural sympathy with the subject of the biography; and that he is more than compensated for any bias by the increased vividness of the personal view. Impersonal history, he will declare, is too often history robbed of all color and immediacy. When I read a general description of Waterloo I am not particularly thrilled. But when, approaching the climax of Philip Guedalla's *Wellington,* I sit with the Duke on his hill while the tall bearskins of the Guard follow Ney to break against the British squares, my heart is sick with suspense, and I rise from watching the pursuit roll away with a new sense of the reality of history. When I read Pepys's account of the Great Fire in London—how he lay in a boat on the Thames, shedding tears as he watched the deep red flames destroy the wealth and pride of the city—I feel that spectacle far more keenly than any general record. I would rather have less impartiality and more personal emotion.

The third objection to the biographical approach to history is that it offers no understanding of mass action or social law. The objection is not quite irrefutable. Some writers have welded an examination of a large number of lives into history in such fashion as to yield a new understanding of a special phase of the past. Douglas Freeman did this with great success in *Lee's Lieutenants,* a study in the record of command in the main Confederate army; Sir Lewis Namier did it in his study of the early part of George III's reign, examining the position and careers of scores of men to find out what was the structure of parties and factions, how policy decisions were made, and just what patterns political behavior showed. Arthur Schlesinger, Jr., in treating the age of Roosevelt and A. L. Rowse in dealing with the Elizabethan age have in less analytical fashion, but with sparkling effect, used a composite of short biographies of many men large and small.

I

But, assuming that history and biography are to be used side by side rather than merged, it can still be contended that biography is indispensable to the historical student. It supplies a unique element. It can furnish a knowledge of individual psychology just as history supplies a knowledge of social action and institutions. As history invites us to study the race or mass, good biography invites us to explore the mind and heart of man; it, and still more, any autobiography as honest as John Stuart Mill's, lays bare the will and emotions in relation to events and environment. "Personality was Plutarch's quarry"— and has since been the goal of every good biographer. How can we understand the past without understanding in detail the psychology of its principal agents? What is the Reformation without Luther, Calvin, and Knox? How can we comprehend these three without listening to their table talk, reading their letters, hearing the anecdotes which illustrate their character? It would be going too far to take the advice of Disraeli, who made the father of Contarini Fleming counsel his son: "Read the memoirs of Cardinal de Retz, the life of Richelieu, everything about Napoleon; read works of that kind. Read no history, nothing but biography, for that is life without theory." But, says the general reader, good biography, re-creating the individual, does give us one set of psychological truths for which history has not the time or space. The two are complementary; each is essential.

Even the sociologist, who deprecates emphasis on the individual and calls for ever-greater attention to social and economic elements, must admit the force of these arguments. Herbert Spencer makes some cautious concessions in his *Principles of Ethics*. After registering his objections to the great-man theory of history, "tacitly held by the ignorant in all ages," and declaring that the impersonal

elements of the past should chiefly occupy our attention,
he goes on to say that some study should be given to
personal elements. "While no information concerning kings
and popes, and ministers and generals, even when joined
to exhaustive acquaintance with intrigues and treaties,
battles and sieges, gives any insight into the laws of social
evolution—while the single fact that division of labor has
been progressing in all advancing nations regardless of the
wills of lawmakers, and unobserved by them, suffices to
show that the forces which mold society work out their
results apart from, and often in spite of, the aims of leading men; yet a certain moderate number of leading men
and their actions may properly be contemplated. The past
stages in human progress, which everyone should know
something about, would be conceived in too shadowy a
form if wholly divested of ideas of the persons and events
associated with them. Moreover, some amount of such
knowledge is requisite to enlarge adequately the conception of human nature in general—to show the extremes,
occasionally good but mostly bad, which it is capable of
reaching." If this statement must be questioned, it is only
because it grudgingly allows too little to biography.

For Spencer does not state adequately the historical
values of biography—quite apart from its literary and moral
values. Biography is useful, as we have said, as a means of
breaking down the complexity of wide movements and
crowded periods into parts sufficiently simple to the readily
grasped and long retained. It is useful as a means of gaining a vivid insight into past conditions of life; still more
useful in drenching past events with some poignancy of
personal emotion. It is valuable as a gallery of portraits, a
presentation of character in history. It is generally agreed
that biography in the English tongue is richer and has
reached greater heights than in other languages; that Boswell's *Johnson*, Lockhart's *Scott*, Froude's *Carlyle*, Morley's
Gladstone, Freeman's *Robert E. Lee*, and Beveridge's *John
Marshall* have hardly been equaled by French and German biographers. The reason beyond question lies in the
deep-rooted individualism of the English-speaking peoples, a race especially rich in character. Biography is valu-

able, again, as a means of understanding the psychology of past generations of men. Its best examples lay bare the man's inner soul and explain the motives back of human actions with a finesse that the pen of history, drawing bolder, cruder strokes, cannot match. Particularly instructive in this respect are those great autobiographies which give us authentic human documents, divested of all self-consciousness; books like Cellini's, Rousseau's, Benjamin Franklin's, Aksakov's, and Anthony Trollope's. Finally, biography is valuable as a study of one important form of historical force—for we cannot question the fact that some historic personages have been sufficiently powerful to constitute each a great force in himself. Caesar was a force; Mohammed was a force; Luther was a force; Napoleon was a force. Mussolini, remarking that "I am not a man but an event," would have us believe that he was a force. Still other men, by no means so powerful, have at least been typical of an age and worth studying because they embody so many of its characteristics. Cobden was not in himself a great force, but was admirably representative of the force called Manchester Liberalism. Mazzini, though not a great force, was typical of one entire side of European nationalism.

II

But if biography is well worth studying, only the best biography deserves any sustained attention; and what is the best? Boswell remarked: "Biography occasions a degree of trouble far beyond that of any other species of literary composition"—and it is true that a world of pains must go to the making of any really excellent life of a man. Biography in the modern sense did not appear in the English language until Izaak Walton, beginning in 1640, produced that collection of works known as *The Lives of Dr. John Donne, Sir Henry Wotton, Mr. Richard Hooker, Mr. George Herbert, and Dr. Robert Sanderson*. Even this was not strictly modern biography; he wished to edify a little, to amuse a little, above all to collect and present enough of the acts and virtues of departed friends to save them from oblivion, and he was more eulogist than biographer. Nevertheless, he showed simplicity, genuineness, and vividness, while his use of letters and anecdotes (as in the tale of Donne and the apparition of his wife and dead child) to illustrate character was admirable. Fuller's *Worthies* and John Aubrey's *Minutes of Lives* also evinced an understanding of the personal element essential to good biography. The same element is likewise prominent in Mrs. Lucy Hutchinson's *Memoirs of the Life of Colonel Hutchinson*, written about 1670; a book interesting to historians for its light on the Roundhead side of the English Civil War, but more interesting to general readers for the vividness of its courtship scenes, the pungency of its dialogue, and the pathos of its detailed description of the colonel's imprisonment and death. We all know how highly Charles Lamb thought of the Duchess of Newcastle's intimate biography of her husband—"No casket is rich enough . . . to honour . . . such a jewel."

But as the first great archetypes of modern history appeared in the eighteenth century, so did those of modernized biography. It is customary, after due obeisance to Dr. Johnson's *Life of Richard Savage*, to point to William Mason's *Life and Letters of Thomas Gray* (1774) as breaking the old molds and bringing in a freer, fuller, more truthful form. Mason had the happy idea, never before really used by any writer, of telling the story of Gray's life by means of his letters, with a ribbon of editorial narrative. Unfortunately, he used but a small part of the letters and papers he collected, while he grossly tampered with the correspondence, altering, transposing, omitting, and redating at his own sweet will. Boswell enormously improved upon Mason's example when he published his life of Dr. Samuel Johnson in 1791. With justice he boasted that he had shown Johnson as no man had ever been shown in a book before, and had "Johnsonized the land." This prince of all biographers was, if not a great man, at least a natural artist, with a quick and sure instinct for obtaining the best materials and making the best use of them. To live, talk, and breathe with his subject, "to become strongly impregnated with the Johnsonian aether," to treasure every detail which added to the completeness and truth of the portrait, in the conviction that "every little spark adds something to the general blaze"—this was his method. For the first time the world found in a biography a photographic—nay, a cinematic—delineation of an arresting personality by a minute observer who used dialogue, letters, anecdotes, and a thousand trifles as well as great acts and events to fill out his portrait. After Boswell, the recipe was open to all.

The chief requirement of a really good biography is that it re-create an individual, convincing the reader that he lived, moved, spoke, and enjoyed a certain set of human attributes. We must not merely be shown what he did, but what he was, and why he was that kind of man. In other words, his inner soul, or at least his personality, must be revealed. The task is obviously more difficult with well-balanced, self-contained, and reticent personalities than with those which present deeply stamped traits and picturesque eccentricities. Irving, who in his life of George Washington produced the first great American biography, faced a far more baffling undertaking than Boswell; the first President was notable for the harmony of his traits, the iron restraint of his will, and the smooth dignity of his private and public appearances. Nevertheless, some of Irving's successors, notably Paul Leicester Ford in *The True George Washington*, succeeded in approaching the inner springs of Washington's personality. In general, the portraiture of personality is easier in dealing with literary men than with political, military, or business leaders, because the former usually have richer minds, and almost always have been more articulate, more self-expressive; they have written more letters and more autobiographical passages, have figured in more anecdotes. It is no accident that the best English biographies are of writers: Boswell's *Johnson*, Lockhart's *Scott*, Froude's *Carlyle*, Trevelyan's *Macaulay*, Forster's *Dickens*. It is no accident that the richest American biography is Albert Bigelow Paine's *Mark Twain*. But even when a character has lineaments as strongly marked as those of Walter Savage Landor, Andrew Jackson, or Bismarck, even when a wealth of personalia exists, to seize upon the main elements of character is a task demanding the highest talents—a task that can be executed with perfection only by something like genius.

For personality is an elusive matter, and the best indications of character are often so subtle that they escape all but the keenest observers. What is a man's soul? How can his motives be disentangled? How can his acts be generalized? Perhaps personality, whether developing, static, or deliquescent, is primarily the sum of a man's habits. A kindly man has the habit of doing kindly acts, an avaricious man the habit of avaricious acts, an arrogant man the habit of arrogant acts. But the biographer must realize that cruel men may occasionally do benevolent deeds, a kindly man may once or twice commit a cruel action; that the rogue may meet some compelling crisis with an honest act, like Sidney Carton walking to the guillotine, while the honest man may wreck himself, as Lord Jim did, by a single base deed. An American who gave long years to searching men's hearts, Gamaliel Bradford, has written: "The most minute study, the widest experience in the investigation of human actions and their motives, only make us feel more and more the shifting, terrible uncertainty of the ground under our feet." The keenest perception must be allied with the most rigorous honesty in using the scalpel. Not merely must no significant detail be overlooked, in the spirit of Plutarch's remark that "an act of small note, a short saying, a jest, will distinguish the real character better than the greatest sieges and most decisive battles." Insight must be applied to these details. Bradford observed how much the taciturn Robert E. Lee had revealed of his character in his pregnant remark at Fredericksburg: "It is well that war is so terrible, or else we should grow too fond of it."

Yet biography must do a great deal more than re-create a personality. Essayists, like Sainte-Beuve in his *Monday Chats,* Gamaliel Bradford in his psychographs, and Lord Bryce in *Studies in Contemporary Biography,* can sometimes vividly evoke a character. They can limn a rapid, arresting portrait which reveals essential traits like a miniature by Isabey. But this is far from sufficient. Dr. Johnson wisely remarked that "a character is not a life"; that "a character furnishes so little detail, that scarcely anything is distinctly known, but all is shown confused and enlarged through a mist."

A good biography must also present as complete, accurate, and unbiased an account of the deeds and experiences of its subject as can be executed; provided, of course, that the completeness does not extend to impertinent and tiresome detail. Most great biographies have been planned on full, copious lines. In Lockhart's *Scott*, Froude's *Carlyle*, Morley's *Gladstone*, Monypenny and Buckle's *Disraeli*, James G. Randall's *Lincoln*, Beveridge's *Marshall*, and Arthur Link's *Woodrow Wilson*, exhaustive research was applied to establish and record every useful fact. Douglas Freeman gave twenty years to his *Robert E. Lee* to make every part of the four volumes as nearly definitive as possible. Men of lesser stature than the heroes just named can of course be dismissed more briefly; four volumes on Martin Van Buren or Calvin Coolidge would be ridiculous, as would even two volumes on a career so devoid of external incident as Edward Fitzgerald's or Emily Dickinson's. But in steering the middle course between meagerness and redundancy, the biographer has most to fear from the former. The lives of important men are often so eventful and rich that justice cannot be done them in narrow compass; details are essential to *vitality;* and traits must be illustrated again and again before their force can be grasped. The hurried or indolent reader may think an outline life of Walter Scott or John Marshall—such as John Buchan and E. S. Corwin have ably provided—quite adequate; but the impression made by such brief volumes rapidly fades, while that left by immersion in the full stream of narrative, anecdote, letters, utterances, and comment provided by Lockhart and Beveridge is permanent. A great biography is a creation on the symphonic or operatic order, not a lyric.

To make a biography factually accurate is materially easier, especially in dealing with recent figures, than to make it unbiased. Voltaire was quite just in saying, "We owe consideration to the living; to the dead we owe truth alone." But in addition to all the forms of bias which may injure history, biographical work is subject to some canker-worms peculiarly its own. The most frequent and striking is the family bias. The papers of great men are usually held after death by widows, children, or other close relatives. Not a few important biographies have been written by sons (Alfred Tennyson, Nathaniel Hawthorne); by widows (Charles Kingsley); by widowers (George Eliot); by daughters (Julia Ward Howe); by sons-in-law (Scott, William Cullen Bryant); by daughters-in-law (Joel Chandler Harris); by brothers (Longfellow); by nephews (Washington Irving); and by secretaries (Charles Sumner). It is unnecessary to say that all the figures just named were presented as faultless—some as archangels. Pierre M. Irving, to draw a portrait of his uncle as faithful to the memory of Matilda Hoffman until death, suppressed the evidence of his courtship of other women. Of course it is more frequent for the family to consign its papers to some literary man for the preparation of a life, but this is too often done with express or implied conditions. Burton J. Hendrick's *Carnegie* barely hints that the ironmaster had one small fault, vanity; many "authorized" biographies are of necessity equally eulogistic. The obstacles which widows in particular throw before honest biography sometimes inspire a wish for the revival of *suttee*. One of the last acts of Robert Louis Stevenson's widow was to suppress a book which revealed certain facts about the novelist which a few years later were far more frankly related by others.

Closely allied with this impediment is the bias of official or social decorum. The "authorized" biographer of a man of high station is frequently moved by a false sense of propriety to suppress or color his evidence. He shows his figure in the most dignified light; he omits matter which would reflect on living men. A more sensible attitude was taken by Carlyle when Froude, preparing Mrs. Carlyle's letters for publication, asked whether he had not better exclude some sharp criticisms of a public man still living. Carlyle rejoined that it "would do the public personage no harm to know what a sensible woman thought of him." But some Americans would think it highly improper to

publish an incident, however authentic, which reflected
discredit on George Washington; many Southerners would
think it treason to print anything which derogated from
Robert E. Lee's merit. Still another distortion common in
biography is what Sir Leslie Stephen called the ethical or
edificatory bias—the desire to use a life as an improving
example. Nearly all ecclesiastical biographies fall under
this disability. When Archdeacon Hare wrote the life of his
one-time curate, John Sterling, he treated it as a tragedy of
spiritual torment, a spectacle of the misery caused by religious doubt. Carlyle, who knew that Sterling's life was
not tragic and who honored his honest skepticism, retorted
by a biography which has become classic. The biographer's
business is to tell the truth about Lincoln and Poe, not to
use them respectively to illustrate the glories of patriotism
and the woes of intemperance.

3   Finally, one indispensable requirement of a good biography is that it carefully relate the man it treats to history
—that it define his position and significance in the broad
stream of events. Obviously this is a requirement which
historians will most of all emphasize. They know full well
that much of their material first reaches them through
biographical and autobiographical channels. American history from 1910 to 1920, for example, could not be written
with any approach to completeness until the papers of
Taft, Theodore Roosevelt, Woodrow Wilson, Bryan, Lan-
sing, Baker, and numerous others had become available.
In no instance were these papers released to general historians until biographic use had been made of them, while
in several instances they were withheld even after the
biographies appeared. It was therefore important to history that the biographies be full; but it was also important
to biography. Critics who take a purely literary view sometimes deplore the tendency to write books which treat the
"lives and times" of eminent men; the times, they declare,
should be omitted, the writer confining himself to the depiction of personality and the recital of acts and thoughts.
But to this the historian could never consent, and the
biographer never should. Every life is to a great extent a
reflection of—a response to, or a reaction against—the con-

ditions of its time, whether political, economic, literary, or artistic. And no biography succeeds unless it brings out the import of every life to its own generation and those which follow. A memoir of Howells, Meredith, or Anatole France must relate him accurately and expertly to American, English, or French literature—and to the social life of his own land; a biography of Cleveland, Peel, or Gambetta must relate him to every contemporaneous turn of national politics. This cannot be done by a few brief allusions.

The demand for spare and stripped lives would deprive us of the great panoramic biographies like Morley's *Gladstone*, Monypenny and Buckle's *Disraeli*, J. L. Garvin's *Chamberlain*, Gardiner's *Harcourt*, Spender's *Campbell-Bannerman*, Ronaldshay's *Curzon*; of the six volumes of David Alec Wilson's *Carlyle*, the three of W. L. Cross's *Fielding*; of Freeman's *Lee*, Nicolay and Hay's *Lincoln*, Sandburg's *Lincoln*, Irving Brant's *Madison*, and the volumes on Franklin D. Roosevelt by Frank B. Freidel. Some of these neither biography nor history could well spare. It is true that a certain amount of repetition is involved in long biographies; that readers of the lives of Gladstone, Disraeli, Harcourt, and Chamberlain get the Home Rule quarrel four times over, and readers of biographies of Cleveland, Blaine, McKinley, and Aldrich four treatments of the tariff. But the repetition in good biography is slight. What is a common denominator of knowledge can be very briefly summarized; for the rest, the reader studies Home Rule or the tariff under four lights, from four points of view, each with its own novelty. None of the multitude of intelligent users of Morley's *Gladstone* and Buckle's *Disraeli* has ever complained of irksome duplication; rather, they have been astonished to find how unlike the same issues appear when seen from opposed sides. To be sure, in treating the "times" of a hero all that is irrelevant to his career should be omitted. This Nicolay and Hay's biography does not do, for it is essentially a history of the Civil War; but the younger biographers named above commit no such error. The day that the "life and times" expires and all biographies are reduced to one volume, that day the full-bodied, vigorous, convincing presentation of distinguished men, so depicted that we can walk all around them and see them in their natural surroundings, will be dealt a fatal blow.

III

The mistaken demand for briefer, sketchier lives was connected with the emergence of a so-called New Biography, which André Maurois tells us first originated about 1910. From one point of view, there was less novelty in the short biography fixing its attention upon character alone and presenting personality by a few sharp strokes than its practitioners supposed. Gamaliel Bradford had been anticipated in general fashion by Plutarch, and much more directly by Sainte-Beuve, who was great less as a literary critic than as an exquisitely finished painter of the chief intellectual figures of France. In England a "new biography" had been born soon after 1850, when the scientific spirit was gaining ground fast and Darwin, Huxley, and Spencer had affected all thought. Realism was coming into fiction; sculptors, ceasing to drape their statesmen in togas, were putting them into honest trousers. In biography the result of the new spirit was seen in such books as John Morley's *Voltaire, Burke, Rousseau,* and *Cobden,* works of a type not previously known in English. He abandoned chronological outlines, fixed his attention upon the inner man, and adopted oblique methods of portraiture. A rigidly critical attitude, avoiding all attempt at panegyric, permitted a keener insight. Sir Philip Magnes's *Gladstone* and A. J. P. Taylor's *Bismarck* are good recent examples of an incisive approach. These works were realistic without being irreverent or iconoclastic.

Yet a still newer biography was unquestionably born from the travail of the First World War years, and was closely connected with changes in the spirit of the age.* The principal agent in introducing it to the world was Lytton Strachey, who scored so brilliant a success in 1918 with

* Be it noted that Georg Brandes's incisive works on Goethe, Nietzsche, Voltaire, Caesar, Michelangelo, and Heine all followed 1910.

Eminent Victorians. The date was significant. In that quietly caustic work he registered his protest against the idealization of the past, against the hero-worship which still characterized so much biography and history. His attack on the Victorian era was the voice of a great disillusion, and fell upon the world in the bitterest year of disillusion in modern history. Mr. Strachey directed his readers' gaze at four heroic pieces of statuary—General Gordon, Arnold of Rugby, Florence Nightingale, Cardinal Manning—and by a deft twirl of the pedestal showed the seamed and pitted brass, the hollow artificiality of the image. With artistic skill he indicated that much of seeming greatness was after all mere pomposity; that the Carlylean heroes who pretended to compel the clouds and direct the lightning were after all mere puppets jerked by the great social and economic forces, by fate, or by their own passions. He was happy in his moment. A world looking at Clemenceau, Lloyd George, and Sonnino was quite willing to admit the hollowness of the great. A world helpless under the bludgeonings of circumstance was quite aware that events are greater than men. Even had Strachey's irony been less deft, witty, and entertaining than it was, it would have struck the mood of the age, and have found many imitators.

But Strachey's method no less than his message had a compelling novelty. He carried a long step further the art of Sainte-Beuve in his brief portraits, of Morley in his *Voltaire* and *Rousseau,* of Frederic Harrison's *Cromwell,* of Rosebery's *Pitt* and *Lord Randolph Churchill.* Abandoning chronology, substituting a dexterous, keen-sighted, and highly allusive exposition for narrative, using highlights and shadows as effectively as Velasquez, wringing a world of meaning from a single incident or quotation, and employing a mordant satire where older writers would have sacrificed truth to sympathy, he obtained striking effects by the most delightful means. He was, in fact, a consummate literary artist. Behind the rapid brushwork was a memory packed with learning, and a brain of very exceptional acuteness and power. Unfortunately, just as his ironic attitude could be imitated by anybody, so the superficial quality of his brushwork could be—and was—copied by a host of men who had none of his erudition or insight.

The result was that the newer biography which followed the First World War in a veritable spate of books did much to lower the standards of this branch of literature, and brought in a larger and more unabashed body of charlatans than were produced in the same years by the New Poetry, New Novel, and New History (which also flourished) all combined. Honest, painstaking craftsmanship was for a time shouldered rudely aside; an inexperienced writer would gather a half-dozen books about some great figure of the past, reshuffle the facts, add a strong dash of contempt, lard with epigrams, and turn out a new portrait. Critics appeared who sneered at the dull men who went to the trouble to investigate sources and write thorough, well-documented lives. It is not difficult to understand why, although the New Biography of Froude and Morley in 1870 had produced a restricted and creditable list of imitators, the Newer Biography of Strachey in 1918 loosed such a huge and in part disreputable stream of works. Morley and Froude had offered no easy formula. Their scientific, thoughtful, and learned method obviously required high gifts, prolonged study, and intense intellectual exertion. Strachey, on the contrary, offered a formula which *appeared* easy of imitation.[1]

A lively copy, indeed, such as Maurois's *Ariel: The Life of Shelley*, could be achieved by rather superficial study of the subject and by substituting cleverness for profundity. This statement does not imply that Strachey was a lesser writer than Morley; Rembrandt and Raphael are possibly of equal stature, but Rembrandt defies easy imitation, while Raphael offered a formula which gave birth to a large school. Readers of *Eminent Victorians* saw what effects Strachey had achieved by his ironic detachment—by turning the hero into an unheroic mediocrity—and many writers rushed to choose subjects, and treat them with condescending disrespect. Moreover, Strachey had with enviable skill suppressed all evidence of the more wearisome labors of the historian and biographer. The labor had really been expended, but by delightful anecdote, amusing epigram, unerring selection of facts, and expert interpretation, he concealed it. Some imitators leaped at the conclusion that because the labor had been suppressed it was unnecessary; that they could just dispense with it. Biography was becoming a form which cost neither the writer nor the reader any real effort.

To realize just what harm this facile doctrine did we must recur to our definition of the three principal objects of biography. A good biography must vividly re-create a character; it must present a full, careful, and unbiased record of his acts and experiences; and it must indicate the place of the hero in history. Strachey himself, in the light of these tests, was rather an essayist and interpreter than biographer; and his more reckless followers achieved something like a perversion of biography. Theirs has well been called "plastic biography."

In presenting a personality, the ironic approach has its advantages—especially in depicting a villain or impostor, as Fielding long ago showed in *Jonathan Wild*. But in general, it is much easier for the writer to succeed with his presentation if he happens to be in sympathy with his subject. Boswell was rather unblushingly in sympathy with Dr. Johnson, Lockhart with Walter Scott, Morley with Gladstone, Dr. Harvey Cushing with William Osler—and all the resulting books we count major successes. Indeed, of the principal biographies in English, it would be hard to mention a successful depiction of personality which is malicious rather than sympathetic. Even Lytton Strachey, when he came to Queen Victoria, hauled down his flag, surrendered to the Victorian glamour, and closed in a burst of commemorative eloquence; he had been ironic in spots, but the final effect was of admiration. Even Philip Guedalla, after spending his witty irony upon Napoleon III, made a true hero out of Wellington. It is impossible to present a personality merely by showering it with brickbats. Satire and sarcasm are not biography, and their uses in biography are after all singularly limited. We all know nowadays that Wordsworth had an illegitimate daughter and that Washington apparently fell in love with a neighbor's wife, but these facts tell us more about personality when stated with dignity and sympathy than when offered with a sly jeer. Lord Curzon was a man of many foibles as well as great gifts, but Harold Nicolson makes his personality fully comprehensible by the combination of warmth and frankness in *Curzon: The Last Phase*. Nicolson once specially praised Sidney Lee's method of disclosing, in his life of Edward VII, the fact that the king pounced upon and gobbled the dishes before him. "He had a splendid appetite at all times," wrote Lee, "and never toyed with his food."

But the failure in inexpert hands of this part of the Stracheyan formula—the ironic or satiric detachment—was nothing compared with the failure of another supposed part: the rule that the biographer must be entertaining at all hazards, and that the less labor he gives himself or the reader the better. This rule (to which Strachey himself would have been the last to subscribe) made it impossible to meet the second and third tests of good biography. A distinguished biography, which traces fully a man's career and defines expertly his historical station, is never all entertainment. It demands not merely enormous toil from the author, but a wholesome mental exertion from the reader. It cannot compete with the detective story, the current film, or other forms of intellectual anaesthesia. The books of M. Maurois, assuredly among the ablest of Strachey's successors, are delightful. They give us for a time the virtuous feeling that we are combining instruction and pleasure without baser alloy; but in the end they are hardly more nourishing than ginger ale, for they oversimplify their subjects. We are offered a stream of anecdote about Shelley, Byron, and Disraeli, an engrossing adventure story based upon their careers, and some amusing thumbnail portraits of collateral figures. But we do not attain any particular understanding of the complexities and depths of character, we get a sadly incomplete record of the subject's acts and ideas, and we miss a thorough appraisal of the hero's position in history. We are told nothing about Byron's standing and influence as a poet, Shelley's special role in the romantic movement, or Disraeli's final achievements and failures as a statesman. A Southern professor of philosophy, when his class raised some particularly intricate question, was wont to say, "That is a bit difficult just now; we will come to it later on." M. Maurois never comes to it, and at length, much as we admire his artistry, the fact breeds a certain suspicion. From his *Disraeli* we turn back, with a not unhappy sigh, to the six volumes of Monypenny and Buckle, sure of finding there the real man in his complete setting.

Some defects of another post-Stracheyan author, Emil Ludwig, were traceable to overproduction. Philip Guedalla once caustically referred to the German school of biography, "the day shift of which compiles the life of Napoleon while the night shift is pumping the life out of Lincoln." But the deeper and more vital defects would remain if Ludwig had written no more volumes than Morley. His volume on Napoleon had every ingredient for a popular success. With all the blood and fire, all the charges and retreats, all the amours, all the backstairs gossip, all the horrors of the Moscow debacle, told in a style that now reminded the reader of a George Arliss movie and now of a Bernard Shaw lecture, it was precisely suited to those who had never before opened a book on Napoleon. As history, it was excellent melodrama. Perhaps no deeper meaning inheres in Napoleon's career than such a Sunday-supplement chronicle of his life would indicate, but those who believe that it does would never send amateurs to Emil Ludwig. When Francis Hackett's life of Henry VIII appeared, it was observed that the enthusiasm of the critics was in inverse proportion to their knowledge of Tudor England. When the book was finally reviewed by Wallace Notestein of Yale University, though due tribute was paid to its fine literary qualities, the general verdict upon it was cool. The idea that exact and patient scholarship, the scholarship matured through years of study, can be dispensed with in biography is analogous to the belief that an architect or engineer can raise magnificent structures without long years of training and apprenticeship.

The radical leaders in the newer biography might be regarded with more tolerance had not some of them added critical insults to the injury that was done by meretricious books. The able Lewis Mumford once reviewed a sheaf of biographies in the *Atlantic*. Two kinds of biography existed, he remarked: the good, which was post-Stracheyan in character, and the bad, which was pre-Stracheyan. Pointing to Van Wyck Brooks's *Emerson* as an admirable example of the former, he condemned Burton J. Hendrick's *Carnegie* and Claude G. Bowers's *Beveridge* as deplorable illustrations of the latter—stuffy, pedantic, uncritical, excessively long. It seems not to have occurred to the critic that he was regarding two wholly different types of work. Mr. Brooks's *Emerson*, though possessing numerous excellences, is for whole chapters a close paraphrase of Emerson's journals, letters, and the works of previous biographers. It has hardly more originality, so far as its factual content goes, than Mr. Mumford's own *Herman Melville*, whose reliable materials (for a good deal of hazardous guessing at psychology was added) were very largely borrowed from Raymond Weaver's scholarly biography. Hendrick's *Carnegie* and Bowers's *Beveridge*, on the contrary, were primary works. Each author, writing the life of his subject for the first time, had to be reasonably exhaustive, thoroughly attentive to scholarship, and ready to take the prosaic along with the dramatic. Each was unfortunate, from one point of view, that he could not turn to some previous biographer, borrow his materials, and write a book which played up all the succulent, sparkling parts of the story. Each was fortunate, from another and better point of view, that he could write a book which is likely to remain standard while ephemeral interpretations of the subject appear and fade away.

The fact is, of course, that a distinction must be drawn between three literary types: the source biography, the popular biography, and the critical interpretation of a life. Nothing should be allowed to diminish the respect paid to the original biographer who spends toilsome years in poring over old letter-books and manuscripts, hunting through crackling newspaper files, interviewing ancient survivors— by myriad labors slowly bringing to light the essential facts of a great man's life; particularly if he shows literary art in shaping his results. Every such biographer is a true servant of history. Even greater respect may sometimes be due to the learned and profound interpreter, who takes the salient facts gathered by another and pours a flood of new light through them. But such an interpreter must have both a great mind and a solid foundation of knowledge; he must be a Sainte-Beuve or John Morley. Commanding interpretive studies like W. C. Brownell's volume on six *Victorian Prose Masters,* like Goldwin Smith's *Three English Statesmen,* no more come from hasty amateurs than figs from thistles. The popularizer deserves the least respect, and if he is slipshod and dishonest, the very opposite of respect. He often tends to bring the whole art of biography into disrepute, and to convince lay readers that it and history are without standards or enduring values. It is important to keep in the foreground the trustworthy source biography, and the trustworthy interpretation; important, since neither can be dispensed with, to avoid invidious comparisons between them. Van Wyck Brooks's *Mark Twain* is a stimulating interpretation, beautifully written, and generally adjudged quite sound. Some critics would doubtless assert that it is shapelier, more artistic, and more acute than the work on which it so largely draws, Albert Bigelow Paine's solid volumes on Mark Twain, but they would go too far when they would contemptuously brush Paine from the earth. No Albert Bigelow Paine, no Van Wyck Brooks!

The ideal in biography is the patient investigator who can write lives which combine scholarship, interpretive power, and literary charm; which are thorough, expert, and yet full of popular interest. In the past this ideal has repeatedly been attained. It better than anything else puts the charlatans to shame and deprives the biographical popularizers of their chief excuse for being. Dogmatism as to form and content in this field is as dangerous as in history. A great biography may be as long as Lockhart's ten volumes on Scott, or as short as Edmund Gosse's *Father and Son,* J. E. Neale's *Queen Elizabeth,* or Lloyd Lewis's *Captain Sam Grant;* it may be as acidly critical as Froude's *Carlyle* or as sympathetic as Lord David Cecil's *The Stricken Deer* (William Cowper); it may be as full of in-

terpretation as Lounsbury's admirable life of Fenimore
Cooper, or as devoid of it as Thomas Beer's highly objective life of Stephen Crane. No doubt greater expertness
in employing the technical tools of psychology—most scholars having distrusted the psychoanalytic method because
they do not feel that the data is adequate—will be attained. But as it stands, with much less use of valid psychological tools than modern fiction has made, biography
is the indispensable ally and supporter of history.[2]

XIII
Literary Aspects of History

THERE ARE twenty different ways, says Kipling, of writing tribal lays, and every single one of them is right. The same assertion may be made of history, which is one of the most variegated departments of letters. Yet certain elements do give a common stamp to the work of the greatest historians. Perhaps the chief is suggested by Thackeray in his comment on the genius of Lord Macaulay, whom he praises for his enormous erudition—but also for a much rarer quality than erudition.

"Take at hazard," writes Thackeray, "any three pages of his Essays or History; and, glimmering below the stream of the narrative, you, an average reader, see one, two, three, a half score of allusions to other historic facts, characters, literature, poetry, with which you are acquainted. Your neighbor, who has *his* reading and *his* little stock of literature stored away in his mind, will detect more points, allusions, happy touches, indicating, not only the prodigious memory and learning of this master, but the wonderful industry, the honest, humble previous toil of this great scholar. He reads twenty books to write a sentence, he travels a hundred miles to make a line of description."

Be it noted that Thackeray admired not merely Macaulay's vast learning and toil of research, but his ability to distil the result into tiny compass, and his readiness to present it without ostentation. It was literally true that Macaulay read twenty books to write a sentence, and traveled a hundred miles to make a line of description. Expending endless pains to ascertain a fact, he then set it down with the simplest brevity. In his famous description of the state of England in 1685, for example, he had occasion to note the population of Leeds. His biographer Trevelyan publishes some of the numerous letters which he wrote in an effort to obtain this single figure. He consulted all the books and pamphlets that might be of use; he got the city recorder to have the municipal archives searched; through church officials he ransacked ecclesiastical records. The recorded number of burials in 1685 gave him a statistic which, after various critical tests, he discarded. By continued research he finally found a list of all the houses in Leeds in 1683, numbering 1400, and projecting this indication forward two years, he arrived at an estimate of 8000 people. Having done all this, how much space did Macaulay use in stating his conclusions? Five lines.

Macaulay wrote on February 8, 1849, after publishing his first two volumes: "I have made up my mind to change my whole plan about my history. I will first set myself to know about my whole subject; to get, by reading and travelling, a full acquaintance with William's reign. I reckon that it will take me eighteen months to do this. I must visit Holland, Belgium, Scotland, Ireland, France. The Dutch archives and French archives must be ransacked. I will see whether anything is to be got from other diplomatic collections. I must see Londonderry, the Boyne, Aghrim, Kinsale, Namur again, Landen, Steinkirk. I must turn over hundreds, thousands of pamphlets. Lambeth, the Bodleian and the other Oxford libraries, the Devonshire Papers, the British Museum, must be explored and notes made; and then I shall go to work. When the materials are ready, and the History mapped out in my mind, I ought easily to write on an average two of my pages daily." He added that when the next section of his history had been finished, then "I reckon a year for polishing, retouching, and printing." This arduous program Macaulay duly carried out.

When he studied the disrepute into which the English clergy had fallen under Charles II, he steeped his mind in the ecclesiastical literature of that reign to pen a few pages. When he wrote of the battle of Killiecrankie he paid the field two visits, and employed much of one in a long walk over the pass to write a single sentence upon the time spent by the English army in mounting it.

It is true, as Macaulay's biographer remarks, that few who read such a brief statement in the *History of England* as that upon the population of Leeds can "form a conception of the pains which these clear and flowing periods must have cost an author who expended on the pointing of a phrase as much conscientious research as would have provided some writers, who speak of Macaulay as showy or shallow, with at least half a dozen pages of ostentatious statistics." Macaulay is delightful to read not merely for his full, rich mind, but because he took extraordinary pains to digest his materials. His method of composition was to fill his capacious memory with his subject, until he had completely mastered every part of it. Then, with few notes or books of reference, he would sit down and write off the whole story at a steady pace, securing in black and white each idea, epithet, and turn of phrase as previously thought out. Every part of the exposition had passed through the alchemy of his brain before it was committed to paper, and the dross had been refined away. An inferior writer, yielding to the temptation of showing on the printed page the extent of his labors, would have given his readers a neat dispute on the population of Leeds, peppered with footnotes. But Macaulay was content to thrust the non-essentials out of sight. He was interested in the finished structure, and did not bother his readers with a view of the scaffolding used to put it up, or the shavings and litter discarded in the process.

The same characteristic stamps the work of such literary historians as Parkman and Prescott. The fact that both men were for long periods almost blind and could not refer constantly to notes and printed works made it indispensable for them to master their materials completely before beginning composition. Parkman during most of his active career had to hire an assistant to read every book and document aloud. First came the labor of ferreting out, buying, or copying materials, in which he showed remarkable keenness. Then he had his assistant read the principal materials to him with care, that he might delineate the chief features of his subject—might plan it in his mind. Later came a much more detailed reading, during which he took notes of the details of the story and of background or accessory materials. Finally, a still minuter scrutiny of the most difficult parts of his mass of documents would follow, Parkman trying to fix the whole in his memory. "By this slow method," writes G. H. Farnham, "he acquired perfect possession of the materials needed for a volume. He then set to work at composition, always finishing one volume before touching another. His inability to compose rapidly, as we have already seen, offered some very valuable compensations for difficulties and delays. It forced him to consider well his plan, *to digest his materials thoroughly;* and by keeping him living for some time in each part of his subject as he went along, secured freedom and leisure for the exercise of both imagination and judgment." And emphasizing the fact of Parkman's patient premastery of his materials, his biographer adds:

In the long hours of enforced solitude and illness in the subdued light of his study, or during his sleepless nights, his subject pressed upon him with the insistence of an absorbing interest. It is easy to understand that his hardest effort was to keep his mind at rest. Few men could have sustained their interest and power under such tedious delays; but he had precisely the faculties needed to meet the situation—breadth and firmness of grasp for details and general lines, a retentive memory, great constructive skill, and a vivid imagination—the whole driven by supernormal energy. When it came to writing or dictating the book, he had each day's production already arranged, probably some of it composed and memorized. He dictated at a moderate pace—sometimes holding a few notes in his hand—without hesitation, and with a degree of finish seldom requiring any correction.

Prescott also, with the sight of one eye destroyed and that of the other impaired, had to have most of his historical materials read to him. His subjects, especially in Spanish history, being more complex than Parkman's, he took more detailed notes. If his eyes happened to be sufficiently strong, he studied these notes himself; if not, he had them read aloud repeatedly—rarely less than six times; some, he says, "a dozen times." They were thus stamped upon a memory which he cultivated to very remarkable retentiveness. Having mastered his data, he began the task of mental composition, a difficult process because of the exactness to be observed as he progressed. But he became able to rely upon this faculty more and more heavily, until at last he attained extraordinary power in the application of his richly stored memory. It was never such an astonishing memory as that of Macaulay, who once said that if all copies of Milton's *Paradise Lost* and Bunyan's *Pilgrim's Progress* were destroyed, he would undertake to reproduce these works intact; but training and use had made it a remarkable instrument. George Ticknor writes of Prescott's method of fusing his materials—of Bessemerizing them—mentally:

It was really desirable to write, not almost, but altogether, from memory. He labored, therefore, long for it, and succeeded, by great and continuous efforts, in obtaining the much-coveted power. "Think concentratedly," he says, "when I think at all." And again, "Think closely, gradually concentrating the circle of thought." At last, in 1841, when he was employed on the *Mexico*, he records, after many previous memoranda on the subject: "My way has lately been to go over a large mass—over and over, till ready to throw it on paper." And the next year, 1842, he says: "Concentrate more resolutely my thoughts the first day of meditation —going over and over—thinking once before going to bed, or in bed, or before rising—prefer the latter. And after one day of chewing the cud should be (i.e. ought to be) ready to write. It was three days for this chapter." (*Conquest of Mexico*, Book V, Chapter II.) Sometimes it was longer, but in general a single whole day, or two or three evenings, with the hours of his exercise in riding or walking, were found to be sufficient for such careful meditation.

The result was remarkable—almost incredible—as to the masses he could thus hold in a sort of abeyance in his mind, and as to the length of time he could keep them there, and consider and reconsider them without confusion or weariness. Thus, he says that he carried in his memory the first and second chapters of the fifth book of the *Conquest of Peru*, and ran over the whole ground several times before beginning to write, although these two chapters fill fifty-six pages of printed text; and he records the same thing of chapters fifth, sixth, and seventh, in the second book of *Philip II*, which make together seventy-two pages, and on which he was employed sixty-two days.

He frequently kept about sixty pages in his memory for several days, and went over the whole mass five or six times, moulding and remoulding the sentences at each successive return.

I

Several principal reasons exist why the inexperienced writer fails, and the inferior writer refuses, to digest his materials after this fashion. He may be the victim of a spurious vanity. Having gone to immense pains to ascertain all the facts, he is so anxious to impress the public with the thoroughness of his work that he gives not merely the results of his labor, but the labor itself—discarded data, rejected hypotheses, long citations of authorities. Instances of this tiresome preening lie thick in the work of the more pedantic historians, who thus qualify for the indictment once leveled at German historians: the sentences are too long, the paragraphs are too long, the chapters are too long, and the books are too long. A second reason, however, arises from the converse of vanity—timidity. The amateur may feel distrustful of his ability to take a step unless bolstered on the crutch of a citation of fact. Instead of

saying that Leeds in 1685 had about 8000 people, he sum-
marizes all the data because this makes him feel *safe;* no
critic can accuse him of snap judgments, of haste and
superficiality. The pedantic reviewing still too common in
some historical periodicals encourages this timidity. Such
amateurs should pluck up courage, for Macaulay and Parkman were also accused of superficiality.

Another explanation for the failure to digest historical
material lies in sheer clumsiness, or more exactly, lack of
literary discernment. Persons deficient in literary instinct
undervalue dynamic directness. They will not write, "Lincoln was six feet four," and go on. Instead, they write: "It
is a fact, and a fact of no small significance, that Lincoln
was six feet four inches tall." They think that a patchwork
of quotations and citations, or such crude summaries of
original material as strew John Bach McMaster, are better
history than a fused and digested narrative. They speak of
the flavor which raw materials, such as quotations from an
old document, give. They would do well to read such a
chapter in Herbert J. Muller's *The Uses of the Past* as that
on "The Legacy of Israel," a mighty subject summarized
effectively without any quotation whatever. To be sure, in
biography copious quotations from letters, diaries, and conversations are almost essential to the lifelike presentation
of personality; and even in history limited quotations sometimes help give the color of a varied background, the flavor
of the more salient personalities. Henry Adams uses them
more frequently than Macaulay, Parkman and Froude
more generously than Adams. The point at which to draw
the line is a matter of taste. But it is always best to err on
the side of parsimony in using unsmelted ore.

The ideal in history is a work on which infinite labor
has first been expended to obtain and utilize the materials,
and infinite pains have then been expended to hide the
labor. An effort to attain the ideal is important for two reasons. Not merely does the complete smelting of the ore, the
absorption of the inchoate mass of original fact into the
mind of the author and its conversion there into a harmonious whole, make history more attractive to the reader.
It holds another great benefit. It releases the imagination

and the reflective power of the author. The mind ceases to be tied to mere minutiae. So long as the author plods, fettering himself at every step to his rough materials, his higher faculties must remain in abeyance. When he lifts himself above his materials, seeing them as a whole, fresh significances occur to him; new associations and generalizations become possible; he can act more effectively in applying ideas to history.

II

But the amateur of history who intends to write a paper, a monograph, or a book is carried only a short distance by the advice that he should digest his information thoroughly before he sets pen to paper. For one consideration, few men can ever trust half so much to memory as Macaulay or Prescott; many cannot compose more than a page or two mentally. For another, what is to be done after gaining a grasp of the material to be used? How arrange it, how proportion it, how make it truly interesting? The answer involves study, discipline, and practice.

There is of course no real conflict between literary and scientific history, and if terms are properly defined, there never has been. The most vehement exponent of scientific method admits that literary grace is desirable, and the most ardent apostle of style in history confesses that exact research is also requisite. A spirited quarrel over the relative emphasis to be given these qualities did rage during much of the nineteenth century. The scientific school held that overwhelming weight should be granted the unvarnished record of the precise facts; that matter and substance were all-important, manner and form were but pleasing trifles. This school believed that it was the chief business of history to clear up dark areas and settle disputed points, and that being artistic was unimportant. Von Ranke's idea of history was fairly summed up in his oft-quoted statement that it should describe the past as it actually happened. But literary historians treated this school with contempt as mere fact-grubbers; Carlyle had Von Ranke in mind when he excoriated Professor Dryasdust, while Frederic Harrison wrote scornfully of Stubbs's dullness. The controversy was carried on with an animosity which became theatrical and unreal.

One truth is indubitable: it is possible to be scientific and exact, and also to write with high literary charm. Thucydides, who was scientific in temper, is not less effective as a literary artist than Plutarch, who was unscientific. No man of sense ever esteemed Tacitus inferior in style to the far less accurate Livy. In modern times, such writers as Michelet, Lecky, Mommsen, Villari, John Addington Symonds, Parkman, Prescott, and J. R. Green in varying degrees illustrated the fact that men can be distinguished in research, in insight, and in expression at the same time. Here and there a historian has so sacrificed substance to literary effect that he has become discredited and is little read; some parts of Froude's work fall into this category. At the other extreme are historians who write clearly but with absolute lack of color, or whose style is exasperatingly clumsy. Both extremes are to be avoided; the combination of literary polish and sparkle with scientific adequacy is the true object.

Another truth is almost as indubitable as the first: the world at large will sooner forgive lack of scientific solidity than lack of literary charm. The great preservative in history, as in all else, is style. A book of consummate literary art may abound in passages of bad history, but nevertheless carry generation after generation before it. It is useless to protest that Lord Clarendon was far too biased on the English Civil War; he will be read for centuries by all who savor a close-packed, pithy, eloquent style, full of graphic sketches of men and events. Motley is unscientific in his treatment of Spanish misrule in the Netherlands, but the world will continue to read Motley. If a historian were compelled to take his choice, fame might urge him to select the winged pen rather than the Aristotelian mind, to choose Apollo against Minerva; but he may choose both.

It is not absolutely necessary, remarked Bishop Mandell Creighton, to be dull in order to prove that you can write history. Indeed, we may add that the converse is true. Usually it is the luminous-minded author, whose work satisfies exacting scientific tests, who also writes with color, point, and ease; it is the muddle-headed author, who goes wrong on facts and evidence, who also makes the inferior literary statement.

The first step for the historical amateur is precisely that which the author of any other piece of extended exposition must take. He should resort to the mechanical device by which all writers obtain unity; he should make a written outline. His attempts at mental digestion of his material will have carried him a long way in this direction. But in most tasks it is important to draft the first outline before note-taking has been carried far, so that subsequent notes can be arranged under headings of the outline. Thereafter, as material accumulates, as digestion keeps pace with it, the outline should be drastically revised. It is seldom that even experienced writers are willing to give as much time to outlining their essays or books as they should; however important, it is a piece of drudgery, and it is easy to make a thousand excuses for sidestepping it. It involves slow, careful thought, and thought is always painful. Emerson once remarked that he had trained himself to *think*, with utter absorption, as much as fifteen minutes a day; and that the man who could train himself to think for half an hour daily might rule the world. A good outline for a historical essay or chapter requires fully fifteen minutes of concentrated, laborious thinking.

Impatience often conspires with laziness, for to think any considerable subject through, and then to prepare an analysis as good as the brief of a careful lawyer, may actually require weeks of time. It is much pleasanter to leaf through books, to jot down notes, to gather materials in all possible nooks—for the hunt after materials may be as exciting as a detective story. The amateur does this work in the vague hope that when his files are packed with citations and references, the monograph will somehow emerge without any trouble. Yet this is to make trouble for himself, and ten times as much trouble for the poor reader. If he begins collecting a large body of materials without a careful plan, in the end his helter-skelter, amorphous accumulation of facts is likely to overpower him; they master the author, who should at all times master them.

The amateur who believes that he is above the drudgery of a preliminary outline believes his mind better than Macaulay's; for the clearest evidence exists that Macaulay, retentive as was his memory and lucid as was his brain, carefully outlined his best historical work in advance. His letters speak of his plans and outlines. He tells how he discarded one subject, the early history of George III's reign, because on making a preliminary sketch he found the subject unmanageable. His essay on Machiavelli may be taken as an example of admirably proportioned and arranged historical argument. It is essentially an attempt to vindicate the Italian thinker from the opprobrium in which he has been held—an opprobrium which had converted his last name into a synonym for trickery, and his first into the nickname for the devil, "Old Nick." In a monograph of about 16,000 words, Macaulay develops the thesis that the characteristics which have rendered Machiavelli hateful belonged rather to the age than to the man. He begins with an introduction upon Machiavelli's disrepute, admitting that *The Prince* is indeed a shocking book. He then propounds the historical problem offered by this and other writings: How did Machiavelli come to present such immoral doctrines? He states several hypotheses, only to reject them—the hypothesis that Machiavelli's private character was hypocritical and grasping, and so warped his judgment of right and wrong; that his public conduct lacked integrity, and he therefore laid down the principles of his book to excuse his official behavior. Macaulay then introduces the true explanation of the unethical tone of *The Prince*. It lies in "the state of moral feeling among the Italians of those times," and the desperate disorders of the country, racked by the wars of petty despots and the devastations of mercenary bands, which required a desperate remedy. That remedy, which he was ready to see achieved by fair means or foul, was to solidify the small Italian states under a powerful central ruler upheld by a national army. To the elaboration and proof of his main thesis Macaulay properly devotes most of his essay, about 9000 words. He then adds a vigorous conclusion of perhaps 1000 words. The judgments in the essay have been questioned, but its construction is masterly.

An historian whose plan is always lucid and often impressive (sometimes, alas, its most impressive feature) is John Fiske. Since each of his books contains a detailed table of contents, summarizing nearly every page, it is as easy as it is profitable for students to take his best volumes and study the outlines for each chapter. His strongest book is the two-volume *Discovery of America,* while next in value stands the graphic history of *Old Virginia and Her Neighbours.* These works are marked by symmetry of structure, unity of design, strong narrative interest, and concentration of effect; they sing like Quentin Durward's arrow to the white bull's-eye of the target. But even so inferior a book as *The Critical Period of American History* maintains a certain place by virtue of its effective architecture and charm of style. It has doubtless been more widely read than the far richer volume on the period by Andrew C. McLaughlin, the more stimulating volume by Charles A. Beard—and the ordinary rapid reader will perhaps carry away more from its perusal than from the other two, for it is so arranged that all its values can be seized.

In *The Critical Period,* Fiske begins both dramatically and logically with the surrender at Yorktown and the treaty of peace. He follows this by a chapter on the thirteen States at the end of the Revolution, showing how strongly the people were attached to their own commonwealths, how well most of the new State governments had operated, and how much they had done for liberty, equality, and progress. He then turns by a natural transition to the contrasting clumsiness, inefficiency, and disrepute of the national government under the Articles of Confederation. This requires two chapters, his narrative rising to a climax as he describes the quarrels of the various States, the paper-money craze, and Shays's Rebellion. Then he takes up "The Germs of National Sovereignty"—the national domain steadily built up by State cessions of land beyond the Alleghenies; Washington's interest in the West and in interstate navigation; and the calling of a commercial convention at Annapolis in 1786. This brings him to the Federal Convention which met at Philadelphia in May 1787, and to which he properly devotes his longest chapter, nearly a hundred pages. A final chapter called "Crowning the Work" describes the ratification of the Constitution by the States, and the placing of the new Federal Government in operation. As a piece of exposition, without reference to questions of scholarly completeness or depth, the volume could hardly be better done.

Nearly all writers who have attempted any sustained piece of historical composition will agree upon the principal difficulty they have encountered in planning their books. It lies in the necessity of somehow reconciling the temporal order with the topical order of treatment. In most comprehensive histories a number of topics, let us say politics, religion, education, literature, and art, have to be discussed; with perhaps a war thrown into the beginning of the study, an important Parliamentary election into the middle, and a financial panic near the close. Since such a history extends over a number of years, it is imperative that it give the reader a sense of progression, and highly desirable that it stimulate his interest by employing suspense and climax at various points. Yet if it is given a purely topical pattern, nearly all sense of continuity in the book as a whole will be sacrificed. The writer will carry politics, let us say, from 1789 to 1803; he will then go back and carry the record of education down from 1789 to 1803; and then go back again to 1789 for art. If on the contrary, he attempts to give a broad temporal sweep to his narrative, relating first what was done in all fields from 1789 to 1793, then what was done from 1793 to 1797, and finally from 1797 to 1803, his topical elements must be mingled together in hopeless confusion. Obviously, in nearly all large histories a compromise must be effected. While the nature of the compromise must depend entirely upon the materials, we may assert that one characteristic it should always have—it should be adroit, smooth, and persuasive. Sometimes, however, so difficult is the task that the best historians fail; even Parkman did not solve the problem in his sprawling *Half-Century of Conflict*.

Still another difficulty in planning many historical books lies in the unevenness of materials. It may seem easy to construct an *ideal* outline for the Administration of James Monroe; so much space will go to the decay of Federalism, so much to internal improvements, so much to the defense of the Atlantic seaboard, so much to the purchase of Florida and the Seminole War, so much to Lafayette's tour, so much to South American relations, and so much to the Monroe Doctrine. But what if the writer finds a perfect gold mine of unexploited material upon several topics, say the Monroe Doctrine, internal improvements, and the Seminole War, while he discovers almost nothing new on the others? Shall he sacrifice his materials, or mar the symmetry of his book? The unescapable answer is that he must sacrifice some part of the symmetry of his volume. Nevertheless, he is gravely at fault if he does not attain as much symmetry as possible in view of the capriciousness of his data, and if he does not give an adequate view of the Administration as a whole. A writer in whom the literary instinct is powerful will go to great lengths to keep each part of his work in due proportion to the whole, rigidly compressing and even rejecting rich materials. Harold Nicolson tells a significant anecdote of his book *Byron: The Last Journey:*

> In my researches . . . in the last year of Byron's life I came across certain documents which threw a wholly new light, not only upon Byron's character, but even upon the problem of his separation and departure from England. To have divulged this information would have created a sensation and have destroyed for many romantic people the picture they had formed of Byron's character. I decided that I should make no use of this material except in so far as it colored and confirmed my own estimate of Byron's strangely complicated temperament. I think I was right in so doing, and I should justify myself upon the following biographical principle, listed under the heading of "Truth and the Whole Truth." My principle is as follows: "If a biographer discovers material which is so shocking and sensational that it will

disturb, not only the average reader, but the whole proportion of his own work, then he is justified in suppressing the actual facts. He is not justified, however, in suppressing the conclusions which he draws from those facts, and he must alter his portrait so that it conforms to those facts." That is what I did in my treatment of Byron. Should some future research-worker come upon that same material he will recognize from my book that I also was in possession of that material, that it colored my interpretation of Byron's temperament, but that I suppressed the material itself for perfectly legitimate reasons.

Since an excessively mechanical arrangement of materials is as deadly as a purely mechanical piece of writing, a political history of England arranged according to prime ministries, or of America according to Presidential administrations, would be a poor history for any but those elementary readers who like to get their dates straight. A book which totally lacks plan may sometimes, on the other hand, achieve a curiously high degree of interest, for variety, novelty, and the spice of the unexpected are important elements in interest; but such a book will utterly fail to achieve the effect of an organic whole. Theodore Roosevelt once wrote his friend Lodge: "If all of McMaster's chapters were changed round promiscuously it would not, I am confident, injure the thread of his narrative in the least. He has put much novel matter in a brilliant, attractive way; but his work is utterly disconnected." The successive volumes of Mark Sullivan's *Our Times* are likewise almost totally without plan. A chapter on Republican politics lies cheek by jowl with one on Walter Reed and the conquest of yellow fever, which in turn is followed—with no connection or transition—by a chapter on the early development of the automobile; while at the end of the book a veritable cartload of unrelated facts upon popular songs, successful books, changing fashions, foods, furniture, crime, and passing sensations is lumped together in a hundred pages of potpourri. All this, enlivened by some vivid writing, bountifully illustrated, and dealing with so recent a period that it awakened the adult public's memory, proved highly entertaining. But it left the reflective reader convinced that while the author had collected many valuable materials for history, he had fallen decidedly short of writing history itself.

1. Symmetry Cla
2. Progression
3. Main feature

III

If symmetry and clarity of design are the first essential of good history, progression is the second. The narrative (for all sustained history presupposes a narrative) should move from point to point; the writer must beware of merely marking time. While description, static analysis, and pure exposition have their place in history, they do not suffice, taken alone or together, to make good historical work. Any account of more than a microscopic segment of the past involves time, and time involves movement. In other words, history is dynamic: it deals with mankind in action, and it should trace changes or at least explain the lack of changes resulting from this action. One writer has gone so far as to say that history must make clear three elements: first, the original condition; second, the action; and third, the condition which results, emphasizing the essentially novel features in this resultant condition. While generally sound, this is perhaps too mechanical a rule to be entirely serviceable. It fits some history badly, and a little not at all. For example, an action may end in utter failure and abortion, changing nothing, and yet be well worth recounting. It is simpler and truer to say that any important piece of historical writing must have progression, and that this progression must consist in demonstrating some relation between cause and effect. In other words, we return to the familiar principle that the facts of a piece of history must be synthesized—must be given coherence and significance by some theory of causation.

This is a simple principle, and the theory of causation may be both simple and obvious. A man may be writing a history of Sag Harbor, Long Island, let us say, and decides that the decay of Sag Harbor after 1850 was the result of the decline of whaling. This elementary theory gives him a basis for synthesizing his facts. In any ideal piece of history, no facts fail to possess some causal relation with other facts. Nothing should be left isolated or detached, and nothing thrown in simply because it is interesting or colorful. In some parts of John Bach McMaster's chronicle of the American people many pages have the appearance of a mere historical memorandum-book; confused masses of facts about social life in America are shot at the reader without due effort to relate them to one another, or to the general theme. However interesting in themselves, they lack significance because they are not synthesized, and in such passages McMaster ceases to write history at all. However, a word of warning must be added as to some books. Various ingenious authors show great skill in giving a mutual relationship to matters which on the surface have no relation at all, and the appearance of haphazard disconnection in some subtly-written books is misleading. At first glance G. K. Chesterton and Thomas Beer appear to gain many of the effects of their quasi-historical works by sheer irrelevance. In *The Mauve Decade* Beer passes lightly from topic to topic, and frequently throws into otherwise coherent passages some details which seem as alien as the birds that sing in the spring. It is only when his art is more carefully studied that the reader perceives that there is really little irrelevance, and that both his satiric and historical aims have been furthered by the interjected details.

In the third and last place, it is important that the main architectural elements of any historical work be brought out in bold relief, and the minor appurtenances left in a clearly subordinate position. The commonest defect in the work of novices of history is that they never let the reader see the wood for the trees. They fill their monographs with facts which are all given approximately the same value; they pile dates, statistics, quotations, and assertions upon each other without subordinating them to any key statement; in short, they lose their way. The facts of the past are indeed sometimes a rather confusing maze. But a good history is like a good map; it possesses plenty of detail, but the important features stand out in large type. In any clear presentation of New York State the great cities, New York, Buffalo, and Albany, the principal rivers and mountain chains, are lifted in bold relief; in any good history of the Revolution in New York the great main forces are kept prominent, though the volume may contain an exhaustive statement of minor events as well.

As a means of attaining this necessary proportion, the best advice which can be given the beginner is that he should not be afraid of generalizations, but cultivate them; that he should keep general premises and general conclusions always in mind. If he does this, the petty details will soon assort themselves. When he writes, he should always try to proceed from the general to the particular, or the particular to the general—never merely from the particular to the particular. He will note that nearly all good historians do this. Elie Halévy, for example, begins each section of his *England in 1815* with a clear general statement which strikes the key for all that is to follow:

(1) "Three and only three possible methods are conceivable by which a people could govern itself; and all these three forms of government existed side by side in the British Constitution at the beginning of the nineteenth century."

(2) "Is it not perilous for a nation to sacrifice its agriculture to the development of its industries, and thereby to become dependent upon the foreigner for the satisfaction of its most elementary needs?"

(3) "During the opening years of the nineteenth century Methodism and Evangelism had imbued English society with their *ethos*."

It will also profit the student to study a number of volumes in which broad and intricate subjects, full of confusing detail, are brought into small compass in a clear, luminous fashion. The English language is well endowed with such works. Everyone will agree that the history of the Holy Roman Empire is one of the thorniest and most baffling of subjects, involving a huge mass of dry details; a jungle in which any writer might easily lose himself and his readers. But Lord Bryce's *Holy Roman Empire*, written when the author was twenty-six, makes the whole map of the wood as clearly visible as if we were in an airplane taking a lofty survey of it. In still briefer compass, an excellent treatment of an even larger subject is afforded by J. B. Bury's *History of Freedom of Thought*. Carl Becker's *Beginnings of the American People* shows in striking fashion how the intricate web of colonial history, rent eventually into thirteen segments, can be simplified, and its principal features disengaged from the minutiae that surround them.

IV

High literary merit ought not to be confused with mere entertainment. Some of the most amusing historical writers have no enduring value, while the really conscientious historian does not pass by important subjects because they are essentially dull. Macaulay remarks in his essay on Horace Walpole that this graceful, shallow writer was never tiresome and never tempted readers to skip. He showed a superior talent not in learning, not in accuracy, not in logic, but in writing what people would like to read. "He rejects all but the attractive parts of his subjects. He keeps only what is in itself amusing, or what can be made so by the artifice of his diction. The coarser morsels of antiquarian learning he abandons to others, and sets out an entertainment worthy of a Roman epicure, an entertainment consisting of nothing but delicacies, the brains of singing birds, the roe of mullets, the sunny halves of peaches." But Walpole, and the writers who like him select only what seems diverting, have no standing as historians. The tendency of some authors to take only the juicy parts of a historical era—the anecdotes, the striking personalities, the picturesque social scenes, the bits of drama—is to be condemned. It is not this but something deeper which is implied by the phrase "literary excellence." Similarly, we should condemn the all too prevalent tendency of writers of popular history to seek entertainment by the device of excessive dramatization. Since boredom is a common ingredient of all human life, since some monotony and tedium attend even great events, a high degree of dramatization insidiously falsifies the record of past times.

Yet in political and military history especially, such dramatization is all too frequent. The color even of battles, sieges, and forced marches can be heightened beyond all reason. Guedalla remarked of the author of *How England Saved Europe,* a tub-thumping history of the Napoleonic Wars, that his night encounters were more nocturnal and his scaling parties more scaligerous than any others in literature.[1] Yet Guedalla's own *Second Empire* is not free from the vice of overdramatization. Probably no subject in recent American history has been treated in more histrionic fashion than the impeachment of Andrew Johnson; Claude G. Bowers, for one, exerts all his descriptive powers to make it as striking as the impeachment of Warren Hastings. That it was a momentous trial, and had qualities of grim suspense as men waited to learn whether a two-thirds vote could be mustered against Johnson is undeniable. But the proceedings themselves were drab and tiresome. Johnson did not appear in person. Ben Butler prosecuted the case, in his own words, "just as he would a case of petty larceny in Massachusetts." Save by Evarts, not one brilliant speech was made. Young Moorfield Storey, whose perceptions were keen and whose feelings were strongly enlisted against Johnson, might have been trusted to feel any drama in the affair; yet writing at the time, he called the trial "a fearful bore," with "very mediocre displays," and "eternal speeches all on the same subject." And in its midst he grumbled: "I feel not a little disgusted with the Congress of the United States. The debates in the House for the last two days have been utterly disgraceful." A highly dramatized account misrepresents the event.

It is by more sterling means that literary distinction is attained. No doubt the central structure of history is a plain square edifice built solidly upon the bedrock of factual research. But in its best manifestations history is a capitol with two wings, one looking toward the domain of ideas, the other toward the domain of imagination. Without these wings history would lack all grace, all inspiration, all depth of interest, and would be in fact unworthy of the name of history; it would be annalistic writing alone. Ideas must be combined with research to produce interpretation. Imagination must be combined with research to produce vividness, human warmth, and poetic truth. Add these wings to the edifice, and the reader can pace the halls of history with a sense that all his faculties, intellectual and aesthetic, are being satisfied. He not only feels a granite foundation under his heel, but he can gaze out at one extremity upon the mountain-peaks of thought, and at the other extremity upon the crowded, multicolored stage where fact is stranger than fiction, and where human destinies challenge the pictorial and narrative powers of the greatest artists. From one set of windows, clear as air, he can see the philosophy of history merging with the abstract philosophy of Kant, Hume, and Hegel. From the other, set with prism-panes, he can see the drama of history merging with the plays of Shakespeare, its romance with the novels of Scott and Hugo, its poetry with that of Dante, Milton, and Goethe.*

* Cf. G. M. Trevelyan in *English Social History:* "Truth is the criterion of historical study; but its impelling motive is poetic. Its poetry consists in its being true. There we find the synthesis of the literary and scientific views of history."

XIV

The Reading of History

EVERYONE WILL AGREE that "the horrid tale of perjury and strife, murder and spoil, which men call history," should be read. But just how? What is the best method of attacking it? The failure to answer these questions properly explains why so much good history remains untouched on library shelves while fiction and travel are worn to tatters. History may be read for entertainment. It may be read for instruction about the past, and (though as Coleridge said, most of it is like the sternlights of a ship, illuminating only the course that is past) for guidance to the future. Above all, it may be read for inspiration. "Show me," Walter Savage Landor makes Pericles exclaim, "how great projects were executed, great advantage gained, and great calamities averted . . . Place History on her rightful throne, and at the sides of her Eloquence and War."

These are generalities. To the ordinary reader, even the ordinary college graduate, history is a dim uncharted sea, her ports doubtless full of rich spoils but her waters rough and her headlands forbidding. The amateur goes to the shelves. He plucks down a volume of Tacitus, and turning to the first book, finds himself wandering in a half-understood revolt against Tiberius in Pannonia (where is it?) and Germany; takes down Buckle, and is promptly plunged into a long, dullish, and clearly outdated examination of resources for investigating history; opens Prescott's *Con-*

quest of Mexico, and is daunted by what at first glance seems a highly archaeological chapter on primitive races and institutions. He concludes that those who call history fascinating are indulging in empty rhetoric. But are they? Is not the fault rather with the reader who fails to use a little common sense and show a little patience? The idea that fifteen minutes a day, or ten times fifteen, of aimless, undirected reading among good books will make a man well-read is one of the most misleading ever disseminated under high authority. The idea that much history is "fascinating" in the sense of offering easy entertainment for a casual hour is equally fatuous. But if approached with as careful preparation and precaution as any sensible man uses in approaching a symphony, a masterpiece of art, or the handling of bicycle or skis, and if a little persistent effort is applied to it, ere long it will offer one of the most interesting, varied, and profitable—one of the most truly fascinating—of all employments.

There is but one golden rule in reading history: it should be read by the blazing illumination of a thoroughly aroused intellectual curiosity. Much fiction may be absorbed in lackadaisical mood; pictorial writers like Herodotus and Froissart may be so approached; but nearly all history worthy of the name requires application. Fortunately, the kindling of intellectual curiosity about the past need not be a matter of self-stimulation. Any alert citizen of the modern world should find it constantly aroused by a variety of factors. They include current events at home and abroad —for every newspaper carries great signposts pointing back into history; political issues, which run back to Lincoln and Jackson, Hamilton and Jefferson, Locke and Hobbes; conversations with friends who are interested in ideas and institutions; fresh discoveries in the past as bruited abroad, whether a Tutankhamen's tomb or an unpublished letter by Grover Cleveland; the wave of interest created by any controversial new interpretation of past events, any new fashion in writing history or biography. A self-stimulated interest, one based upon a fixed ambition to master some select period of history, and to do it by systematic, intensive reading, is of course far more valuable. It represents a steady disciplined impulse, not a transient appetite. But some intellectual curiosity, some inner dissatisfaction leading to effort, is indispensable.

In certain minds intellectual curiosity plays like an unceasing fountain. That fact explains the rather jaunty tone of Theodore Roosevelt's observations upon reading history. In his impetuous offhand way he wrote that every serious man should apply himself to serious books. "He ought to read interesting books on history and government, and books of science and philosophy; and really good books on these subjects are as thrilling as any fiction ever written in prose or verse. Gibbon and Macaulay, Herodotus, Thucydides, and Tacitus, the Heimskringla, Froissart, Joinville and Villehardouin, Parkman and Mahan, Mommsen and Ranke—why! there are scores and scores of solid histories, the best in the world, which are as absorbing as the best of all the novels, and of as permanent value." Roosevelt could write like this because he knew an immense deal about certain eras of European and American history, and his incessantly active mind was eager to extend this knowledge. But other men do not have his grounding; even if they have part of his incessant mental activity, it may normally be channeled into non-historical directions—whereas Roosevelt began life as a writer of history. It is usually necessary to take a small flame of intellectual curiosity, and feed it higher and brighter. It may be necessary to take a distinct channel of professional activity and relate it to the nearest branch of history. The businessman has every reason to be interested in economic history and the careers of industrial leaders; the lawyer, in constitutional history.

Those who seek entertainment in history will have no great difficulty in finding it. They should be warned that Clio has never given up much of her domain to mere diversion. Yet by careful selection a good deal of pure description and pure narrative, delightful to peruse, can be found. Herodotus certainly falls in that category; he hardly penned a paragraph that is analytical. Many of the memoir writers of medieval or early modern times are also found there. Take the chronicles of the crusades by Villehardouin

and Joinville mentioned by Roosevelt. They are picturesque and stirring accounts by eye-witnesses of different
aspects of one of the most striking movements in history, the effort of the Christian world to recapture "those
holy fields over whose acres walked the blessed feet" of
Christ. Philip de Commines is sometimes analytical and
much of his detail is dull, but in Froissart we see all the
brilliancy of court life, all the glamour of chivalry, and
dimly in the background, the bloody misery of battles,
sieges, and spoliations, in the period when feudalism was
fast decaying. Some of Hakluyt's voyages, not so much
travel as history, are irresistibly entertaining, while they
convey the very essence of the Elizabethan era.

Thus we come down to the modern period, with whole
shelves of interesting memoirs, and an increasing number
of writers who bring to history a brilliant style and a desire
to interest large popular audiences. Several of Parkman's
books, notably his *La Salle and the Great West*, and his
masterpiece *Montcalm and Wolfe*, are written with the
rarest descriptive and narrative power, and are difficult to
surpass in interest. Trevelyan's three volumes on the campaigns of Garibaldi are rich in adventurous incident. Gabriel Hanotaux's *Contemporary France*, with its clarity of
style, its rich gallery of personalities, and its flashes of insight, is—despite an inadequate translation—full of diversion to almost anyone.

One way of making the past entertaining is to approach
it through historical novels. A course of reading in the
American Revolution may be prefaced by Paul Leicester
Ford's *Janice Meredith*, with its portraits of Washington,
Hamilton, and other heroes, showing their faults as well
as virtues; by J. P. Kennedy's *Horseshoe Robinson*, a romance which culminates with the battle of King's Mountain; and by Kenneth Roberts's lively *Rabble in Arms*. It
ought to be difficult for anyone to read *The Cloister and
the Hearth* without wishing to know more in general about
the years which ushered in the Renaissance, and in particular about Erasmus; to read the two parts of Stevenson's
David Balfour without a curiosity about Scottish affairs
just after the rebellion of 1745; to read Dumas's *Margue-*

rite de Valois without keener interest in the massacre of St. Bartholomew's. Who has closed Joel Chandler Harris's *Free Joe, and Other Sketches* without wondering exactly what slavery was like in the old South?—a wonder that might well lead to the ante-bellum travels of Frederick Law Olmsted, and the histories of Ulrich B. Phillips. Who has finished the earliest and best tales of Bret Harte without an interest in California civilization in the days of its lawless beginnings? To be sure, most historical fiction does not carry us far into history, and the invented elements are frequently misleading. But some of it is really admirable— Scott's *Fortunes of Nigel*, for example, contains the best portrait of James I to be found anywhere; Shorthouse's *John Inglesant* reproduces the manners, ideas and religious feeling of seventeenth century England and Italy with accuracy and artistry—while much of it may whet an appetite for more solid fare.

So also may the newspaper. It is as true to say that current events cast their shadows backward as that coming events cast their shadows before. No informed man read of the abdication of Edward VIII without thinking of previous dethronements—Richard II, James II—and some must have gone to J. R. Green's *Short History* and to Macaulay, if not further. The civil war in Spain with the participation of Moors and Italians—what vistas these events call up! Several of them have been ably treated by American writers. No one needs to be reminded of Irving's *Conquest of Granada*, that lively work of the fictitious Fray Antonio Agapida which catches so faithfully the spirit of the final struggle between Cross and Crescent in the Peninsula. Not many people, unfortunately, are acquainted with the almost equally interesting and far more scholarly sequel, Henry C. Lea's *Moriscoes of Spain, Their Conversion and Expulsion;* a book which takes up the sad history of the conquered Moors, tracing their chequered fortunes from the fall of Granada in 1492 to their expulsion in 1609, and describing the heavy economic and artistic loss which their ejection cost Spain. Prescott's *Ferdinand and Isabella*, probably his masterpiece, covers a much broader canvas. It relates how the various states into which Spain had long been divided were brought under one rule; how the kingdom of Naples was conquered; how the ancient empire of the Moors was overthrown; how the New World was discovered; how the dire engine of the Inquisition was set up; and how the Jews, with all their wealth and culture, were banished. In short, it gives us a secure grip upon many threads which run down to the present-day position of Spain. And if the reader wishes more light upon Italian-Spanish relations, he need only turn for a beginning to two other American books: W. R. Thayer's admirable *Dawn of Italian Independence,* and his *Cavour.*

The newspaper, the weekly magazine, the monthly review, are indeed full of hints which ought to send alert men delving occasionally into the past. Is Abyssinia in the news? For a mere general background, the reader may begin with Sir Harry Johnston's *Opening Up of Africa,* a standard work by one who helped in the opening; go on to Charles P. Lucas's *Partition and Colonization of Africa;* and conclude with a realistic analysis of the selfish factors at work, L. S. Woolf's *Empire and Commerce in Africa, A Study in Economic Imperialism.* Has a Polish statesman died? Georg Brandes wrote an eloquent book on Poland— the land, the people, the literature—full of sympathy for her long struggle for freedom; in its English translation it is still well worth reading. The brilliant and stimulating book by Kazimierz Waliszewski on the unknown Poland offers a defense of the nation's history against hostile Russian and German interpretations. And Monica Gardner's well-known biography of the great national hero, Kosciusko, is supplemented by her book on the nineteenth century poets, Mickiewicz and others, who held the torch of national feeling aloft in the country's darkest hours. Are the origins of the American Constitution being debated? Someone might care to look up a vivid but neglected novel of Shays's Rebellion, Edward Bellamy's *The Duke of Stockbridge,* and thence go on to McMaster, McLaughlin, Beard, and others who have treated the Constitutional Convention. Historical reading born of passing events is likely to be haphazard and sketchy, but it is certainly better than none.

Somewhat better is the curiosity kindled by a striking new historical or biographical work, which sets critics quarreling and dinner-tables talking. Works full of vitality are likely to do precisely this. Many of the great nineteenth century histories did not slip into the world, but exploded upon it. So it was with the nationalistic histories, the democratic histories, the Communistic histories, of Europe. While some of the old quarrels are completely dead, others still reverberate with diminishing thunder. No one cares much today about the battle between Freeman, who held the Germanic theory of the origin of the village community, and Frederic Seebohm, who in *The English Village Community* retorted by defending Roman influences. But other disputes are unending. Froude's *The English in Ireland in the 18th Century* reflected, along with a liking for the Irish people, a contempt for their political activities; Lecky made an able rejoinder in the second volume of his history of eighteenth century England; books as old as Goldwin Smith's *Irish History and Irish Character,* and as recent as Stephen Gwynn's bear on the subject. The controversy covered in Andrew D. White's *Warfare of Science With Theology,* two volumes as fascinating as they are learned, goes on forever.

New quarrels are constantly beginning. In American history, how many myths about the Revolution have been struck down, and how many keep their defenders! The writers who maintain, and plausibly, that Andrew Jackson sprang from an aristocratic instead of democratic social background; that Polk and the United States had ample justification for war with Mexico; that Supreme Court majorities have usually obeyed the public will in the background; that tariff battles after the Civil War were a disaster because they diverted popular attention from the great issues of business control that should have been faced promptly; that Taft was an efficient and constructive President—these all arouse controversy. Has our literary history been as rich as Van Wyck Brooks believes, or as thin as Ludwig Lewisohn intimates? Is the value of our cultural traditions as slight as many young radicals assert, or as great as Vernon L. Parrington and Henry S. Canby maintain? These disputes ought to provoke people to reading.

Yet reading thus provoked is likely again to be too topical, too hurried to be valuable; it will lack depth, consistency, and steady purpose. The world is so full of a number of things that those who do not exercise discipline in controlling their interests will remain superficial and scatterbrained. Anything that arouses intellectual curiosity is praiseworthy. But the man inspired by the latest archaeological find to take up Breasted's history of Egypt, by some church celebration to tackle Williston Walker's life of Calvin, and by a club dispute over the battle of Jutland to hurry through Winston Churchill's *World Crisis*, is likely to suffer from intellectual dyspepsia. Interest in the past should be marked by a sensible dichotomy. Part of it should certainly be based upon the present, for the man who does not do *some* historical reading with reference to the problems of the day misses a great deal. But after all, the more solid magazines exist in part to relate the present to the past—to indicate the larger implication of current issues; and in any event no one should read too much with his eye on the passing show. Part of his reading should deal with the past as welded into the substructure of the present, not as related to its superstructure.

A casual, *ad hoc* type of reading is far from likely to yield the deeper results of historical study. The best fruits of such study do not lie in mere information, but in the wisdom taught by combining long and accurate historical views with reflection. It is often said that reading history enlarges the mind, and makes the spirit broader and more tolerant. But why and how? This end cannot be achieved by dipping here and there, but only by the planned study of considerable periods in the life of populous and important nations.

Only by such study, to begin with, are streams of tendency, economic, social, and cultural, to be discerned in history. These can be defined in brief textbooks but they can be illustrated only by ample narratives. As an example, we may take Motley's *Rise of the Dutch Republic* and *United Netherlands,* works which, with some superficialities and many inadequacies and inaccuracies, nevertheless furnish an impressive panorama. The titles are somewhat unfortunate. They have led many people to think of these works as essentially Dutch history, whereas Motley deals with Spain, France, and England almost as fully as with Holland. His seven volumes go far beyond an eloquent and vivid record of the struggle of the Dutch people against civil and ecclesiastical tyranny. They were intended to illustrate some great philosophical truths. In effect, he offers us a history of the later phases of the Reformation, of the triumph of religious freedom in various lands over clerical absolutism, and of the emergence of Europe from the Middle Ages into the full light of modern times. He presents the birth of a new era in religion, social life, and politics. No one can read the work through without feeling his spirit as well as mind enriched.

Motley's stage is well set; he presents Philip II and William the Silent as the two principal antagonists in a complex struggle in which, directly or indirectly, half a dozen nations participated. After describing the land, people, and civilization of Holland during the first half of the sixteenth century, *The Rise of the Dutch Republic* begins with the abdication of Charles V as Holy Roman Emperor in 1555. Motley relates how Philip II took up the reins of government in Spain and Holland, how the Reformation, the true cause of the Dutch revolt, spread steadily, and how the Inquisition scattered oil on the flames it was meant to quench. In the background, at this beginning of the story, we see many elements of a feudal civilization still persisting: Holland enchained, England weak, Spain holding sway over a vast empire; pre-Copernican ideas of this world and medieval ideas of the next still in the ascendancy. From this point the story proceeds with graphic and original detail drawn by Motley from every available archive. He traces the activities of Egmont, Horn, and the Prince of Orange; tells of Philip's resolve to enforce the decrees of the Council of Trent; describes the popular storm aroused by his torturings and executions; relates how

Alva was sent into the Netherlands to crush the revolt; and tells of the years of war that followed, with the heroic feats of the Dutch, the defense of Haarlem, the defeat of Alva's fleet, and other stirring events, till, when freedom was in sight, William of Orange was assassinated. With this calamity of 1584, the first three volumes end.

The four volumes of the *United Netherlands* cover the second great epoch in what Motley expected to be his record of "the eighty years' war for liberty." They open with the independence of Holland practically achieved, though not recognized, and extend from the murder of William the Silent to the Twelve Years' Truce in 1609. The first half of the work is as much English history as Dutch. It deals with the period when the alliance of England and Holland against Spain was almost a political union, the Earl of Leicester becoming governor of the United Provinces; and it culminates in a stirring chapter on the defeat of the Great Armada. Motley never wrote anything better than his description of the tragic siege and loss of Antwerp, or his narrative of the destruction of the great Spanish fleet in 1588. The second half of the *United Netherlands* is somewhat inferior in interest. It contains no events which catch at the heart like the relief of Leyden or the cruel massacre at Naarden, and no personalities which win our regard as do William of Orange and Leicester. Still, Philip and Queen Elizabeth and Bloody Mary are present, and the story reaches a logical conclusion with the Dutch triumph of 1609. In the background, as the history closes, is a very different scene from that described at the beginning. The modern lineaments of society, such as town life, are distinctly marked; science is making steady progress; while Holland has been gaining her freedom, England, triumphant over the Armada, has been reaching the front rank of nations; France has become the political leader of the Continent, and Spain is sinking toward decay. The great central gain of the period, the triumph of Protestantism in most of northern Europe, seems assured. Motley meant to go on with the history of the Thirty Years' War in Germany, a continuation of the titanic religious struggle, but death intervened.

Motley's seven volumes have many faults, for his research was far from exhaustive, and his strong prejudices, especially on the Protestant side, made him unfair to Philip II and Spain. Even Froude, as it has been said, saw the golden thread in the gown of the Dominican monk, but to Motley the gown seemed wholly black. Nevertheless, he told a magnificent story, with half of Europe as a background and some of the main forces of modern civilization hanging in the balance; and his style has force and a dignity that sometimes rises to eloquence. The reader gains more than information. He obtains a broad view of a critical period of European history, a deeper insight into some of the central tendencies of Occidental civilization. He rises with judgment a little more matured, with wisdom a little riper. So, in still greater degree, readers of Mommsen's *Rome*, of Gibbon's *Decline and Fall*, of Michelet's *History of France*, gain a comprehension of the main streams of tendency in history, and a wisdom born of that understanding.

Another object of historical reading is to obtain a view of the conditions, limitations, and potentialities of leadership in any sphere, whether political, economic, or cultural. Of necessity, it must be a view with breadth and depth. Here again extended and planned study is almost essential; a considerable period in the life of a considerable civilization must be given thorough examination. In the political sphere, the history of mankind is strewn with instances in which true statesmanship has produced prosperity and happiness, while its lack has brought about terrible calamities. Was it impossible for wise leadership in Washington to have averted the Civil War, which ruined half the South, degraded the whole country morally for years, and left upon American life debilitating effects which are still plainly visible? Not in the eyes of some good observers of that day; Hamilton Fish declared that if about 1850 a large carriage had been filled with the worst of the Northern and Southern extremists and plunged for ten minutes beneath the surface of the Potomac, the nation might have been spared that staggering calamity. Or could the American Revolution, which from the point of view of the British Empire was certainly a calamity, have been avoided? On this point we have the judgment of the British historian who wrote one of the very best studies of the event. Lecky tells us that "there has scarcely been a great revolution in the world which might not at some stage have been averted, materially modified, or at least greatly postponed, by wise statesmanship." He goes on:

Take, for example, the American Revolution, which destroyed the political unity of the English race. You will often hear this event treated simply as if it were simply due to the wanton tyranny of an English government, which desired to reduce its colonies to servitude by taxing them without their consent. But if you will look closely into the history of that time—and there is no history which is more instructive—you will find that this is a gross misrepresentation. What happened was essentially this. England, under the guidance of the elder Pitt, had been waging a great and most successful war, which left her with an enormously extended Empire, but also with an addition of more than seventy millions to National Debt. That debt was now nearly £400 millions, and England was reeling under the taxation it required. The war had been waged largely in America, and its most brilliant result was the conquest of Canada, by which the old American colonies had benefited more than any other part of the Empire, for the expulsion of the French from North America put an end to the one great danger which hung over them. It was, however, extremely probable that if France ever regained her strength, one of her first objects would be to recover her dominion in America.

Under these circumstances the English government concluded that it was impossible that England alone, overburdened as she was by taxation, could undertake the military defence of her greatly extended Empire. Their object, therefore, was to create subsidiary armies for its defence. Ireland already raised by the vote of the Irish Parliament, and out of exclusively Irish resources, an army consisting of from twelve to fifteen thousand men, most of whom were available for the general purpose of the Empire. In India, under a despotic system, a separate army was maintained for the protection of India. It was the strong belief of the English Government that a third army should be maintained in America for the defence of the American colonies and of the neighboring islands, and that it was just and reasonable that America should bear some part of the expense of her own defence. She was charged with no part of the interest of the National Debt; she paid nothing towards the cost of the navy which protected her coast; she was the most lightly taxed and the most prosperous portion of the Empire; she was the part which benefited most by the late war, and she was the part which was most likely to be menaced if the war was renewed. Under these circumstances Grenville determined that a small army of ten thousand men should be kept in America, under the distinct promise that it was never to serve beyond that country, and the West Indian Isles, and he asked America to contribute 10,000 pounds a year, or about a third part of its expense.

But here the difficulty arose. The Irish army was maintained by the vote of the Irish Parliament; but there was no single parliament representing the American colonies, and it soon became evident that it was impossible to induce thirteen State legislatures to agree upon any scheme for supporting an army in America. Under these circumstances Grenville in an ill-omened moment resolved to revive a dormant power which existed in the Constitution, and levy this new war-tax by Imperial taxation. He at the same time guaranteed the colonists that the proceeds of this tax should be expended solely in America; he intimated to them in the clearest way that if they would meet his wishes by themselves providing the necessary sum, he would be abundantly satisfied, and he delayed the enforcement of the measure for a year in order to give them ample time for doing so.

Such and so small was the original cause of difference between England and her colonies. Who can fail to see that it was a difference abundantly susceptible of compromise, and that a wise and moderate statesmanship might easily have averted the catastrophe?

To understand this failure of British statesmanship no summary view will serve; the reader must go through some work as searching as Lecky's *History of England in the 18th Century*. So to understand properly the failure of American statesmanship just before the Civil War it is necessary to read some history of the fifties as extensive as James Ford Rhodes, and to supplement it by at least a few biographies. The extremes to which the French Revolution was pressed constituted a terrible calamity to Europe. They too can be understood only by sustained examination of several volumes, a process more absorbing, by far, once interest is fully aroused, than any dilettantish excursion into the period.

Still another utility of the "sustained" reading of history —of following a nation through many mutations and over a considerable period of time—is that this alone exhibits the rise, development, and decay of institutions; and what is more important, shows how much institutions depend upon national tradition, character, and habit, as well as upon physical and economic circumstances. Men untrained in history are wont to take contracted views of institutions. They suppose that because universal suffrage works well in Australia, it might be a great blessing in Egypt. They think that because modern legislatures have almost always been bicameral, they ought never to become unicameral. They believe that the American Constitution is a model of perfection, and that if it were introduced into other lands (perhaps with free schools and free speech thrown in), order, liberty, and prosperity would result; though they need only look at Cuba and some South American republics to see that this is not so.

People who read little history seldom comprehend, again, how greatly the different nations of men differ—how widely the average psychology of the Spaniard diverges from the average psychology of the Russian; or how much variation arises between different human types within the same nation. They are therefore nonplused by the extreme divergences of motive, the eccentricities of conduct, often displayed in world affairs. They seldom realize, in consequence, that the institution which in one nation proves highly successful may be a calamity in another. Parliamentary institutions work well in the various nations of the British Commonwealth but almost nowhere else. The Presidential system of government has on the whole served the United States admirably, but south of the Rio Grande it has been an easy stepping-stone to dictatorships. A failure to grasp this elementary truth leads European dictators into foolish denunciations of democracy, and some democratic leaders into only less shortsighted denunciations of the totalitarian forms.

But the greatest lessons of history, as writers from Thucydides to Woodrow Wilson have pointed out, are the moral lessons; and here again some sustained reading is absolutely essential to a full grasp of truth. Such reading helps men a little to measure time against eternity; to rise above the heat and dust of ephemeral issues into a serener atmosphere. Who wins the next election may *seem* a matter of desperate concern; who wins the war of really overwhelming importance. But the first may be trivial in its bearing upon national destiny, and the second of no lasting significance in its bearing upon human destiny. In moments of party triumph or national exaltation, history teaches a wise humility; in moments of darkness, confusion, or pain it teaches a wise patience. It shows Americans that the corruption, greed, and hatred of Reconstruction days were but an evanescent obscuration of the true national spirit; it shows them equally that the strut, fanfare, and arrogance of 1898 was an inglorious rather than a glorious moment in the national record. History has a moral lesson, again, in demonstrating that the immediate results of a national policy are frequently of slight account compared with the remote results. It is for this reason that those who prefer principle to expediency in the conduct of human affairs are usually right. The immediate gain from seizing

CONSERVATIVE.

THE GATEWAY TO HISTORY

upon expediency may appear greater than any possible
loss; but respect for tradition, the value of continuity in
affairs, the importance of dependable habits to a community as to a man, the close connection between principle and rectitude—all this weighs heavily in the balance.
When a Napoleon III or Mussolini arises who charts his
course by expediency alone, his nation is in grave peril.

Not least of the moral lessons derived from any prolonged perusal of history is that which relates to the character of nations. No one can read much in this department
of literature without being profoundly impressed by the
mutability of all human fortunes, the constant alternations
of prosperity and disaster in the record of nearly all peoples. Nor can anyone read much of it without feeling the
hollowness of a vast deal that is called glory and greatness.
Little Athens may be more truly great than Rome, little
Denmark than imperial Germany. When even the greatest
Powers are essentially insecure, when military disasters,
economic collapses, territorial losses so frequently befall
the strongest nations, it behooves a country to seek its enduring welfare in quarters not too grossly material. Americans rightly pride themselves upon the idealism of their
national character; Britons upon their national integrity
and steadfastness; Frenchmen upon their devotion to light
and culture. The permanent well-being of peoples, one
historian assures us, "is essentially the outcome of their
moral state. Its foundation is laid in pure domestic life, in
commercial integrity, in a high standard of moral worth
and of public spirit; in simple habits, in courage, upright-
ness, and self-sacrifice, in a certain soundness and modera-
tion of judgment, which springs quite as much from character as from intellect."[1] There is a great deal in history,
read *in extenso,* to support this thesis. It is not difficult,
over long periods, to tell when a nation is rising or when it
is decaying, and almost invariably the rise or decay is
connected with a development or deliquescence of the national character.

This thesis is nowhere better expounded than in the
famous introduction of Polybius to the first book of his
history. The Greek author, who had stood by Scipio's side

while Carthage was burning, and had been at Corinth during or just after its sack by Mummius, knew the Romans of his day thoroughly. Writing about 150 B.C., he called the attention of Greek readers to the immense change wrought in half a century in the Mediterranean world. Who does not wish to understand just how "the Romans in less than fifty-three years have succeeded in subjecting nearly the whole inhabited world to their sole government—a thing unique in history"? In these fifty-three years the entire face of the known earth had been altered. If Rome was not everywhere sovereign, at any rate she was everywhere dominant. Polybius remarks that a man must be not only a dullard but morally deficient if he does not wish to understand this amazing achievement, this "spectacle so striking and grand." What is the explanation of it? To supply an answer is the purpose of his history. It is not mere events, he writes, that are interesting, but their causes. The causes of the rise of Rome were primarily moral, and these moral causes he elucidates.

To plan the extensive reading of history offers no great difficulty. It is not old-fashioned advice to say that the best step that the ordinary amateur can take is to provide himself with complete sets of some of the classic historians, and read them through. Thus the amateur may make himself acquainted with large periods, with great convulsions and their causes, and with vast changes for good or ill in the fortune of nations. What, he may ask, read all of Prescott? He wrote nothing that is not worth reading; in fact he wrote but four books, each of which might nowadays be printed in one volume. Read all of Parkman? He also wrote nothing that is not worth reading. Read all of Mommsen's *Rome* or Macaulay's *England*? Why not? Is not Gibbon a little too difficult for the plain man? His style is certainly tiring in its pomposity, and may best be taken in moderate quantities. But two plain hardfisted men of affairs, Cecil Rhodes and Tom Johnson, made Gibbon almost a Bible, and the latter could quote the *Decline and Fall* with word-perfect familiarity. Let readers but experiment a little—let them take Milman's *History of the Jews*, or Henry Adams's *History of the United States* under Jefferson and Madison, and see if when fully launched they can lay it down unfinished; if the experiment fails let them take up something else till their taste is met.

Apart from this initial reliance upon the great standard writers, it is usually a common sense rule to approach any historical period by reading trustworthy books in the order of their literary attractiveness. There are recent books upon the American Revolution which possess greater authoritativeness than any of their predecessors, but which are not precisely delightful to read. One older work, however, is fascinating in style and presentation. No man, however scant his knowledge of the period or his interest in history in general, ever expressed disappointment in George Otto Trevelyan's volumes; hundreds of thousands have expressed the delight which led Theodore Roosevelt to invite the author to visit America and stay in the White House. Why not, then, take Trevelyan first? It is also a wise rule to follow any vein of ore for some distance by the connected but not necessarily systematic reading of various books, one suggesting another. A man may begin with John Addington Symonds's brightly colored and beautifully written work on the Renaissance. From this he may go to other books upon the same beguiling period. Or, with equal logic and in some instances greater profit, he may turn into some side-road. Symonds's account of the cruelties and crimes perpetrated by church and state in the age of the despots may send him to a biography of the reformer Savonarola; then from that to Henry C. Lea's *Superstition and Force*, a striking record of the conflicts and exertions, the advances and defeats, by which the progress of humane legislation and exact justice was slowly forwarded; and then to Sir James Fitzjames Stephen's history of the criminal law in England, with its impressive exhibition of the growth of equity and justice. The large number of feasible and attractive roads through the domain of history will soon impress any diligent reader; and presently he will find how frequently they offer stimulating intersections.

But after all, the essential advice is—Read! There are the varied shelves, rich in works from Herodotus and Thu-

cydides to the ten thousand writers of today; there are
guides and handbooks which anyone can find. There is
wealth it were a shame to neglect—wealth

> Compact of Rainbow Gold and of Fire
> Of sorrow and sin and of heart's desire,
> Of good and of evil and of things unknown.

Notes

CHAPTER 1

1. Paul Leicester Ford, *The True George Washington*, 203–4.
2. *Statesman and Friend: Correspondence of John Adams with Benjamin Waterhouse*, 57.
3. *Notes on Virginia* (Jefferson's *Works*, Memorial Edition, II, 206, 207).
4. E. L. Pierce, *Memoir and Letters of Charles Sumner*, I, 80–82.
5. Emerson's *Works*, Concord Ed., II, 4.
6. In *Works*, National Ed., XII, 23, 24; "History as Literature."
7. August Fournier, *Napoleon the First: A Biography*, one-volume edition (1903), 743.

CHAPTER 2

1. James MacGregor Burns, *Roosevelt: The Lion and The Fox*, 484.
2. Notably, in England, G. F. Tout's six-volume *Chapters in English Administrative History*.
3. George Otto Trevelyan, *Life of Lord Macaulay*, II, 174.
4. Sir Charles Oman, "Cataclysmic History," address to the 23rd annual meeting of the British Historical Association.
5. See James Cotter Morison, *Gibbon*, 144 ff.
6. See Charles A. Beard, "That Noble Dream," *American Historical Review*, XLI, 74–87 (October 1935).
7. Parkman, *Montcalm and Wolfe*, Ch. VII.

CHAPTER 3

1. James Ford Rhodes, *Historical Essays*, 35 ff.
2. Richard Crawley's translation, Bk. I, Ch. I.
3. James Bryce, *Biographical Studies*, 266, 267, quoting
George T. Clark.
4. Cf. Theodore A. Willard, *The Lost Empire of the Itzaes
and the Mayas* (1933).
5. See Morgan's "Houses of the Mound-Builders," *North
American Review*, July 1876.
6. September 28, 1876.

CHAPTER 4

1. In *De Tranquillitate Animi*.
2. Ernest A. Savage, *The Story of Libraries and Book Collecting*, 19.
3. M. R. James, *The Wanderings and Homes of Manuscripts*,
22, 23.
4. M. R. James, op. cit., 36.
5. George Matthew Dutcher and others, *A Guide to Historical Literature*, 477, 478.
6. R. D. W. Connor, in *Minnesota History*, XVII, No. 1,
March 1936.
7. W. L. Langer, *European Alliances and Alignments, 1871–
90*, Preface.

CHAPTER 5

1. See John Fiske on Mandeville in *The Discovery of America*, I, 290, 291.
2. On Morley's errors see *Philosophical Review*, XXVI,
214 ff., January 1917.
3. Lord Rosebery, *Napoleon: The Last Phase*, 26–38, for a
long discussion of the spurious letters.
4. For Schapira and others see Waldemar Kaempffert, "The
World's Most 'Cultured' Criminals," *Saturday Review*, June 3,
1944.
5. *The New York Times*, June 18, 1936, contains an account
of Spring's activities.
6. For example, into Emanuel Hertz's two volumes, *Abraham Lincoln: A New Portrait*.
7. The full Ireland story is told by John Mair in *The Fourth
Forger* (1930); see also Chapter VI of Richard D. Altick's *The
Scholar Adventurers* (1950). For pictorial forgery see C. H.

Hart's "Frauds in Historical Portraiture" in *Annual Report,* American Historical Association, I, 87–99 (1913).

8. Paul Angle examines these forgeries in *The Atlantic Monthly,* CXLIII, 516 ff., April 1929.

9. The book *Thomas J. Wise: Centenary Studies,* edited by William B. Todd (1960), contains essays by John Carter, Graham Pollard, and Professor Todd.

10. See, for example, T. F. Henderson, *The Casket Letters.*

11. Encyclopaedia Britannica, 11th Ed., V, 449–52.

12. L. M. Larson, "The Kensington Rune Stone," *Minnesota History,* XVII, No. 1, March 1936, p. 14.

13. See the discussion of Hennepin's brazen forgery in Reuben Gold Thwaites's introduction to his two-volume edition of Hennepin's *A New Discovery of a Vast Country in America* (1903). Thwaites riddles it through and through.

14. Louis Gottschalk, *Lafayette Comes to America,* p. 123.

15. Bertram D. Wolfe, "Adventures in Forged Sovietica," *The New Leader,* August 8, 1955.

CHAPTER 6

1. Max Farrand, *Records of the Federal Convention of 1787,* I, Introduction, xviii; see also note 23.

2. Howard K. Beale, "Is the Printed Diary of Gideon Welles Reliable?" *American Historical Review,* XXX, 547 ff., April 1925.

3. John Thomas Lee, "The Authorship of Gregg's Commerce of the Prairies," *Mississippi Historical Review,* XVI, 451 ff., March 1930.

4. See Walter E. Bundy, *Jesus and the First Three Gospels* (Cambridge, Mass.), 1955.

5. William A. Foran, "John Marshall as a Historian," *American Historical Review,* XLIII, 51–64, October 1937.

6. Jacob E. Cooke, in his fully edited volume of *The Federalist* (1961), while discounting the value of internal evidence, declares that the presumption of authorship for No. 58 must be in favor of Madison's claim.

7. Edmund Wilson, "Gorky on Lenin," *New Republic,* February 15, 1933.

CHAPTER 7

1. Philip S. Van Cise, *Fighting the Underworld* (1936), p. 70.

2. Charles Godfrey Leland, *Memoirs,* pp. 201, 202.

3. "Dissolution of the Monasteries," *Short Studies on Great*

Subjects, First Series, World Classics Ed., p. 286. Any reader will profit from a study of the chapter "On Plurality of Causes" in John Stuart Mill's *Logic*.

4. Review of Sister Mary Augustina Ray's "American Opinion of Roman Catholicism in the Eighteenth Century," *New England Quarterly*, X, 143–46, March 1937.

5. Arthur Edward Rowse, *Slanted News, a Case Study of the Nixon and Stevenson Fund Stories*, Boston, 1953. Treatments of news coloration useful to the historian are Norman Angell, *The Press and the Organization of Society*, Cambridge, England, 1933, and Irwin D. Davidson and Richard Gehman, *The Jury Is Still Out*, 1959, this last centering on crime news.

6. Students of history will find Leo Rosten's *The Washington Correspondents*, and Douglass Cater's *The Fourth Branch of Government* perceptive and expertly informed.

7. Albert Bigelow Paine, *Joan of Arc*, I, 352–58.

8. Harold L. Ickes's *Secret Diary* (1953–54) offers illustrations of bias rein–forced by misanthropy. See, for example, his preposterous account of Governor Herbert H. Lehman's opposition to Roosevelt's Supreme Court bill as motivated by political jealousy; Lehman's reverence for the judiciary was well known, and his brother was Chief Judge of the New York Court of Appeals.

9. Henry Villard, *Memoirs*, I, 93, 94.

10. For an interesting analysis of national bias in history, see Hugh Miller's *Macaulay on Scotland, a Critique*. This tracks Macaulay through old newspapers and pamphlets, and attempts to prove him anti-Scottish from the very sources he used.

11. *The Study of Sociology*, pp. 294, 295. For a recent exploration of some of the complexities of causation see the papers of Clyde Kluckhohn and Henry A. Murray, *Personality in Nature, Society and Culture* (1948).

CHAPTER 8

1. The works of Ulrich B. Phillips and Kenneth Stampp on American Negro slavery, which any student may profitably compare, seem hardly to describe the same institution.

2. Profitably re-evaluated by Howard H. Peckham in *Pontiac and the Indian Uprising* (1947).

3. Alfred Cobban in *London Times Literary Supplement*, January 6, 1956.

4. See the chapter on "Plurality of Causes" in John Stuart Mill's *Logic*.

5. *Short Studies on Great Subjects*, First Series, World Classics Ed., pp. 284, 285.

6. Herbert Spencer, *The Study of Sociology*, p. 73.

7. George E. Warren and Frank A. Pearson, *Prices* (1933).

8. *London Times Literary Supplement.*

9. H. A. L. Fisher, *History of Europe,* 3 vols., 1938.

10. Carter Goodrich and Sol Davidson, "The Wage-Earner in the Westward Movement," *Political Science Quarterly,* June 1935, XL, 161 ff.

11. Studies of leadership now emphasize the "situationist" approach; see James MacGregor Burns, *Roosevelt: The Lion and the Fox* (1956), Appended Note, and Hans Gerthe and C. Wright Mills, *Character and Social Structure* (1953).

12. John Fiske, *The Discovery of America,* I, 472, note.

13. Ashton Sanborn, *Saturday Review of Literature,* June 27, 1931, reviewing Sir E. D. Ross, *The Art of Egypt Through the Ages.*

14. W. L. Langer, *European Alliances and Alignments, 1871–90,* Preface.

15. Herbert Butterfield, *History and Human Relations* (1951).

16. William James, *Principles of Psychology,* II, 365.

CHAPTER 9

1. For a more thorough account of the philosophy of history than is here possible, see Vladimir G. Simkhovitch on "Approaches to History" in the *Political Science Quarterly,* Vols. XLIV, XLV, XLVII, and XLVIII. See also R. G. Collingwood, *The Idea of History* (1946), and W. H. Walsh, *An Introduction to Philosophy of History* (1951).

2. Dr. Simkhovitch, in the fourth article of his "Approaches to History," *Political Science Quarterly,* XLVIII, 23 ff., names and describes lesser exponents of a rhythmical philosophy—Scherer, Karl Joel, O. Lorenz, and others.

3. Henry Adams, *Degradation of the Democratic Dogma,* p. 127.

4. Voltaire, *Essai sur les Moeurs,* pp. 1, 2.

5. Voltaire, ibid., p. 9.

6. Lord Morley, *Collected Works,* VII, 249, 250.

7. Encyclopaedia Britannica, Ninth Ed., VI, 234.

8. Cf. Emile Durkheim's *De la Division du Travail Social* (1893).

CHAPTER 10

1. John Richard Green, *The Making of England,* pp. 95, 96.

2. A striking analysis of geographic influences upon the settlement of the Kentucky-Tennessee country is given in the

chapter "Rocks and Earth" in Harriette Simpson Arnow's beautifully written *Seedtime on the Cumberland* (1960).

3. John D. Barnhart, "Rainfall and the Populist Party in Nebraska," *American Political Science Review,* August 1925, XIX, 527 ff.

CHAPTER 11

1. For a capital exposition of this fact see Dirk J. Struik's *Yankee Science in the Making* (1948), a treatment of the flowering of science and technology in New England to 1860.

2. In G. P. Gooch's *History and Historians in the Nineteenth Century,* second edition, 1952, p. xiii.

CHAPTER 12

1. Strachey's work did much to inspire two interesting and provocative books, Harold Nicolson's *The Development of English Biography,* and Maurois's *Aspects of Biography.* A brief but especially penetrating discussion may be found in Leon Edel's *Literary Biography* (1957). Donald O. Stauffer's two volumes on *English Biography Before 1700* and *The Art of Biography in 18th Century England* cover the background.

2. Cf. Herbert Butterfield, *History and Human Relations.*

CHAPTER 13

1. Philip Guedalla, *Supers and Supermen,* p. 19.

CHAPTER 14

1. W. E. H. Lecky, *History and Political Essays,* p. 38.

Bibliographical Aids to Research

I GENERAL BIBLIOGRAPHIES OF BIBLIOGRAPHIES

Besterman, Theodore, A World Bibliography of Bibliographies, 3rd and final ed. Geneva, Societas Bibliographica, 1955–56. 4 vols. Records 84,403 separately published bibliographies by subject.

Bibliographic index; A Cumulative Bibliography of Bibliographies, 1937– , New York, Wilson, 1938– . Issued semi-annually with annual cumulations. Cumulative permanent vols. issued: V.1, 1938–42; V.2, 1943–46; V.3, 1947–50; V.4, 1951–55; V.5, 1956–59.

II GENERAL GUIDES TO BOOKS

A London Bibliography of the Social Sciences, London School of Economics, 1931–60. 11 vols. (to be continued). Largest bibliography of its kind; arrangement is chronological under subject. Covers the holdings of the British Library of Political and Economic Science and the Edward Fry Library of International Law. Vols. I–IV listed the holdings of seven other London libraries. Author indexes are included for vols. I–IV. Vol. XI, 1960, lists holdings through 1955.

British Museum, Dept. of Printed Books. *General Catalogue of Printed Books.* Photolithographic edition to 1955, London, 1959–61. Vols. 52–85 expected to be completed in 1967, at which time the first 51 volumes will be reproduced with the addition of entries to the end of 1955.

When completed the *Catalogue* will be in about 300 volumes and contain about 5,500,000 entries.

British Museum, Dept. of Printed Books. *General Catalogue of Printed Books.* London, 1931–54. Vols. 1–51, A–De. Ceased publication. Superseded by photolithographic edition, 1959– . Previous edition as *Catalogue of Printed Books*, 95 vols., 1881–1900 (photographic reprint, Ann Arbor, Michigan, Edwards, 1946, 58 vols.). Supplement, 1900–5, 13 vols. (reprint 1950, 10 vols.).

British Museum, Dept. of Printed Books. *Subject Index to Modern Works Acquired*, London, 1902–53. 14 vols., 1881–1945. A supplement to the 1916–20 vol., *European War, 1914–18*, was published separately in 1922.

British National Bibliography, London, Whitaker, 1950– . There are three, six, nine, and twelve monthly cumulations of both main entries and index. Arrangement is by Dewey classification. Based on copyright deposit.

Cumulated Subject Catalogue, 1951–54, London, 1958, 2 vols. A cumulation of the material appearing in the 1951–54 volume.

The British Nation Bibliography Cumulated Index, 1950–54 (1955) serves as a key to both of the above works.

Robert A. Peddie, *A Subject Index of Books Published Up to and Including 1880*, London, Grafton, 1933–48, 4 vols. Supplements the *British Museum Subject Index* by recording earlier books, but is not confined to British Museum holdings. Each volume is an alphabetical subject list.

The English Catalogue of Books, 1801– , London, Publisher's Circular, 1837– . Main entry is under author with title and catchword subject entries (1837–89 had separate subject indexes). Since 1957, published quarterly with six months, nine months, annual and four year cumulations.

United States Catalogue; books in print, 4th ed., New York, Wilson, 1928.

The Cumulative Book Index: World List of Books in the English Language, New York, Wilson, 1898– . Supersedes and supplements the *United States Catalogue*. Main entry is under author with short title and subject entries.

Monthly issues, six months, annual, and two year cumulations are superseded by permanent five year cumulations.

United States Library of Congress, *A Catalogue of Books Represented by Library of Congress Printed Cards* (cards issued from August 1898 through July 1942), Ann Arbor, Michigan, Edwards, 1942–46, 167 vols. Author entries only, except for titles of periodicals and anonymous works.

Supplement (cards issued from August 1942 through December 1947), Ann Arbor, Edwards, 1948, 42 vols.

United States Library of Congress, *Library of Congress, Books: Subjects,* a cumulative list of works represented by Library of Congress printed cards, 1950–54, Ann Arbor, Michigan, Edwards, 1955, 20 vols. 1955–59, Paterson, New Jersey, Pageant, 1960, 22 vols. This work is kept up to date by quarterly issues and annual cumulations.

United States Library of Congress. *The Library of Congress Author Catalogue,* 1948–52, Ann Arbor, Michigan, Edwards, 1953, 24 vols.

The National Union Catalogue, a cumulative author list, 1953–57, Ann Arbor, Michigan, Edwards, 1958, 28 vols. *The National Union Catalogue* includes, in addition to the printed cards of the Library of Congress, works in 729 (in 1960) libraries in the United States and Canada which are not represented in the Library of Congress' collection. This work is kept up to date by monthly issues, and quarterly and annual cumulations.

III GENERAL GUIDES TO REFERENCE BOOKS

Albert J. Walford, *Guide to Reference Material,* London, the Library Association, 1959. This work includes fewer books than Winchell's *Guide,* but it provides fuller annotations. Emphasis is on British publications.

Constance M. Winchell, *Guide to Reference Books,* 7th ed., Chicago, American Library Association, 1951. Supplement, 1950–52, 1954; second supplement, 1953–55, 1956; third supplement, 1956–58, 1960. This work is further kept up to date by supplements appearing in the January and July issues of *College and Research Libraries.*

Louise-Noëlle Malclès, *Les Sources du Travail Biblio-graphique,* Geneva, Droz; Lille, Giard, 1950–58, 3 vols., in 4. A major guide to reference material of all kinds.

Paris, Bibliothèque Nationale, Catalogue Général des Livres Imprimés: *Auteurs,* Paris, Imprimerie Nationale, 1897 (in progress), vols. 1–186 (1897–1960), A-Thirty.

IV GENERAL GUIDES TO PERIODICALS

British Union Catalogue of Periodicals, a record of the periodicals of the world from the seventeenth century to the present day in British libraries, London, Butterworth, 1955–58, 4 vols. Lists more than 140,000 titles contained in about 440 British libraries with indication of holdings.

Eric H. Boehin, and Adolphus Lalit, Historical periodicals; an annotated world list of historical and related serial publications. Munich, Clio Press, 1961. In progress. Will list about 5000 periodicals.

New Serial Titles; a union list of serials commencing publication after December 1949. Washington, The Library of Congress, 1960. 2nd ser., cumulation through 1958 which is supplemented by monthly issues and annual cumulations. Continues *Union List of Serials.*

Ulrich's Periodical Directory; a classified guide to a selected list of current periodicals, foreign and domestic. 9th ed., New York, Bowker, 1959.

Union List of Serials in libraries of the United States and Canada. 2nd ed., New York, Wilson, 1943. Supplements: 1941–43 (1945); 1944–49 (1953).

V PERIODICAL INDEXES

Annual Magazine Subject Index: a subject index to a selected list of American and English periodicals and society publication, 1907–49. Boston, Faxon, 1908–52. An annual which covered periodicals not included in other indexes except that it aimed to cover all historical periodicals. A reissue in one cumulated alphabet is being published by G. K. Hall & Co.

Book Review Digest. New York, Wilson, 1905– .
Monthly issues and six-month cumulations are superseded
by annual cumulations. Guide to book reviews in periodicals. Alphabetical arrangement by author of book with
subject and title index.

Index to the Times. London, The Times, 1906– .
Monthly with annual cumulations, 1906–June 1914;
quarterly, July 1914–56; bi-monthly, 1957– .

International Index; a guide to periodical literature in
the social sciences and humanities. New York, Wilson,
1916– . Published quarterly with bound annual and two-
year cumulations. Covers period of 1907 to date with emphasis on scholarly periodicals. Originally published as a
supplement to the *Reader's Guide.*

New York Times Index. 1913– . Now issued semi-
monthly with annual cumulations. 1913–29, quarterly issues only. A very detailed index.

*Nineteenth-Century Reader's Guide to Periodical Litera-
ture,* 1890–99, with supplementary indexing, 1900–22.
New York, Wilson, 1944. 2 vols.

Palmer's Index to the Times newspaper. London, Palmer, 1868–1943. Quarterly volumes cover the period of
1790–June 1941. Valuable because of its retrospective indexing.

Poole's index to periodical literature. Revised ed. Boston, Houghton, 1891–1908. 6 vols. Indexes 479 English
and American periodicals for the period 1802–1907.

Reader's Guide to periodical literature. New York, Wilson, 1905– . Semi-monthly issues and frequent cumulations are superseded by permanent two-year cumulations.
Indexing begins in 1900 and is confined to general and
popular American periodicals.

Subject Index to periodicals. London, Library Association, 1915– . Now issued quarterly with annual cumulations. Indexes about 330 British periodicals.

VI GENERAL GUIDES TO HISTORY

American Universities Field Staff. *A select bibliography:
Asia, Africa, Eastern Europe, Latin America.* New York,

1960. Lists about 6000 useful books and journals in western languages on the civilization of these areas.

Guide to Historical Literature. New York, Macmillan, 1961. A classified bibliography of world history sponsored by the American Historical Association. Index of authors and subjects. Successor to *A Guide to historical literature*, (1930).

Hannah Lofas. *Historical Non-Fiction;* an organized, annotated, supplementary reference book. 7th revision, enlarged. Phil., McKinly, 1960. A general classified listing.

Historical Association. *Annual Bulletin of Historical Literature,* 1911– . London, 1912– . Annual. Highly selective and strong on British materials. Classified arrangement.

International Bibliography of Historical Sciences, 1926– . Washington, International Committee of Historical Sciences, 1930– . Vol. 21, 1954, published in 1956, vol. 15 for period of 1940–46 not yet published. Selected classified lists.

Jahresberichte der Geschichtswissenschaft, 1878–1913. Berlin, 1880–1916. 36 vols. Excellent record of the historical literature for the period covered, however it is not exhaustive.

Louis B. Frewer. *Bibliography of historical writings published in Great Britain and the Empire,* 1940–45. Oxford, Blackwell, 1947. Covers books and periodical articles. Systematically arranged. Partially fills the gap for the period in which the *International bibliography of historical sciences* was not published.

VII GUIDES TO ANCIENT HISTORY

August F. Pauly and George Wissowa. *Pauly's Realencyclopadie der Elassischen Alterumswissenschaft.* Stuttgart, Metzler, 1893– . (In progress.) Published in two series concurrently. Comprehensive articles covering classical literature, history, and civilization. Bibliographies.

Charles Daremberg and Edmond Saglio. *Dictionnarie des Antiquites Grecques and Romaines.* Paris, Hatchette,

1813–1919. 5 vols. and index. A very authoritative work with signed articles. Includes detailed bibliographies.

Jules Marouzeau. *Dix Années de Bibliographie Classique;* bibliographie critique and analytique de l'antiquité gréco-latine pour la période 1914–24. Paris, Soc. d'Edition, 1927. 2 vols. Covers the whole field of history and culture of the classical world.

L'année Philologique: bibliographie critique and analytique de l'antiquité gréco-latine, 1924–26. Paris, Soc. d'Edition, 1928–   . An annual continuation of *Dix années de bibliographie classique.*

Louis Laurand, *Manuel des Études Grecques et Latines.* Nouv. ed., Paris, Picard, 1957, 2 vols. An earlier ed. published in 1938–49 was in 4 vols. Arranged as a syllabus with bibliographies.

History of the Greek and Roman World, New York, Macmillan, 1934–   . 7 vols. Originally published by Methuen (London). Vol. 1 is in preparation. Vols. 2–6 revised 1948–53. Each volume includes a bibliography at the end.

The Cambridge Ancient History. New York, Macmillan, 1923–39. 12 vols. and 5 vols. of plates. Extensive chapter bibliographies at the end of each volume.

VIII GUIDES TO MEDIEVAL HISTORY

A. Molinier. *Les Sources de l'Histoire de France Depuis les Origines Jusqu'au 1815.* Paris, Picard, 1901–35. A critical bibliography of the printed narrative sources for the history of France. The last part, covering the period 1715–1815, was never published.

August Potthast. *Bibliotheca Historica Medii Aevi.* Wegweiser durch die Geschichtswerke des Guropaischen Mittelalters bis 1500. Berlin, Weber, 1896. Reprinted 1955. 2 vols. A comprehensive guide to sources of medieval history. Part 1 lists important printed collections of sources. Part 2 lists the works of individual medieval authors.

Cambridge Medieval History. New York, Macmillan, 1911–36, 8 vols. Chapter bibliographies included at the end of each volume.

Cyr Ulysse Chevalier. *Répertoire des sources historiques du moyen âge.* Nouv. ed., Paris, Picard, 1894–1904. 2 vols. in 4. An important guide to the literature of medieval history.

Dahlmann-Waitz. *See under Modern History.*

Francesco Cognasso. *Avviamento Agli Studi di Storia Medieval.* Torino, Gheromi, 1951. Bibliographical manual for students of medieval history.

Louis J. Paetow, *Guide to the Study of Medieval History.* Rev. ed., New York, Crofts, 1931. A valuable guide to bibliographies, printed sources and secondary works on the history of medieval Europe and its Eastern neighbors.

Pierre Caron and Henri Stein. *Répertoire Bibliographique de l'Histoire de France.* Paris, Picard, 1923–38. 6 vols. Standard bibliography of the history of France from the beginning to 1914. In 1959, volumes 7, 8, and 9 were supposedly in publications covering the period 1933–45.

IX GUIDES TO MODERN HISTORY

André Monglond. *La France Révolutionnaire et Impériale;* Annales de bibliographie methodique et description des livres illustrés.

B. Sanchez Alonso. *Fuentas de la historia española e hispano-americana.* 3rd ed. Madrid Consejo Superior de Investigaciones Cientificas, 1952, 3 vols. Most comprehensive bibliography of Spanish history.

Cambridge Modern history. New York, Macmillan, 1902–26. 13 vols. and atlas. Chapter bibliographies included at ends of each volume.

Frederich C. Dahlmann. Dahlmann-Waitz. *Quellenkunde der Deutschen Geschichte.* 9th ed. Leipzig, Koehler, 1931–32. 2 vols. Standard bibliography of German history through World War I.

Historical Abstracts; a quarterly, covering the world's periodical literature, 1775–1945. Munich-Solln, 1955– . Provides abstracts on history of the period 1774–1945 appearing in periodicals since June 1954.

X GENERAL GUIDES TO BRITISH HISTORY

Bibliography of British history; Tudor period, 1485–1603. 2nd ed. edited by Conyers Read. London, Oxford University Press, 1959.

Stuart Period, 1603–1714. Edited by Godfrey Davies. London, Oxford University Press, 1928.

The eighteenth century, 1714–1789. Edited by Stanley Pargellis and D. J. Medley. London, Oxford University Press, 1951.

Charles Cross. *The Sources and Literature of English History from the Earliest Times to about 1485.* 2nd ed. New York, Longmans, 1915. Reprinted in 1951 by Peter Smith. A comprehensive and systematically arranged bibliography for the period covered. The three volumes of *Bibliography of British history* do the same for the period each covers.

Great Britain. H. M. Stationery Office. *A Brief Guide to Official Publications.* London, 1960. Not a catalogue but a descriptive guide to the various types of publications. Titles of important series and monographs are cited.

The Cambridge History of the British Empire. Cambridge University Press, 1929–59. Comprehensive bibliographies accompany each volume.

The Cambridge Bibliography of English Literature: 600–1900. New York, Macmillan, 1941–57, 5 vols. Systematically arranged. Volume 4 is an index to the first 3 volumes, and volume 5 is a supplement to the entire work.

XI GUIDES TO AMERICAN HISTORY

Carnegie Institution. *Guides to Manuscript Materials for the History of the United States.* Washington, 1906–43. 23 vols. Covers material in American and European archives.

Evarts B. Greene, and Richard B. Morris. *A Guide to*

the Principal Sources for Early American History (1600–1800) in the City of New York. 2nd ed. revised by Richard B. Morris, New York, Columbia University Press, 1953.

Harry J. Carman, and Arthur W. Thompson. *A Guide to Principal Sources for American Civilization (1800–1900) in the City of New York: Manuscripts.* New York, Columbia University Press, 1960.

Harvard Guide to American History. Cambridge, Belknap Press, of Harvard University Press, 1954. A selective guide to books and articles.

Henry P. Beers. *Bibliographies in American History; guide to materials for research.* Rev. ed., New York, Wilson, 1942. Classified list of over 11,000 bibliographies. Author and subject index.

Laurence F. Schmeckebier and Roy B. Eastin. *Government Publications and Their Use.* Rev. ed. Washington, Brookings Institute, 1961. An excellent guide to the use of U. S. Government publication.

Philip M. Hamer, ed. *A Guide to Archives and Manuscripts in the United States.* New Haven, Yale University Press, 1961. A comprehensive guide to approximately 1300 archive collections. A 132-page index serves as a guide to subjects.

The New York Public Library. Dictionary Catalogue of the History of the Americas Collection. Boston, G. K. Hall, 1961. 28 vols. The 594,000 entries cover both North and South America, and in addition to book materials, indexes important articles in scholarly journals.

United States National Archives. *List of National Archives Microfilm publications: 1961.* Washington, 1961. Detailed list of microfilms made since 1940, giving price. Frequently revised.

U. S. Library of Congress. General Reference and Bibliography Division. *A Guide to the Study of the United States of America; representative books reflecting the development of American life and thought.* Washington, 1960.

Writings on American History, 1906– . New York, 1908–10; Washington, 1911–13; New Haven, 1914–19;

Washington, 1921. Supplemented by an earlier annual, under same title, for 1902 and 1903. Now issued as part of the annual report of the American Historical Association. No volumes issued for 1941–47.

Writings on American History, Index, 1902–40, Washington, American Historical Association, 1956. Author and subject index to works listed in annual volumes.

XII GUIDES TO LATIN AMERICAN HISTORY

Jose T. Medina. *Biblioteca Hispano-Americana,* 1493–1810. Santiago, Chile, 1898–1907. 7 vols. Lists 8481 titles for the period covered.

Handbook of Latin-American Studies. Gainsville, University of Florida Press, 1936–   . A comprehensive annual bibliography. Vol. 22, covering the period 1956–59, published in 1960, includes citation to five hundred journals and the publications of 2500 authors in fifteen contemporary languages.

Robert A. Humphreys. *Latin American History,* a guide to the literature in English. Rev. ed. London, Oxford University Press, 1958.

XIII GUIDES TO SLAVIC AND RUSSIAN HISTORY

Akademiia Nauk USSR. Fundamental'naia Biblioteka Obshchestvennykh Neuk. *Prilozhenie,* Skhema klassifikatsii. Vspomogatel'nye Ukazateli. Moskva, 1956–58. 2 vols. (In progress.) A major bibliography of Soviet historical writings published between 1917 and 1952 on Russian history.

New York Public Library. *Dictionary Catalogue of the Slavonic collection.* G. K. Hall, 1959. 26 vols. Approximately 500,000 entries for works in Lettish, Lithuanian, and Slavonic languages. Covers books on all subjects.

Philip Grierson. *Books on Soviet Russia;* 1917–42; a bibliography and a guide to reading. London, Methuen, 1943. An annotated classified guide to books and pamphlets, most of which were published in Great Britain.

Robert J. Kerner. *Slavic Europe;* a selected bibliography in the Western European languages, comprising history, languages, and literature. Cambridge, Harvard University Press, 1918.

Index

Abbotsford Club, 130
Abernethy, Thomas P., 229
Acquisitive Society . . . , 45, 343
Acton, John, Lord, 40, 54, 67, 70, 258–59
Adams, Charles F., 212–14, 244
Adams, Henry, 16, 77, 250, 274–75, 295, 377
Adams, James Truslow, 244
Adams, John, 16
Adams, John Q., 162, 163, 215–17, 238
Adams family, 183
Adventure in Constructive Finance, 162
Advocates' Library, 114
Africa, books on, 398
Aftermath, The, 253
Age of Louis XIV, 277
Agrarian Problem . . . , 343
Alcibiades, 89
Alcuin, 111
Alexander the Great, 51
Alexandria library, 104
Alfred the Great, 113
Allen, Frederick Lewis, 233
Allen, Grant, 321
Allen and Muratoff, 154
Alpatov, M. A., 25
Alphabets, 91, 100–1
American Antiquarian Society, 132
American Archives, 130
American Doctor's Odyssey, 169
American History and Its Geographic Conditions, 309–10
Ancient and Modern Imperialism, 22
Ancient Law, 45
Angle, Paul, 156–57
Anglo-Saxon Chronicles, 113
Annals, 84–86, 112–14, 127 ff., 174
Ansel, Walter, 247–48
Anthropogeography, 308 ff.
Antiquities of Rome, 86
Antislavery Impulse of 1830–44, 298
Apologia Pro Vita Sua, 291 n.
Appleton's Cyclopaedia . . . , 151–52
Arabs, 22–23, 52, 108–9, 330–31. See also Moors; Saracens

Arber, Edward, 161
Archaeology, 72–77
Archives, 114, 120–36 *passim*
Ariel: The Life of Shelley, 363
Aristotle, 103, 104, 108, 301
Arnold, Thomas, 257
Art, Egyptian, 255–56
Art of the Netherlands, 293
Ashe, Thomas, 152
Asquith, H. H., 348
Assurbanipal, 102
Atlantic Crossings . . . , 84 n.
Atlantic Monthly, and Lincoln forgery, 143
Aubrey, John, 354
Audience of Beowulf, 82 n.
Augustine, St., 264, 265
Augustus, 90, 105
Aulard, François V. A., 233
Autobiographies, 160 ff., 209–25

Babcock, Orville E., 197
Babylonia, 99, 100, 102–3
Bacon, Delia, 246
Bacon, Francis, 242, 246, 302
Bagehot, Walter, 61, 266–68
Bakunin, Michael, 341
Balfour, David, 396
Ballads, 79–80, 143
Bancroft, Frederick, 55, 57
Bancroft, George, 20, 21, 32, 59, 281, 290
Bannatyne Club, 130
Baring-Gould, Sabine, 81, 83
Barnes, Gilbert H., 298
Barraclough, Geoffrey, 273
Bates, Edward, 183
Bayeux tapestry, 95
Beale, Howard K., 255
Beard, Charles A. and Mary R., 55, 175, 263, 264, 343, 382
Beaumont, Francis, 176
Becker, Carl, 340–41, 389
Bede, Venerable, 110
Beer, George Louis, 295
Beer, Thomas, 369, 387
Beginnings of the American People, 389
Behistun Rock, 21–22, 100
Belgium, 129, 131 n., 297–98

Bell, Whitfield J., Jr., 183
Bellamy, Edward, 398
Belloc, Hilaire, 55, 194, 291
Benedict, St., 109
Benedict Biscop, 110
Benedictine Order, 109–10
Bennett, C. H., 185
Bennett, James Gordon, 154
Bentham, Jeremy, 281
Bentley, Richard, 117
Beowulf, 81, 82
Bergson, Henri, 80 n.
Berlin, 89, 90, 119
Berlin, Isaiah, 272
Beveridge, Albert J., 35, 41, 54–55, 357, 367
Bias, historians and. *See* Evidence
Bible, 170–73, 178–80
Bibliothèque Nationale, 115–16
Biedermann, Karl, 294
Bigelow, John, 167–68, 184–85
Bilharzia, 312
Biography, 347–69
Biology, 46–47
Bismarck, Otto von, 361
Blaine, James G., 197
Boccaccio, Giovanni, 109
Boeckh, Augustus, 87–88
Boethius, 109
Bohemia, medieval, 146
Bollandists, 131 n.
Bologna, book trade in, 112
Borghesi, Conte Bartolommeo, 89
Bossuet, Jacques, 265
Boswell, James, 185, 353, 354
Bothwell, James, Lord, 147
Boulainvilliers, Perceval de, 210–12
Bowers, Claude G., 229, 367, 390
Boyd, Julian, 183
Bracciolini, Poggio, 89
Braddock, Edward, 62–63, 256–57
Bradford, Gamaliel, 356, 361
Brady, Mathew B., 127
Brandes, Georg, 293, 361 n., 398
Breasted, James H., 38, 74
Bridge, Norman, 166
Brigham, R. H., 293
Bristow, Benjamin H., 190
British Museum, 102, 117, 118, 144, 145; defrauded, 141
Brookings Institute, 297
Brooks, Van Wyck, 367, 368, 399
Brown, Alexander, 161
Brownell, W. C., 368
Browning, Robert, 97
Brunhes, Jean, 308
Bryce, James, Lord, 318, 356, 388–89
Buckle, Henry T., 283–85, 304–5
Buell, A. C., 151
Burbank, Luther, 79
Burckhardt, Jacob, 293, 338, 340
Burke, Edmund, 15, 361
Burlingame, Roger, 208 n.
Burr, Aaron, 229
Burr, George L., 334
Bury, J. B., 339, 389
Bush, Douglas, 83 n.
Butler, Ben, 390
Byron, George, Lord, 192, 384–85
Byron: The Last Journey, 384–85

Cabral, Pedro Alvarez, 50
Caesar, Julius, 105, 332–33, 361 n.
Calhoun, John C., 217–18

Cambridge Modern History, 263
Camden Society, 130
Canada, archives in, 132–33
Capgrave, John, 129
Carlyle, Thomas, 19, 39 ff., 50–51, 323–25, 378–79; and authenticity, 358, 359; and "Right," 290
Carnegie, Andrew, 358, 367
Carr, E. H., 154
Carter, John, 144
"Casket Letters," 147–48
Cason, Clarence, 318 n.
Cassiodorus, 110
Cather, Willa, 13
Catholics, 57, 200, 222
Causation, 222 ff., 247 ff.
Cavour, Camillo, Conte di, 398
Caxton Society Publications, 131
Caylus, Anne Claude, Comte de, 73
Cecil manuscripts, 122
Censorships, 180–82
Ceolfrid, 110
Chain of Error and the Mecklenburg Declaration of Independence, 138 n.
Chalmers, George, 175
Chamberlain, John, 170
Champlain Society, 133
Champollion, Jean François, 100
Chandler, Zachariah, 214
Channing, Edward, 161, 231–32, 238–42, 243–44, 263, 295
Charlemagne, 111
Charles I, 30
Charles V, 92, 129, 289 n., 401
Charles XII, 277
Charles Albert, King, 128
Charnwood, Godfrey, Lord, 54, 219
Chatterton, Thomas, 143
Chesterton, G. K., 46, 387
Chevy Chase, ballad of, 80
Cheyney, E. P., 242
Chicago Tribune, 205
China, 255, 317–18
Christianity, 52–53, 81, 135–36, 264–65. *See also* Bible; Catholics; Gibbon on, 56, 104, 280
Chronicles, 112–14, 127 ff.
Churchill, Winston, 198, 207, 253
Cicero, 103, 104, 105, 110
Cid, El, 82
Civil War, U.S., 23, 46, 263, 403. *See also* specific books; Channing on, 231–32, 238–42, 243–44
Clarendon, Edward, Lord, 16, 379
Claudius, Emperor, 91
Cleveland, Grover, 168, 238
Climate, 292–93, 310–12
Clodd, E., 99 n.
Cloister and the Hearth, 40, 396
Cnossus, 73–74
Cobbett, William, 123
Cobden, Richard, 319, 320, 353, 361
Cohen, Morris L., 46 n.
Coins, 91–95
Colbert, Jean Baptiste, 116
Coleridge, Samuel, 176, 393
Colin Clout's Come Home Again, 246
Collection of Inedited Documents for the History of Spain, 129
Collis, Maurice, 77 n.
Columbus, Christopher, 50, 254
Commerce of the Prairies, 167
Commines, Philip de, 396

Communism, 341–42. *See also* Russia

Communist Manifesto, 25

Comparative history, 336 ff.

Comte, August, 285–87, 326

Congressional Globe, 130, 199

Congressional Library, 118 ff., 125

Congressional Record, 130, 199

Connecticut, 149

Conquest of Granada, 397

Conquest of Mexico (Prescott), 21, 76–77, 375

Conquest of Peru, 21, 376

Conspiracy of Pontiac, 231

Constantine, 107, 145–46

Constitution, U.S., 162–63, 398

Contemporary France, 396

Contes, Louis de, 212

Coquelle, M., 230

Cordova, libraries in, 109

Corpus Inscriptionum Graecarum, 87

Corpus Inscriptionum Latinarum, 89–90

Cortés and Montezuma, 77 n.

Corwin, E. S., 357

Cosmos, 303

Cotton, Sir Robert, 117

Cottonian Library, 117–18

Coulanges, Fustel de, 25

Courthope, W. J., 293

Creighton, Mandell, 40, 379

Crimea, 26–27, 126

Critical Period of American History, 382

Critique of Political Economy, 269

Croesus, 67–68

Cromer, Evelyn, Lord, 22, 50

Cromwell, Oliver, 51, 323–24

Cromwell, Richard, 51

Crowther, Samuel, 168

Cultural history, 293–94

Cumont, Franz, 90 n.

Cuneiform writing, 99–100

Cunningham, Alan, 143

Curry, J. L. M., 240

Curzon, George, Lord, 365

Curzon, Robert, 107

Curzon: The Last Phase, 365

Cyriac of Ancona, 87

Cyrus the Great, 68

Czechoslovakia, 146–47, 317

Dana, Charles A., 168

Darius the Great, 22

Darnley, Henry, Lord, 147

Darwin, Charles, 285, 288, 329

David Balfour, 396

Davis, Elmer, 208 n.

Davis, Jefferson, 239, 241

Dawn of Conscience, 38

Dawn of Italian Independence, 398

De Re Diplomatica, 124

Decline and Fall of the Roman Empire, 30–31, 56, 114, 279–80, 409

Decline of the West, 263

Defoe, Daniel, 137

Depression of 1929, 245

Deutsche Geschichte (Lamprecht), 339–40

Deutsche Geschichte (Treitschke), 57

De Witt, James, 142

Diaries, 120 ff., 166 ff., 192, 209 ff.

Diary of a Young Lady . . . , 143

Dickens, Charles, 154

Dickson, William P., 185

Dionysius of Harlicarnassus, 86

Discovery of America, 254, 382

Disease, 312

Disraeli, Benjamin, 39, 351, 366

Doctrina Numorum Veterum, 93

Donne, John, 353, 354

Don't Let Them Scare You . . . , 208 n.

Douglas, Stephen A., 46, 54, 55, 218–19

Doylestown, Pa., 79

Drake, Sir Francis, 149 n.

Du Bois, W. E. B., 222

Du Châtelet-Lomont, Marquise, 277

Duke of Stockbridge, 398

Dumas, Alexandre, 396

Dunning, W. A., 41 n.

Durant, Will, 43

Duranty, Walter, 203

Durkheim, Emile, 292

Ecclesiastical History . . . , 110

Eckhel, J. H., 92–93

École de Chartes, 124

Economic Interpretation of the Constitution, 343

Economic Interpretation of Jeffersonian Democracy, 343

Economic and Social History of Medieval Europe, 297

Economics, 263, 268–70, 280–81, 292, 341–45; coins and, 93–94; press and, 204

Edison, Thomas A., 79

Editing, 182–85

Edmunds, George F., 192

Education of Cyrus, 37

Education of Henry Adams. See Adams, Henry

Edward VII, 365

Edward VIII, 397

Egbert, 110

Egmont, John, Earl of, 123

Egypt, 50, 99 ff., 255–56, 312

Eight Years with Wilson's Cabinet, 164

Einhard, 111

Eisenhower, Dwight D., 126, 333 n.

Eisenhower's Six Great Decisions . . . , 333 n.

Elgin, Thomas Bruce, Lord, 73

Elizabeth I, 242, 368

Ellwood, C. A., 337

Emerson, Ralph Waldo, 20, 367, 380

Emerson, Ephraim, 334

Eminent Victorians, 257, 362

Empire and Commerce in Africa, 398

Energy, 313–14, 315

Engels, Friedrich, 25, 28

England, 20, 31, 120–24, 129–31, 253, 319–20. *See also* Archaeology; Newspapers; British Museum

English Historical Ass'n, 231

English in Ireland . . . , 399

English Literature, 185

English Literature and Society . . . , 293

English Local Government, 38

English Social History, 391 n.

English Village Community, 399

Enlightenment, 15, 16

Epic of America, 244
Epinay, Louise d', 141
Erdkunde, Die, 304
Essai sur les Moeurs, 265
Essays, Moral, Political . . . , 279
Essex, Robert, Earl of, 242
Evans, Arthur, 73–74
Evelyn, John, 182
Evidence, 189–225, 297
Evolution, 49 ff., 266–68, 270, 287–89
Excursions of an Evolutionist, 321
Expansionists of 1812, 298

Fabius Pictor, Quintus, 85
Fairgrieve, James, 317
"Falstaff," 187
Farnham, G. H., 374
Farrand, Max, 163, 185
Federalist, The, 176–78
Federalists, The, 345
Fenton, Roger, 126–27
Ferdinand and Isabella, 397–98
Fersen, Count Hans Axel, 194
Fiction, 40, 42–43, 396–97
Fielding, Henry, 43, 364
Fingal, 147
First World War, 15, 205, 312, 319
Firth, C. H., 59
Fischer, Kuno, 266
Fish, Hamilton, 403
Fisher, H. A. L., 50, 251
Fisher, Sydney George, 298
Fiske, John, 114, 161, 254, 321–22, 330–32; and evolution, 266–67, 288; and literary style, 382–83
Fitzpatrick, John C., 184
Fletcher, John, 176
Fling, Fred Morrow, 335–36
Folklore, 79–86
Force, Peter, 130
Ford, Henry, 79, 168
Ford, Paul L., 143, 176, 355, 396
Ford, Worthington C., 131, 184
Forgeries, 137 ff.
Formation of the Alphabet, 99 n.
Forrest, J. Donald, 294
Fortunes of Nigel, 397
Fox (English historian), 117
Fox, Dixon Ryan, 294
France, 124, 128, 131 n., 201, 305, 319; libraries, 115–17; Revolution, 41, 116, 233, 282, 290, 324–25
Francis I, 116
Franciscans, 110
Franklin, Benjamin, 183, 184–85
Fraud, 137 ff.
Free Joe, and Other Sketches, 397
Freeman, Douglas, 350, 357
Freeman, Edward A., 60, 72, 399
Frémont, John C., 127
Froissart, Jean, 396
Froude, James A., 20, 332, 358, 379, 399; quoted, 194, 235–36
Fuller, Thomas, 354
Fulvio, Andrea, 92
Furness, H. H., 186, 187

Gallatin, Albert, 118
Gardiner, Samuel R., 42, 58, 291
Gardner, Alexander, 127
Gardner, Monica, 398
Garibaldi, Giuseppe, 396
Gebauer (philologist), 146
Gellius, Aulus, 103, 106
General Historie (Smith), 160–61

General History of Connecticut, 149
General History of the United States, 265
Geniuses. *See* Heroes
Geography, 292–93, 301–22
George, St., 81
George II, 117, 118, 130
George IV, 161–62
Germania, 37
Germany, 23, 57, 247–48, 295, 339–40; archives, 124–25, 127–28
Germany in the 18th Century, 294
Geyl, Pieter, 273
Ghost writers, 167–70
Gibbon, Edward, 30–31, 52–53, 114, 279–80, 409; convictions of, 56–57
Giddings, Franklin H., 294, 326, 334
Gladstone, Wm. E., 61, 155, 360, 361
Glass, Carter, 162, 246
Godkin, E. L., 206 n.
Gogol, Nikolai, 42
Golden Legend, 81
Goltz, Hubert, 92
Gooch, G. P., 345
Gordon, William, 175–76
Gorgas, Josiah, 240
Gorky, Maxim, 181–82
Governments, 120–34, 198–200, 208–9
Grant, Ulysses S., 165–66, 192, 368
Gray, Thomas, 354
Great Britain. *See* England
Great Plains, 314
Greece, ancient, 73–74, 101, 103–5, 312; inscriptions, 86–89, 90–91
Green, John R., 51, 284–85, 305–8
Greenfield Village, Mich., 79
Gregg, Josiah, 167–68
Gregory VII, Pope, 330
Grimm, Jacob, 128
Griswold, Rufus Wilmot, 192–93
Grote, George, 21, 56
Gsell, Stéphane, 74
Guedalla, Philip, 60, 364, 366, 390
Guizot, François, 20, 42, 128, 291
Gwynn, Stephen, 399

Hackett, Francis, 366
Hakluyt, Richard, 302, 396
Hakluyt Society Publications, 131
Halévy, Elie, 37, 338, 388
Half-Century of Conflict, 383
Hallam, Henry, 41
Halstead, Murat, 206 n.
Hamilton, Alexander, 17, 119, 176–78
Hammond, J. B., 38
Hannibal, 37, 61
Hanotaux, Gabriel, 396
Hansard, Thomas C., 124
Hardee, William J., 241
Hare, Archdeacon, 359
Harleian Library, 117–18
Harley, Robert, 117
Haroun-al-Raschid, 109
Harris, Joel Chandler, 358, 397
Harrison, Frederic, 40–41, 108, 379
Harrison, William Henry, 17
Harte, Bret, 397
Hay, John, 255
Hearst press, 205, 206
Heeren, Arnold H. L., 281

Hegel, Georg, 266
Heiser, Victor G., 169
Helen of Troy, 82
Hendrick, Burton J., 168, 358, 367
Hennepin, Father Louis, 152–53, 157
Henry, Patrick, 143
Henry V, 187
Henzen, William, 89
Herman Melville, 367
Herndon, William, 192 n.
Herodotus, 37, 65, 67, 86, 395
Heroes, 50 ff., 82, 323–32, 351 ff.
Hertz, Emanuel, 192 n.
Heylyn, Peter, 302
Hidden Lincoln, 192 n.
Hieroglyphics, 99 ff.
Hilprecht, H. V., 103
Histoire Générale, 263
Histoire Universelle, 265
Historical Inevitability, 272–73
History (periodical), 231
History of American Life, 294
History of Belgium, 297–98
History of Civilization . . . , 283–85, 304
History of England (Hume), 79, 114
History of England (Macaulay), 294, 372–73
History of England from the Ascension of James II, 40
History of England in the 18th Century, 406
History of the English People in 1815, 37, 338, 388
History of English Poetry, 293
History of France, 305
History of Freedom of Thought, 389
History of the French Revolution, 41, 324–25
History of the Jews, 409
History of the People of the United States, 284
History of the United States from the Compromise of 1850, 41
History of the United States, 295, 409–10
Hitler, Adolph, 23, 30, 247–48
Hitler Confronts England, 247–48
Hodgkin, Thomas, 42, 110
Hoffman, Matilda, 358
Holand, H. R., 148
Holst, Hermann von, 61
Holy Roman Empire, 388–89
Homer, 74, 101, 296–97
Homer and His Age, 296
Hone, Philip, 182
Hooker, Joseph, 225
Hookworm, 312
Hoover, Herbert, 209, 222
Horace, 105
Horseshoe Robinson, 396
Hotson, Leslie, 187 n.
House, Edward M., 162
Houston, David F., 164
How England Saved Europe, 390
Hugo, Victor, 78
Hull, Cordell, 209
Human Geography of the South, 321
Humboldt, Alexander von, 76, 303
Hume, David, 114, 279
Humphrey Clinker, 43

Huntington, Ellsworth, 292–93, 310–12
Hutchinson, Lucy, 354
Huxley, T. H., 44
Hypothesis, 238–42 ff.

Icelandic sagas, 83–84
Ideas, 261–300
Ideen über Politik . . . , 281
Idomeneus, King, 74
Iliad, 101, 296
Illinois library, 132
Illustrium Imagines, 92
India, 22, 141
Indians, 75–76, 84, 160–61
Individuals. *See* Heroes
Induction, 237–38
Influence of Geographical Environment, 309
Influence of Seapower . . . , 296
Inquisition, 253–54
Inscriptions, 86–91, 141
Inspiration, history as, 19–21
Interpretation, 262 ff., 275–95
Intimate Papers of Colonel House, 162
Io, legend of, 68
Ireland, William, 143
Ireland, 110, 131, 253, 399
Irish History . . . , 399
Irving, Pierre M., 358
Irving, Washington, 21, 254, 355, 358, 397
Israel, 22–23
Italy, 124, 125, 128, 201, 274

James, William, 260, 321–22, 327–30
James of Varagium, 81
Jameson, J. Franklin, 57
Janice Meredith, 396
Jaurés, Jean, 233
Jay, John, 176
Jefferson, Thomas, 17, 118, 150, 215–17; papers of, 119, 183
Jesuits, Parkman on, 57, 296
Jesus, 171 ff.
Jews, 22–23, 150, 409
Joan of Arc, 210–12, 289 n.
John Inglesant, 397
Johnson, Andrew, 247, 390
Johnson, Clifford, 168–69
Johnson, Samuel, 147, 205, 354, 356–57
Johnson, Tom, 409
Johnston, Sir Harry, 398
Johnston, Joseph E., 239, 240
Joinville, Jean, sire de, 396
Jones, John Paul, 151
Jonson, Ben, 246
Journal of a Tour to the Hebrides, 185
Jowett, Benjamin, 89
Julian the Apostate, 107

Kant, Immanuel, 302–3
Kennan, George, 154
Kennedy, J. P., 396
Kennedy, John F., 18
Kensington Stone, 148
Kent, Chancellor, 16
Keynes, John M., 46 n.
Khafra, 102
Khufu, 102
Kidd, Benjamin, 294, 326–27
King Cotton Diplomacy, 298

Klebansky, R., 80 n.
Knox, Cleone, 143
Kosciusko, Thaddeus, 398
Kraljevitch, Marko, 82
Krock, Arthur, 209
Krylov, Ivan, 154

Labaree, Leonard W., 183
Labrousse, M., 234
Lafayette, Marie Joseph, Marquis
  de, 154
Lahey, Edwin A., 208
Lamb, Charles, 354
Lamprecht, Karl, 37, 339–40, 341
Landor, Walter Savage, 393
Lang, Andrew, 80, 147, 296–97
La Salle, Robert, 152–53, 157
La Salle and the Great West, 396
Las Cases, Emmanuel, Comte de,
  141
Laval, Gui de, 212
Law, history of, 38, 345
Layard, Sir Austen, 102
Lea, Henry C., 30, 397, 410
Lebfevre, Georges, 234
Lecky, W. E. H., 43, 399, 404–6
Lectures on the History of France,
  83
Lee, Robert E., 239, 356, 357, 359
Lee, Sidney, 365
Lee at Appomattox . . . , 244
Lee's Lieutenants, 350
Legends, 80–86
Leif Ericson, 84 n.
Leland, Charles Godfrey, 192–93
Lenin, Vladimir, 25, 154, 181–82
Leo IX, Pope, 148
Leo XIII, Pope, 115
Letters, 120 ff., 127 ff.; forged,
  141 ff.; integrity of, 166 ff., 182 ff.,
  192 ff., 209 ff.
Leupp, Francis E., 209
Leverrier, U. J. J., 238
Lewisohn, Ludwig, 399
Libraries, 102–7 ff.
Life of Charlemagne. See Charle-
  magne
Ligorio, Pirro, 89
Lincoln, Abraham, 23, 54, 150, 246,
  247, 290; forged letters, 142, 143–
  44, 156–57; papers destroyed,
  192 n.; and Seward, 212–14; Vil-
  lard on, 218–19
Lincoln, Robert, 192 n.
Lincoln and Seward, 214
Lippmann, Walter, 205
Literature, 20–21, 44–45, 60 ff., 293,
  371–91
Literature of Europe . . . , 41
Litvinov, Maxim, 154
Lives of Dr. John Donne . . . ,
  353–54
Lives of the Saints, 81
Lives of the Twelve Caesars, 348
Livy, 36, 71, 84–86, 173–74, 379
Locke, John, 143
Lockhart, John G., 357, 368
London, 243, 306–8
London Times, 201–2
Lucas, Charles P., 398
Lucian, 15
Lucullus, Licinius, 104
Ludwig, Emil, 348, 366
Luke, 170–73
Lyman (author), 183

Lynd, Robert and Helen, 337–38

Mabillon, Jean, 124
MacArthur, Douglas, 169–70
Macaulay, John Babington, 20–21,
  40–41, 56, 294, 371–73; and Mc-
  Carthyism, 30; memory, 375; use
  of outlines, 381–82; on Walpole,
  389
McCaleb, Walter F., 229
McClure, A. K., 192 n.
McClure, S. S., 168
Machiavelli, Niccolò, 381
Mackinder, Halford J., 309
McLaughlin, Andrew C., 382
MacLaurin, C., 289
McLean, Evalyn Walsh, 168
McMaster, John Bach, 41, 284–85,
  341, 377, 387; T. Roosevelt on, 385
Macpherson, James, 147
Madison, James, 119, 163–64, 176–
  78
Magnes, Sir Philip, 361
Mahan, Alfred T., 13, 296
Mahomet. See Mohammed
Main Currents in American
  Thought, 338–39
Main Currents in Nineteenth Cen-
  tury Literature, 293–94
Maine, Sir Henry, 45
Maitland, Frederic W., 38, 61
Making of England, 305–8
Malaria, 312
Manchester Guardian, 202, 203–4
Mandeville, Sir John, 138–39
Marching Years, 166
Marguerite de Valois, 396–97
Marie Antoinette, 141, 194
Marini, and inscriptions, 89
Mark, 170–73
Mark Twain, 355, 368
Marshall, John, 174–76, 357
Martyrdom of Man, 288
Marx, Karl, 25, 28, 268–70, 342
Mary Queen of Scots, 147–48
Masaryk, Thomas G., 146
Mason, William, 354
Massachusetts Historical Society,
  131, 132
Mathiez, Albert, 233
Matilda, Queen, 95
Matthew, 170–73
Maurists, 131 n.
Maurois, André, 348, 361, 363, 365–
  66
Mauve Decade, 387
Maxim, Hudson, 168–69
Mayas, 75
Mazzini, Giuseppe, 353
Mechanistic view, 49–50
Mecklenburg County, 138
Medicine, 289
Medieval Mind, 297
Melville, Herman, 367
Memoirs, integrity of, 160 ff., 209–
  25
Memoirs of the Life of Colonel
  Hutchinson, 354
Memoirs of Socrates, 347
Memorial de Ste-Helene, 141
Memories of Travel, 318
Mencken, H. L., 138
Menitt, V. V., 138 n.
Mere Mortals, 289 n.
Mexico, 76–77

Michelet, Jean, 42, 63, 291, 305
Microcosmus, 302
Midsummer-Night's Dream, 187–88
Mill, J. S., 234, 237, 304, 351
Milman, Henry H., 409
Milton, John, 246
Minutes of Lives, 354
Misprinting, 186
"Mr. Dooley," 96
Mitchill, Samuel Latham, 118
Mitford, William, 56
Moabite Stone, 101
Mohammed (Mahomet), 51–52, 330–31
Mollenhoff, Clark, 208
Molotov, V. M., 27, 198
Mommsen, Theodor, 89, 185, 332–33
Monasteries, 107, 109–10, 235–36
Mont St.-Michel and Chartres, 77
Montaigne, Michel, seigneur de, 115
Montcalm and Wolfe, 396
Monte Cassino, 109, 112
Montesquieu, Charles, Baron de, 276
Monumenta Germaniae Historica, 127
Monumenta Historica Patriae, 128
Monypenny and Buckle, 366
Moore, Tom, 192
Moors, 30, 109, 397
Moral lessons, 407 ff.
Morals, 258–59
"Morey letter," 141
Morgan, Lewis H., 75–76
Morgenthau, Henry, 168
Moriscoes of Spain . . ., 397
Morison, John Cotter, 39
Morison, Samuel Eliot, 294
Morley, Henry, 80
Morley, John, 141, 155, 320, 360, 361; quoted, 278–79, 286
Morris, Robert, 193 n.
Morrow, Honoré Willsie, 219
Morse, John T., Jr., 165
Moscow library, 119
Moss, John E., 208
Motley, John L., 21, 32, 379, 401–3
Mound Builders, 75–76
Mount Athos, 107
Muller, Herbert J., 377
Mulligan, Jacob, 197
Mumford, Lewis, 367
Munsterberg, Hugo, 66
Muratori, Ludovico, 131 n.
Murray, Gilbert, 38
My Life and Opinions, 168
Mystery of the Pinckney Draught, 163 n.
Mythology and the Romantic Tradition in English Poetry, 83 n.

Namier, Sir Lewis, 350
Napoleon I, 33, 141, 230, 289 n., 366; bibliography on, 155; Hegel and, 266
Napoleon III, 128, 364
National character, 318–19
Nationalism, 18–19, 271
Nazism, 23–24, 273–74
Neptune (planet), 237–38
Netherlands, 124, 129, 293, 401–2
New Bedford, Mass., 79
New History, 61–62
New Republic, 205

New York (city): Public Library, 141–42
New York (state): archives, 132
New York Times, 201 ff., 209
Newcastle, Margaret, Duchess of, 354
Newman, John Henry, 290, 291 n.
Newspapers, 39–40, 65–66, 200–9, 397–99
Nicolson, Harold, 365, 384–85
Nietzsche, Friedrich, 23, 361 n.
Nightingale, Florence, 257
90° in the Shade, 318 n.
Nineveh, 102
Nippur, 102
Nissen, H., 174
Nixon, Richard M., 206
Notestein, Wallace, 366
Nôtre Dame de Paris, 78
Nott, C. C., 163 n.
Novels, 40, 42–43, 396–97
Nunc pro tunc fallacy, 253 ff.

Oberholtzer, E. P., 341
Occo, Adolph, 92
Ocmulgie National Monument, 76
Odyssey, 296
Office of War Information, 208 n.
O'Higgins, Harvey J., 246
Old Regime in Canada, 13
Old Virginia . . ., 382
Olmsted, Frederick Las, 298, 397
Oman, Sir Charles, 51
Oncken, Wilhelm, 23
Only Yesterday, 233
Opening Up of Africa, 398
Origin of Species, 285, 288
Origins of the Second World War, 246
Orsini, Fulvio, 92
Osgood, Herbert L., 42, 60
Oshkosh, Wisconsin, 79
Ossianic Society, 131
Otterburn, battle of, 80
Our Times, 385–86
Outline of History, 270
Outlines of Cosmic Philosophy, 266–67, 330–32
Outremeuse, Jean d', 139
Owsley, Frank L., 298
Oxford, Edward, Earl of, 246

Pacificus (archdeacon), 112
Paine, Albert B., 355, 368
Pareto, Vilfredo, 264, 274, 333
Paris, 112, 124
Parker, Alton B., 195
Parkman, Francis, 21, 63, 71–72, 231, 373–74, 383, 396; on Jesuits, 57, 296; Willa Cather and, 13
Parliamentary debates, 123–24
Parliamentary History of England . . ., 123
Parmenides, 301
Parr, Samuel, 142
Parrington, Vernon, 294, 338–39, 400
Partition and Colonization of Africa, 398
Paul, St., 52, 53, 171, 178–80
Peel, Sir Robert, 319
Peisistratus, 103
Penn, William, 143
Pepys, Samuel, 150, 185
Pericles, 393

Periodicals, 230–31
Peters, Samuel A., 149
Petrarch, 92
Petrie, Sir W. Flinders, 99 n., 100–1
Philip II, 129, 259, 376, 401
Phillips, Ulrich B., 55, 397
Philochoros, 86
Philosophy and History, 80 n.
Philosophy of history, 263–75, 335 ff.
Philosophy of History, 266
Photographs, 126–27
Physical remains, 70 ff.
Physics and Politics, 266–68
Pinckney, Charles, 162–63
Pinckney, Charles C., 137
Pintard, John, 131, 132
Pipe Rolls Society, 131
Pirenne, Henri, 249, 297–98
Pitt, William, 253
Plain Folk of the Old South, 298
Platina, 115
Platonov, Sergey, 25
Plutarch, 104–5, 347, 379
Pocahontas, 160, 161
Poe, Edgar A., 192–93
Poetry, history in, 42
Pohl, Frederic, 84 n.
Pokrovsky, M., 25, 26, 28, 269
Poland, 316, 398
Polemon, 86
Politics, 26, 38, 281–82, 291, 345; coins and, 93, 94; press and, 204
Polk, James K., 217–18
Pollard, Graham, 144
Pollio, Caius Asinius, 105
Polybius, 86, 174, 408–9
Popes, 145–46. *See also* by name
Popper, Karl, 48
Portraits, forged, 142–43
Positive Philosophy, 285–87
Post Mortem, 289 n.
Pottle, F. A., 185
Poverty of Historicism, 48–49
Powhatan, 160, 161
Pratt, Julius W., 298
Prescott, William H., 41, 76–77, 375–76, 397–98, 409; book sales, 21
Presidential libraries, 126
Press agents, 207 ff.
Prince, The, 381
Principles of Ethics, 351–52
Problems, historical, 229–60
Profiles in Courage, 18
Prolegomena to Homer, 296
Propagandists, 207 ff.
Protestant Ethic . . . , 345
Psychology, 289
Ptolemy I, 104
Ptolemy II, 104
Putnam, Herbert, 119
Pyramids, 65–66

Quay, Matthew, 190

Rabble in Arms, 396
Raglan, Lord, 82
Raleigh, Sir Walter, 16, 246
Rameses II, 102
Randolph, John, 16
Random Recollections . . . , 168
Ranke, Leopold von, 42, 44, 54, 58–59, 291, 378–79
Rationalism, 276 ff.
Rats, Lice and History, 289

Ratzel, Friedrich, 308–9
Rawlinson, Sir Henry, 100
Read, George Meredith, 193 n.
Reade, Winwood, 288
Reading, 393–411
Reason and Nature, 46 n.
Reclus, Elisée, 309
Recollections of the Civil War, 168
Reformation, The, 253
"Reign of the Lie," 22
Religion, 47, 81–82, 222, 271–72, 290–91. *See also* Christianity; coins and Roman, 94–95
Renan, Ernest, 109, 178
Republic, 110
Rerum Britannicorum Aevi . . . , 129
Reviews, historical, 230–31
Revolutions, 48. *See also* France; U.S.
Rhodes, Cecil, 409
Rhodes, James Ford, 41, 65, 291, 406
Richard de Bury, 110
Rienzi, Cola di, 89
Rise of American Civilization, 263
Rise of the Dutch Republic, 401
Ritter, Carl, 303–4
Robert E. Lee, 357
Roberts, Kenneth, 396
Robinson, James Harvey, 60 ff., 338
Rockefeller, John D., 168
Roland, 81
Rollins, Charles, 21
Rolls Series, 129
Rome, ancient, 30–31, 52–53, 84–85, 246, 312, 316; coins, 92, 94–95; inscriptions, 89–90, 91; libraries, 103, 104–7
Roosevelt, Franklin D., 50, 126, 203, 208 n., 245, 320
Roosevelt, Theodore, 13, 32, 209–10, 255, 395; birthplace, 79; on McMaster, 385; and Trevelyan, 410
Rosetta Stone, 100
Rousseau, Jean Jacques, 141, 361
"Rowley Papers," 143
Rowse, A. L., 350–51
Royal Historical Society, 65
Rukopis Královedvorský, 146
Runciman, Steven, 35
Ruskin, John, 77, 319
Russia, 24–28, 128, 154–55, 203, 255, 269, 341–42; *New Republic* and, 205
Russia Leaves the War, 154
Russian Campaigns of 1941–43, 154
Rutledge, Ann, 143–44, 156–57

Saga of Eric the Red, 83–84
Saint Paul, 178
Sainte-Beuve, Charles, 356, 361
Saints, 81, 83, 131 n.
Salisbury, Marquis of, 122
Saracens, 53, 108–9, 182, 316
Saul of Tarsus. *See* Paul, St.
Schlesinger, Arthur M., 294, 350
Schouler, James, 41 n., 291
Science, 29, 43–49, 237–38, 289–95, 378–79. *See also* Economics
Scientific Study of Human Society, 326
Scope and Method of Political Economy, 46 n.
Scotland, 130

Scott, Walter, 161, 357, 358, 368, 397
Second Empire, 390
Second World War, 15, 130, 169–70, 247–48, 333 n.; OWI, 208 n.
Sedgwick, Ellery, 144
Seebohm, Frederic, 399
Selden Society, 131
Seligman, E. R. A., 269, 342
Semple, Ellen C., 293, 309–10
Seward, William H., 165–66, 212–14
Seymour, Charles, 162
Shadows on the Rock, 13
Shakespeare, William, 43, 142, 176, 186–88, 246
Shakespeare Restored, 187
Shea, John G., 152
Short History of the English . . . ., 284
Shorthouse, Joseph, 397
Siegfried, André, 319
Silvester, Pope, 145
Sisson, Edgar, 154
Sixtus IV, 115
Sixtus V, 115
Sloane, Sir Hans, 118
Smith, Adam, 280–81
Smith, Cecil Woodham, 257
Smith, Goldwin, 368, 399
Smith, J. Allen, 339, 343
Smith, Captain John, 160–61
Smith, Sidney, 61
Smith, W. Robertson, 38
Smith, Walter Bedell, 333 n.
Smoot-Hawley Tariff, 242
Social Evolution, 294, 326–27
Social History of England, 37, 295 n.
Societies, historical, 130–33
Society of Antiquaries, 130
Society of Dilettanti, 73
Sociology, 47–48, 285 ff., 294–95, 326–32, 351
Sociology in Its Psychological Aspects, 337
Solon, 67–68
Sorokin, Pitrim, 274
Soviet Communism . . . ., 342
Spain, 30, 109, 128–29, 397–98
Sparkes, Boyden, 168
Sparks, Jared, 154, 175, 183–84, 193 n.
Spencer, Herbert, 220–21, 223–24, 243, 285, 287–88, 351–52
Spengler, Oswald, 263, 264, 273–74
Spenser, Edmund, 246
Spirit of the Laws, 276
Spofford, A. R., 119
Spring, Robert, 142
Stalin, Josef, 26, 27, 30, 155, 181–82
Stanton, Edwin M., 165–66, 247
Stein, Heinrich von, 127
Stephen, Sir James F., 38, 83, 410
Stephen, Sir Leslie, 293, 359
Stephenson, Carl, 249
Sterling, John, 359
Stevenson, Adlai, 206
Stevenson, Robert L., 358, 396
Stiles, Charles, 312
Stith, William, 175
Stones of Venice, 77
Storey, Moorfield, 390
Story of the Alphabet, 99 n.
Story of Civilization, 43
Stow, John, 117

Strabo, 301–2
Strachey, Lytton, 42, 242, 257, 361–64
Struggle for American Independence, 298–99
Stuart and Revett, 73
Stuart manuscripts, 123
Stubbs, William, 40, 60, 379
Study of Greek Inscriptions, 88 n.
Study of History, 271–73
Study of Sociology, 220
Südenhorst, Hans von, 23
Suetonius, 347–48
Sullivan, Mark, 209, 385–86
Sumner, Charles, 17, 358
Superstition and Force, 410
Switzerland, 124, 316–17, 319
Symonds, John A., 108, 293, 410
Synthesis, 262 ff., 295 ff.

Tacitus, 37, 137, 277–78, 379
Taine, Hippolyte, 185, 293, 338, 339
Tale of the Greenlanders, 83–84
Tan Shih-hua, 186
Taras Bulba, 42
Tarbell, Ida M., 168
Tarle, Eugene, 25
Tatars, 27
Taussig, F. W., 228
Tawney, R. H., 45, 292, 343
Taylor, A. J. P., 246, 361
Taylor, Henry Osborn, 297
Textiles, 95
Thackeray, William, 202, 371
Thayer, W. R., 398
Theobald, Lewis, 187
Theodore Roosevelt and the Rise of America . . . ., 255
Thesis, 295 ff.
Three English Statesmen, 368
Thucydides, 37, 68–69, 71, 379; and inscriptions, 86, 89
Thwaites, Reuben, 114, 131, 152, 157
Tiberius, 37, 278
Ticknor, George, 375–76
Tides, 313–14
Tocqueville, Alexis de, 25
Todd, Robert Levi, 192 n.
Tom Jones, 43
Tools, 314–15
Towns, medieval, 249
Toynbee, Arnold, 40 n., 271–73
Trajan, Emperor, 106
Translations, 185–86
Travels in America . . . ., 152
Treitschke, Heinrich von, 57, 295
Trevelyan, George M., 37, 295 n., 391 n.
Trevelyan, George O., 372, 410
Troy, 81
True George Washington, 143, 355
True Relation, A, 160, 161
Trotsky, Leon, 154, 181–82
Truman, Harry, 18, 126
Trumbull, Benjamin, 265
Truth in History . . . ., 41 n.
Turner, Frederick J., 19, 132, 251, 295–96
Twain, Mark, 57, 62, 151, 246; books on, 355, 368
Two Noble Kinsmen, 176

United Netherlands, 401, 402
United States, 15 ff., 31–33, 38, 78–79, 83–84, 118–19, 125–27, 131–33,

73

United States (cont'd)
  314–15, 318 ff., 341 ff. See also
  Civil War; Constitution; etc.;
  specific books; labor, 251–52;
  Revolution, 21, 29, 298–99, 319,
  403–6; South, 22, 23, 312, 321
Untersuchungen, 174
Uses of the Past, 377

Valla, Laurentius, 146
Vance, Rupert B., 321
Van Praet (librarian), 116–17
Varro, Terentius, 105
Vatican Library, 110, 115, 124
Ventris, Michael, 74
Victoria, Queen, 122, 348, 364
Victorian Prose Masters, 368
Villard, Henry, 218–19
Villehardouin, Geoffroi de, 395–96
Voltaire, François de, 15, 114, 265,
  276–79, 357–58, 361
Vortigern, 142

Waliszewski, Kazimierz, 398
Walker, Williston, 253–54
Walpole, Horace, 389
Walton, Izaak, 354–55
Wanderings and Homes of Manu-
  scripts, 111–12
Warfare of Science . . . , 399
Warren and Pearson, 245
Washington, Bushrod, 183
Washington, George, 143, 150, 183–
  84, 355, 359, 364; cherry-tree tale,
  139–40; Marshall biography, 174–
  76
Washington National Intelligencer,
  201
Watson, James E., 242
Wealth of Nations, 280
Weather, 319–20

Weaver, Raymond, 367
Webb, Sidney and Beatrice, 38, 342
Webb, Walter P., 314
Weber, Max, 345
Webster, Daniel, 14, 17
Wedgwood, C. V., 58
Weems, Mason Locke, 139–40
Weik, Jesse W., 192 n.
Welles, Gideon, 165–66, 214
Wellington, Arthur, Duke of, 137,
  364
Wells, David A., 221
Wells, H. G., 270, 292
West, Willis M., 334
White, Andrew D., 399
White, Leonard D., 345
Whitelocke, Dorothy, 82 n.
William the Conqueror, 95
Willoughby, C. A., 170
Wilson, Woodrow, 17–18, 61, 186,
  291
Winckelmann, J. J., 73
Winning of the West, 209
Winsor, Justin, 114, 175
Wisconsin Hist. Society, 132
Wise, Thomas J., 144–45
Wolf, Friedrich A., 296
Woodhead, A. G., 88 n.
Woolf, L. S., 398
Wordsworth, William, 41, 364
Worthies of England, 354
Wrenn, John Henry, 144–45
Writers, biographies of, 355–56
Writing, ancient, 74, 97–101 ff.
Writing of History, 335–36

Xenophon, 37, 347

Zelenohorský, 146
Zinsser, Hans, 289
Zweig, Arnold, 194